FRIENDLY SETTLEMENTS BEFORE THE EUROPEAN COURT OF HUMAN RIGHTS

Friendly Settlements before the European Court of Human Rights

Theory and Practice

HELEN KELLER
Professor of Public, European and International Law,
University of Zurich

MAGDALENA FOROWICZ
University of Zurich

LORENZ ENGI
University of Zurich

OXFORD
UNIVERSITY PRESS

OXFORD
UNIVERSITY PRESS

Great Clarendon Street, Oxford OX2 6DP

Oxford University Press is a department of the University of Oxford.
It furthers the University's objective of excellence in research, scholarship,
and education by publishing worldwide in

Oxford NewYork

Auckland Bangkok Buenos Aires Cape Town Chennai
Dar es Salaam Delhi Hong Kong Istanbul Karachi Kolkata
Kuala Lumpur Madrid Melbourne Mexico City Mumbai Nairobi
São Paulo Shanghai Taipei Tokyo Toronto

With offices in

Argentina Austria Brazil Chile Czech Republic France Greece
Guatemala Hungary Italy JapanPolandPortugal Singapore
South Korea Switzerland Thailand Turkey Ukraine Vietnam

Oxford is a registered trade mark of Oxford University Press
in the UK and certain other countries

Published in the United States
by Oxford University Press Inc., New York

British Library Cataloguing in Publication Data
Data available

Library of Congress Cataloging in Publication Data
Data available

Typeset by Michael Anderau
and by Newgen Imaging Systems Pvt. Ltd
Printed in Great Britain
on acid-free paper by
MPG Books Group, Bodmin and King's Lynn

ISBN 978–0–19–960097–7

1 3 5 7 9 10 8 6 4 2

Contents

Acknowledgements   ix
Table of Cases   xi

PART I: FOUNDATIONS, PRACTICE AND BEYOND

1. **Introduction**   3
   I. Old Instrument – New Use   4
   II. Research Questions   5
   III. Questions of Legitimacy   7
   IV. Research Method   8
   V. Aim, Content and Responsibility   10

2. **Legal Framework and Practice**   14
   I. Reform History   14
   II. Before Protocol No 11   18
   III. After Protocol No 11   31
   IV. After Protocol No 14bis   57
   V. After Protocol No 14   57

3. **Beyond Doctrine – The Strasbourg Realities**   59
   I. Typology   59
   II. States' Policy, Interests and Trust   75
   III. The Registry's Proactive Approach   77
   IV. Written Procedures and Negotiations   79

4. **Philosophical Background**   85
   I. Human Rights and Ethics   86
   II. Philosophical Foundations   87
   III. Conflict of Interests   91
   IV. Concerns of Justice   95
   V. Finding the Balance   98
   VI. The Specific Case of Unilateral Declarations   103
   VII. Considering Specific Cases   106

5. **Analysis of the Court's Practice in Selected Areas**   108

   I. General Overview of the Statistics   110

   II. Turkish Settlement Practice under Articles 2 and 3 ECHR   116

   III. Polish Settlement Practice under Article 6 (1) ECHR   127

   IV. A Multitude of Factors   134

6. **Future of Friendly Settlements**   138

   I. Understanding, Potential and Limits   139

   II. Basic Assumptions Partially Refuted   140

   III. Professionalizing the Handling   140

   IV. Distribution of Tasks   148

   V. Confidentiality and Disclosure   150

   VI. New Competencies for Old and New Actors   151

   VII. Friendly Settlements in the Future Court   152

PART II: ANNEXES

1. **Interviews**   157

   I. Interview with Elisabet Fura   157

   II. Interview with Jakub Wołąsiewicz   169

   III. Entretien avec Frank Schürmann   183

   IV. Interview with Serkan Cengiz   193

2. **Statistics**   199

   I. Explanatory Note   199

   II. Overall Statistics   203

   III. Poland – Yearly Statistics Concerning Friendly Settlements and Arrangements   208

   IV. Poland – Cumulative Statistics Concerning Friendly Settlements and Arrangements   220

   V. Poland – Yearly Statistics Concerning Judgments   222

   VI. Poland – Cumulative Statistics Concerning Judgments   235

   VII. Poland – Yearly Statistics Concerning Unilateral Declarations   237

VIII. Poland – Cumulative Statistics Concerning Unilateral Declarations 241

IX. Turkey – Yearly Statistics Concerning Friendly Settlements and Arrangements 243

X. Turkey – Cumulative Statistics Concerning Friendly Settlements and Arrangements 257

XI. Turkey – Yearly Statistics Concerning Judgments 261

XII. Turkey – Cumulative Statistics Concerning Judgments 281

XIII. Turkey – Yearly Statistics Concerning Unilateral Declarations 283

XIV. Turkey – Cumulative Statistics Concerning Unilateral Declarations 286

3. **Legal Basis for Friendly Settlements** 288

I. European Convention on Human Rights 288

II. Rules of the European Court of Human Rights 290

III. Rules of Procedure of the European Commission of Human Rights 297

4. **Charts for the Use of Friendly Settlements** 298

I. In General under Protocol No 11 299

II. In General under Protocol No 14 300

III. Unilateral Declaration 301

IV. After a Pilot Judgment by the Grand Chamber 302

Bibliography 303

Index 309

Acknowledgements

The research for this book would not have been possible without the enormous help and support of the Judges, State Agents, human rights lawyers and Registry personnel that work at or appear before the European Court of Human Rights. We wish to thank all those who agreed to be interviewed and generously shared their views on friendly settlements with us. Heartfelt thanks are due to Elisabet Fura, Judge at the Court, Jakub Wołasiewicz, Polish State Agent at the Court, Frank Schürmann, Swiss State Agent at the Court, and Cerkan Cengiz, Turkish human rights lawyer, for kindly permitting us to reprint the transcripts of their interviews in the annex to this volume. Some of the Registry's personnel gave us their insights in a more informal manner. Among them was Magda Mierzewska-Krzyżanowska who read parts of the manuscript and examined them from an insider's perspective. We owe much to the generosity of Jean-Paul Costa, President of the Court, and Erik Fribergh, Registrar of the Court, for hosting Helen Keller as a Visiting Professor at the Court from January until August 2009. This position afforded us precious office space, which we used for conducting interviews. The friendly assistance of support staff and use of some of the Court's internal resources were indispensable preconditions for this kind of scientific endeavour.

We thank the Swiss Research Foundation, which provided a considerable part of the funding for this book. We are also indebted to additional sponsors, in particular the Hermann and Marianne Straniak Foundation (Sarnen/Switzerland). We also want to express our gratitude to Andreas Follesdal and Geir Ulfstein for hosting Helen Keller as a research fellow at the Centre of Advanced Study (CAS) at the Norwegian Academy of Science and Letters. The excellent research conditions and facilities at the CAS rendered the final polishing of this volume possible.

We extend our deepest gratitude to the following members of Helen Keller's Chair at the University of Zurich: Maya Sigron, Luca Cirigliano, David Suter, Nicole Bürli, Andreas Fischer and Daniela Kühne. Throughout, they supported our project by collecting data, footnoting texts and editing draft chapters. Maya Sigron provided in addition assistance at all levels until the very last moments of the editing phase. We deeply appreciated her efforts and dedication. Research does not only happen in the library and lonely scriptorium. The interviews at the Court gave this group of young scholars the opportunity to see the Court from the inside and to meet its main actors, which will hopefully inspire their future research and work. Finally, the manuscript benefited greatly from the work of Michael Anderau who was responsible for the layout of the entire book.

Last but not least, we would like to thank Mark Villiger, Judge at the Court, for his continuous support in completing this book. In many conversations, he gave us both the necessary insight into the Court's machinery and critical feedback for our provisional research results.

Helen Keller, Magdalena Forowicz and Lorenz Engi, April 2010

Table of Cases

I. EUROPEAN COMMISSION OF HUMAN RIGHTS[1]

A. v. Sweden (Appl. No. 14293/88), Decision (Commission–Arrangement),
14 January 1991, not reported 29
A. v. United Kingdom (Appl. No. 6840/74), Report (Commission–Friendly Settlement),
6 July 1980, D.R. 20, 5 24
A.K. v. Austria (Appl. No. 19630/92), Report (Commission–Friendly Settlement),
25 January 1996, not reported 22
A.S. v. Austria (Appl. No. 15220/89), Report (Commission–Friendly Settlement),
15 October 1993, D.R. 75, 30 22
Abbas v. France (Appl. No. 15671/89), Report (Commission–Friendly Settlement),
7 July 1992, not reported 21
Abbott v. United Kingdom (Appl. No. 15006/89), Decision (Commission–Arrangement),
10 December 1990, D.R. 67, 290 20
Aires v. Portugal (Appl. No. 13387/87), Report (Commission–Friendly Settlement),
31 May 1991, not reported 26
Alagöz v. Netherlands (Appl. No. 24205/94), Report (Commission–Friendly Settlement),
2 July 1996, not reported 22
Aldrian v. Austria (Appl. No. 10532/83), Report (Commission–Arrangement),
17 March 1989, not reported 21, 30
Alva Torres v. Portugal (Appl. No. 14836/89), Report (Commission–Friendly Settlement),
31 May 1991, not reported 25
Andersson and 28 Others v. Sweden (Appl. No. 14740/89), Report (Commission–Friendly
Settlement), 19 January 1994, not reported 25
Arrondelle v. United Kingdom (Appl. No. 7889/77), Decision (Commission),
15 July 1980, D.R. 19, 186 195
Ayadi v. France (Appl. No. 18000/91), Report (Commission–Arrangement),
1 September 1993, not reported 9, 61
Ayala v. Portugal (Appl. No. 23663/94), Report (Commission–Friendly Settlement),
21 October 1996, D.R. 87-B, 38 22
B.H. v. United Kingdom (Appl. No. 30307/96), Report (Commission–Friendly
Settlement), 30 June 1998, D.R. 94-B, 82 20
Baumgartner a. O. v. Austria (Appl. No. 23085/93), Report (Commission–Friendly
Settlement), 16 October 1996, not reported. 25
Boeckmann v. Belgium (Appl. No. 1727/62), Report (Commission–Friendly Settlement),
17 February 1965, Y.B. 8, 370 15
Bozovic v. Austria (Appl. No. 21684/93), Decision (Commission–Arrangement),
29 June 1994, not reported 62
Brant v. United Kingdom (Appl. No. 9303/81), Report (Commission–Friendly
Settlement), Report adopted on 16 July 1987, D.R. 52, 21 28
Bulus v. Sweden (Appl. No. 9330/81), Report (Commission–Friendly Settlement),
8 December 1984, D.R. 39, 75 22

---

[1] The Decisions and Reports of the Commission were published until 1 November 1999 (Article 5 (3) of Protocol no 11 to the ECHR (entered into force on 1 November 1998)).

C. and O. v. Portugal (Appl. Nos. 12934/87; 12935/87), Report (Commission–Friendly
Settlement), 31 May 1991, not reported 26
C.Z. v. Austria (Appl. No. 21874/93), Decision (Commission–Arrangement),
2 March 1994, not reported 63
Cagirga v. Turkey (Appl. No. 21895/93), Report (Commission–Friendly Settlement),
7 July 1995, D.R. 82-B, 20 . . . . 19, 70
Campbell and Cosans v. United Kingdom (Appl. Nos. 7511/76; 7743/77), Report
(Commission), 16 May 1980, Series B, Vol. 42 28
Campbell v. United Kingdom (Appl. No. 11240/84), Report (Commission–Friendly
Settlement), 13 May 1988, D.R. 56, 108 20
Constantinou v. Cyprus (Appl. No. 28209/95), Decision (Commission–Arrangement),
21 May 1997, not reported 29–30
Correia Dias v. Portugal (Appl. No. 14904/89), Report (Commission–Friendly
Settlement), 31 May 1991, not reported 25
Crook and National Union of Journalists v. United Kingdom (Appl. No. 11552/85),
Decision (Commission–Arrangement), 15 July 1988, D.R. 56, 148 . . . . 20, 62
D. v. Switzerland (Appl. No. 15736/89), Report (Commission–Friendly Settlement),
1 April 1992, D.R. 73, 102 . . . . 183, 185
De Oliveira Barros v. Portugal (Appl. No. 20502/92), Report (Commission–Friendly
Settlement), 7 December 1994, not reported 26
De Vos v. Belgium (Appl. No. 20597/92), Decision (Commission–Arrangement),
5 July 1994, not reported 62
Dunkel v. Germany (Appl. No. 10812/84), Report (Commission–Friendly Settlement),
14 May 1987, D.R. 52, 188 23
Durairaj, Baker (formerly Durairaj) and Durairaj v. United Kingdom (Appl. No.
9114/80), Report (Commission–Friendly Settlement), Report adopted on
16 July 1987, D.R. 52, 13 28
F.V.B. v. Portugal (Appl. No. 13774/88), Report (Commission–Friendly Settlement),
8 July 1991, D.R. 70, 198 26
Farrell v. United Kingdom (Appl. No. 9013/80), Report (Commission–Friendly
Settlement), 2 October 1984, D.R. 38, 44 27
Fidalgo Martins v. Portugal (Appl. No. 13874/88), Report (Commission–Friendly
Settlement), 31 May 1991, not reported 25
Flattery v. Ireland (Appl. No. 28995/95), Decision (Commission–Arrangement),
8 July 1998, not reported 23
Fraisse v. France (Appl. No. 26512/95), Report (Commission–Friendly Settlement),
4 July 1995, not reported 26
France, Norway, Denmark, Sweden, Netherlands v. Turkey (Appl. Nos. 9940–9944/82),
Report (Commission–Friendly Settlement), 7 December 1985, D.R. 44, 31 74–75
G.D., C.T. and D.D. v. Belgium (Appl. No. 16909/90), Report (Commission–Friendly
Settlement), 6 April 1993, D.R. 74, 111 20
G.T. v. Netherlands (Appl. No. 15416/89), Report (Commission–Arrangement),
19 January 1994, not reported 61
Geerk v. Switzerland (Appl. No. 7640/76), Report (Commission–Friendly Settlement),
4 May 1979, D.R. 16, 56 19
Georgsson v. Iceland (Appl. No. 22103/93), Report (Commission–Friendly Settlement),
15 April 1997, not reported 30
Giama v. Belgium (Appl. No. 7612/76), Report (Commission–Friendly Settlement),
17 July 1980, D.R. 21, 73 22
Grabemann v. Germany (Appl. No. 12748/87), Report (Commission–Friendly
Settlement), 11 October 1989, D.R. 63, 137 20

Harman v. United Kingdom (Appl. No. 10038/82), Report (Commission–Friendly
   Settlement), 15 May 1986, D.R. 46, 57 20
Hazar, Hazar and Açik v. Turkey (Appl. Nos. 16311/90; 16312/90; 16313/90), Report
   (Commission–Friendly Settlement), 10 December 1992, D.R. 73, 111 122
Heikel v. Finland (Appl. No. 30511/96), Decision (Commission–Arrangement),
   9 September 1998, not reported 29
Higgins v. United Kingdom (Appl. No. 14778/89), Report (Commission–Friendly
   Settlement), 13 February 1992, D.R. 73, 95 24
Holzinger v. Austria (Appl. No. 20204/92), Decision (Commission–Arrangement),
   13 April 1994, not reported 61
I. v. Austria (Appl. No. 10215/82), Report (Commission–Arrangement),
   13 March 1986, not reported 21
Isiyok v. Turkey (Appl. No. 22309/93), Report (Commission–Friendly Settlement),
   31 October 1997, D.R. 91-A, 5 70
J. and R. S. v. United Kingdom (Appl. No. 12676/87), Report (Commission–Friendly
   Settlements), 11 May 1988, not reported 28
J.P.R. and M.C.L. v. Portugal (Appl. No. 15046/89), Report (Commission–Friendly
   Settlement), 31 May 1991, not reported 25
J.S. a. O. v. Netherlands (Appl. Nos. 14561/89; 14657/89; 15105/89; 15343/89;
   15712/89; 15908/89; 15988/90; 16118/90; 16513/90; 16583/90; 16843/90;
   16896–97/90; 17001/90; 17241/90; 17252/90; 17675/91; 17883/91; 18615/91;
   19590–91/92; 20311/92; 22532/ 93), Report (Commission–Friendly Settlement),
   23 January 1996, not reported 25
Jädergård a. O. v. Sweden (Appl. No. 13247/87), Report (Commission–Friendly
   Settlement), 1 July 1992, not reported 25
Jäger v. Switzerland (Appl. No. 13467/87), Report (Commission–Friendly Settlement),
   11 December 1989, D.R. 63, 156 21
Jensen v. Denmark (Appl. No. 14063/88), Decision (Commission), 7 January 1991,
   D.R. 68, 182 148
K. v. United Kingdom (Appl. No. 11468/85), Report (Commission–Friendly Settlement),
   15 April 1988, D.R. 56, 138 20
Karrer a. O. v. Austria (Appl. No. 7464/76), Report (Commission–Friendly Settlement),
   4 May 1979, D.R. 16, 42 22
Khristianso Sdruzheni "Svideteli Na Iehova" v. Bulgaria (Appl. No. 28626/95), Report
   (Commission–Friendly Settlement), 9 March 1998, D.R. 92-A, 44 23
Kurtz and Seltmann v. Germany (Appl. No. 2707/66), Decision (Commission–
   Arrangement), 4 April 1967, Y.B. 10, 320 60
Ländström v. Sweden (Appl. No. 29105/95), Report (Commission–Friendly Settlement),
   21 October 1998, not reported 23
Larsen v. Denmark (Appl. No. 23871/94), Report (Commission–Friendly Settlement),
   15 April 1997, not reported 30
Laurant v. France (Appl. No. 26295/95), Report (Commission–Friendly Settlement),
   4 July 1995, not reported 26
Leterme v. France (Appl. No. 26387/95), Report (Commission–Friendly Settlement),
   4 July 1995, not reported 26
Liebig v. Germany (Appl. No. 6650/74), Report (Commission–Friendly Settlement),
   11 May 1978, D.R. 17, 5 . . . . 19, 21
Luciano Sernache v. Portugal (Appl. No. 14548/89), Report (Commission–Friendly
   Settlement), 8 July 1991, not reported 26
Lund and Walker v. United Kingdom (Appl. No. 12674/87), Report (Commission–
   Friendly Settlements), 11 May 1988, not reported 28

M. v. United Kingdom (Appl. No. 15861/89), Report (Commission–Friendly Settlement),
   8 September 1992, not reported. 24
M.A.R. v. United Kingdom (Appl. No. 28038/95), Report (Commission–Friendly
   Settlement), 19 September 1997, not reported. 21
M.M. v. Bulgaria (Appl. No. 27496/95), Report (Commission–Friendly Settlement),
   9 July 1997, D.R. 90-B, 56 24
M.O.N. v. Portugal (Appl. No. 12745/87), Report (Commission–Friendly Settlement),
   31 May 1991, D.R. 69, 135. 25
Mansi v. Sweden (Appl. No. 15658/89), Report (Commission–Friendly Settlement),
   9 March 1990, not reported. 22
Marcos Cordeiro v. Portugal (Appl. No. 12746/87), Report (Commission–Friendly
   Settlement), 31 May 1991, not reported 26
Marquet v. France (Appl. No. 26266/95), Report (Commission–Friendly Settlement),
   4 July 1995, not reported. 26
Mattsson v. Sweden (Appl. No. 13425/87), Decision (Commission–Arrangement),
   27 May 1991, not reported 29
Maycock and Maycock v. United Kingdom (Appl. No. 12675/87), Report (Commission–
   Friendly Settlements), 11 May 1988, not reported. 28
McComb v. United Kingdom (Appl. No. 10621/83), Report (Commission–Friendly
   Settlement), 15 May 1986, D.R. 50, 81. 24
Mesquita v. France (Appl. No. 21433/93), Report (Commission–Friendly Settlement),
   4 July 1995, not reported. 26
Min, Min and Min Paik v. United Kingdom (Appl. No. 10204/82), Report (Commission–
   Friendly Settlement), 7 October 1986, D.R. 48, 58. 21
Moosmann v. Austria (Appl. No. 14093/88), Report (Commission–Friendly Settlement),
   9 July 1992, D.R. 73, 19 . . . . 22, 24
Mora do Vale a. O. v. Portugal (Appl. Nos. 33329/96; 34140/96; 34796/97;
   36003797; 36166/97), Report (Commission–Friendly Settlement),
   15 September 1998, not reported. 25
N.V. Televizier v. Netherlands (Appl. No. 2690/65), Report (Commission–Arrangement),
   3 October 1968, Y.B. 11, 782 62–63
Nagel v. Germany (Appl. No. 7641/76), Report (Commission–Friendly Settlement),
   2 May 1978, D.R. 12, 97. 21
Nyssen v. Belgium (Appl. No. 10574/83), Report (Commission–Friendly Settlement),
   8 July 1987, D.R. 52, 140 21
O'Brien v. United Kingdom (Appl. No. 20121/92), Decision (Commission–Arrangement),
   8 September 1993, not reported. 61
Ofner and Hopfinger v. Austria (Appl. Nos. 524/59; 617/59), Report (Commission–
   Friendly Settlement), 23 November 1962, Y.B. 6, 680. 26
Oliveira Pinto v. Portugal (Appl. No. 12918/87), Report (Commission–Friendly
   Settlement), 31 May 1991, not reported 26
O'Reilly v. Ireland (Appl. No. 24196/94), Report (Commission–Friendly Settlement),
   3 December 1996, D.R. 87-A, 58 26
P.P.P. v. Portugal (Appl. No. 13526/88), Report (Commission–Friendly Settlement),
   31 May 1991, not reported 26
Paal v. Portugal (Appl. No. 14659/89), Report (Commission–Friendly Settlement),
   8 July 1991, not reported. 26
Peschke v. Austria (Appl. No. 8289/78), Report (Commission–Friendly Settlement),
   13 October 1981, D.R. 25, 182. . . . . 20, 21
Poláková and Machová v. Slovak Republic (Appl. No. 30903/96), Decision
   (Commission–Arrangement), 3 December 1997, not reported. 23, 61

R.R. v. Germany (Appl. No. 14446/88), Decision (Commission–Arrangement),
13 July 1990, not reported 22

Reed v. United Kingdom (Appl. No. 7630/76), Report (Commission–Friendly
Settlement), 12 December 1981, D.R. 25, 5 20

Reis Antunes v. Portugal (Appl. No. 20844/92), Report (Commission–Friendly
Settlement), 7 December 1994, not reported 26

Ritchie v. United Kingdom (Appl. No. 16212/90), Report (Commission–Friendly
Settlement), 13 February 1992, not reported 24

Rogers and Rogers v. United Kingdom (Appl. No. 12677/87), Report (Commission–
Friendly Settlements), 11 May 1988, not reported 28

Roux v. United Kingdom (Appl. No. 25601/94), Report (Commission–Friendly
Settlement), 16 September 1997, not reported 20

S. v. United Kingdom (Appl. No. 11756/85), Decision (Commission–Arrangement),
13 March 1989, not reported 28

S.L. v. France (Appl. No. 26365/95), Report (Commission–Friendly Settlement),
4 July 1995, not reported 26

S.P., D.P. and A.T. v. United Kingdom (Appl. No. 23715/94), Report (Commission–
Friendly Settlement), 11 April 1997, D.R. 89-A, 31 24

Sami El-Makhour v. Germany (Appl. No. 14312/88), Report (Commission–Friendly
Settlement), 10 July 1989, not reported 22

Samková v. Slovak Republic (Appl. No. 26384/95), Report (Commission–Friendly
Settlement), 15 January 1997, D.R. 88-A, 67 23–24

Santos Marques v. Portugal (Appl. No. 20381/92), Report (Commission–Friendly
Settlement), 7 December 1994, not reported 26

Sarialtun a. O. v. Germany (Appl. No. 37534/97), Report (Commission–Friendly
Settlement), 18 September 1998, D.R. 94-B, 113 21

Sätterlund v. Sweden (Appl. No. 30157/96), Decision (Commission–Arrangement),
9 July 1997, not reported 29, 62

Sawicki v. Poland (Appl. No. 25085/94), Report (Commission–Friendly Settlement),
14 January 1997, D.R. 88-B, 42 22

Schaden v. Austria (Appl. No. 12896/87), Report (Commission–Friendly Settlement),
12 February 1990, D.R. 65, 165 23

Seale v. United Kingdom (Appl. No. 9466/81), Report (Commission–Friendly
Settlement), 15 May 1986, D.R. 50, 70 24

Stoutt v. Ireland (Appl. No. 10978/84), Report (Commission–Friendly Settlement),
17 December 1987, D.R. 54, 43 20

Sverrisson v. Iceland (Appl. No. 13291/87), Report (Commission–Friendly Settlement),
6 February 1990, D.R. 65, 192 23

T. v. Netherlands (Appl. No. 13143/87), Report (Commission–Friendly Settlement),
12 February 1990, D.R. 65, 184 21

T.O.A. v. United Kingdom (Appl. No. 27559/95), Decision (Commission–Arrangement),
8 July 1998, not reported 21

Teixeira da Mota v. Portugal (Appl. No. 18866/91), Report (Commission–Friendly
Settlement), 7 December 1994, not reported 26

Ten Berge v. Netherlands (Appl. No. 20929/92), Report (Commission–Friendly
Settlement), 5 December 1995, not reported 29

Thomaz dos Santos S.A. v. Portugal (Appl. No. 19372/92), Report (Commission–Friendly
Settlement), 7 December 1994, not reported 26

Three members of the A. family v. United Kingdom (Appl. No. 10592/83), Report
(Commission–Friendly Settlement), Report adopted on 16 July 1987, D.R. 52, 150 28

Todescato v. Italy (Appl. No. 24307/94), Decision (Commission–Arrangement),
    11 April 1995, not reported 62
Townend Sr. and Townend Jr. v. United Kingdom (Appl. No. 9119/80), Report
    (Commission–Friendly Settlement), 23 January 1987, D.R. 50, 36 28
Uppal a. O. v. United Kingdom (Appl. No. 8244/77), Report (Commission–Friendly
    Settlement), 9 July 1980, Y.B. 23, 444 21
Valada v. Portugal (Appl. No. 18581/91), Report (Commission–Friendly Settlement),
    7 December 1994, not reported 26
Van Waegeningh v. Netherlands (Appl. No. 10535/83), Report (Commission–Friendly
    Settlement), 7 March 1985, not reported 20
Vieira v. Portugal (Appl. No. 20879/92), Report (Commission–Friendly Settlement),
    7 December 1994, not reported 26
W.W. v. United Kingdom (Appl. No. 18123/91), Report (Commission–Friendly
    Settlement), 6 April 1993, not reported 24
Ward v. United Kingdom (Appl. No. 19526/92), Report (Commission–Friendly
    Settlement), 5 July 1993, D.R. 75, 217 24
Wiener Stadtische Wechselseitige Versicherungsanstalt v. Austria (Appl. No. 2076/63),
    Decision (Commission–Arrangement), 30 May 1967, Y.B. 10, 136 62
Wilson v. United Kingdom (Appl. No. 30535/96), Decision (Commission–Arrangement),
    4 March 1998, not reported 61
X. v. United Kingdom (Appl. No. 7907/77), Report (Commission–Friendly Settlement),
    17 December 1981, Y.B. 24, 402 28
Yağcı and Sargın v. Turkey (Appl. Nos. 16419/90; 16426/90), Report (Commission),
    30 November 1993, not reported 194
Zeidler, Strauss and Puhm v. Austria (Appl. Nos. 17755/91, 17756/91; 17757/91),
    Decision (Commission–Arrangement), 7 December 1994, not reported 62
Zimmermann v. Austria (Appl. No. 8490/79), Report (Commission–Friendly
    Settlement), 6 July 1982, D.R. 30, 15 21

II. EUROPEAN COURT OF HUMAN RIGHTS

A. v. Italy (Appl. No. 40453/98), Judgment (First Section–Arrangement),
    9 October 2003, not reported 62
A.S. v. Italy (Appl. No. 43077/98), Judgment (Second Section–Friendly Settlement),
    22 June 2000, not reported 112
Abbas v. France (Appl. No. 35783/97), Judgment (Third Section–Friendly Settlement),
    20 July 2000, not reported 41
Abdurrahim Incedursun v. Netherlands (Appl. No. 33124/96), Judgment (Grand
    Chamber–Friendly Settlement), 22 June 1999, not reported 41, 53
Abid v. France (Appl. No. 3541/05), Decision (Third Section–Arrangement),
    5 July 2007, not yet reported 101
Abraham v. Serbia (Appl. No. 33430/05), Decision (Second Section–Arrangement),
    4 March 2008, not yet reported 44
Acar v. Turkey (Appl. No. 24940/94), Judgment (Second Section–Friendly Settlement),
    18 December 2001, not reported 45
Acar v. Turkey (Appl. No. 74941/01), Decision (Third Section–Arrangement),
    30 August 2007, not yet reported 101
Adali v. Turkey (Appl. No. 31137/96), Judgment (Third Section–Friendly Settlement),
    12 December 2002, not reported 48, 101
Aggiato v. Italy (Appl. No. 36822/97), Judgment (Second Section–Arrangement),
    29 February 2000, not reported 62

Agibalova a. O. v. Russia (Appl. No. 26724/03), Decision (First Section–Arrangement),
13 April 2006, not reported 82
Akbaş v. Turkey (Appl. No. 42744/98), Decision (Third Section–Friendly Settlement),
21 November 2002, not reported 111
Akbay v. Turkey (Appl. No. 32598/96), Judgment (First Section–Friendly Settlement),
2 October 2001, not reported 45
Akimova v. Azerbaijan (Appl. No. 19853/03), Judgment (First Section–Friendly
Settlement), 9 October 2008, not yet reported 142
Akman v. Turkey (Appl. No. 37453/97), Judgment (First Section–Unilateral
Declaration), 26 June 2001, Reports 2001-VI, 223 . . . . 5, 9, 51, 67, 103–104, 119, 147
Albayrak v. Turkey (Appl. No. 70151/01), Decision (Fourth Section–Arrangement),
21 March 2006, not reported 193
Alekhina a. O. v. Russia (Appl. No. 22519/02), Judgment (First Section), 13 April 2006,
not reported 115
Aleksentseva and 28 Others v. Russia (Appl. Nos. 75025–38/01; 75136/01; 76386/01;
76542/01; 76736/01; 77049/01; 77051–53/01; 3999/02; 5314/02; 5384/02;
5388/02; 5419/02; 8190/02; 8192/02), Decision (First Section–Unilateral
Declaration), 4 September 2003, not reported 56
Aleksentseva a. O. v. Russia (Appl. Nos. 75025–26/01; 75028–29/01; 75036/01;
75031/01; 75033–34/01; 8192/02; 5314/02; 77049/01; 76386/01; 77051–53/01;
3999/02; 5384/02; 5388/02; 5419/02), Judgment (First Section), 17 January 2008,
not yet reported 56–57
Alfatli a. O. v. Turkey (Appl. No. 32984/96), Judgment (Third Section–Friendly
Settlement), 2 October 2003, not reported. 65
Alfatli a. O. v. Turkey (as regards Mahmut Memduh Uyan) (Appl. No. 32984/96),
Judgment (Third Section), 30 October 2003, not reported. 66, 150
Ali Erol v. Turkey (Appl. No. 35076/97), Judgment (First Section–Arrangement),
20 June 2002, not reported 63
Altan v. Turkey (Appl. No. 32985/96), Judgment (First Section–Arrangement),
14 May 2002, Reports 2002-III, 341 51
Amnesty International (United Kingdom) v. United Kingdom (Appl. No. 38383/97),
Decision (Third Section–Arrangement), 18 January 2000, not reported. 53
Amorim Gomes v. Portugal (Appl. No. 40311/98), Decision (Fourth Section–
Arrangement), 21 September 1999, not reported 62
Andrzejewska v. Poland (Appl. No. 15153/02), Decision (Fourth Section–Arrangement),
18 November 2003, not reported. 55
Antkowiak v. Poland (Appl. No. 14056/06), Decision (Fourth Section–Arrangement),
22 April 2008, not yet reported 131
Antoszczuk a. O. v. Poland (Appl. No. 15230/04), Decision (Fourth Section–
Arrangement), 11 December 2007, not yet reported 51, 73
Arkwell a. O. v. United Kingdom (Appl. No. 47289/99), Judgment (Fourth Section–
Arrangement), 25 September 2007, not yet reported 64
Arslan and Arslan v. Turkey (Appl. No. 57908/00), Judgment (Fourth Section–
Friendly Settlement), 10 January 2006, not reported 46, 47, 150
Aruç v. Turkey (Appl. No. 39675/98), Decision (Fourth Section–Arrangement),
6 April 2004, not reported 45, 63, 102
Arvaniti v. Poland (Appl. No. 20797/06), Decision (Fourth Section–Unilateral
Declaration), 18 March 2008, not yet reported 132
Ascierto v. Italy (Appl. No. 40363/98), Judgment (Second Section–Friendly Settlement),
22 June 2000, not reported 112

Aspichi Dehwari v. Netherlands (Appl. No. 37014/97), Judgment (First Section–
Arrangement), 27 April 2000, not reported 38, 41, 62
Ateş v. Turkey (Appl. No. 28292/95), Judgment (Second Section–Friendly
Settlement), 22 April 2003, not reported 46
Ateş v. Turkey (Appl. No. 42144/98), Decision (Third Section–Friendly Settlement),
23 October 2003, not reported 50
Atkinson a. O. v. United Kingdom (Appl. Nos. 63587/00, 28034/02; 30478/02), Decision
(Fourth Section–Arrangement), 26 September 2006, not reported. 64
Avci v. Turkey (Appl. No. 24935/94), Judgment (First Section–Friendly Settlement),
10 July 2001, not reported 44, 122
Ayan v. Turkey (Appl. No. 73789/01), Decision (Third Section–Friendly Settlement),
21 November 2002, not reported. 111
Aydın v. Turkey (Appl. Nos. 28293/95; 29494/95; 30219/96), Judgment (First
Section–Friendly Settlement), 10 July 2001, not reported 44–45, 125
Aydın v. Turkey (Appl. No. 29289/95), Judgment (Second Section–Friendly
Settlement), 16 July 2002, not reported 101
Aydın v. Turkey (Appl. No. 42747/98), Decision (Third Section–Friendly Settlement),
21 November 2002, not reported. 111
Baciu v. Romania (Appl. No. 21440/03), Decision (Third Section–Friendly Settlement),
6 July 2006, not reported 45, 49
Bağatur a. O. v. Turkey (Appl. No. 42847/98), Decision (Third Section–Arrangement),
7 November 2002, not reported. 69
Bąk v. Poland (Appl. No. 21092/04), Decision (Fourth Section–Arrangement),
16 October 2007, not yet reported. 131
Balasoiu v. Romania (Appl. No. 37424/97), Judgment (Second Section–Friendly
Settlement), 20 April 2004, not reported 45
Başak a. O. v. Turkey (Appl. No. 29875/96), Judgment (Third Section–Friendly
Settlement), 16 October 2003, not reported. 125
Beard v. United Kingdom (Appl. No. 27951/02), Decision (Fourth Section–
Arrangement), 24 June 2008, not yet reported. 116
Beau v. Germany (Appl. No. 16996/03), Decision (Fifth Section–Arrangement),
11 September 2007, not yet reported. 113
Bello v. Italy (Appl. No. 43063/98), Judgment (Second Section–Friendly Settlement),
22 June 2000, not reported 112
Beneficio Cappella Paoloni v. San Marino (Appl. No. 40786/98), Judgment (Second
Section–Arrangement), 3 May 2007, not yet reported 42
Ben Yaacoub v. Belgium (Appl. No. 9976/82), Judgment (Chamber–Friendly Settlement),
27 November 1987, Series A, Vol. 127-A. 31
Benzan v. Croatia (Appl. No. 62912/00), Judgment (First Section–Friendly Settlement),
8 November 2002, not reported. 101
Berk v. Turkey (Appl. No. 41973/98), Judgment (Third Section–Friendly Settlement),
20 April 2006, not reported 46
Bieńkowski and Bieńkowska v. Poland (Appl. No. 39010/05), Decision (Fourth Section–
Arrangement), 17 June 2008, not yet reported. 131
Bilby v. United Kingdom (Appl. No. 76944/01), Decision (Fourth Section–Arrangement),
24 June 2008, not yet reported. 116
Binbay v. Turkey (Appl. No. 24922/94), Judgment (First Section–Arrangement),
21 October 2004, not reported 49, 126
Birou v. France (Appl. No. 13319/87), Judgment (Chamber–Arrangement),
27 February 1992, Series A, Vol. 232-B 23

Blagovestnyy v. Russia (Appl. No. 72558/01), Judgment (Second Section), 4 July 2006,
not reported 115
Blakemore and 41 Others v. United Kingdom (Appl. Nos. 10471/0; 10467/05; 10474/05;
10478/05; 10480/05; 10483/05; 10541/05; 10546/05; 10550/05; 10553–54/05;
10556/05; 10558/05; 10565–66/05; 10568/05; 10572/05; 10573/05; 10575–76/05;
10579/05; 10581/05; 10583–85/05; 10589/05; 10591/05; 10593/05; 10595–97/05;
10602/05; 10607/05; 10609/05; 10611–13/05; 10616/05; 10619/05; 10622–23/05;
16517/05), Decision (Fourth Section–Friendly Settlement), 11 December 2007,
not yet reported 54
Bochkov v. Russia (Appl. No. 58826/00), Decision (Second Section–Arrangement),
10 February 2004, not reported 75
Bódiné Bencze v. Hungary (Appl. No. 42373/98), Judgment (Second Section–
Arrangement), 1 October 2002, not reported 61
Boğ v. Turkey (Appl. No. 24946/94), Judgment (First Section–Friendly Settlement),
10 July 2001, not reported 45
Boğa v. Turkey (Appl. No. 24938/94), Judgment (First Section–Friendly Settlement),
10 July 2001, not reported 44, 122
Bogdan v. Moldova (Appl. No. 148/05), Decision (Fourth Section–Arrangement),
16 October 2007, not yet reported 44
Bohunický v. Slovakia (Appl. No. 36570/97), Judgment (Second Section–Friendly
Settlement), 13 September 1999, not reported 40
Bojagić v. Croatia (Appl. No. 37421/04), Decision (First Section–Arrangement),
23 October 2007, not yet reported 101
Boltyonkov v. Ukraine (Appl. No. 35113/03), Decision (Fifth Section–Arrangement),
19 June 2007, not yet reported 44
Bottazzi v. Italy (Appl. No. 34884/97), Judgment (Grand Chamber), 28 July 1999,
Reports 1999-V, 1 . . . . 71, 113
Bouamar v. Belgium (Appl. No. 9106/80), Judgment (Chamber–Arrangement),
27 June 1988, Series A, Vol. 136-F. 23, 30
Bozkurt v. Turkey (Appl. No. 35851/97), Judgment (First Section–Arrangement),
31 March 2005, not reported 101
Brocco v. Italy (Appl. No. 68074/01), Judgment (Third Section–Arrangement),
7 April 2005, not reported 69
Brodtmann v. Germany (Appl. No. 47389/99), Decision (Third Section–Arrangement),
16 June 2005, not reported 42
Broniowski v. Poland (Appl. No. 31443/96), Judgment (Grand Chamber–Pilot Judgment),
22 June 2004, Reports 2004-V, 1 . . . . 4, 11, 47, 72–73, 111, 136, 144, 173–174, 180
Broniowski v. Poland (Appl. No. 31443/96), Judgment (Grand Chamber–Friendly Settlement),
28 September 2005, Reports 2005-IX, 1 . . . . . . 4, 11, 47, 72–73, 83, 111, 136, 144, 173–174, 180
Broszczakowska v. Poland (Appl. No. 18262/05), Decision (Fourth Section–Arrangement),
13 March 2007, not yet reported 131
Brumarescu v. Romania (Appl. No. 28342/95), Judgment (Grand Chamber),
28 October 1999, Reports 1999-VII, 201 165
Burdov v. Russia (No. 2) (Appl. No. 33509/04), Judgment (First Section–Pilot
Judgment), 15 January 2009, not yet reported 39, 72
C.B. v. Italy (Appl. No. 43094/98), Judgment (Second Section–Friendly Settlement),
22 June 2000, not reported 112
Caliński v. Poland (Appl. No. 4744/03), Decision (Fourth Section–Arrangement),
11 December 2007, not yet reported 51
Can v. Austria (Appl. No. 9300/81), Judgment (Chamber–Arrangement),
30 September 1985, Series A, Vol. 96. . . . . 8, 20, 27, 30

Can, Can, Güneş, Menteşe, Kasap, Akgök, Kasap, Daimi, Tosun and Tanriverdi v. Turkey
(Appl. Nos. 30662–30667/96; 30669/96; 30670/96; 30672/96; 30673/96), Decision
(Second Section–Friendly Settlement), 22 March 2001, not reported. 123
Canpolat v. Turkey (Appl. Nos. 28506/95; 30780/96), Decision (Second Section–Friendly
Settlement), 22 March 2001, not reported 101
Cantürk v. Turkey (Appl. No. 30779/96), Decision (Second Section–Friendly Settlement),
22 March 2001, not reported 101
Cardoso and Johansen v. United Kingdom (Appl. No. 47061/99), Decision (Third
Section–Arrangement), 5 September 2000, not reported 43
Carević v. Slovenia (Appl. No. 17314/03), Decision (Third Section), 3 June 2008,
not yet reported 104
Carrozza v. Italy (Appl. No. 43598/98), Judgment (Second Section–Friendly Settlement),
19 October 1999, not reported 50
Charzyński v. Poland (Appl. No. 15212/03), Decision (Fourth Section), 1 March 2005,
Reports 2005-V, 323 129
Ciaramella v. Italy (Appl. No. 43035/98), Judgment (Second Section–Friendly
Settlement), 22 June 2000, not reported 112
Ciechanowski v. Poland (Appl. No. 2863/06), Decision (Fourth Section–Arrangement),
16 September 2008, not yet reported 131
Circelli v. Italy (Appl. No. 43107/98), Judgment (Second Section–Friendly Settlement),
22 June 2000, not reported 112
Cojocaru v. Romania (Appl. No. 39184/03), Decision (Third Section–Friendly
Settlement), 18 October 2007, not yet reported 48
Colangelo v. Italy (Appl. No. 29671/96), Judgment (Second Section–Arrangement),
31 May 2001, not reported 62
Colman v. United Kingdom (Appl. No. 16632/90), Judgment (Chamber–Arrangement),
28 June 1993, Series A, Vol. 258-D 62
Constantini v. Romania (Appl. No. 49145/99), Judgment (Third Section–Friendly
Settlement), 17 February 2005, not reported 45
Cornwell v. United Kingdom (Appl. No. 36578/97), Judgment (Third Section–Friendly
Settlement), 25 April 2000, not reported 41
Crew v. United Kingdom (Appl. No. 61928/00), Judgment (Fourth Section–
Arrangement), 9 January 2007, not yet reported 116
Croke v. Ireland (Appl. No. 33267/96), Judgment (Fourth Section–Friendly Settlement),
21 December 2000, not reported 41, 43
Crossland v. United Kingdom (Appl. No. 36120/97), Judgment (Third Section–
Arrangement), 9 November 1999, not reported 63
Crouch v. United Kingdom (Appl. No. 39472/98), Decision (Third Section–
Arrangement), 18 September 2001, not reported 63
Cruz da Silva Coelho v. Portugal (Appl. No. 9388/02), Judgment (Second Section–
Friendly Settlement), 13 December 2005, not reported 49
Czemarnik-Noga v. Poland (Appl. No. 21905/06), Decision (Fourth Section–
Arrangement), 2 September 2008, not yet reported 131
Çardakçi a. O. v. Turkey (Appl. No. 39224/98), Judgment (Fourth Section–
Arrangement), 23 January 2007, not yet reported 46, 101
Çavuşoğlu v. Turkey (Appl. No. 32983/96), Judgment (Third Section–Friendly
Settlement), 6 March 2001, not reported 101
Çiçek and Öztemel and 6 other cases v. Turkey (Appl. Nos. 74069/01; 74703/01;
76380/01; 16809/02; 25710/02; 25714/02; 30383/02), Judgment (Second Section),
3 August 2007, not yet reported. 38–39

D.L. and M.A. v. Italy (Appl. No. 31926/96), Judgment (Second Section–Arrangement),
19 April 2001, not reported 69

D'Adonna v. Italy (Appl. No. 43031/98), Judgment (Second Section–Friendly
Settlement), 22 June 2000, not reported 112

Dakman, Özsucu, Bilal, Aytek, Hocaoğlu, Öztürk and Ersancan v. Turkey (Appl. Nos.
30741–30743/96; 30745/96; 30747–30752/96), Decision (Second Section–Friendly
Settlement), 22 March 2001, not reported 123

Danielsson v. Sweden (Appl. No. 38458/04), Decision (Second Section–Arrangement),
12 September 2006, not reported 115

Dănilă v. Romania (Appl. No. 28220/03), Decision (Third Section–Friendly Settlement),
23 October 2007, not yet reported 48

De Becker v. Belgium (Appl. No. 214/56), Judgment (Chamber–Friendly Settlement),
27 March 1962, Series A, Vol. 4 15

Değer v. Turkey (Appl. No. 24934/94), Judgment (First Section–Friendly Settlement),
10 July 2001, not reported 44, 122

Değirmenci a. O. v. Turkey (Appl. No. 31879/96), Judgment (Second Section–Friendly
Settlement), 23 September 2003, not reported 50

Demades v. Turkey (Appl. No. 16219/90), Judgment (Third Section), 31 July 2003, not
reported 197

Demai v. France (Appl. No. 22904/93), Judgment (Chamber–Arrangement),
28 October 1994, Series A, Vol. 289-C 62

Demir v. Turkey (Appl. No. 24990/94), Judgment (First Section–Friendly Settlement),
10 July 2001, not reported 45

Demir v. Turkey (Appl. No. 22280/93), Judgment (First Section–Friendly Settlement),
5 December 2002, not reported 52, 125

Denmark v. Turkey (Appl. No. 34382/97), Judgment (First Section–Friendly
Settlement), 5 April 2000, Reports 2000-IV, 1 . . . . 74–75, 99, 122

Di Mauro v. Italy (Appl. No. 34256/96), Judgment (Grand Chamber),
28 July 1999, Reports 1999-V, 31 113

Dimitrov, Savov and Vishanov v. Bulgaria (Appl. Nos. 37358/97; 37988/97; 39565/98),
Decision (Fourth Section–Arrangement), 10 April 2001, not reported 47, 63

Dinić v. Netherlands (Appl. No. 7137/07), Decision (Third Section–Arrangement),
1 July 2008, not yet reported 41

Djeroud v. France (Appl. No. 13446/87), Judgment (Chamber–Arrangement),
23 January 1991, Series A, Vol. 191-B 19, 21, 31

Doğan v. Turkey (Appl. No. 24939/94), Judgment (First Section–Friendly Settlement),
10 July 2001, not reported 44, 122

Doğan v. Turkey (Appl. No. 73675/01), Decision (Third Section–Friendly Settlement),
21 November 2002, not reported 111

Doğan a. O. v. Turkey (Appl. Nos. 8803-11/02; 8813/02; 8815-19/02), Judgment
(Third Section), 29 June 2004, Reports 2004-VI (extracts), 81. 197

Dömel v. Germany (Appl. No. 31828/03), Decision (Fifth Section–Arrangement),
9 May 2007, not yet reported 51, 70, 149

Draon v. France (Appl. No. 1513/03), Judgment (Grand Chamber–Arrangement),
21 June 2006, Reports 2006-IX, 5 48

Dremlyugin v. Russia (Appl. No. 75136/01), Judgment (First Section–Arrangement),
12 April 2007, not yet reported 114

Đorić-Francuski v. Serbia (Appl. No. 712/06), Decision (Second Section–Arrangement),
4 March 2008, not yet reported 44

Enrico Cecere v. Italy (Appl. No. 70585/01), Judgment (Third Section–Arrangement),
24 November 2005, not reported 69

Erat and Sağlam v. Turkey (Appl. No. 30492/96), Judgment (Fourth Section–Friendly
Settlement), 26 March 2002, not reported 46, 102
Ercolani v. San Marino (Appl. No. 35430/97), Judgment (Second Section–Arrangement),
25 November 2003, not reported 42
Erdogan v. Turkey (Appl. No. 26337/95), Judgment (Third Section–Friendly Settlement),
20 June 2002, not reported 52
Ergüne a. O. v. Turkey (Appl. No. 42838/98), Decision (Third Section–Arrangement),
7 November 2002, not reported. 69
Erkanli v. Turkey (Appl. No. 37721/97), Judgment (Second Section–Friendly Settlement),
13 February 2003, not reported 36, 41
Erkner and Hofauer v. Austria (Appl. No. 9616/81), Judgment (Chamber–Arrangement),
29 September 1987, Series A, Vol. 124-D 23, 30
Esmaili v. Netherlands (Appl. No. 23254/05), Decision (Third Section–Arrangement),
23 May 2006, not reported 41
Estate of Nitschke v. Sweden (Appl. No. 6301/05), Judgment (Third Section),
27 September 2007, not yet reported 68, 104
Eugenia Michaelidou Developments Ltd and Michael Tymvios v. Turkey
(Appl. No. 16163/90), Judgment (Fourth Section–Arrangement),
22 April 2008, not yet reported 70, 80
F.C. v. United Kingdom (Appl. No. 37344/97), Decision (Third Section–Arrangement),
7 September 1999, not reported. 41, 53
F.F. v. Italy (Appl. No. 30133/96), Decision (Second Section–Arrangement),
27 January 2000, not reported 41, 63
Fahriye Calişkan v. Turkey (Appl. No. 40516/98), Judgment (Fourth Section),
2 October 2007, not yet reported. 196
Falkowski v. Poland (Appl. No. 32743/06), Decision (Fourth Section–Arrangement),
23 October 2007, not yet reported. 131
Faulkner v. United Kingdom (Appl. No. 30308/96), Judgment (Third Section–
Arrangement), 30 November 1999, not reported 42, 63
Fedotova v. Russia (Appl. No. 73225/01), Judgment (First Section), 13 April 2006,
not reported. 115
Ferrari v. Italy (Appl. No. 33440/96), Judgment (Grand Chamber),
28 July 1999, not reported 113
Fielding v. United Kingdom (Appl. No. 36940/97), Judgment (Second Section–
Arrangement), 29 January 2002, not reported 64
Figiel v. Poland (Appl. No. 10281/03), Decision (Fourth Section–Unilateral Declaration),
8 July 2008, not yet reported 132
Figiel v. Poland (No. 1) (Appl. No. 38190/05), Judgment (Fourth Section),
17 July 2008, not yet reported 104, 132
Finucane v. United Kingdom (Appl. No. 29178/95), Judgment (Fourth Section),
1 July 2003, Reports 2003-VIII, 1 . . . . , ... 27
Foti a. O. v. Italy (Appl. Nos. 7604/76; 7719/76; 7781/77; 7913/77), Judgment
(Chamber–Arrangement), 21 November 1983, Series A, Vol. 69 . . . . 23, 30
Fouquet v. France (Appl. No. 20398/92), Judgment (Chamber–Arrangement),
31 January 1996, Reports 1996-I, 19. . . . . 30, 62
Franosz and Franosz v. Poland (Appl. No. 17992/03), Decision (Fourth Section–
Arrangement), 2 October 2007, not yet reported 130
Friedl v. Austria (Appl. No. 15225/89), Judgment (Chamber–Arrangement),
31 January 1995, Series A, Vol. 305-B 62
Fusco v. Italy (Appl. No. 43049/98), Judgment (Second Section–Friendly Settlement),
22 June 2000, not reported 112

G.A. v. Italy (Appl. No. 43096/98), Judgment (Second Section–Friendly Settlement),
22 June 2000, not reported 112
G.P. v. Italy (Appl. No. 43093/98), Judgment (Second Section–Friendly Settlement),
22 June 2000, not reported 112
Galietti v. Italy (Appl. No. 43104/98), Judgment (Second Section–Friendly Settlement),
22 June 2000, not reported 112
Galusiewicz v. Poland (Appl. No. 8651/04), Decision (Fourth Section–Unilateral
Declaration), 9 December 2008, not yet reported 132
Gamble v. United Kingdom (Appl. No. 68056/01), Judgment (Fourth Section–
Arrangement), 9 January 2007, not reported 116
Gapicheva v. Russia (Appl. No. 34746/04), Decision (First Section–Arrangement),
2 March 2006, not reported. 82
Gaulieder v. Slovakia (Appl. No. 36909/97), Judgment (Second Section–Friendly
Settlement), 18 May 2000, not reported 43
Gaydukov v. Russia (Appl. No. 75038/01), Judgment (First Section–Arrangement),
12 April 2007, not yet reported 114
Gelgeç and Özdemir v. Turkey (Appl. No. 27700/95), Judgment (Second Section–
Friendly Settlement), 1 March 2001, not reported. 102
Gianazza v. Italy (Appl. No. 69878/01), Judgment (Second Section–Arrangement),
14 October 2008, not yet reported. 70
Göçmen a. O. v. Turkey (Appl. No. 19279/92), Judgment (First Section),
30 January 2001, not reported. 166
Göktaş a. O. v. Turkey (Appl. No. 31787/96), Judgment (First Section–Arrangement),
25 September 2001, not reported. 50
Golob and 5 Others v. Slovenia (Appl. Nos. 2589/03; 2590/03; 3051/03; 3882/03;
10405/03; 14197/03), Decision (Third Section–Arrangement), 4 March 2008,
not yet reported 65
Görgülü v. Turkey (Appl. No. 6802/03), Decision (Third Section–Arrangement),
30 September 2008, not yet reported. 164
Grechko v. Russia (Appl. No. 75037/01), Judgment (First Section–Arrangement),
12 April 2007, not yet reported 114
Greig v. United Kingdom (Appl. No. 10567/05), Decision (Fourth Section–
Arrangement), 7 October 2008, not yet reported 44
Grill v. Sweden (Appl. No. 38503/02), Decision (Second Section–Arrangement),
22 November 2005, not reported. 115
Grimm v. Germany (Appl. No. 27696/05), Decision (Fifth Section–Arrangement),
13 March 2007, not yet reported 113
Groza a. O. v. Romania (Appl. No. 28139/04), Decision (Third Section–Arrangement),
10 January 2008, not yet reported 50
Güler v. Germany (Appl. No. 48967/99), Decision (Fourth Section–Arrangement),
13 September 2001, not reported. 41, 61
Gülhan a. O. v. Turkey (Appl. No. 42839/98), Decision (Third Section–Arrangement),
7 November 2002, not reported. 69
Gündan, Karadag, Can, Canpolat, Şaşmaz, Şaşmaz, Izgi and Tasdemir v. Turkey
(Appl. Nos. 30674–30677/96; 30679/96; 30680/96; 30682–30685/96),
Decision (Second Section–Friendly Settlement), 22 March 2001, not reported 123
Gündüz a. O. v. Turkey (Appl. No. 31249/96), Judgment (First Section–Friendly
Settlement), 14 November 2000, not reported. 104
Guttschuss v. Germany (Appl. No. 771/04), Decision (Fifth Section–Unilateral
Declaration), 8 January 2008, not yet reported 114, 146

H.D. v. Poland (Appl. No. 33310/96), Judgment (Fourth Section–Friendly Settlement),
20 June 2002, not reported 101
H.K. a. O. v. Turkey (Appl. No. 29864/96), Judgment (Second Section–Friendly
Settlement), 14 January 2003, not reported 125
Hacioğlu a. O. v. Turkey (Appl. Nos. 7253/04; 7260/04; 7266/04; 7268/04; 7270/04;
7272/04; 14873/04; 15047/04; 15071/04; 15093/04; 15113/04), Decision
(Second Section–Friendly Settlement), 4 January 2007, not yet reported 45
Hadri-Vionnet v. Switzerland (Appl. No. 55525/00), Judgment (Fifth Section),
14 February 2008, not yet reported 186
Halil v. Cyprus (Appl. No. 33981/96), Decision (Third Section–Arrangement),
7 December 1999, not reported 53
Hanim Tosun v. Turkey (Appl. No. 31731/96), Judgment (First Section–Arrangement),
6 November 2003, not reported 126
Haran v. Turkey (Appl. No. 25754/94), Judgment (Fourth Section–Unilateral
Declaration), 26 March 2002, not reported 119, 147
Hassdenteufel v. Germany (Appl. No. 21214/03), Decision (Fifth Section–Unilateral
Declaration), 6 November 2007, not yet reported 113
Hatami v. Sweden (Appl. No. 32448/96), Judgment (Chamber–Arrangement),
9 October 1998, Reports 1998-VII, 3038 21
Hattatoğlu v. Turkey (Appl. No. 37094/97), Judgment (Third Section–Friendly
Settlement), 26 June 2003, not reported 48
Hegnar and Periscopus AS v. Norway (Appl. No. 38638/02), Decision (Third Section–
Arrangement), 14 October 2004, not reported. 64
Heron v. United Kingdom (Appl. No. 66181/01), Decision (Fourth Section–
Arrangement), 24 June 2008, not yet reported 116
Hryniewicki v. Poland (Appl. No. 18779/02), Decision (Fourth Section–Unilateral
Declaration), 22 April 2008, not yet reported 146
Huber v. Switzerland (Appl. No. 12794/87), Judgment (Plenary), 23 October 1990,
Series A, Vol. 188. 183
Hulki Güneş v. Turkey (Appl. No. 28490/95), Judgment (Third Section), 19 June 2003,
Reports 2003-VII (extracts), 187 196
Hurtado v. Switzerland (Appl. No. 17549/90), Judgment (Chamber–Arrangement),
28 January 1994, Series A, Vol. 280-A 62
Hutten-Czapska v. Poland (Appl. No. 35014/97), Judgment (Grand Chamber–Pilot
Judgment), 19 June 2006, Reports 2006-VIII, 57 . . . . 4, 165, 174, 180
Hutten-Czapska v. Poland (Appl. No. 35014/97), Judgment (Grand Chamber–
Friendly Settlement), 28 April 2008, not yet reported 4, 73, 76, 83, 165, 174, 180
Hutton v. United Kingdom (Appl. No. 28014/02), Decision (Fourth Section–
Arrangement), 24 June 2008, not yet reported 195
İ.İ., İ.Ş., K.E. and A.Ö. v. Turkey (Appl. Nos. 30953/96; 30954/96; 30955/96;
30956/96), Judgment (First Section–Friendly Settlement), 6 November 2001,
not reported 45, 120
I.O. v. Switzerland (Appl. No. 21529/93), Judgment (Second Section–Friendly
Settlement), 8 March 2001, not reported. 77, 189
İçen and İçen v. Turkey (Appl. No. 10268/02), Decision (Second Section–
Arrangement), 6 May 2008, not yet reported. 46, 102, 150
Institute of French Priests a. O. v. Turkey (Appl. No. 26308/95), Judgment (Fourth
Section–Arrangement), 14 December 2000 42
Ireland v. United Kingdom (Appl. No. 5310/71), Judgment (Plenary), 18 January 1978,
Series A, Vol. 25. 71

J.M. v. United Kingdom (Appl. No. 41518/98), Decision (Fourth Section–Arrangement),
28 September 2000, Reports 2000-X, 561 48

J.M. v. United Kingdom (Appl. No. 47014/99), Decision (Fourth Section–Arrangement),
15 January 2002, not reported 42

J.T. v. United Kingdom (Appl. No. 26494/95), Judgment (Fourth Section–Arrangement),
30 March 2000, not reported 53, 63

Jaffredou v. France (Appl. No. 39843/98), Judgment (Third Section–Friendly Settlement),
19 Mai 1999, not reported 53

Jordan v. United Kingdom (Appl. No. 24746/94), Judgment (Third Section), 4 May 2001,
not reported 27

Josefsson v. Sweden (Appl. No. 38477/04), Decision (Second Section–Arrangement),
12 September 2006, not reported 115

K. v. Austria (Appl. No. 16002/90), Judgment (Chamber–Arrangement),
2 June 1993, Series A, Vol. 255-B 20, 27–28, 29, 61, 63

Kabul a. O. v. Turkey (Appl. No. 24873/02), Decision (Second Section–
Arrangement), 4 September 2007, not yet reported 42, 46, 101

Kanoš v. Slovakia (Appl. No. 67037/01), Decision (Fourth Section–Arrangement),
15 March 2005, not reported 55

Kaplan v. Turkey (Appl. No. 24932/94), Judgment (Second Section–Friendly Settlement),
26 February 2002, not reported 101

Kaplan v. Turkey (Appl. No. 38578/97), Judgment (Third Section–Friendly Settlement),
10 October 2002, not reported 52–53

Kaptan v. Turkey (Appl. No. 46749/99), Judgment (Third Section–Friendly Settlement),
22 December 2004, not reported 45

Kara a. O. v. Turkey (Appl. No. 42849/98), Decision (Third Section–Arrangement),
7 November 2002, not reported 69

Karakoç v. Turkey (Appl. No. 28294/95), Judgment (Third Section–Friendly Settlement),
2 November 2004, not reported 49

Karakoyun v. Turkey (Appl. No. 51285/99), Decision (Third Section–
Arrangement), 30 March 2006, not reported 45, 101, 126

Karci a. O. v. Turkey (Appl. No. 42841/98), Decision (Third Section–
Arrangement), 7 November 2002, not reported 69

Karlsson v. Sweden (Appl. No. 68721/01), Decision (Second Section–Arrangement),
4 October 2005, not reported 115

Karner v. Austria (Appl. No. 40016/98), Judgment (First Section), 24 July 2003, Reports
2003–IX, 199. 38

Kastrati v. Bulgaria (Appl. No. 41348/98), Decision (Fourth Section–Arrangement),
30 November 2000, not reported 54

Katić v. Serbia (Appl. No. 13920/04), Decision (Second Section–Arrangement),
4 March 2008, not yet reported 20, 55

Katić v. Serbia (Appl. No. 13920/04), Decision (Second Section), 7 July 2009,
not yet reported 55

Katikaridis a. O. v. Greek (Appl. No. 19385/92), Judgment (Chamber–Arrangement),
31 March 1998, Reports 1998-II, 699 23

Kaya v. Turkey (Appl. No. 22729/93), Judgement (Chamber), 19 February 1998,
Reports 1998-I, 297. 120

Kaya v. Turkey (Appl. No. 20981/03), Decision (Second Section–Arrangement),
13 May 2008, not yet reported. 46, 102

Keçeci v. Turkey (Appl. No. 38588/97), Judgment (Fourth Section–Friendly Settlement),
26 November 2002, not reported 102, 103

Kessler v. Switzerland (Appl. No. 10577/04), Judgment (First Section),
26 July 2007, not yet reported 185, 188
Kiliç v. Turkey (Appl. No. 22492/93), Judgment (Grand Chamber),
28 March 2000, Reports 2000-III, 75 120
Kiliç and Kiliç v. Turkey (Appl. No. 42715/98), Decision (Third Section–Arrangement),
13 May 2004, not reported 50
Kinay and Kinay v. Turkey (Appl. No. 31890/96), Judgment (Second Section–Friendly
Settlement), 26 November 2002, not reported 43
Kiraç v. Turkey (Appl. No. 30844/96), Decision (Second Section–Friendly Settlement),
22 March 2001, not reported 101
Kizilgedik v. Turkey (Appl. No. 24944/94), Judgment (First Section–Friendly
Settlement), 10 July 2001, not reported 45, 123
Klavdianos v. Greece (Appl. No. 38841/97), Judgment (Third Section–Arrangement),
17 October 2000, not reported 47
Köksal v. Netherlands (Appl. No. 31725/96), Judgment (First Section–Friendly
Settlement), 20 March 2001, not reported 19
Kölge v. Turkey (Appl. No. 20227/02), Decision (Second Section–Arrangement),
21 November 2006, not reported 46, 101
Kolona v. Cyprus (Appl. No. 28025/03), Judgment (First Section–Arrangement),
2 October 2008, not yet reported 70
Korkusuz, Suiçmez, Canpolat, Karaman, Bayhan, Delidere and Orakçi v. Turkey
(Appl. Nos. 30763–30772/96), Decision (Second Section–Friendly Settlement),
22 March 2001, not reported 123
Kornacki v. Poland (Appl. No. 2967/05), Decision (Fourth Section–Arrangement),
27 March 2008, not yet reported 131
Korva v. Sweden (Appl. No. 27818/04), Decision (Second Section–Arrangement),
9 May 2006, not reported 115
Kos v. Poland (Appl. No. 36240/03), Decision (Fourth Section–Arrangement),
26 June 2007, not yet reported 130
Kósa v. Hungary (Appl. No. 43352/98), Judgment (Second Section–Arrangement),
1 October 2002, not reported 61
Kostovski v. Netherlands (Appl. No. 11454/85), Judgment (Plenary–Arrangement),
29 March 1990, Series A, Vol. 170-B 23, 30
Kotsidis v. Sweden (Appl. No. 9933/03), Decision (Third Section–Arrangement),
20 February 2007, not yet reported 116
Kozlowski v. Germany (Appl. No. 23462/03), Decision (Fifth Section–Arrangement),
15 May 2007, not yet reported 113
Krächan v. Germany (Appl. No. 39644/03), Decision (Fifth Section–Arrangement),
27 November 2007, not yet reported 113
Krasuski v. Poland (Appl. No. 61444/00), Judgment (Fourth Section), 14 June 2005,
Reports 2005-V, 1 129
Krawczak v. Poland (Appl. No. 40387/06), Judgment (Fourth Section), 8 April 2008,
not yet reported 104
Krzysztof Kaniewski v. Poland (Appl. No. 49788/06), Judgment (Fourth Section),
30 September 2008, not yet reported 104
Kuberski v. Poland (Appl. No. 33099/03), Decision (Fourth Section–Arrangement),
2 October 2007, not yet reported 130
Kudła v. Poland (Appl. No. 30210/96), Judgment (Grand Chamber),
26 October 2000, Reports 2000-XI, 197 . . . . 71, 128–129
Kukalo v. Russia (Appl. No. 63995/00), Judgment (First Section),
3 November 2005, not reported 115

Külekçi a. O. v. Turkey (Appl. No. 39330/98), Decision (First Section–Arrangement),
  12 December 2002, not reported 63
Kurier Zeitungsverlag und Druckerei GmbH v. Austria (Appl. No. 48481/99),
  Decision (Third Section–Arrangement), 20 March 2001, not reported. 54, 62
Kwaśnik v. Poland (Appl. No. 6480/04), Decision (Fourth Section–Unilateral
  Declaration), 20 May 2008, not yet reported 132, 146
Kyzioł v. Poland (Appl. No. 24203/05), Judgment (Fourth Section),
  12 February 2008, not yet reported 132
L.M.G. v. Italy (Appl. No. 32655/96), Judgment (Second Section–Arrangement),
  19 April 2001, not reported 69
Lamguindaz v. United Kingdom (Appl. No. 16152/90), Judgment (Chamber–
  Arrangement), 23 June 1993, Series A, Vol. 258-C. 21, 62
Laskowski v. Poland (Appl. No. 17220/03), Decision (Fourth Section–Arrangement),
  12 February 2008, not yet reported 131
Leber and 5 Others v. Slovenia (Appl. Nos. 17520/03; 18425/03; 21523/03;
  22641/03; 31198/03; 33936/03), Decision (Third Section–Arrangement),
  11 March 2008, not yet reported 65
Lee v. Ukraine (Appl. No. 7697/02), Decision (Fifth Section–Arrangement),
  6 November 2006, not reported. 46–47, 101
Leggett v. United Kingdom (Appl. No. 37517/97), Decision (Third Section–
  Arrangement), 31 August 1999, not reported. 42, 53
Lendzion v. Poland (Appl. No. 41587/05), Decision (Fourth Section–Arrangement),
  30 January 2007, not yet reported 131
Leonov v. Russia (Appl. No. 16606/02), Decision (First Section–Arrangement),
  10 November 2005, not reported. 81
Leppänen and Aittamäki v. Finland (Appl. No. 30271/96), Decision (Fourth Section–
  Arrangement), 13 January 2000, not reported 41
Levin v. Russia (Appl. No. 33264/02), Judgment (First Section),
  2 February 2006, not reported 115
Lewandowska v. Poland (Appl. No. 55204/00), Decision (Fourth Section–Arrangement),
  27 November 2001, not reported. 61
Lindelöf v. Sweden (Appl. No. 22771/93), Judgment (First Section–Friendly Settlement),
  20 June 2000, not reported 43
Lipcan v. Moldova (Appl. No. 32737/03), Decision (Fourth Section–Arrangement),
  9 October 2007, not yet reported. 101
Lisiecki v. Poland (Appl. No. 18034/05), Decision (Fourth Section–Arrangement),
  6 May 2008, not yet reported. 130
Löhr v. Germany (Appl. No. 10465/05), Decision (Fifth Section–Arrangement),
  4 December 2007, not yet reported 113
Loizidou v. Turkey (Appl. No. 15318/89), Judgment (Grand Chamber),
  23 March 1995, Series A, Vol. 310. 74
Loizidou v. Turkey (Appl. No. 15318/89), Judgment (Grand Chamber),
  18 December 1996, Reports 1996-VI, 2216 197
Lombardi and 7 Others v. Italy (Appl. No. 43103/98), Judgment (Second Section–
  Friendly Settlement), 22 June 2000, not reported. 112
Lotter and Lotter v. Bulgaria (Appl. No. 39015/97), Judgment (First Section–
  Arrangement), 19 May 2004, not reported. 41
Lück v. Germany (Appl. No. 58364/00), Judgment (Fifth Section–Unilateral
  Declaration), 15 May 2008, not yet reported 146
Luedicke, Belkacem & Koc v. Germany (Appl. Nos. 6210/73; 6877/75; 7132/75),
  Judgment (Chamber–Arrangement), 10 March 1980, Series A, Vol. 36 . . . . 15, 30

M. v. United Kingdom (Appl. No. 30357/03), Decision (Fourth Section–Friendly
   Settlement), 13 February 2007, not yet reported 41
M.M. v. Poland (Appl. No. 37850/03), Decision (Fourth Section–Unilateral
   Declaration), 4 January 2008, not yet reported 132
M.R. and C.S. v. Italy (Appl. No. 42286/98), Decision (First Section–Arrangement),
   17 October 2002, not reported 61
M.S. v. Bulgaria (Appl. No. 40061/98), Judgment (First Section–Arrangement),
   4 July 2002, not reported 52
Macir v. Turkey (Appl. No. 28516/95), Judgment (Second Section–Friendly Settlement),
   22 April 2003, not reported 125
Mączyński v. Poland (Appl. No. 1084/02), Decision (Fourth Section–Arrangement),
   7 February 2006, not reported 130
Madi v. France (Appl. No. 51294/99), Judgment (Second Section–Friendly Settlement),
   27 April 2004, not reported 45, 49
Makowska v. Poland (Appl. No. 34762/06), Decision (Fourth Section–Arrangement),
   16 September 2008, not yet reported 131
Małagocki v. Poland (Appl. No. 53122/07), Decision (Fourth Section–Arrangement),
   21 October 2008, not yet reported 131
Malone v. United Kingdom (Appl. No. 8691/79), Judgment (Chamber–Arrangement),
   26 April 1985, Series A, Vol. 95 . . . . 23, 30
Manasson v. Sweden (Appl. No. 41265/98), Judgment (Fourth Section–Friendly
   Settlement), 20 July 2004, not reported 115
Marchel v. Poland (Appl. No. 31119/02), Decision (Fourth Section–Arrangement),
   13 November 2007, not yet reported 130
Maria Castelli v. Italy (Appl. No. 30920/96), Judgment (Second Section–Arrangement),
   31 May 2001, not reported 62
Marian v. Romania (Appl. No. 42239/04), Decision (Third Section–Arrangement),
   10 January 2008, not yet reported 69
Markieta v. Poland (Appl. No. 49718/06), Decision (Fourth Section–Arrangement),
   21 October 2008, not yet reported 130
Marković v. Serbia (Appl. No. 27919/05), Decision (Second Section–Unilateral
   Declaration), 10 June 2008, not yet reported 146
Marlhens v. France (Appl. No. 22862/93), Judgment (Chamber–Arrangement),
   24 May 1995, Series A, Vol. 317-A 19, 62
Mathiasson v. Sweden (Appl. No. 6161/04), Decision (Second Section–Arrangement),
   9 May 2006, not reported 115
Matkowska v. Poland (Appl. No. 18410/06), Decision (Fourth Section–Arrangement),
   19 June 2007, not yet reported 131
Maurice v. France (Appl. No. 11810/03), Judgment (Grand Chamber–Arrangement),
   21 June 2006, Reports 2006-IX, 33 48
McCann a. O. v. United Kingdom (Appl. No. 18984/91), Judgment (Grand Chamber),
   27 September 1995, Series A, Vol. 324 120
McErlane a. O. v. United Kingdom (Appl. Nos. 67777/01; 68429/01; 68430/01),
   Decision (Fourth Section–Arrangement), 3 May 2007, not yet reported 64
McKerr v. United Kingdom (Appl. No. 28883/95), Judgment (Third Section),
   4 May 2001, Reports 2001-III, 475 27
McShane v. United Kingdom (Appl. No. 43290/98), Judgment (Fourth Section),
   28 May 2002, not reported 27
Mehmet Özcan v. Turkey (Appl. No. 29856/96), Judgment (Second Section–Friendly
   Settlement), 9 April 2002, not reported 45, 101

Melnic v. Moldova (Appl. No. 6923/03), Judgment (Fourth Section),
 14 November 2006, not reported 104
Memiş v. Turkey (Appl. No. 42593/98), Judgment (Second Section–Arrangement),
 21 February 2006, not reported 46, 101
Militowska v. Poland (Appl. No. 10002/05), Decision (Fourth Section–Arrangement),
 11 December 2007, not yet reported 131
Millan I Tornes v. Andorra (Appl. No. 35052/97), Judgment (First Section–Friendly
 Settlement), 6 July 1999, Reports 1999-IV, 1, para. 21 41
Miragall v. Spain (Appl. Nos. 38366/97; 38688/97; 40777/98; 40843/98;
 41015/98; 41400/98; 41446/98; 41484/98; 41487/98 and 41509/98),
 Judgment (Fourth Section–Arrangement), 25 May 2000, Reports 2000-I, 275 54
Mlynek v. Austria (Appl. No. 15016/89), Judgment (Chamber–Arrangement),
 27 October 1992, Series A, Vol. 242-C 22
Mocanu v. Romania (Appl. No. 56489/00), Judgment (Third Section–Friendly
 Settlement), 24 May 2006, not reported 45, 49
Modłkowska v. Poland (Appl. No. 6420/02), Decision (Fourth Section–Unilateral
 Declaration), 29 January 2008, not yet reported 132, 146
Moldovahidromaş v. Moldova (Appl. No. 30475/03), Judgment (Fourth Section–
 Arrangement), 13 May 2008, not yet reported 43
Moldovan a. O. v. Romania (Appl. Nos. 41138/98; 64320/01), Judgment
 (Second Section–Friendly Settlement), 5 July 2005, not reported 42, 46–47
Morea v. Italy (Appl. No. 69269/01), Judgment (Second Section–Arrangement),
 29 April 2008, not yet reported 70
Morris v. United Kingdom (Appl. No. 31701/96), Decision (Fourth Section–
 Arrangement), 27 November 2001, not reported 62
Mosgöller & Partner Engineering GmbH v. Austria (Appl. No. 640/03), Decision
 (First Section–Arrangement), 16 June 2005, not reported 55
Mrkonjić a. O. v. Croatia (Appl. No. 16725/02), Decision (First Section–Arrangement),
 13 May 2004, not reported 8
Muyldermans v. Belgium (Appl. No. 12217/86), Judgment (Chamber–Arrangement),
 23 October 1991, Series A, Vol. 214-A. 20, 63
N.Ö. v. Turkey (Appl. No. 33234/96), Judgment (First Section–Friendly Settlement),
 17 October 2002, not reported 102, 125
Nepomuceno Mora a. O. v. Portugal (Appl. No. 38780/97), Decision (Fourth Section–
 Arrangement), 21 September 1999, not reported 62
Notar v. Romania (Appl. No. 42860/98), Judgment (Second Section–Friendly
 Settlement), 20 April 2004, not reported 46, 47, 49
Novicov v. Moldova (Appl. No. 507/04), Decision (Fourth Section–Arrangement),
 20 May 2008, not yet reported. 44
Nowiński v. Poland (Appl. No. 14883/04), Decision (Fourth Section–Unilateral
 Declaration), 7 October 2008, not yet reported 132
Nugent v. United Kingdom (Appl. No. 77423/01), Decision (Fourth Section–
 Arrangement), 24 June 2008, not yet reported. 116
Oates v. Poland (Appl. No. 35036/97), Decision (Fourth Section–Arrangement),
 7 September 2000, not reported. 43
Oganov v. Russia (Appl. No. 53826/00), Decision (First Section–Arrangement),
 23 May 2006, not reported 54, 82, 143
Ogloblin v. Russia (Appl. No. 30028/02), Decision (First Section–Arrangement),
 23 November 2006, not reported. 81–82
Oğraş a. O. v. Turkey (Appl. No. 39978/98), Judgment (Fourth Section–
 Arrangement), 28 October 2003, not reported. 101, 126

Okatan v. Turkey (Appl. No. 40996/98), Judgment (Third Section–Friendly Settlement),
13 July 2006, not reported 46

Oleksiw v. Germany (Appl. No. 31384/02), Decision (Fifth Section–Unilateral
Declaration), 11 September 2007, not yet reported 113

Oliver and Britten v. United Kingdom (Appl. Nos. 61604/00; 68452/01), Judgment
(Fourth Section–Arrangement), 25 April 2006, not reported 64

Olivera Neves v. Portugal (Appl. No. 11612/85), Judgment (Chamber–Friendly
Settlement), 25 May 1989, Series A, Vol. 153-B. 29

Orak v. Turkey (Appl. No. 24936/94), Judgment (First Section–Friendly Settlement),
10 July 2001, not reported 44, 122

Oral a. O. v. Turkey (Appl. No. 27735/95), Judgment (First Section–Friendly
Settlement), 28 March 2002, not reported 46, 101

Orha v. Romania (Appl. No. 1486/02), Judgment (Third Section–Arrangement),
4 November 2008, not reported 42

Orlowski v. Germany (Appl. No. 35000/05), Decision (Fifth Section–Unilateral
Declaration), 1 April 2008, not yet reported 146

Osman v. United Kingdom (Appl. No. 23452/94), Judgment (Grand Chamber),
28 October 1998, Reports 1998-VIII, 3124. 120

Önder v. Turkey (Appl. No. 31136/96), Judgment (Third Section–Friendly Settlement),
25 July 2002, not reported 102

Önsöz v. Turkey (Appl. No. 73676/01), Decision (Third Section–Friendly Settlement),
21 November 2002, not reported 111

Özbey v. Turkey (Appl. No. 31883/96), Judgment (First Section–Friendly Settlement),
31 January 2002, not reported 101

Özgür Kiliç v. Turkey (Appl. No. 42591/98), Judgment (Second Section–Arrangement),
22 July 2003, not reported 47, 102

Özkan Kiliç v. Turkey (Appl. Nos. 27209/95; 27211/95), Judgment (Second Section–
Arrangement), 26 November 2002, not reported 63

Özkur and Göksungur v. Turkey (Appl. No. 37088/97), Judgment (Second Section–
Friendly Settlement), 4 March 2003, not reported 46

P.K. v. Poland (Appl. No. 37774/97), Judgment (First Section–Arrangement),
6 November 2003, not reported. 101

Paritchi v. Moldova (Appl. No. 54396/00), Decision (Fourth Section–Arrangement),
1 March 2005, not reported. 81

Parlak a. O. v. Turkey (Appl. Nos. 24942/94; 24943/94; 25125/94), Judgment
(First Section–Friendly Settlement), 10 July 2001, not reported. 44, 123

Parry v. Germany (Appl. No. 24378/02), Decision (Fifth Section–Unilateral
Declaration), 16 October 2007, not yet reported 113

Pavel v. Romania (Appl. No. 28709/04), Decision (Third Section–Arrangement),
10 January 2008, not yet reported 69

Pawłowska v. Poland (Appl. No. 37991/04), Decision (Fourth Section–Arrangement),
10 June 2008, not yet reported. 130

Pektaş a. O. v. Turkey (Appl. No. 73722/01), Decision (Second Section–
Arrangement), 4 December 2007, not yet reported 46, 101

Petrini v. Italy (Appl. Nos. 66292/01; 66299/01), Judgment (First Section–
Arrangement), 22 April 2004, not reported 47

Piccinini v. Italy (No. 2) (Appl. No. 28936/95), Judgment (Second Section–Friendly
Settlement), 11 April 2000, not reported 50

Piekarczyk v. Poland (Appl. No. 47727/06), Decision (Fourth Section–Arrangement),
29 January 2008, not yet reported 131

Pitsillos v. Cyprus (Appl. No. 41854/98), Judgment (Third Section–Arrangement),
  28 March 2000, not reported 62
Pla and Puncernau v. Andorra (Appl. No. 69498/01), Judgment (Fourth Section–
  Arrangement), 10 October 2006, not reported 48
Podbolotova v. Russia (Appl. No. 26091/02), Decision (First Section–Arrangement),
  24 November 2005, not reported 81
Pohlen v. Slovenia (Appl. No. 28457/03), Decision (Third Section), 3 June 2008,
  not yet reported 104
Poiss v. Austria (Appl. No. 9816/82), Judgment (Chamber–Arrangement),
  29 September 1987, Series A, Vol. 124-E 23, 30
Pokorny v. Austria (Appl. No. 57080/00), Judgment (Fourth Section–Friendly
  Settlement), 16 December 2003, not reported 47
Polupanova v. Russia (Appl. No. 21447/04), Judgment (Fifth Section),
  13 July 2006, not reported 115
Popescu v. Romania (Appl. No. 3831/04), Decision (Third Section–Arrangement),
  10 January 2008, not yet reported 69
Popov v. Russia (Appl. No. 34310/06), Decision (First Section–Arrangement),
  10 January 2008, not yet reported 41
Prokudin v. Russia (Appl. No. 24408/02), Decision (Third Section–Arrangement),
  7 December 2006, not reported 79–80
Pyatko a. O. v. Russia (Appl. No. 38374/02), Decision (First Section–Arrangement),
  14 September 2006, not reported 54, 143
Ramazan Sari v. Turkey (Appl. No. 41926/98), Judgment (First Section–Arrangement),
  31 July 2003, not reported 101
Ratajczyk v. Poland (Appl. No. 11215/02), Decision (Fourth Section),
  31 May 2005, Reports 2005-VIII, 379. 129
Rathfelder v. United Kingdom (Appl. No. 63507/00), Judgment (Fourth Section–
  Arrangement), 9 January 2007, not yet reported 116
Rebocho v. Portugal (Appl. No. 34562/97), Judgment (Fourth Section–Friendly
  Settlement), 30 April 1999, not reported 40
Remesz v. Poland (Appl. No. 32224/04), Decision (Fourth Section–Arrangement),
  9 December 2008, not yet reported 130
Revina v. Russia (Appl. No. 32150/03), Decision (First Section–Arrangement),
  9 November 2006, not reported 82
Robson v. United Kingdom (Appl. No. 7112/06), Decision (Fourth Section–
  Arrangement), 9 September 2008, not yet reported 64
Rocca v. Italy (Appl. No. 59452/00), Judgment (First Section–Arrangement),
  27 November 2003, not reported 62
Rogalev v. Russia (Appl. No. 55941/00), Decision (Third Section–Arrangement),
  3 March 2005, not reported 54–55, 143
Romlin v. Sweden (Appl. No. 48630/99), Judgment (Fourth Section–Arrangement),
  15 June 2004, not reported 40
Rosival a. O. v. Slovakia (Appl. No. 17684/02), Judgment (Fourth Section–Arrangement),
  23 September 2008, not yet reported 42
Rudeanu v. Romania (Appl. No. 21428/03), Decision (Third Section–Arrangement),
  2 September 2008, not yet reported 48, 101
Rugină v. Romania (Appl. No. 21863/04), Decision (Third Section–Friendly Settlement),
  23 October 2007, not yet reported. 48
S.A. and D.D.L. v. Italy (Appl. No. 30973/96), Judgment (Second Section–
  Arrangement), 12 April 2001, not reported 69

S.B. a. O. v. Italy (Appl. No. 62976/00), Decision (Second Section–Arrangement),
17 May 2001, not reported 62
Sadura v. Poland (Appl. No. 35382/06), Judgment (Fourth Section), 1 July 2008,
not yet reported 104, 132
Sahli v. Belgium (Appl. No. 38707/97), Judgment (Third Section–Friendly Settlement),
9 January 2001, not reported 41
Saki v. Turkey (Appl. No. 29359/95), Judgment (First Section–Friendly Settlement),
30 October 2001, not reported 45
Sakowski and Sakowska v. Poland (Appl. No. 5201/06), Decision (Fourth Section–
Unilateral Declaration), 10 June 2008, not yet reported 132
Salkič v. Slovenia (Appl. No. 76508/01), Decision (Third Section–Arrangement),
21 October 2004, not reported 50
Salman v. Turkey (Appl. No. 63745/00), Decision (Fourth Section–Arrangement),
3 April 2007, not yet reported 46, 102
Samoylenko v. Russia (Appl. No. 7366/04), Decision (First Section–Arrangement),
8 November 2007, not yet reported 82, 115
Sarnowski v. Poland (Appl. No. 3879/05), Decision (Fourth Section–Arrangement),
12 December 2006, not reported 131
Sartorelli v. Italy (Appl. No. 42357/98), Judgment (First Section–Arrangement),
9 October 2003, not reported 62
Schisas v. Cyprus (Appl. No. 62078/00), Decision (First Section–Arrangement),
25 October 2005, not reported 53
Schuler-Zgraggen v. Switzerland (Appl. No. 14518/89), Judgment (Chamber),
24 June 1993, Series A, Vol. 263 187
Schuler-Zgraggen v. Switzerland (Appl. No. 14518/89), Judgment (Chamber),
31 January 1995, Series A, Vol. 305-A 187
Scoppola v. Italy (No. 2) (Appl. No. 10249/03), Judgment (Grand Chamber),
17 September 2009, not yet reported 39
Scott v. United Kingdom (Appl. No. 62688/00), Decision (Fourth Section–Arrangement),
25 August 2005, not reported 44
Selim v. Cyprus (Appl. No. 47293/99), Judgment (Fourth Section–Arrangement),
16 July 2002, Reports 2002-VI, 179 63
Sevostyanov v. Russia (Appl. No. 76736/01), Judgment (First Section–Arrangement),
12 April 2007, not yet reported 114
Seweryn v. Poland (Appl. No. 38620/06), Decision (Fourth Section–Unilateral
Declaration), 13 May 2008, not yet reported 132, 146
Shabani v. Switzerland (Appl. No. 29044/06), Judgment (First Section),
5 November 2009, not yet reported 187
Shamina v. Russia (Appl. No. 70501/01), Judgment (Fifth Section),
13 July 2006, not reported 115
Shanaghan v. United Kingdom (Appl. No. 37715/97), Judgment (Third Section),
4 May 2001, not reported 27
Sharomova v. Russia (Appl. No. 34750/04), Decision (First Section–Arrangement),
23 May 2006, not reported 82
Shishlov v. Russia (Appl. No. 75035/01), Judgment (First Section–Arrangement),
12 April 2007, not yet reported 114
Shpynov v. Russia (Appl. No. 21940/03), Decision (First Section–Arrangement),
23 May 2006, not reported 8, 54, 143
Shvetsova v. Russia (Appl. No. 18967/04), Decision (First Section–Arrangement),
8 February 2007, not yet reported 54, 144

Siddik Yasa v. Turkey (Appl. No. 22281/93), Judgment (First Section–Friendly Settlement), 27 June 2002, not reported 101

Siglfirdingur Ehf v. Iceland (Appl. No. 34142/96), Judgment (First Section–Friendly Settlement), 30 May 2000, not reported 41

Singh a. O. v. United Kingdom (Appl. No. 60148/00), Judgment (Fourth Section–Arrangement), 8 June 2006, not reported. 48, 51

Sisák v. Slovakia (Appl. No. 73532/01), Decision (Fourth Section–Arrangement), 1 March 2005, not reported. 55

Skoogström v. Sweden (Appl. No. 8582/79), Judgment (Chamber–Arrangement), 2 October 1984, Series A, Vol. 83 . . . . 20, 27, 30, 31

Skórzybót v. Poland (Appl. No. 3858/05), Decision (Fourth Section–Arrangement), 21 November 2006, not reported. 130

Slavgorodski v. Estonia (Appl. No. 37043/97), Judgment (First Section–Arrangement), 12 September 2000, not reported. 43

Soğukpinar v. Turkey (Appl. No. 31153/96), Judgment (Third Section–Friendly Settlement), 12 December 2002, not reported 48, 52, 101

Solovyev v. Russia (Appl. No. 52339/99), Decision (Second Section–Arrangement), 11 October 2001, not reported 75

Spišák v. Slovakia (Appl. No. 43730/98), Decision (Second Section–Arrangement), 7 December 2000, Reports 2000-XII, 493. 43

Stanek v. Poland (Appl. No. 16244/03), Decision (Fourth Section–Arrangement), 6 November 2007, not yet reported 131

Stankiewicz v. Poland (Appl. No. 25217/02), Decision (Fourth Section–Arrangement), 11 December 2007, not yet reported 51, 73

Staroszczyk v. Poland (Appl. No. 59519/00), Judgment (First Section), 22 March 2007, not yet reported 171

Starshova and Starshov v. Russia (Appl. No. 8333/05), Decision (First Section–Arrangement), 8 September 2005, not reported. 8, 54, 143

Steno Monit v. Italy (Appl. No. 63833/00), Judgment (First Section–Arrangement), 27 May 2004, not reported 47

Strzelecki v. Poland (Appl. No. 23051/05), Decision (Fourth Section–Arrangement), 12 December 2006, not reported. 130

Süleyman Kaplan v. Turkey (Appl. No. 38578/97), Judgment (Third Section–Friendly Settlement), 10 October 2002, not reported. 102

Sumak v. Turkey (Appl. No. 29735/03), Decision (Third Section–Arrangement), 11 October 2007, not yet reported. 101

Sünnetçi v. Turkey (Appl. No. 28632/95), Judgment (Second Section–Arrangement), 22 July 2003, not reported. 47, 102

Sur v. Turkey (Appl. No. 21592/93), Judgment (Chamber–Arrangement), 3 October 1997, Reports 1997-VI, 2034 . . . . 19, 62

Sürek v. Turkey (No. 5) (Appl. Nos. 26976/95; 28305/95; 28307/95), Judgment (Second Section–Arrangement), 16 July 2002, not reported. 63

Szymanowicz v. Poland (Appl. No. 16658/04), Decision (Fourth Section–Arrangement), 20 March 2007, not yet reported 130

Szymańska-Baier v. Poland (Appl. No. 12935/03), Decision (Fourth Section–Arrangement), 11 December 2007, not yet reported 51, 73

Śliwa v. Poland (Appl. No. 6738/07), Decision (Fourth Section–Arrangement), 1 July 2008, not yet reported 131

Śliwa v. Poland (Appl. No. 10265/06), Judgment (Fourth Section), 2 December 2008, not yet reported 104, 132

Şahmo v. Turkey (Appl. No. 37415/97), Judgment (Fourth Section–Friendly Settlement),
    22 June 2004, not reported 46
Şaşmaz, Karadağ, Özsucu, Vuran, Yalçin and Taşkaya v. Turkey (Appl. Nos. 30652–
    30661/96), Decision (Second Section–Friendly Settlement), 22 March 2001,
    not reported 123
Şen v. Turkey (Appl. No. 31154/96), Judgment (Third Section–Friendly
    Settlement), 12 December 2002, not reported 49, 52, 101
Şenses v. Turkey (Appl. No. 24991/94), Judgment (First Section–Friendly Settlement),
    10 July 2001, not reported 45
Şevčíková v. Slovakia (Appl. No. 1928/04), Decision (Fourth Section–Unilateral
    Declaration), 1 April 2008, not yet reported 146
T.A. v. Turkey (Appl. No. 26307/95), Judgment (Second Section–Unilateral
    Declaration), 9 April 2002, not reported 67, 104, 106
Tahraoui v. France (Appl. No. 39776/04), Decision (Fifth Section–Arrangement),
    17 June 2008, not yet reported 41
Tahsin Acar v. Turkey (Appl. No. 26307/95), Judgment
    (Grand Chamber), 6 May 2003, Reports 2003-VI, 1 .... 67, 68, 104, 120, 146, 150, 194
Talankovs v. Latvia (Appl. No. 5001/04), Decision
    (Third Section–Arrangement), 4 January 2008, not yet reported 101
Talewski v. Germany (Appl. No. 16308/05), Decision (Fifth Section–Unilateral
    Declaration), 6 November 2007, not yet reported 113
Tarducci v. Italy (Appl. No. 31460/96), Judgment (Second Section–Arrangement),
    19 April 2001, not reported 69
Tatete v. Switzerland (Appl. No. 41874/98), Judgment (Second Section–Arrangement),
    6 July 2000, not reported 41, 188
Taykov v. Russia (Appl. No. 48498/99), Decision (First Section–Arrangement),
    28 March 2000, not reported 75
Tekmek v. Turkey (Appl. No. 50035/99), Decision (Second Section–Arrangement),
    28 November 2006, not reported 46, 101
Temel v. Turkey (Appl. No. 37047/97), Judgment (Second Section–Friendly
    Settlement), 13 July 2004, not reported 46
Terekhova v. Russia (Appl. No. 21425/04), Judgment (Fifth Section), 13 July 2006,
    not reported 115
The Holy Monasteries v. Greece (Appl. Nos. 13092/87, 13984/88), Judgment
    (Chamber–Arrangement), 1 September 1997, Reports 1997-V, 1565 8
Toğcu v. Turkey (Appl. No. 27601/95), Judgment (Second Section–Unilateral
    Declaration), 9 April 2002, not reported 56, 67, 104, 119
Toğcu v. Turkey (Appl. No. 27601/95), Judgment (Second Section),
    31 May 2005, not reported 56, 119, 284
Trome S.A. v. Spain (Appl. No. 27781/95), Judgment (Fourth Section–
    Arrangement), 1 April 1999, Reports 1999-III, 1 .... 42, 62
Trybus v. Poland (Appl. No. 31503/03), Decision (Fourth Section–Arrangement),
    15 May 2007, not yet reported 102
Trygve Hegnar and Periscopus AS v. Norway (Appl. No. 38638/02), Decision
    (Third Section–Arrangement), 14 October 2004, not reported...................... 48
Tsavachidis v. Greece (Appl. No. 28802/95), Judgment (Grand Chamber–
    Arrangement), 21 January 1999, not reported 43, 62
Tsomtsos a. O. v. Greece (Appl. No. 20680/92), Judgment (Chamber–Arrangement),
    31 March 1998, Reports 1998-II, 705 25
Tur v. Poland (Appl. No. 21695/05), Judgment (Fourth Section), 23 October 2007,
    not yet reported 104, 132

Türkoğlu and Turan v. Turkey (Appl. No. 42745/98), Decision (Third Section–Friendly
Settlement), 21 November 2002, not reported 111

Tyrer v. UK (Appl. No. 5856/72), Judgment (Chamber), 25 April 1978,
Series A, Vol. 26 38

Tysiąc v. Poland (Appl. No. 5410/03), Judgment (Fourth Section), 20 March 2007,
not yet reported 179

Ukrainian Media Group v. Ukraine (Appl. No. 72713/01), Judgment (Former
Second Section), 29 March 2005, not reported 38, 150

Uluğkay v. Turkey (Appl. No. 9782/02), Decision (Third Section–Arrangement),
8 February 2007, not yet reported 48

Ülke v. Turkey (Appl. No. 39437/98), Judgment (Second Section),
24 January 2006, not reported 196

Üstün a. O. v. Turkey (Appl. No. 44056/98), Decision (Second Section–Arrangement),
22 February 2005, not reported 55

Vallon v. Italy (Appl. No. 9621/81), Judgment (Chamber–Arrangement),
3 June 1985, Series A, Vol. 95 25

Varey v. United Kingdom (Appl. No. 26662/95), Judgment (Grand Chamber–
Arrangement), 21 December 2000, not reported 35

Vefa v. Turkey (Appl. No. 31139/96), Decision (Fourth Section–Arrangement),
2 December 2003, not reported 55

Velcea v. Romania (Appl. No. 60957/00), Judgment (Third Section–Friendly Settlement),
22 December 2005, not reported 45

Venera-Nord-Vest Borta A.G. v. Moldova (Appl. No. 31535/03), Judgment (Fourth
Section), 13 February 2007, not yet reported 104

Vilborg Yrsa Sigurdardóttir v. Iceland (Appl. No. 32451/96), Judgment (First Section–
Friendly Settlement), 30 May 2000, not reported. 43

Virdi v. United Kingdom (Appl. No. 58851/00), Decision (Fourth Section–Arrangement),
8 October 2002, not reported 61

Vogel v. Romania (Appl. No. 46633/99), Decision (Second Section–Friendly Settlement),
8 April 2003, not reported 42

Vogt v. Germany (Appl. No. 17851/91), Judgment (Grand Chamber–Arrangement),
2 September 1996, Reports 1996-IV, 1086 23

Von Hannover v. Germany (Appl. No. 59320/00), Judgment (Third Section–
Arrangement), 28 July 2005, not reported 70

Walder v. Poland (Appl. No. 45032/06), Decision (Fourth Section–Arrangement),
26 June 2007, not yet reported. 131

Waser and Steiger v. Switzerland (Appl. No. 31990/02), Decision (Fifth Section–
Arrangement), 23 October 2006, not reported. 188

Watson v. United Kingdom (Appl. No. 41379/98), Decision (Third Section–
Arrangement), 10 May 2001, not reported. 61

Wawrzynowicz v. Poland (Appl. No. 73192/01), Judgment (Fourth Section),
17 July 2007, not yet reported 104, 132

Waza v. Poland (Appl. No. 11602/02), Decision (Fourth Section–
Unilateral Declaration), 26 June 2007, not yet reported. 132

Weeks v. United Kingdom (Appl. No. 9787/82), Judgment (Plenary–Arrangement),
5 October 1988, Series A, Vol. 145-A. 23, 30, 150

Wessels-Bergervoet v. Netherlands (Appl. No. 34462/97), Judgment (Second Section–
Arrangement), 12 November 2002, not reported 40

Wiktor v. Poland (Appl. No. 42178/05), Decision (Fourth Section–Arrangement),
10 June 2008, not yet reported. 131

Willis v. United Kingdom (Appl. No. 36042/97), Judgment (Fourth Section),
    11 June 2002, Reports 2002-IV, 311 64
Wintersberger v. Austria (Appl. No. 57448/00), Judgment (Third Section–Friendly
    Settlement), 5 February 2004, not reported 8
Winterwerp v. Netherlands (Appl. No. 6301/73), Judgment (Chamber–Arrangement),
    27 November 1981, Series A, Vol. 47. . . . . 23, 30
Wiśniewski v. Poland (Appl. No. 64205/01), Decision (Fourth Section–Arrangement),
    17 October 2006, not reported 130
Witer v. Poland (Appl. No. 39814/03), Decision (Fourth Section–Arrangement),
    18 September 2007, not yet reported. 130
Witkowska-Tobola v. Poland (Appl. No. 11208/02), Decision (Fourth Section–
    Arrangement), 4 December 2007, not yet reported 144
Wolkenberg a. O. v. Poland (Appl. No. 50003/99), Decision (Fourth Section–
    Arrangement), 4 December 2007, not yet reported 51, 73, 144
Worsley v. United Kingdom (Appl. No. 71758/01), Decision (Fourth Section–
    Arrangement), 24 June 2008, not yet reported. 116
Woukam Moudefo v. France (Appl. No. 10868/84), Judgment (Chamber–
    Arrangement), 11 October 1988, Series A, Vol. 141-B. 29
Woźniak v. Poland (Appl. No. 10511/07), Decision (Fourth Section–Arrangement),
    14 October 2008, not yet reported. 131
Wróblewski v. Poland (Appl. No. 9359/03), Decision (Fourth Section–Arrangement),
    12 April 2007, not yet reported 130
Y. v. United Kingdom (Appl. No. 14229/88), Judgment (Chamber–Arrangement),
    29 October 1992, Series A, Vol. 247-A. 28
Yağci a. O. v. Turkey (Appl. No. 5974/02), Decision (Third Section–Arrangement),
    22 March 2007, not yet reported 45
Yakar v. Turkey (Appl. No. 36189/97), Judgment (Fourth Section–Friendly
    Settlement), 26 November 2002, not reported. 101
Yalçin v. Turkey (Appl. No. 31152/96), Judgment (Third Section–Friendly
    Settlement), 12 December 2002, not reported 48, 52, 101
Yaman v. Turkey (Appl. No. 37049/97), Judgment (First Section–Arrangement),
    22 May 2003, not reported 101, 126
Yazici v. Turkey (Appl. No. 73033/01), Decision (First Section–Arrangement),
    11 July 2006, not reported. 46, 101
Yedikule Surp Pirgiç Ermeni Hastanesi Vakfi v. Turkey (Appl. Nos. 50147/99;
    51207/99), Judgment (Second Section–Friendly Settlement),
    26 June 2007, not yet reported. 42
Yildiz v. Turkey (Appl. No. 32979/96), Judgment (Fourth Section–Friendly
    Settlement), 16 July 2002, not reported. 101
Yücetürk v. Turkey (Appl. No. 76089/01), Decision (Third Section–Arrangement),
    4 October 2005, not reported 46, 101
Yüksel Erdoğan a. O. v. Turkey (Appl. No. 57049/00), Judgment (Third Section),
    15 February 2007, not yet reported 278
Yurtseven a. O. v. Turkey (Appl. No. 31730/96), Judgment (First Section–
    Arrangement), 18 December 2003, not reported 63, 126
Z.E. a. O. v. Turkey (Appl. No. 35980/97), Judgment (Second Section–
    Arrangement), 7 June 2001, not reported. 62
Z.Y. v. Turkey (Appl. No. 27532/95), Judgment (Second Section–Friendly
    Settlement), 9 April 2002, not reported 46, 101

Zagožen and Suhoveršnik and 4 Others v. Slovenia (Appl. Nos. 4497/03; 5177/03;
  5584/03; 10880/03; 14191/03), Decision (Third Section–Arrangement),
  4 January 2008, not yet reported 64
Zając v. Poland (Appl. No. 19817/04), Judgment (Fourth Section), 29 July 2008,
  not yet reported 104, 132
Zawadzka a. O. v. Poland (Appl. No. 10476/02), Decision (Fourth Section–
  Arrangement), 15 January 2008, not yet reported 73
Zeman v. Austria (Appl. No. 23960/02), Judgment (First Section–Arrangement),
  10 January 2008, not yet reported 70
Zielonkiewicz v. Poland (Appl. No. 25656/05), Decision (Fourth Section–Arrangement),
  19 September 2006, not reported.. 130
Zingraf v. Germany (Appl. No. 27156/05), Decision (Fifth Section–Unilateral
  Declaration), 12 February 2008, not yet reported............................... 114
Zu Leiningen v. Germany (Appl. No. 59624/00), Decision (Third Section–Arrangement),
  17 November 2005, Reports 2005-XIII, 183 48

III. INTER-AMERICAN COURT OF HUMAN RIGHTS

Velásquez Rodriguez Case (Preliminary Objections), Inter-Am. Ct. H. R. (Ser. C.)
  No. 1 (1994), 26 June 1989.. 7, 99

PART I

FOUNDATIONS, PRACTICE AND BEYOND

1

Introduction

The European Convention on Human Rights (ECHR, Convention)[1] is both the most prominent human rights treaty in Europe and the most effective human rights regime in the world. The European Court of Human Rights (ECtHR, Court) benefits from a history of 50 years of unprecedented success. There is a great deal of legal doctrine focussing on the reasons for this success.[2] However, on the flip side, there is a dramatically heavy caseload before the Court and, since 2009, more than 100,000 cases have been pending in Strasbourg.[3]

Against this background, the possibility of settling a case before the ECtHR becomes an attractive alternative to ordinary judicial proceedings. With the conclusion of a friendly settlement, the Court can pursue a three-fold goal: Although the Court does not hand down a judgment on the alleged human rights violation, the parties receive compensation and the case is settled with a strike out decision. Several reform projects for the Court stress the utility of friendly settlements and favour an expansion of this practice.[4] In 2002, the Committee of Ministers explained the new approach to friendly settlements as follows:

Considering that the conclusion of a friendly settlement, while remaining a matter left entirely to the discretion of the parties to the case, may constitute a means of alleviating the workload of the Court, as well as a means of providing a rapid and satisfactory solution for the parties,

Underlines the importance:

– of giving further consideration in all cases to the possibilities of concluding friendly settlements and,
– if any such friendly settlement is concluded, of ensuring that its terms are duly fulfilled.[5]

---

[1] Convention for the Protection of Human Rights and Fundamental Freedoms, as amended by Protocol no 11, entered into force on 1 November 1998. The Convention is cited throughout this volume as amended by Protocol no 11.

[2] Greer, S. (2006), p. 60 et seq.; Keller, H./Stone Sweet, A. (2008), pp. 677–710.

[3] European Court of Human Rights, Pending Applications Allocated to a Judicial Formation, 31 December 2009, available at <http://www.echr.coe.int/NR/rdonlyres/BBFE7733-3122-40F5-AACA-9B16827B74C2/0/Pending_applications_chart.pdf> (last visited 15 April 2010).

[4] See for example, Review of the Working Methods of the European Court of Human Rights – Lord Woolf Report, p. 458.

[5] Resolution Res(2002)59 concerning the practice in respect of friendly settlements, Committee of Ministers, 18 December 2002.

I. Old Instrument – New Use

Although the availability of friendly settlement is as old as the Convention system itself, the broader use of this tool in the Court's daily life is a recent development. As early as in 1995, Vincent Berger, at the time Head of Division at the Registry of the Court stated laconically: *"Force est de constater que les règlements amiables sont apparus tardivement devant la Cour et n'occupent encore qu'une place modeste dans son activité."*[6] Since then, we have witnessed a dramatic increase in the use of friendly settlements – for some countries even an exponential growth.[7] What made the situation change so radically? Is it only the enormous caseload before the Court that explains this development?

Two new phenomena show the clear correlation between the expanding caseload of the Court on the one hand, and the increasing number of friendly settlements on the other. Since the new millennium, the Court has not only tackled systemic human rights problems in certain countries through a, so-called, pilot judgment but has also completed the case with a *pilot friendly settlement (règlement amiable pilote)*.[8] The Court followed this approach for the first time in the cases of *Hutten-Czapska* and *Broniowski*.[9] In such situations, the friendly settlement procedure has become an instrument for the Court to deal with domestic systemic deficiencies on sociological, historical and political levels. At the same time, a pilot friendly settlement can prevent hundreds of applicants from bringing their claims to Strasbourg.

As well as the pilot judgment procedure, the Court recently developed an additional tool for coping with the ever-growing caseload. In areas of established case law in which the State Party is normally prepared to acknowledge a violation of the Convention and to make up for it with an *ex gratia* payment, the Court decides the case on the basis of a, so-called, unilateral declaration.[10] Unilateral declarations are usually a by-product of failed settlement negotiations. In other words, the Court accepts the offer for a friendly settlement from the State Party

---

[6] Berger, V. (1995), p. 783.

[7] See the statistics in annex 2, "Table II/1. Statistics 1998–2008", "Table II/2. Statistics per Country 1998–2008: Friendly Settlements" and "Table III/3. Statistics per Country 1998–2008: Arrangements". Ang, F./Berghmans, E. (2005), p. 92; Zwaak, L. (2006), p. 226.

[8] Garlicki, L. (2007), pp. 177–192; Gattini, A. (2007), pp. 276–294; Sadurski, W. (2009), pp. 397–453; Wildhaber, L. (2009), pp. 69–75; Zagrebelsky, V. (2007), pp. 521–535.

[9] *Broniowski v. Poland* (Appl. No. 31443/96), Judgment (Grand Chamber–Pilot Judgment), 22 June 2004, Reports 2004-V, 1; *Broniowski v. Poland* (Appl. No. 31443/96), Judgment (Grand Chamber–Friendly Settlement), 28 September 2005, Reports 2005-IX, 1; *Hutten-Czapska v. Poland* (Appl. No. 35014/97), Judgment (Grand Chamber–Pilot Judgment), 19 June 2006, Reports 2006-VIII, 57; *Hutten-Czapska v. Poland* (Appl. No. 35014/97), Judgment (Grand Chamber–Friendly Settlement), 28 April 2008, not yet reported. For the different categories of friendly settlements, see the chapter "Beyond Doctrine", section I.

[10] Ang, F./Berghmans, E. (2005), pp. 98–104; Myjer, E. (2007), pp. 318–327; Rozakis, C. L. (2007), pp. 1003–1014; Zwaak, L. (2006), pp. 233–235.

and closes the case on this (sometimes slightly changed) basis, even if the applicant does not accept it. The Court used this tool for the first time in *Akman v. Turkey*[11] in 2001. Since then, unilateral declarations have become by sheer numbers an effective tool to increase the number of cases that can be struck out of the Court's list. Statistics show that in the very early years of this century only a handful of applications were terminated via a unilateral declaration. However, their number rose to 47 in 2007 and to 78 in 2008.[12]

II. Research Questions

Seen from a domestic perspective, friendly settlements in the human rights field are entirely extrinsic. Alternative dispute resolution is well established in most Western European countries in areas including family law (divorces, visiting rights), commercial law (arbitration), and increasingly more in administrative law (environmental or construction law) and in criminal law (plea bargaining).[13] This practice is nonetheless not applied to the resolution of human rights disputes. The situation is quite different at the international level where several human rights treaties provide a framework for the conclusion of friendly settlements, e.g. in Article 63 of the Rules of Procedure of the Inter-American Court of Human Rights;[14] Article 9 of the Protocol to the African Charter on Human Rights and Peoples' Rights on the Establishment of an African Court on Human and Peoples' Rights;[15] or Rule 79 of the Rules of Procedure of the Human Rights Committee.[16]

The conclusion of an arrangement between the parties to an international dispute follows a well-established rule in international dispute resolution: Whenever possible, the parties should settle the case without the assistance of an international court or tribunal. A settlement gives the State Party one last opportunity to adequately redress the wrong done before the Court undertakes its final task of finding a violation on the merits.[17] The instrument of friendly settlement introduces a peculiar element to the otherwise rigid judicial nature

[11] *Akman v. Turkey* (Appl. No. 37453/97), Judgment (First Section–Unilateral Declaration), 26 June 2001, Reports 2001-VI, 223.

[12] See the statistics in annex 2, "Table II/1. Statistics 1998–2008".

[13] Brown, H. J./Marriott, A. L. (1999), p. 189 et seq.

[14] Rules of Procedure of the Inter-American Court of Human Rights, approved by the Court during its LXXXV Regular Period of Sessions, held from 16–28 November 2009. For the practice of the Inter-American bodies, see Reisman, W. M./Benesch, S. (2003), pp. 741–769; Standaert, P. E. (1999), pp. 519–542.

[15] Protocol to the African Charter on Human and Peoples' Rights on the Establishment of an African Court on Human and Peoples' Rights, 9 June 1998, OAU Doc. OAU/LEG/EXP/AFCHPR/PROT (III), entered into force 25 January 2004.

[16] Rules of Procedure of the Human Rights Committee, 22 September 2005, CCPR/C/3/Rev.8.

[17] Rozakis, C. L. (2007), p. 1004.

of the Court proceedings by transforming it into a mechanism of good offices. This logic makes the most sense in an interstate dispute. However, it has also infiltrated human rights proceedings in cases brought by individuals before international treaty bodies. The contrast between domestic procedures not providing the opportunity to settle human rights cases and the ECHR system offering this possibility is not devoid of irony. An applicant who went through all the domestic instances and who fought for years for his, or her, human rights on the basis of a purely adversarial procedure is suddenly confronted with an entirely new approach upon arrival in Strasbourg: The Court invites him to settle the case. There are hurt feelings and there is "no such thing as a 'friendly settlement'" for such an applicant.[18] In such a situation, convincing the applicant and his lawyer to settle is above all a psychological challenge for the Court and its Registry.

In the framework of the Convention, it is important to bear in mind that any friendly settlement should be seen against the background of a functioning judicial system having jurisdiction to issue a binding legal decision in each case that is not settled. The conciliatory function of the system is carried out within a setting of rule enforcement. Therefore, they are strictly distinct from the conciliation of general political interstate disputes.[19]

The increasing use of friendly settlements before the ECtHR raises a series of questions that go to the core of the Court's function, mission and current predicament: Does Article 39 ECHR as a minimal legal parameter offer all the necessary guidelines for the conclusion of friendly settlements or is it rather a *carte blanche* for the Court? Do friendly settlements imperil the Court's first and foremost duty of protecting and developing human rights? Is the large amount of friendly settlements counterproductive because it encourages lawyers to bring claims to Strasbourg and compounds the Court's actual workload problems? Are friendly settlements suitable in all human rights areas, such as in cases concerning very serious human rights violations under Articles 2 and 3 ECHR? If yes, is there a different examination threshold in these cases? More generally, are there limits for the settlement of human rights cases on ethical or philosophical grounds? Or in other words, can the Court monetize all kinds of human rights violations? Can friendly settlements raise specific enforcement problems? On a more practical level, is the Court – and its Registry in particular – well-trained and equipped for the negotiation and handling of friendly settlements, and especially of pilot friendly settlements? Finally, can friendly settlements in such situations fulfil the function of transitional justice?

---

[18] Elisabeth Fura, Judge at the ECtHR, information given in her interview of 12 January 2009, reprinted in annex 1.
[19] Koopmans, S. M. G. (2008), p. 184.

III. Questions of Legitimacy

Friendly settlements are controversial when they are employed in the context of human rights violations. In general, fundamental legal norms do not allow for a compromise. The human rights guarantee is either violated or respected, *tertium non datur*. It is especially in cases involving serious human rights violations (such as the right to life and the prohibition of torture and inhuman treatment) that the negotiation of the alleged violations calls into question the very idea of friendly settlements.[20] However, the question of whether human rights cases can be settled cannot be considered in light of only one criterion, namely the nature of the underlying human rights violations.[21]

From a philosophical point of view, the unbalanced power situation in the negotiation process is a sensitive issue. The political dimension of settlements is most noticeable in interstate settlements. In these cases, the power balance between the parties is more even than in cases brought by individuals. We have to bear in mind that the equality of States is a principle which is guaranteed before the Court. Nonetheless, in reality it would be naïve to consider all States equal in terms of influence and power.

This unbalanced situation becomes even more apparent in cases brought by individual applicants to Strasbourg. In general, an individual applicant and a Government Agent are not on an equal footing. The applicant is generally a one-shot player, whereas the Government Agent is a repeat player. In terms of influence, experience and resources, the Government is in a much more favourable position than the individual applicant.[22] However, interestingly, none of our interview partners ever encountered a situation where the outcome of the case was unfavourable for the applicant due to an unbalanced situation between the parties. This can be explained in part by the prevalence of routine friendly settlements where no real negotiations take place and where the outcome is more or less determined by existing case law.[23]

In pilot friendly settlements, the outcome of the negotiations between the parties is likely to influence the situation of many other actors. This begs the question whether such a procedure is a legitimate remedy for the potential applicants who are not involved in the negotiation process.

---

[20] According to the Inter-American Commission on Human Rights, disputes concerning grave human rights violations cannot be resolved through conciliation: *Velásquez Rodriguez Case (Preliminary Objections)*, Inter-Am. Ct. H. R. (Ser. C.) No. 1 (1994), 26 June 1989, para. 43. Cf. Standaert, P. E. (1999), p. 529.

[21] Reisman, W. M./Benesch, S. (2003), p. 743.

[22] Ang, F./Berghmans, E. (2005), p. 95; Standaert, P. E. (1999), pp. 529–532; De Schutter, O. (2000), pp. 234–237.

[23] For the different categories of friendly settlements, see the chapter "Beyond Doctrine", section I.

IV. Research Method

The legal framework of friendly settlements is minimal.[24] A deeper understanding of friendly settlements called for an approach other than a purely jurisprudential one, and this reasearch borrowed several elements from other fields of social science. We collected data on the use of friendly settlements in the Court's and the Commission's practice. Analytically, we focused mainly on the practice of the new Court. Our research concentrated on the first ten years of the new Court.[25] This data showed both the dramatic increase in friendly settlements and the considerable differences in the practice of several Contracting States. Furthermore, the length of proceedings and the amount of financial awards were of general interest.

Our hypothesis was that the Registry is in one way or another actively involved in settling cases before the Court.[26] However, there is little official information to verify this hypothesis. As the Registrar dismissed our request for access to the confidential files,[27] we could only rely on the information that was publicly available. In general, the description of a friendly settlement in the official publication of the Court's decisions and judgments is limited to a short summary (that has become even shorter in very recent years[28]). We tried to distinguish the nature of the proceedings on the basis of the Registry's involvement. When the files indicated a clear engagement of the Registry, we classified the settlement as a "friendly settlement" (*règlement amiable*). When we had indications that the parties reached an agreement on their own, we identified this settlement as an "arrangement" (*arrangement*). The latter term has mostly been used by the Commission and

---

[24] For the changes in the Convention and the Rules of Court over time, see annex 3.

[25] The overall statistics and the statistics per country (friendly settlements and arrangements) reprinted in annex 2 cover the period between 1 November 1998 and 1 January 2009, whereas the country-specific statistics concerning Poland and Turkey encompass the period between 1 January 1999 and 1 January 2009. In addition, we collected statistics on friendly settlements from the very beginning of the old Court and the former Commission (1951–2008). These statistics are on file with the authors.

[26] Cf. Ang, F./Berghmans, E. (2005), p. 91; Cabral Barreto, I. (2000), p. 53; Mahoney, P. (2001), p. 447.

[27] Letter of 9 September 2008, on file with the authors.

[28] See for examples, *Can v. Austria* (Appl. No. 9300/81), Judgment (Chamber–Arrangement), 30 September 1985, Series A, Vol. 96 and *The Holy Monasteries v. Greece* (Appl. Nos. 13092/87, 13984/88), Judgment (Chamber–Arrangement), 1 September 1997, Reports 1997-V, 1565 where the published files contain the negotiation process, and compare these cases with, for example, *Wintersberger v. Austria* (Appl. No. 57448/00), Judgment (Third Section–Friendly Settlement), 5 February 2004, not reported, or even *Mrkonjić and Others v. Croatia* (Appl. No. 16725/02), Decision (First Section–Arrangement), 13 May 2004, not reported where the whole case is summarized on three pages. In *Starshova and Starshov v. Russia* (Appl. No. 8333/05), Decision (First Section–Arrangement), 8 September 2005, not reported and *Shpynov v. Russia* (Appl. No. 21940/03), Decision (First Section–Arrangement), 23 May 2006, not reported, the published files basically solely contain the information that a friendly settlement has been concluded.

by the old Court in the early cases.[29] This typically occurs in situations where the parties concluded an arrangement before the case was declared admissible. It seemed to us remarkable that after having fought for so long at the domestic level the parties were able to reach an arrangement concerning eventual ECHR proceedings without the assistance of a mediator from the Court.[30] The parties sometimes agreed to withdraw the application as part of the deal accepted. This was not usually included in a friendly settlement and we classified these cases as arrangements.[31]

We were fully aware of the difficulties in drawing a clear distinction between arrangements and friendly settlements on the basis of the scant information officially available. We maintained this differentiation in the country-specific and overall statistics collected as part of our research. The increase in friendly settlement is intrinsically linked to a new phenomenon, namely the acceptance of unilateral declarations by the Court.[32] The statistics showing the growing use of friendly settlements and arrangements, on the one hand, and unilateral declarations, on the other, best depict the broad use and function of friendly settlements in the most recent years.[33]

Thus far, the content of friendly settlements has been largely neglected in academic publications.[34] Therefore, we also collected data about the specific content of friendly settlements. We were particularly interested to see whether the parties agreed on benefits other than financial awards and whether this inventiveness was accepted by the Court.[35]

In recent years, the Court struck out hundreds of cases on the basis of a friendly settlement. As part of our interviews, we explored the practical knowledge and experiences of Judges, the Registry's staff, attorneys and representatives of the Governments. In total, we contacted 49 persons with a request for an interview. Twenty-eight were able and willing to give us an oral interview, among them five Judges, nine Registry employees, four State Agents and six human rights lawyers. Among our interview partners, there were 16 men and 12 women with an average age of 52. The youngest partner was 36 and the oldest 72.

A few days before our meeting, every interview partner received a questionnaire in French or in English for his, or her, preparation. We always used the same

---

[29] See for example, *Ayadi v. France* (Appl. No. 18000/91), Report (Commission–Arrangement), 1 September 1993, not reported, para. 13: "*Conformément à l'article 30 par. 1 a) et b) de la Convention, la Commission constate que le requérant ne souhaite plus maintenir sa requête au motif que le litige avait été résolu sur la base de l'arrangement ci-dessus exposé.*" (available only in French).

[30] This criterion explains why some concrete cases might appear differently in our statistics than in the Court's own official records.

[31] See the chapter "Beyond Doctrine", section I.1.

[32] *Akman v. Turkey* (Appl. No. 37453/97), Judgment (First Section–Unilateral Declaration), 26 June 2001, Reports 2001-VI, 223.

[33] See the statistics in annex 2, "Table II/1. Statistics 1998–2008".

[34] Weber, G. S. (2007), pp. 217, 239.

[35] See the chapter "Legal Framework and Practice", sections II. and III.

questionnaire, but not all questions applied to all interview partners. Different groups of interview partners played various roles in the conclusion of a friendly settlement. In our interviews, we followed the questionnaire loosely in the sense of qualified interview techniques.[36] We encouraged the interview partners to add information we did not ask for directly in the questionnaire since this was the only way to obtain a full picture of the current use of friendly settlements before the Court, in the various Sections and in the different State Parties. All the transcripts are on file with the authors. Out of a total of 28 interview partners, five persons wished to keep their interviews confidential.

With the permission of the interview partners, we cited some of their statements. As a sample, four transcripts have been printed in annexes to this work.[37] The interviews we published were chosen on the basis of the following criteria: First, we tried to give a representative sample by choosing interviews from the different groups of interview partners involved in the research project. Second, the quality of the content depended widely on the character and experience of the person involved. Thirdly, the interview transcript was only reprinted with the permission of the person concerned. As a matter of course, all information concerning confidential negotiations has been deleted from the published transcripts.

V. Aim, Content and Responsibility

The aim of this book is to provide an insight into a fascinating area of the ECtHR's practice which has been much neglected in the scholarly world. Friendly settlements are an unexpectedly flexible tool for resolving human rights problems and they are thus of outmost interest to lawyers representing applicants before the ECtHR. The flexibility of friendly settlements is, however, a double-edged sword; while it is its most important advantage, it also represents its major risk. The current use mirrors the Court's predicament. Faced with an ever growing docket, the Registry uses friendly settlements primarily as a case management tool. Thereby, the original intent of this legal instrument – i.e. the resolution of an alleged human rights violation on an individual basis without a final judgment on the merits – is much neglected.

Friendly settlements are often a viable solution for applicants wishing to lodge an application before the ECtHR. However, not every case, at any stage of the proceedings, is suitable for a friendly settlement. Applicants thus need professional advice. The aim of this book is to give interested lawyers the necessary information as to when and how a friendly settlement should be negotiated. The

---

[36] Bryman, A. (2008), pp. 435–471; Chesebro, J. W./Borisoff, D. J. (2008), pp. 449–486; Denzin, N. K./Lincoln, Y. S. (2008), pp. 1–43; Doucet, A./Mauthner, N. (2008), pp. 328–343.

[37] See annex 1.

choice between a friendly settlement and ordinary proceedings has to be made carefully, as it has important legal and practical implications for the applicant. For easy reference, the annex provides four charts where the different stages of friendly settlements proceedings are illustrated.[38]

The book is divided into six chapters. Our starting point was the legal framework of friendly settlements. Against this background, we analysed the practice of the former Commission of Human Rights, the old Court and the new Court. The last ten years have demonstrated that there are constant features in the Strasbourg settlement practice. Friendly settlements are primarily associated with financial awards. A systematic survey of the content revealed that friendly settlements can achieve much more than settle an alleged human rights violation through compensation. The 887 friendly settlements and 2,113 arrangements that we examined showed that a wide variety of individual non-pecuniary measures were agreed on by the parties. This vast range of individual measures underlines one of the biggest advantages of friendly settlements: When properly handled, friendly settlements offer to the parties much more flexibility than ordinary proceedings. However, some individual measures (reduction of penal sentences, granting of pardon, granting of residence permit, etc.) raise important theoretical questions regarding legitimacy, competence and separation of powers between the Court and the State Parties as well as the Court and the different State branches. These concerns might also explain why individual measures other than financial awards have been used less frequently in the most recent years. Through the survey of the Court's practice we also found that some time before the *Broniowski* case the Court started using general measures in friendly settlements. Finally, the systematic analysis of the Court's practice showed the significant financial dimension that friendly settlements played for particular Contracting Parties (e.g. Italy, Turkey and Poland).

The Court's Registry developed friendly settlements in the most recent years in order to deal with repetitive cases. In addition, friendly settlements form an essential component in the follow-up of pilot judgment procedures. Finally, the parties might – although rather seldom – decide to close a disputed matter with a real settlement. The diversity of friendly settlements in appearance and function lies at the heart of Chapter 3 of this work. Interestingly, the diverse use of friendly settlements has gone unnoticed by the world outside of the Court. This chapter shows the subtle difference between the various forms of friendly settlements and arrangements. Finally, it also connects these practices to the phenomenon of unilateral declarations based on a failed friendly settlement.

Chapter 4 of this work sheds light on the question of whether friendly settlements are legitimate from an ethical point of view. Two lines of philosophical thought are applied to our basic problem. The first is whether all human rights violations should be settled via financial awards, even the most serious ones. The

---

[38] See annex 4.

result is not unambiguous and makes clear that the procedural requirements for a fair settlement play an essential role in the ethical assessment. The second is whether a concrete friendly settlement fulfils this high standard of procedural fairness and substantive justice and this can only be answered on an individual basis. As a matter of course, the Court cannot limit itself to a solution *ex bono et gratia* because friendly settlements often do not just have implications for the individual applicant, but also for a larger group of individuals. Ultimately, it is the Court's primary task to ensure that human rights are respected in the settlement. This is the equally prominent and difficult duty that the Court has to fulfil in each and every single case endorsed by a friendly settlement.

In Chapter 5 of this work, we tried to verify two basic assumptions, namely whether in a friendly settlement an applicant can receive in a shorter period of time more compensation than in ordinary proceedings. The systematic analysis of the financial awards granted and the length of proceedings before the Court should provide the required evidence as to these two common assumptions which speak very much in favour of friendly settlements. Naturally, such a systematic collection of data was not feasible for all areas and for all Contracting Parties. We selected cases concerning the most serious substantive violations and the less serious procedural violations. We reviewed Turkish cases concerning the right to life and the prohibition of torture and inhuman treatment (Article 2 ECHR, Article 3 ECHR and combined applications) as well as Polish cases on the length of proceedings in civil matters (Article 6 (1) ECHR). The Turkish and Polish cases provided a sufficiently large sample for a deeper analysis. Surprisingly, the data collected rebutted in part and in some areas the above-mentioned basic assumptions of the Strasbourg case law. For those readers interested in the social sciences, we reprinted the statistical data in annex 2 of this work.

The last chapter summarizes our basic results and makes reform proposals for a better management of friendly settlements. The proper handling of friendly settlements requires a high degree of professionalism. This holds true for both the Registry's personnel and for the applicant's lawyers. In this regard, there is still much to be done in future years.

This volume is published under the co-authorship of Helen Keller, Magdalena Forowicz and Lorenz Engi. However, the three authors contributed differently to the outcome of this study. Helen Keller was the *spiritus rector* of this research project. During her sabbatical, she spent eight months at the Court and conducted the interviews. She is mainly responsible for the text of this volume. Magdalena Forowicz was in charge of collecting the statistical data – a time-consuming and burdensome task. She is mainly responsible for the chapter "Analysis of the Court's Practice in Selected Areas" and the editing of the whole volume. Lorenz Engi completes the triumvirate and is the author of the chapter entitled

"Philosophical Background". Only the collective efforts enabled us to give a full picture of the multifaceted phenomenon of friendly settlements. Although we contributed differently, we share the ideas expressed in this volume.

2

Legal Framework and Practice

The starting point for the analysis of the legal framework was the fact that the Convention does not provide a distinct legal framework for the settling of cases. From the wording of Article 38 ECHR, it appears that any case can be settled at any time. The only given limit is the respect of human rights as guaranteed in the Convention and the Additional Protocols.[1] As the legal setting is so sparse, examining the practice of the Court and its Registry is crucial for developing a deeper understanding of the vital role that friendly settlements play in the handling of the enormous caseload of the Court.

This chapter describes the standard development of a case that arrives in Strasbourg. The main goal is to show the various opportunities for the settlement of a case in the different phases of the proceedings. Our main intent was to examine when friendly settlements come into play in the normal progression of an application before the Court. As the legal framework has changed in the last 20 years, this chapter reflects the roles of the different actors involved in friendly settlements following the various reforms. Further, it reviews the practice of the former European Commission of Human Rights by showing the peculiarities and the continuation of the scheme. The main focus is, however, the period from 1998 until 2009 and the legal framework in force at that time. At first glance, this chapter may appear more descriptive than analytical. However, the descriptive part provides a crucial basis for the classification of friendly settlements on a non-doctrinal level, which is discussed in a later chapter of this work.[2]

I. Reform History

The development of friendly settlements before the European Court of Human Rights reflects the various developments and reforms that the Strasbourg institutions have undergone in the last 50 years. Since the entry into force of the ECHR in 1950, the legal regime for the protection and control of human rights has changed several times. In the early years of the Convention, the former Commission of Human Rights was responsible for the conclusion of friendly

---

[1] Zwaak, L. (2006), p. 223.
[2] See the chapter "Beyond Doctrine", section I.

settlements.[3] The Commission held its first sessions in July 1954 and decided the first friendly settlements in 1965.[4] The growing caseload before the Strasbourg institutions provided good reasons for several minor reforms and finally for a radical reorganization of the Court. With the entry into force of Protocol no 11, both the former Commission and the old Court were abolished. A single full-time institution, composed of one Judge from each ECHR Contracting Party, was established, retaining the name of the "European Court of Human Rights". Protocol no 11 centralized the administrative authority to process claims to this new Court and its staff, the Registry. This new Court inherited all matters relating to the filtering of applications, fact-finding and determining admissibility. Consequently, the Court also formally took over the leading role in processing friendly settlements.

The events of 1989 and 1990 brought about vast changes in the Council of Europe. A rapid increase in the number of Member States followed, from 23 at the end of 1989 to 47 in 2008. The Council of Europe decided that the ratification of the Convention shortly after joining the Organization should be a precondition for accession thereto. With the enlargement of membership to Central and Eastern European countries, the number of potential applicants calculated on the basis of the Contracting States' population had nearly doubled. Transition countries generated cases that raised different and more complex issues than those found in cases originating from the older State Parties, especially when structural problems were involved (such as grievous deficiencies in the judiciary, brutal police practice, deplorable prison conditions, insufficient protection of property rights, etc.). In recent years, the human rights system has been flooded with hundreds of virtually identical complaints generated by systemic defects on the domestic level.

Between 2006 and 2009, the Court experienced for the first time in its reform history an absolute deadlock. For years, Russia's veto blocked the reform process despite an ever-mounting flood of applications lodged in Strasbourg. In 2008, the evolution of a quasi-supranational jurisdictional scheme reached its inter-governmental limits. This strained situation could only be overcome by unusual methods. The Council of Europe examined *inter alia* the possibility of Protocol

---

[3] For the various changes of the Convention in the 60s and 70s, see Fribergh, E./Villiger, M. E. (1993), p. 605.

[4] *Boeckmann v. Belgium* (Appl. No. 1727/62), Report (Commission–Friendly Settlement), 17 February 1965, Y.B. 8, 370. Although it is correct to say that at the time the Commission played a leading role in the conclusion of friendly settlements, the Court was not completely excluded from this procedure, see for example, *Luedicke, Belkacem & Koc v. Germany* (Appl. Nos. 6210/73; 6877/75; 7132/75), Judgment (Chamber–Arrangement), 10 March 1980, Series A, Vol. 36. However, it was not the case in *De Becker v. Belgium* (Appl. No. 214/56), Judgment (Chamber–Friendly Settlement), 27 March 1962, Series A, Vol. 4. In this case, there was no friendly settlement concluded, but the Survey 1959–1998 has nevertheless listed it as a friendly settlement, see European Court of Human Rights, Survey, Forty Years of Activity 1959–1998, 22 September 1998, pp. 27, 120, available at <http://www.echr.coe.int/NR/rdonlyres/66F2CD35-047E-44F4-A95D-890966820E81/0/Surveyapercus_19591998.pdf> (last visited 15 April 2010).

no 14[5] entering into force for all Contracting States except Russia, but finally abandoned the idea. From a purely international point of view, this option was not convincing and it would have created confusion. It was considered that a solution to overcoming the deadlock was to adopt Protocol no 14[bis].[6] Rather than being a compromise, it embodied the lowest common denominator among the circle of Contracting States in the Council of Europe. Protocol no 14[bis] contained the few non-disputed reforms included in Protocol no 14 and thereby helped the Court to increase its capacity in the short-term. In order to deprive a single State of its veto power, Protocol no 14[bis] needed to be ratified by only three Contracting States.

Protocol no 14[bis] had two aims. First, it was a tool to overcome the deadlock in the ratification process of Protocol no 14. Second, it provided the Court with the necessary instruments to cope with the growing caseload, even if only on a short-term basis. Article 9 of the Protocol makes its provisional character explicit: "This Protocol shall cease to be in force or applied on a provisional basis from the date of entry into force of Protocol no 14 to the Convention." The two Protocols are clearly interconnected and Protocol no 14[bis] includes two provisions from Protocol no 14. The first provision enables single-judge formations to deal with plainly inadmissible applications. Under the regime of Protocol no 11, these applications were dealt with by Committees of three Judges where such decisions could be taken "without further examination".[7] The second provision extends the competence of the three-judge Committees to handle manifestly well-founded and repetitive cases deriving from structural or systemic defects. Under the old regime, these cases would have been disposed of by the Chambers of the Court, composed of seven Judges. Although these measures did not provide a final answer to the Court's problem, they were considered to have increased the efficiency of the Court by 20–25 per cent.

Protocol no 14[bis] followed the direction taken in earlier reforms. As a result, it increasingly closed the door to applicants bringing clone or repetitive cases to Strasbourg. For that purpose, it transferred certain competences from the Chamber to the Committee and from the Committee to the single Judge. Additionally, Protocol no 14[bis] foresaw a novelty. Article 25 of the Convention, as amended by Protocol no 14[bis], introduced the function of Rapporteurs: When sitting in a single-judge formation, the Court is assisted by Rapporteurs who are under the authority of the President of the Court. They form part of the

[5] Protocol no 14 to the Convention for the Protection of Human Rights and Fundamental Freedoms, amending the control system of the Convention, CETS 194, was opened for signature on 13 May 2004, and entered into force on 1 June 2010.

[6] Protocol no 14[bis] to the Convention for the Protection of Human Rights and Fundamental Freedoms, CETS 204, was opened for signature on 27 May 2009. It required only three ratifications and it entered into force on 1 October 2009.

[7] Article 28 (1) ECHR, as amended by Protocol no 14[bis].

Court's Registry.[8] The Rapporteur knows the language and the legal system of the respondent State Party. However, the function of Rapporteur in this sense would never be carried out by a Judge.[9] With the entering into force of Protocol no 14[bis], the Convention – for the first time in its history – explicitly stated that the Registry had quasi-judicial power. The circle of Registry Rapporteurs constitutes the administrative body of the Court that filters the applications. Thus, in clear-cut inadmissibility cases, Judges were relieved of their Rapporteur role when sitting in a single-judge formation.

At first glance, the solutions provided in Protocol no 14bis to the Court's fundamental problems seem to be convincing for being both creative and pragmatic. However, Protocol no 14bis also came at a high price. For the first time in the new Court's history, a Europe *à deux vitesses* has been accepted. There was a quick way to move through the Court's machinery for cases coming from States that had ratified Protocol no 14bis and a slower route for the others.

The curious two tier system created by Protocol no 14bis eventually led to a significant development: By mid-January 2010 in the run-up to the Interlaken Conference, the State *Duma* of the Russian Federation voted in favour of the draft Statute ratifying Protocol no 14. This vote finally cleared the way for the entry into force of Protocol no 14 in June 2010. Following this, the new procedures described above came into force and the remaining provisions of Protocol no 14 could be applied. Among these, there is the highly disputed new admissibility criterion. Pursuant to Protocol no 14, the Court can declare any individual application inadmissible if it considers that "the applicant has not suffered a significant disadvantage, unless respect for human rights as defined in the Convention and the Protocols thereto requires an examination of the application on the merits and provided that no case may be rejected on this ground which has not been duly considered by a domestic tribunal."[10] We assume that the Court first has to define the required standards for this new admissibility criterion which would therefore only alleviate the Court's backlog following a consolidation of the new case law.

In these last two reform steps, the regime for the settlement of cases has not been completely altered. However, friendly settlements are promoted as much as possible. Although their legal basis did not change drastically, the Court found a way of using friendly settlements in a creative way which was not explicitly foreseen by the Convention. This new development in relation to friendly settlements has to be seen against the background of a growing docket and the need for a triage of the cases. The Court and its Registry have pursued a policy of declaring the bulk of cases lodged as inadmissible (approximately 94 per cent in

---

[8] Article 25 (2) ECHR, as amended by Protocol no 14[bis].
[9] Explanatory Report to Protocol no 14[bis] by the Council of Europe, available at:
<http://conventions.coe.int/Treaty/EN/Reports/Html/194.htm> (last visited 15 April 2010).
[10] Article 35 (3) (b) ECHR, as amended by Protocol no 14.

2008).[11] For the rest, the strategy is obvious: In all areas with established case law and concerning reliable State Parties, the cases shall be settled whenever possible. If no settlement can be reached, but the Government is willing to make a unilateral declaration, the Court accepts this and strikes the case out of the list. As a result, only a small percentage of all cases reaching Strasbourg are examined by a Chamber or Grand Chamber. Since the 90s, this closing door policy has evolved outside of a formal amendment of the Convention. It is the Court's quiet answer to the need to keep the human rights system effective. The Court's practice has been to some extent *ex post* legitimized and legalized through the adoption of Protocol no 14[bis], Protocol no 14 and the corresponding formal amendment of the Convention.

II. Before Protocol No 11

Before the entry into force of Protocol no 11, the Commission was responsible for negotiating and concluding friendly settlements.[12] It was an established practice to share with the parties the Commission's opinion as to whether or not there was a violation of the Convention.[13] This provisional view on the merits of the case was used as an incentive for the State Party concerned to enter into settlement negotiations. In terms of numbers, friendly settlements played at that time a modest role.[14] Both the Commission and the Court accepted relatively few friendly settlements. However, those friendly settlements concluded were often the final solution of a real mediation process under the direction of a representative of the Registry and the Commission. The negotiations are well-documented in the Commission's reports. The information available to the public about friendly settlements is much more detailed than current publications.

---

[11] European Court of Human Rights, Annual Report 2008, Registry of the European Court of Human Rights, Strasbourg 2009, p. 36.

[12] Krüger, H. C./Nørgaard, C. A. (1988), p. 329. For the legal basis of friendly settlements in general, see annex 3. Article 28 ECHR read at the time as: "In the event of the Commission accepting a petition referred to it:

a. it shall, with a view to ascertaining the facts, undertake together with the representatives of the parties an examination of the petitions and, if need be, an investigation for the effective conduct of which the States concerned shall furnish all necessary facilities, after an exchange of views with the Commission;

b. it shall at the same time place itself at the disposal of the parties concerned with a view to securing a friendly settlement of the matter on the basis of respect for Human Rights as defined in this Convention."

[13] Ang, F./Berghmans, E. (2005), pp. 91–92; Cabral Barreto, I. (2000), p. 38; Courell, A. M. (2006), p. 44; Fribergh, E./Villiger, M. E. (1993), p. 612.

[14] Berger, V. (1995), p. 783.

An illustrative example of the Commission's practice is the friendly settlement concluded in *Cagira v. Turkey*.[15] Interestingly, the case concerned issues related to *inter alia* Articles 2 and 3 ECHR where the financial award was accepted *ex gratia* (i.e. without the acknowledgment of a violation of the Convention).[16] The *Köksal v. Netherlands* case[17] is a rare friendly settlement concluded before the Court prior to the reform of Protocol no 11. In both cases, the facts were complicated and disputed among the parties. This could be considered as a typical situation where the Court itself had an important interest in settling the case in order to avoid a costly and cumbersome fact-finding mission.

1. Content of Friendly Settlements

Under the Commission's and the old Court's practice, friendly settlements have been primarily understood as an individual solution in a case in which the financial award was the predominant element. In terms of sheer numbers, however, the settlements did not provide for high financial awards.[18] Surprisingly, the question of default interest was usually not explicitly included in the friendly settlement.[19]

In the Commission's and the old Court's practice, some elements have been developed and copied over the years. The *ex gratia* payment or a claims waiver (i.e. the applicant agrees not to appeal the friendly settlement before either national or international court or tribunals) was normally included as a standard measure.[20] Further, it was understood that the friendly settlement terminated the

---

[15] *Cagirga v. Turkey* (Appl. No. 21895/93), Report (Commission–Friendly Settlement), 7 July 1995, D.R. 82-B, 20.

[16] Compare with the different approach in such cases taken by the new Court, section III.4. *infra*.

[17] *Köksal v. Netherlands* (Appl. No. 31725/96), Judgment (First Section–Friendly Settlement), 20 March 2001, not reported.

[18] See for some exceptions, *Djeroud v. France* (Appl. No. 13446/87), Judgment (Chamber–Arrangement), 23 January 1991, Series A, Vol. 191-B, para. 11: 150,000 FF (Article 3 and 8 ECHR); *Marlhens v. France* (Appl. No. 22862/93), Judgment (Chamber–Arrangement), 24 May 1995, Series A, Vol. 317-A, para. 19: 150,000 FRF (Article 6 (1) ECHR).

[19] See for an exception, *Sur v. Turkey* (Appl. No. 21592/93), Judgment (Chamber–Arrangement), 3 October 1997, Reports 1997-VI, 2034, para. 29: "In case the Government fail to make the aforesaid payment within three months, they shall pay 3.5 (three and a half) per cent annual default interest on the unpaid sums in French francs."

[20] See for examples, *Liebig v. Germany* (Appl. No. 6650/74), Report (Commission–Friendly Settlement), 11 May 1978, D.R. 17, 5, p. 19 [no paragraphs]: "I (sc. the applicant) furthermore declare that I will not, either by way of legal proceedings before a German Court or before an international tribunal or otherwise, make against the Federal Republic of Germany or the Land of Niedersachsen any Claims (…) which are in any way connected with the subject of the proceedings before the European Commission of Human Rights or the proceedings discontinued by decision of the Oldenburg District Court (…)." *Geerk v. Switzerland* (Appl. No. 7640/76), Report (Commission–Friendly Settlement), 4 May 1979, D.R. 16, 56, p. 67 [no paragraphs]: "He (sc. the applicant) declares that he will not put forward other claims before the national or international authorities based on the facts which gave rise to the said application." Of course, the waiver of national proceedings is by no

case. Also, the State Party was only under an international law obligation to pay a certain amount of money and did not need to acknowledge any breach of the Convention.[21]

While financial awards were included as part of the friendly settlements endorsed by the Commission and the old Court, other individual measures were also agreed upon. A survey of the older friendly settlements suggests that the parties' creativity had no limits. The very individual character of friendly settlements, as understood by the Commission, might explain the wide range of possible individual measures.

From the very beginning, the Commission and the Court were ready to accept a friendly settlement where the State Party intended to amend national law.[22] During the negotiations, the applicant sometimes asked for a commitment to amend the national statute.[23] This old practice, followed by the new Court, has ultimately paved the way to the pilot judgments and pilot friendly settlements which were concluded in the new millennium.

In criminal matters concerning procedural guarantees, the Commission and the old Court endorsed a series of individual measures, such as:

means mandatory, see for example, *Katić v. Serbia* (Appl. No. 13920/04), Decision (Second Section–Arrangement), 4 March 2008, not yet reported [no paragraphs]: "The applicants' domestic ... [claim] shall be considered by the Serbian courts separately and is not affected by this declaration."

[21] See for the more differentiated practice of the new Court, section III.4. *infra.*

[22] *Peschke v. Austria* (Appl. No. 8289/78), Report (Commission–Friendly Settlement), 13 October 1981, D.R. 25, 182, p. 188 [no paragraphs]; *Reed v. United Kingdom* (Appl. No. 7630/76), Report (Commission–Friendly Settlement), 12 December 1981, D.R. 25, 5, p. 13 [no paragraphs]; *Skoogström v. Sweden* (Appl. No. 8582/79), Judgment (Chamber–Arrangement), 2 October 1984, Series A, Vol. 83, paras. 22, 24; *Van Waegeningh v. Netherlands* (Appl. No. 10535/83), Report (Commission–Friendly Settlement), 7 March 1985, not reported, para. 15; *Can v. Austria* (Appl. No. 9300/81), Judgment (Chamber–Arrangement), 30 September 1985, Series A, Vol. 96, para. 14; *Harman v. United Kingdom* (Appl. No. 10038/82), Report (Commission–Friendly Settlement), 15 May 1986, D.R. 46, 57, para. 16; *Stoutt v. Ireland* (Appl. No. 10978/84), Report (Commission–Friendly Settlement), 17 December 1987, D.R. 54, 43, para. 18; *K. v. United Kingdom* (Appl. No. 11468/85), Report (Commission–Friendly Settlement), 15 April 1988, D.R. 56, 138, para. 21; *Campbell v. United Kingdom* (Appl. No. 11240/84), Report (Commission–Friendly Settlement), 13 May 1988, D.R. 56, 108, para. 13; *Crook and National Union of Journalists v. United Kingdom* (Appl. No. 11552/85), Decision (Commission–Arrangement), 15 July 1988, D.R. 56, 148, p. 151 [no paragraphs]; *Grabemann v. Germany* (Appl. No. 12748/87), Report (Commission–Friendly Settlement), 11 October 1989, D.R. 63, 137, para. 13; *Abbott v. United Kingdom* (Appl. No. 15006/89), Decision (Commission–Arrangement), 10 December 1990, D.R. 67, 290, p. 291 et seq. [no paragraphs]; *Muyldermans v. Belgium* (Appl. No. 12217/86), Judgment (Chamber–Arrangement), 23 October 1991, Series A, Vol. 214-A, para. 17 et seq.; *K. v. Austria* (Appl. No. 16002/90), Judgment (Chamber–Arrangement), 2 June 1993, Series A, Vol. 255-B, para. 13 et seq.; *Roux v. United Kingdom* (Appl. No. 25601/94), Report (Commission–Friendly Settlement), 16 September 1997, not reported, para. 22; *B.H. v. United Kingdom* (Appl. No. 30307/96), Report (Commission–Friendly Settlement), 30 June 1998, D.R. 94-B, 82, para. 12. Cf. Krüger, H. C./Nørgaard, C. A. (1988), p. 331.

[23] *G.D., C.T. and D.D. v. Belgium* (Appl. No. 16909/90), Report (Commission–Friendly Settlement), 6 April 1993, D.R. 74, 111, para. 17. However, this proposal was not accepted in the final settlement.

- stay of the enforcement of a prison sentence through use of pardon powers together with a certain period of probation;[24]
- sentence reduction granted through use of pardon powers;[25]
- closing of criminal proceedings against the applicant;[26]
- reduction of a lifelong prison sentence to 15 years of imprisonment through use of pardon powers;[27]
- quashing of a conditional prison sentence through use of pardon powers;[28]
- release of the applicant from a ten-year prison sentence by use of pardon powers, provided that he renounces any claims for financial award and refrains from any legal step against the Netherlands;[29]
- extraordinary re-opening of criminal proceedings.[30]

It is apparent that these measures are critical from the point of view of the separation of powers at the national level. It is, of course, for the national courts to consider criminal proceedings. In most cases, however, the authorities used the pardon, a power that is usually attributed to the Government or the President.

Another area in which the range of individual measures was significantly wide concerns proceedings relating to residence permits and asylum status:

- repeal of a deportation order and granting of residence permit;[31]

---

[24] *Nagel v. Germany* (Appl. No. 7641/76), Report (Commission–Friendly Settlement), 2 May 1978, D.R. 12, 97, p. 102 [no paragraphs].
[25] *Peschke v. Austria*, note 22 *supra*, p. 188 [no paragraphs]; *Nyssen v. Belgium* (Appl. No. 10574/83), Report (Commission–Friendly Settlement), 8 July 1987, D.R. 52, 140, para. 14.
[26] *Liebig v. Germany*, note 20 *supra*, p. 18 [no paragraphs].
[27] *Aldrian v. Austria* (Appl. No. 10532/83), Report (Commission–Arrangement), 17 March 1989, not reported, para. 17.
[28] *Zimmermann v. Austria* (Appl. No. 8490/79), Report (Commission–Friendly Settlement), 6 July 1982, D.R. 30, 15, p. 20 et seq. [no paragraphs].
[29] *T. v. Netherlands* (Appl. No. 13143/87), Report (Commission–Friendly Settlement), 12 February 1990, D.R. 65, 184, para. 15.
[30] *Jäger v. Switzerland* (Appl. No. 13467/87), Report (Commission–Friendly Settlement), 11 December 1989, D.R. 63, 156, para. 14.
[31] *Uppal and Others v. United Kingdom* (Appl. No. 8244/77), Report (Commission–Friendly Settlement), 9 July 1980, Y.B. 23, 444, p. 452 [no paragraphs]; *I. v. Austria* (Appl. No. 10215/82), Report (Commission–Arrangement), 13 March 1986, not reported [no paragraphs]; *Min, Min and Min Paik v. United Kingdom* (Appl. No. 10204/82), Report (Commission–Friendly Settlement), 7 October 1986, D.R. 48, 58, para. 12 et seq.; *Djeroud v. France*, note 18 *supra*, para. 11; *Abbas v. France* (Appl. No. 15671/89), Report (Commission–Friendly Settlement), 7 July 1992, not reported, para. 20; *Lamguindaz v. United Kingdom* (Appl. No. 16152/90), Judgment (Chamber–Arrangement), 23 June 1993, Series A, Vol. 258-C, para. 13; *M.A.R. v. United Kingdom* (Appl. No. 28038/95), Report (Commission–Friendly Settlement), 19 September 1997, not reported, para. 13; *T.O.A. v. United Kingdom* (Appl. No. 27559/95), Decision (Commission–Arrangement), 8 July 1998, not reported [no paragraphs]; *Sarialtun and Others v. Germany* (Appl. No. 37534/97), Report (Commission–Friendly Settlement), 18 September 1998, D.R. 94-B, 113, para. 18; *Hatami v. Sweden*, (Appl. No. 32448/96), Judgment (Chamber–Arrangement), 9 October 1998, Reports 1998-VII, 3038, para. 26.

- granting of visa and residence permit;[32]
- issuing of travel documents for leaving the Contracting State and travelling to an African country.[33]

Other individual measures included in friendly settlements were:

- destruction of the applicant's file card established in the course of criminal investigations;[34]
- transfer of the applicant to a prison of his choice and apologies from the Government for the interference with his correspondence;[35]
- termination of a contractual relationship and interruption of civil proceedings before national courts;[36]
- transfer of the applicant (a Turkish national) to Turkey for the execution of his prison sentence combined with a so-called declaration of undesirability;[37]
- transfer of the applicant (a U.S. national) to the United States for the serving of his prison sentence;[38]
- waiver of interpretation costs in court proceedings,[39] waiver of expert costs and fees in a criminal procedure;[40]
- return of a fine;[41]
- granting of a special right to be heard in administrative proceedings;[42]

---

[32] *Bulus v. Sweden* (Appl. No. 9330/81), Report (Commission–Friendly Settlement), 8 December 1984, D.R. 39, 75, para. 16; *Sami El-Makhour v. Germany* (Appl. No. 14312/88), Report (Commission–Friendly Settlement), 10 July 1989, not reported, para. 12; *Mansi v. Sweden* (Appl. No. 15658/89), Report (Commission–Friendly Settlement), 9 March 1990, not reported, para. 16.

[33] *Giama v. Belgium* (Appl. No. 7612/76), Report (Commission–Friendly Settlement), 17 July 1980, D.R. 21, 73, para. 43 in a case concerning Article 3 ECHR.

[34] *A.S. v. Austria* (Appl. No. 15220/89), Report (Commission–Friendly Settlement), 15 October 1993, D.R. 75, 30, para. 10.

[35] *Sawicki v. Poland* (Appl. No. 25085/94), Report (Commission–Friendly Settlement), 14 January 1997, D.R. 88-B, 42, para. 14. Interestingly, no financial compensation was included in this friendly settlement.

[36] *Karrer and Others v. Austria* (Appl. No. 7464/76), Report (Commission–Friendly Settlement), 4 May 1979, D.R. 16, 42, p. 47 [no paragraphs].

[37] *Alagöz v. Netherlands* (Appl. No. 24205/94), Report (Commission–Friendly Settlement), 2 July 1996, not reported, para. 20.

[38] *Ayala v. Portugal* (Appl. No. 23663/94), Report (Commission–Friendly Settlement), 21 October 1996, D.R. 87-B, 38, para. 31.

[39] *R.R. v. Germany* (Appl. No. 14446/88), Decision (Commission–Arrangement), 13 July 1990, not reported [no paragraphs].

[40] *Mlynek v. Austria* (Appl. No. 15016/89), Judgment (Chamber–Arrangement), 27 October 1992, Series A, Vol. 242-C, para. 13.

[41] *A.K. v. Austria* (Appl. No. 19630/92), Report (Commission–Friendly Settlement), 25 January 1996, not reported, para. 12.

[42] *Moosmann v. Austria* (Appl. No. 14093/88), Report (Commission–Friendly Settlement), 9 July 1992, D.R. 73, 19, para. 8.

- definition of the right to visit a child;[43]
- re-opening of restitution proceedings;[44]
- acknowledgement of a religious group according to national statutes;[45]
- conclusion of an arbitration agreement;[46]
- repeal of a decision to destroy the applicant's dog;[47]
- requirement that the applicant withdraws the application.[48]

A typical situation where a friendly settlement appears to be appropriate is when a violation of the Convention has been authoritatively declared but the question of just satisfaction is not yet ripe. Both the Commission[49] and the old Court[50] used the opportunity to settle purely financial matters in the form of follow-up friendly settlement.[51]

In the large majority of cases, friendly settlements contained only individual measures.[52] However, the Government agreed in rare cases to extend its efforts to more general measures.[53] A good example of this practice would be *Samková v. The Slovak Republic* where the Parties agreed upon the following terms: "The Government of the Slovak Republic, shall, in an adequate manner, draw the

---

[43] *Dunkel v. Germany* (Appl. No. 10812/84), Report (Commission–Friendly Settlement), 14 May 1987, D.R. 52, 188, para. 12.

[44] *Poláková and Machová v. Slovak Republic* (Appl. No. 30903/96), Decision (Commission–Arrangement), 3 December 1997, not reported [no paragraphs].

[45] *Khristianso Sdruzheni "Svideteli Na Iehova" v. Bulgaria* (Appl. No. 28626/95), Report (Commission–Friendly Settlement), 9 March 1998, D.R. 92-A, 44, para. 17.

[46] *Flattery v. Ireland* (Appl. No. 28995/95), Decision (Commission–Arrangement), 8 July 1998, not reported [no paragraphs].

[47] *Ländström v. Sweden* (Appl. No. 29105/95), Report (Commission–Friendly Settlement), 21 October 1998, not reported, para. 10.

[48] *Sverrisson v. Iceland* (Appl. No. 13291/87), Report (Commission–Friendly Settlement), 6 February 1990, D.R. 65, 192, para. 11; *Birou v. France* (Appl. No. 13319/87), Judgment (Chamber–Arrangement), 27 February 1992, Series A, Vol. 232-B, para. 11.

[49] *Schaden v. Austria* (Appl. No. 12896/87), Report (Commission–Friendly Settlement), 12 February 1990, D.R. 65, 165.

[50] *Winterwerp v. Netherlands* (Appl. No. 6301/73), Judgment (Chamber–Arrangement), 27 November 1981, Series A, Vol. 47; *Foti and Others v. Italy* (Appl. Nos. 7604/76; 7719/76; 7781/77; 7913/77), Judgment (Chamber–Arrangement), 21 November 1983, Series A, Vol. 69; *Malone v. United Kingdom* (Appl. No. 8691/79), Judgment (Chamber–Arrangement), 26 April 1985, Series A, Vol. 95; *Erkner and Hofauer v. Austria* (Appl. No. 9616/81), Judgment (Chamber–Arrangement), 29 September 1987, Series A, Vol. 124-D; *Poiss v. Austria* (Appl. No. 9816/82), Judgment (Chamber–Arrangement), 29 September 1987, Series A, Vol. 124-E; *Bouamar v. Belgium* (Appl. No. 9106/80), Judgment (Chamber–Arrangement), 27 June 1988, Series A, Vol. 136-F; *Weeks v. United Kingdom* (Appl. No. 9787/82), Judgment (Plenary–Arrangement), 5 October 1988, Series A, Vol. 145-A; *Kostovski v. Netherlands* (Appl. No. 11454/85), Judgment (Plenary–Arrangement), 29 March 1990, Series A, Vol. 170-B; *Vogt v. Germany* (Appl. No. 17851/91), Judgment (Grand Chamber–Arrangement), 2 September 1996, Reports 1996-IV, 1086; *Katikaridis and Others v. Greek* (Appl. No. 19385/92), Judgment (Chamber–Arrangement), 31 March 1998, Reports 1998-II, 699.

[51] For the terminology, see the chapter "Beyond Doctrine", section I.4.

[52] Cabral Barreto, I. (2000), p. 42.

[53] Ibid., pp. 37, 43.

attention of the national judicial authorities to the urgent need of the respect of the requirements contained in Article 6 para. 1 of the Convention when applying the provision of Section 250f of the Code of Civil Procedure."[54] In other cases, the State Party agreed to provide general information and guidelines concerning the use of seclusion in a hospital,[55] on the amendment of circular instruction to prison staff,[56] or the circulation of a practice note to all appeal court chairmen and clerks on legal aid.[57]

Normally, the friendly settlement did not specify which national authority was responsible for paying out the financial awards. It was intended that the national (federal) Government would handle it as an international commitment in accordance with national law. However, in rare cases where the authorities at the local or State level (in the meaning of the *Länder* or *Cantons*) were responsible for the alleged ECHR violation, the settlement was directly binding on the *Länder* authorities.[58] The Commission also used friendly settlements as a means for resolving problems on a transitional basis.[59] This feature of the friendly settlement strategy has played an important role before the new Court.[60]

---

[54] *Samková v. Slovak Republic* (Appl. No. 26384/95), Report (Commission–Friendly Settlement), 15 January 1997, D.R. 88-A, 67, para. 21. Similar also *S.P., D.P. and A.T. v. United Kingdom* (Appl. No. 23715/94), Report (Commission–Friendly Settlement), 11 April 1997, D.R. 89-A, 31, para. 10: "By letter dated 4 December 1996, the applicants accepted the offer of the Government of 21 November 1996 to settle the case on the basis of an *ex gratia* payment to the applicants of £ 3000, payment of reasonable legal costs and the Government's confirmation that they are taking steps to implement the recommendations made by Dame Margaret Booth DBE in her report investigating the delay in Children Act cases and reviewing the administrative procedures for listing cases (...)." *M.M. v. Bulgaria* (Appl. No. 27496/95), Report (Commission–Friendly Settlement), 9 July 1997, D.R. 90-B, 56, para. 15: "The Government undertake to draft, in consultation with the applicant's representative, and submit to the National Assembly a legislative proposal for the amendment of the relevant provisions concerning the enforcement of judicial decisions providing for personal contact between a child and a non-custodial parent, with a view to guaranteeing enforceability of such decisions."

[55] *A. v. United Kingdom* (Appl. No. 6840/74), Report (Commission–Friendly Settlement), 6 July 1980, D.R. 20, 5, p. 8 et seq. [no paragraphs].

[56] *Seale v. United Kingdom* (Appl. No. 9466/81), Report (Commission–Friendly Settlement), 15 May 1986, D.R. 50, 70, para. 18; *McComb v. United Kingdom* (Appl. No. 10621/83), Report (Commission–Friendly Settlement), 15 May 1986, D.R. 50, 81, para 16.

[57] *Ritchie v. United Kingdom* (Appl. No. 16212/90), Report (Commission–Friendly Settlement), 13 February 1992, not reported, para. 10; *Higgins v. United Kingdom* (Appl. No. 14778/89), Report (Commission–Friendly Settlement), 13 February 1992, D.R. 73, 95, para. 10; *M. v. United Kingdom* (Appl. No. 15861/89), Report (Commission–Friendly Settlement), 8 September 1992, not reported, para. 15; *W.W. v. United Kingdom* (Appl. No. 18123/91), Report (Commission–Friendly Settlement), 6 April 1993, not reported, para. 17.

[58] *Moosmann v. Austria*, note 42 *supra*, para. 8: "The applicant (...) will be paid Austrian Shillings 80'280.-. This sum will be paid in equal amounts both by the Regional State (Land) and the Federal State (Bund) (Federal Ministry of Economic Affairs)."

[59] See for example, *Ward v. United Kingdom* (Appl. No. 19526/92), Report (Commission–Friendly Settlement), 5 July 1993, D.R. 75, 217, para. 16: "(...) the Government proposed to settle the case on the basis of section 34 of the Criminal Justice Act 1991 (in force since October 1992) which provision is intended to give the Parole Board the powers and functions of a court."

[60] See section III.7. *infra*.

2. Characteristics of the Practice

Several characteristics of the Commission's and the old Court's practice appear to be important, as they are also decisive for the understanding of the use of friendly settlements before the new Court. Much of the settlement work was delegated. It was the Secretariat rather than the Commission Members that would contact the parties.[61] Furthermore, unless the case had a major political or legal significance, it was also the Secretariat (rather than the Commission Members) that would conduct the negotiations.[62] In many cases, the involvement of the Commission was limited to a written invitation sent to the parties suggesting the terms of a settlement. However, it was the Commission's responsibility to verify whether the proposed settlement was reached on the basis of respect for human rights.[63] Most settlements consisted of financial compensation for the applicant, without an acknowledgement of a violation by the respondent Government.[64]

Friendly settlements were regularly concluded between a State Party and a single applicant.[65] Mass friendly settlements or pilot friendly settlements were unknown at that time. However, the Commission occasionally adopted several friendly settlements on the same date,[66] or rationalized the procedure by merging several applications in the area of lengthy proceedings.[67]

---

[61] Krüger, H. C./Nørgaard, C. A. (1988), p. 331.

[62] Koopmans, S. M. G. (2008), p. 188.

[63] Cabral Barreto, I. (2000), p. 40. See Article 28 (1) (b) ECHR in force at that time, reprinted in annex 3.

[64] The Government was prepared, however, to acknowledge a violation of the Convention in rare cases. See for example, *Vallon v. Italy* (Appl. No. 9621/81), Judgment (Chamber–Arrangement), 3 June 1985, Series A, Vol. 95, para. 21: "The Government have acknowledged that there has been violation on their part of the European Convention on Human rights in the criminal proceedings instituted against the applicant." See for the development section III.4. *infra*.

[65] For the rare exception of a settlement concluded by several applicants see for examples, *Jädergård and Others v. Sweden* (Appl. No. 13247/87), Report (Commission–Friendly Settlement), 1 July 1992, not reported, which settled cases of seven applicants; *Andersson and 28 Others v. Sweden* (Appl. No. 14740/89), Report (Commission–Friendly Settlement), 19 January 1994, not reported, which was a settlement for 28 applicants; *J.S. and Others v. Netherlands* (Appl. Nos. 14561/89; 14657/89; 15105/89; 15343/89; 15712/89; 15908/89; 15988/90; 16118/90; 16513/90; 16583/90; 16843/90; 16896–97/90; 17001/90; 17241/90; 17252/90; 17675/91; 17883/91; 18615/91; 19590–91/92; 20311/92; 22532/93), Report (Commission–Friendly Settlement), 23 January 1996, not reported, which resulted in the settlement of 23 similar cases; *Baumgartner and Others v. Austria* (Appl. No. 23085/93), Report (Commission–Friendly Settlement), 16 October 1996, not reported, which was a settlement of 41 applicants; *Tsomtsos and Others v. Greece* (Appl. No. 20680/92), Judgment (Chamber–Arrangement), 31 March 1998, Reports 1998-II, 705, which settled 101 applications; *Mora do Vale and Others v. Portugal* (Appl. Nos. 33329/96; 34140/96; 34796/97; 36003797; 36166/97), Report (Commission–Friendly Settlement), 15 September 1998, not reported, which closed five applications. See also the cases cited in note 78 and 79 *infra*.

[66] See for examples, *M.O.N. v. Portugal* (Appl. No. 12745/87), Report (Commission–Friendly Settlement), 31 May 1991, D.R. 69, 135; *J.P.R. and M.C.L. v. Portugal* (Appl. No. 15046/89), Report (Commission–Friendly Settlement), 31 May 1991, not reported; *Correia Dias v. Portugal* (Appl. No. 14904/89), Report (Commission–Friendly Settlement), 31 May 1991, not reported; *Alva Torres v. Portugal* (Appl. No. 14836/89), Report (Commission–Friendly Settlement), 31 May 1991, not reported; *Fidalgo Martins v. Portugal* (Appl. No. 13874/88), Report (Commission–

The applicants occasionally refused to conclude a friendly settlement in spite of the State Party's willingness to settle on reasonable and favourable terms. We assume that the individual applicant sometimes preferred to obtain an authoritative judgment acknowledging the violation of the Convention.[68]

The negotiations were – as they are still today – confidential, and this very fact was sometimes specifically mentioned in the agreement.[69]

3. Critical Areas

In the Commission's and the old Court's practice, friendly settlements – containing purely financial awards – were also concluded in cases concerning allegations

---

Friendly Settlement), 31 May 1991, not reported; *Aires v. Portugal* (Appl. No. 13387/87), Report (Commission–Friendly Settlement), 31 May 1991, not reported; *C. and O. v. Portugal* (Appl. Nos. 12934/87; 12935/87), Report (Commission–Friendly Settlement), 31 May 1991, not reported; *Oliveira Pinto v. Portugal* (Appl. No. 12918/87), Report (Commission–Friendly Settlement), 31 May 1991, not reported; *Marcos Cordeiro v. Portugal* (Appl. No. 12746/87), Report (Commission–Friendly Settlement), 31 May 1991, not reported; *P.P.P. v. Portugal* (Appl. No. 13526/88), Report (Commission–Friendly Settlement), 31 May 1991, not reported; all reports concerned the length of proceedings in different areas of the Portuguese judicial system. It was also similar in *Luciano Sernache v. Portugal* (Appl. No. 14548/89), Report (Commission–Friendly Settlement), 8 July 1991, not reported; *F.V.B. v. Portugal* (Appl. No. 13774/88), Report (Commission–Friendly Settlement), 8 July 1991, D.R. 70, 198; *Paal v. Portugal* (Appl. No. 14659/89), Report (Commission–Friendly Settlement), 8 July 1991, not reported. For similar cases, see also *Reis Antunes v. Portugal* (Appl. No. 20844/92), Report (Commission–Friendly Settlement), 7 December 1994, not reported; *Vieira v. Portugal* (Appl. No. 20879/92), Report (Commission–Friendly Settlement), 7 December 1994, not reported; *Teixeira da Mota v. Portugal* (Appl. No. 18866/91), Report (Commission–Friendly Settlement), 7 December 1994, not reported; *Thomaz dos Santos S.A. v. Portugal* (Appl. No. 19372/92), Report (Commission–Friendly Settlement), 7 December 1994, not reported; *De Oliveira Barros v. Portugal* (Appl. No. 20502/92), Report (Commission–Friendly Settlement), 7 December 1994, not reported; *Santos Marques v. Portugal* (Appl. No. 20381/92), Report (Commission–Friendly Settlement), 7 December 1994, not reported; *Valada v. Portugal* (Appl. No. 18581/91), Report (Commission–Friendly Settlement), 7 December 1994, not reported, all reports concerned the length of proceedings. See also *S.L. v. France* (Appl. No. 26365/95), Report (Commission–Friendly Settlement), 4 July 1995, not reported; *Leterme v. France*, (Appl. No. 26387/95), Report (Commission–Friendly Settlement), 4 July 1995, not reported; *Fraisse v. France* (Appl. No. 26512/95), Report (Commission–Friendly Settlement), 4 July 1995, not reported; *Mesquita v. France* (Appl. No. 21433/93), Report (Commission–Friendly Settlement), 4 July 1995, not reported; *Marquet v. France* (Appl. No. 26266/95), Report (Commission–Friendly Settlement), 4 July 1995, not reported; *Laurant v. France* (Appl. No. 26295/95), Report (Commission–Friendly Settlement), 4 July 1995, not reported; all reports concerned the length of proceedings.

[67] For example, the reports adopted by the Commission in 1999 against France concerning the length of proceedings are quite striking: On 22 April, 16 Reports with a total amount of 475,000 FF; on 3 June, 18 reports with a total amount of 540,000 FF; on 9 September, 22 Reports with a total amount of 660,000 FF; and on 25 October, three reports with a total amount of 100,000 FF.

[68] We do not have evidence for this assumption since the applicants' preferences were not spelled out in the decisions or judgments of the Court. Of course, the State Party refused from time to time to settle a case as well, see for example, *Ofner and Hopfinger v. Austria* (Appl. Nos. 524/59; 617/59), Report (Commission–Friendly Settlement), 23 November 1962, Y.B. 6, 680, para. 51.

[69] *O'Reilly v. Ireland* (Appl. No. 24196/94), Report (Commission–Friendly Settlement), 3 December 1996, D.R. 87-A, 58, para. 15.

of serious human rights abuses or ongoing human rights violations.[70] In this context, the case of *Farrell v. United Kingdom*[71] raised some criticism. The UK security forces had mistakenly killed a man in Northern Ireland. The UK Government concluded a friendly settlement with the deceased's wife for the amount of 37,500 GBP, without acknowledging a breach of Article 2 ECHR or taking any additional measures. However, the settlement was followed by several cases suggesting that there may have been a broader issue concerning the use of force by UK soldiers in Northern Ireland.[72]

In *Skoogström v. Sweden*,[73] the issue was whether the applicant had been brought promptly before a Judge or another officer authorized by law to exercize judicial power, as required by Article 5 (3) ECHR. In particular, the case provided an opportunity to evaluate whether the district prosecutor could be regarded as a judicial officer according to the national law at that time. The Court accepted the friendly settlement in spite of the fact that the settlement indicated neither the nature of the amendment to the Code of Judicial Procedure nor when those amendments would be proposed. Three Judges criticized the findings of the majority: "(...) such a decision does not seem to us to be consonant with the general interest attaching to observance of human rights (...)".[74] Similarly, in *Can v. Austria*,[75] the Court agreed to strike the case out of its list following a friendly settlement on the basis that any lingering doubts about the legislative programme announced therein must be put aside, because there was clear case law on the issue of Articles 5 (3) and 6 (3) ECHR giving sufficient guidance to the respondent Government.[76]

---

[70] Ang, F./Berghmans, E. (2005), p. 93.
[71] *Farrell v. United Kingdom* (Appl. No. 9013/80), Report (Commission–Friendly Settlement), 2 October 1984, D.R. 38, 44, para. 10 et seq.
[72] *Jordan v. United Kingdom* (Appl. No. 24746/94), Judgment (Third Section), 4 May 2001, not reported; *McKerr v. United Kingdom* (Appl. No. 28883/95), Judgment (Third Section), 4 May 2001, Reports 2001-III, 475; *McShane v. United Kingdom* (Appl. No. 43290/98), Judgment (Fourth Section), 28 May 2002, not reported; *Shanaghan v. United Kingdom* (Appl. No. 37715/97), Judgment (Third Section), 4 May 2001, not reported; *Finucane v. United Kingdom* (Appl. No. 29178/95), Judgment (Fourth Section), 1 July 2003, Reports 2003-VIII, 1; see also Koopmans, S. M. G. (2008), p. 193.
[73] *Skoogström v. Sweden* (Appl. No. 8582/79), Judgment (Chamber–Arrangement), 2 October 1984, Series A, Vol. 83.
[74] Ibid., joint dissenting opinion of Judges Wiarda, Ryssdal and Ganshof van der Meersch.
[75] *Can v. Austria* (Appl. No. 9300/81), Judgment (Chamber–Arrangement), 30 September 1985, Series A, Vol. 96.
[76] See also subsequently *K. v. Austria* (Appl. No. 16002/90), Judgment (Chamber–Arrangement), 2 June 1993, Series A, Vol. 255-B, where the Commission's Delegate expressed serious doubts: "The Delegate has considerable doubts as to whether the settlement can be regarded as being 'on the basis of respect for human rights' (see Eur. Court H. R., Can judgment of 30 September 1985, Series A no. 96, pp. 10–11, paras. 17 and 18 [*Can v. Austria*, ibid.]. He therefore considers that, in the absence of any commitment on the part of the Austrian Government regarding the general interest, the case should not be struck out of the record as it raises important issues of principle." (text inserted by the authors).

Another sensitive issue concerned corporal punishment in schools in the United Kingdom. As early as 1980, the Commission acknowledged a violation of Article 2 of Protocol no 1 in *Campbell and Cosans v. United Kingdom*.[77] Although the Report made it clear that corporal punishment was a widespread practice in schools across the United Kingdom at the time, the Commission accepted the settlement of similar cases in 1981 and 1987.[78] Shortly after, in July 1987, the UK Government announced an amendment of the national statutes in several friendly settlement cases.[79] This was sufficient for the Commission to resolve 13 applications concerning the same matter by holding that: "(...) given the reform of the law on corporal punishment in state schools, (...) there are no reasons of a general character affecting the observance of the Convention which necessitate the further retention of this case."[80] Subsequent applications were settled on the same grounds.[81] In 1992, the Court still accepted a friendly settlement, although the Commission had expressed its doubts: "Y's case (...) clearly demonstrates the inadequacy of the civil remedy for treatment which, in the Commission's view, was in breach of Article 3 (art. 3) of the Convention. (...) The Delegate [sc. of the Commission] therefore concludes, albeit reluctantly, that he has no formal objection to make should the Court, in its wisdom, decide to endorse the settlement and strike the case out of the list."[82]

In the light of notorious problems concerning the length of national proceedings in Portugal, France and Italy, the question arises whether friendly settlements in this area and concerning these countries were justified. It sometimes seemed that certain State Parties preferred to conclude a friendly settlement rather than to tackle the underlying problem.[83]

From the publicly available case file, it seems that the old Court rarely refused to endorse a friendly settlement, even in cases in which the Commission had

---

[77] *Campbell and Cosans v. United Kingdom* (Appl. Nos. 7511/76; 7743/77), Report (Commission), 16 May 1980, Series B, Vol. 42.

[78] *X. v. United Kingdom* (Appl. No. 7907/77), Report (Commission–Friendly Settlement), 17 December 1981, Y.B. 24, 402; *Townend Sr. and Townend Jr. v. United Kingdom* (Appl. No. 9119/80), Report (Commission–Friendly Settlement), 23 January 1987, D.R. 50, 36.

[79] *Three members of the A. family v. United Kingdom* (Appl. No. 10592/83), Report (Commission–Friendly Settlement), Report adopted on 16 July 1987, D.R. 52, 150, para. 13; *Brant v. United Kingdom* (Appl. No. 9303/81), Report (Commission–Friendly Settlement), Report adopted on 16 July 1987, D.R. 52, 21, para. 14; *Durairaj, Baker (formerly Durairaj) and Durairaj v. United Kingdom* (Appl. No. 9114/80), Report (Commission–Friendly Settlement), Report adopted on 16 July 1987, D.R. 52, 13, para. 12.

[80] Identical formulation in all Reports (Commission–Friendly Settlements) adopted by the Commission on 11 May 1988: *Lund and Walker v. United Kingdom* (Appl. No. 12674/87), not reported; *Maycock and Maycock v. United Kingdom* (Appl. No. 12675/87), not reported; *J. and R. S. v. United Kingdom* (Appl. No. 12676/87), not reported; *Rogers and Rogers v. United Kingdom* (Appl. No. 12677/87), not reported.

[81] See for example, *S. v. United Kingdom* (Appl. No. 11756/85), Decision (Commission–Arrangement), 13 March 1989, not reported [no paragraphs].

[82] *Y. v. United Kingdom* (Appl. No. 14229/88), Judgment (Chamber–Arrangement), 29 October 1992, Series A, Vol. 247-A, para. 16 (text inserted by the authors).

[83] Dollé, S. (1998), p. 244.

expressed clear doubts as to whether the settlement respected human rights.[84] Sometimes, the Court simply accepted the friendly settlement, recalling its juris-prudence on the matter.[85]

4. Form of the Friendly Settlement

The Commission usually concluded a procedure in the form of a Report stating that the settlement reached by the parties had been secured on the basis of respect for human rights, as defined in the Convention.[86] Before Protocol no 11 entered into force, the applicant had no right to bring his case before the old Court. There was therefore no need to waive this possibility. Sometimes, however, the parties agreed on a friendly settlement and the Commission decided to strike the case out of its list.[87] From the case files, it is not entirely clear what made the Commission choose one form of closing the case over another. Sometimes, it seems that the Commission was not much involved in the negotiation process and therefore preferred to strike the case out of the list.[88] Sometimes, the parties simply agreed to the strike out.[89] However, this practice was not always applied consistently.[90]

---

[84] *K. v. Austria,* note 76 *supra*, para. 13. Cf. Cabral Barreto, I. (2000), pp. 44, 47; Krüger, H. C./ Nørgaard, C. A. (1988), p. 332; Reisman, W. M./Benesch, S. (2003), p. 756; Zwaak, L. (2006), p. 224.

[85] *Woukam Moudefo v. France* (Appl. No. 10868/84), Judgment (Chamber–Arrangement), 11 October 1988, Series A, Vol. 141-B, para. 15; *Olivera Neves v. Portugal* (Appl. No. 11612/85), Judgment (Chamber–Friendly Settlement), 25 May 1989, Series A, Vol. 153-B, para. 11: "The Court takes formal note of the friendly settlement reached by the Government and the applicant. It would nevertheless be open to the Court, having regard to its responsibilities under Article 19 (art. 19) of the Convention, to decide to continue its examination of the case if a reason of public policy appeared to necessitate such a course (Rule 48 para. 4). However, it finds no such reason. In this connection, the Court notes that it has had to review the 'reasonableness' of the length of 'civil' proceedings, in Portugal (…) [citing several cases]. In so doing, it clarified the nature and extent of the obligations undertaken in this area by the Contracting States." (text inserted by the authors).

[86] Fribergh, E./Villiger, M. E. (1993), p. 613; Ovey, C./White, R. (2006), p. 374. See for ex-ample, *Ten Berge v. Netherlands* (Appl. No. 20929/92), Report (Commission–Friendly Settlement), 5 December 1995, not reported, para. 16: "(…) having regard to Article 28 para. 1 (b) of the Convention, that the friendly settlement of the case had been secured on the basis of respect for Human Rights as defined in the Convention."

[87] See for examples, *A. v. Sweden* (Appl. No. 14293/88), Decision (Commission–Arrangement), 14 January 1991, not reported [no paragraphs]: "Having regard to Article 30 para. 1 of the Conven-tion, the Commission notes that the matter has been resolved. Furthermore, it finds no special circumstances regarding respect for human rights as defined in the Convention which require the continuation of the examination of the application." *Sätterlund v. Sweden* (Appl. No. 30157/96), Decision (Commission–Arrangement), 9 July 1997, not reported; *Heikel v. Finland* (Appl. No. 30511/96), Decision (Commission–Arrangement), 9 September 1998, not reported.

[88] See for example, *Constantinou v. Cyprus* (Appl. No. 28209/95), Decision (Commission–Arrangement), 21 May 1997, not reported [no paragraphs]: "By letter dated 24 February 1997, the applicant's lawyer informed the Secretariat that the parties have reached an out-of-court settlement which provides that the Cypriot Government will pay the applicant 55 000 CYP£ and costs. There-fore, the applicant has decided to withdraw his application."

[89] *Mattsson v. Sweden* (Appl. No. 13425/87), Decision (Commission–Arrangement), 27 May

The difference between the two forms is purely formalistic: Under the former, the Commission examined the settlement reached on the basis of Article 28 (1) (b) ECHR, and under the latter it evaluated it on the basis of Article 30 (1) ECHR (in force at that time). From a functional point of view, the friendly settlements adopted in a strike out decision fulfill the same aim as the settlements adopted in a formal Report in that the parties agreed to resolve the case.[91]

One should bear in mind that the mediator plays a crucial role in the context of friendly settlements, which are judicially endorsed decisions. If the Commission controls the negotiation process, the respect for human rights is more institutionalized. This control may even have a preventive function. If the parties conclude a friendly settlement on their own, however, the danger of misgivings is inherent. In these instances, the only control is exercised *ex post* and it might suffer from the strong incentive of all stakeholders to get rid of the case as quickly as possible.[92]

The old Court adopted friendly settlements in the form of judgments and decided to strike the case out of its list independently of whether it only concerned financial matters (Article 50 ECHR in force at that time)[93] or the settlement as a whole.[94] The old Court deliberately chose to strike the case out in the form of

---

1991, not reported [no paragraphs]: "The parties agree that the application is struck out of the Commission's list of cases." The contrary was also possible, i.e., the applicant insisted on a Report of the Commission, see *Larsen v. Denmark* (Appl. No. 23871/94), Report (Commission–Friendly Settlement), 15 April 1997, not reported, para. 15: "My client expects to receive a report from the [Commission], cf. Article 28 of the Convention."

[90] See for examples, *Aldrian v. Austria* (Appl. No. 10532/83), Report (Commission–Arrangement), 17 March 1989, not reported, para. 22: The Commission decided to strike the decision off its list and to adopt the report; *Georgsson v. Iceland* (Appl. No. 22103/93), Report (Commission–Friendly Settlement), 15 April 1997, not reported, para. 13: "In signing this Settlement, Mr Sigurdur Georgsson furthermore declares that he approves that this Settlement be submitted to the European Commission of Human Rights in confirmation of the fact that he revokes his application against the Icelandic Government." Nonetheless, these settlements were adopted in the form of a report. Similar also a case decided by the old Court, *Fouquet v. France* (Appl. No. 20398/92), Judgment (Chamber–Arrangement), 31 January 1996, Reports 1996-I, 19, para. 16: Although the applicant did explicitly agree to withdraw his application, the Court examined the friendly settlement.

[91] See for more details the chapter "Beyond Doctrine", section I.1.

[92] See for the same problem under the new Court section III.8. *infra*.

[93] *Luedicke, Belkacem and Koc v. Germany* (Appl. Nos. 6210/73; 6877/75; 7132/75), Judgment (Chamber–Arrangement), 10 March 1980, Series A, Vol. 36; *Winterwerp v. Netherlands* (Appl. No. 6301/73), Judgment (Chamber–Arrangement), 27 November 1981, Series A, Vol. 47; *Foti and Others v. Italy* (Appl. Nos. 7604/76; 7719/76; 7781/77; 7913/77), Judgment (Chamber–Arrangement), 21 November 1983, Series A, Vol. 69; *Malone v. United Kingdom* (Appl. No. 8691/79), Judgment (Chamber–Arrangement), 26 April 1985, Series A, Vol. 95; *Erkner and Hofauer v. Austria* (Appl. No. 9616/81), Judgment (Chamber–Arrangement), 29 September 1987, Series A, Vol. 124-D; *Poiss v. Austria* (Appl. No. 9816/82), Judgment (Chamber–Arrangement), 29 September 1987, Series A, Vol. 124-E; *Weeks v. United Kingdom* (Appl. No. 9787/82), Judgment (Plenary–Arrangement), 5 October 1988, Series A, Vol. 145-A; *Bouamar v. Belgium* (Appl. No. 9106/80), Judgment (Chamber–Arrangement), 27 June 1988, Series A, Vol. 136-F; *Kostovski v. Netherlands* (Appl. No. 11454/85), Judgment (Plenary–Arrangement), 29 March 1990, Series A, Vol. 170-B.

[94] *Skoogström v. Sweden* (Appl. No. 8582/79), Judgment (Chamber–Arrangement), 2 October 1984, Series A, Vol. 83; *Can v. Austria* (Appl. No. 9300/81), Judgment (Chamber–Arrangement),

a judgment in order to ensure that it would be enforced by the Committee of Ministers.[95] Sometimes, the old Court would also strike the case out on the basis of a settlement reached by the parties.[96]

The policy that friendly settlements are adopted both in the form of judgments and decisions is also applied by the new Court. Under Protocol no 11, it is quite obvious that this practice evolved rather inconsistently and was not very transparent to the outsiders.

III. After Protocol No 11

Protocol no 11 was originally the most radical step in the Court's reform history. As part of this drastic development, the old Commission was abolished. The new Court, composed of professional Judges with substantial staff at their disposal, became a fully-fledged international human rights adjudicative body. The judicial character of the Convention was enhanced in comparison to the original 1950s model. The Court's jurisdiction to handle both individual and interstate petitions became compulsory and the adjudicative role of the Committee of Ministers was abolished. As a result, the full judicalization of the European human rights protection system was completed in 1998.

During the reform discussions, friendly settlements were in jeopardy following the abandonment of the practice of sharing with the parties the Commission's opinion as to whether or not there was a violation of the Convention. The rational behind this previous practice was that the Government would have no incentive to enter into a settlement without the signal of a probable violation of the Convention. From its very beginning, the new Court rejected this practice on grounds that it was not compatible with its judicial nature.[97] The transfer of responsibility had a significant impact on task sharing. In most friendly settlement proceedings,

---

30 September 1985, Series A, Vol. 96, para. 15: "The Court takes formal note of the friendly settlement reached by the Government and the applicant. The applicant regards the settlement as being clearly in accordance with his own interest; nevertheless, the Court must satisfy itself that there are no reasons of public policy (ordre public) of a kind which would necessitate the continuation of the proceedings (Rule 48 para. 4)." *Ben Yaacoub v. Belgium* (Appl. No. 9976/82), Judgment (Chamber–Friendly Settlement), 27 November 1987, Series A, Vol. 127-A.

[95] Rule 49 (3) Rules of Court A and Rule 51 (3) Rules of Court B at the time in force, reprinted in annex 3.

[96] See for examples, *Skoogström v. Sweden*, note 94 *supra*; *Muyldermans v. Belgium* (Appl. No. 12217/86), Judgment (Chamber–Arrangement), 23 October 1991, Series A, Vol. 214-A; *Djeroud v. France* (Appl. No. 13446/87), Judgment (Chamber–Arrangement), 23 January 1991, Series A, Vol. 191-B, para. 12: "The Court takes formal note of the friendly settlement reached by the Government and the applicant. It discerns no reason of ordre public militating against striking the case out of the list (Rule 49 §§ 2 and 4 of the Rules of Court)."

[97] Ang, F./Berghmans, E. (2005), p. 91 et seq.; Courell, A. M. (2006), p. 65; Mahoney, P. (2001), p. 447; Myjer, E. (2007), p. 315. However, we currently have a similar situation. Although the Registry does not indicate a violation in the case formally, it signals clearly by sending a friendly settlement proposal to the parties, that the case is considered to be clear-cut. The Government Agent

the Registry took the lead and the Judges only gave their final approval. In sheer numbers, friendly settlements therefore started to play a much more prominent role in the early years of the new millennium.[98]

1. Progression of an Application before the Court

An application passes through several stages of proceedings before the Court. In order to understand both the fate of an application and the different possibilities of entering into negotiations for a friendly settlement, we use the normal life of an application as a reference for the structure of this section. The main purpose of this part is to demonstrate which actors are involved in the proceedings and when the settlement would come into play. In the different procedural phases, settlements have various functions that will be analysed.[99]

A second element that plays an important role in the handling of cases is the growing number of applications.[100] Currently, the Court deals with about 30,000 cases a year.[101] By December 2009, 119,300 applications were pending before the Court.[102] The Court receives roughly 1,000 letters a day – in other words, approximately every two minutes somebody in Europe writes to the Court.[103] The Court's attempt to render its machinery more effective had a strong impact on the procedural level. At the beginning of the new millennium, the idea that the 47 Judges would be able to resolve each and every single human rights case arriving in Strasbourg proved to be both unrealistic and unfeasible. Over the years, the Court's administrative and assisting bodies – the Registry, translation services, etc. – have been considerably enlarged. In the course of this enlargement, much work, competence and power had been delegated downwards. This also holds for the settling of disputes.

a) Registration

Once an application is received in Strasbourg, it is not immediately registered. The Registry sometimes gets in touch with the person concerned, whose attention will be drawn to matters that may render the application inadmissible (e.g., failure to exhaust domestic remedies or comply with the time-limit for applying;

---

can then anticipate that there would be a violation in the case. He, or she, can also predict the level of compensation that would have to be granted (cf. Courell, op. cit.).

[98] Zwaak, L. (2006), p. 226.

[99] See also for a schematic overview the charts in annex 4.

[100] Stone Sweet, A./Keller, H. (2008), p. 12; Weber, G. S. (2007), p. 221.

[101] European Court of Human Rights, Annual Report 2008, Registry of the European Court of Human Rights, Strasbourg 2009, p. 137. In 2008, the Court disposed of 32,045 cases by decision or judgment.

[102] European Court of Human Rights, Pending Applications Allocated to a Judicial Formation, 31 December 2009, available at <http://www.echr.coe.int/NR/rdonlyres/BBFE7733-3122-40F5-AACA-9B16827B74C2/0/Pending_applications_chart.pdf> (last visited 15 April 2010).

[103] Villiger, M. E. (2009), p. 94.

allegations having no connection with a right guaranteed by the Convention or ill-founded in the light of the existing case law).[104] This practice may lead some applicants to abandon their claim.

All applications requiring a Court examination are allocated to a decision-making body. According to Rule 25 Rules of Court, the Court is divided into at least four Sections.[105] A fifth Section was created on 1 January 2005.[106] Once an application is registered, the President of one of the five Sections of the Court to which the case is assigned nominates a Member of the Section as the Judge Rapporteur. In Grand Chamber cases, the President of the Court designates the Rapporteur and in interstate applications, one or several Judges are designated as Judge Rapporteurs.[107] The identity of the Judge Rapporteur is confidential. He, or she, works closely with the Case Lawyer in the Registry to whom the case has been allocated. When a case reaches a three-judge Committee, the lawyer prepares a one-page proposal (maximum) in which the salient points are summarized.[108] The Judge Rapporteur, who is responsible for the examination and the preparation of the case, channels the case towards a Committee of three Judges or a Chamber of seven Judges.

b) *Inadmissible Cases*

The Judge Rapporteur seizes one of the three-judge Committees in the same Section.[109] Pursuant to Article 28 ECHR, the Committee can declare an application inadmissible or strike it out of the list of cases if such a decision can be taken without further examination. These cases are decided on the basis of a Committee note containing a brief description of the facts, the allegations made and the reasons for inadmissibility or strike out. Any requirement concerning Articles 34 or 35 ECHR could be a reason for the inadmissibility or strike out of the case: Anonymity, manifest ill-foundedness, six-month time period elapsed, *ratione materiae, ratione temporis, ratione personae* or the lack of victim status. The Committee's decision is final. In practice, roughly 90 per cent of the applications are declared inadmissible at this stage.[110]

---

[104] Cf. Ovey, C./White, R. (2006), p. 476.

[105] Weber, G. S. (2007), p. 220.

[106] For the organization of the Court, see the chart "Composition of the Sections" on the Court's website, available at <http://www.echr.coe.int/ECHR/EN/Header/The+Court/The+Court/The+Sections/> (last visited 15 April 2010).

[107] Rule 48–50 Rules of Court.

[108] Villiger, M. E. (2009), p. 96.

[109] Rule 27 (1) Rules of Court. For those countries that ratified Protocol no 14[bis] this procedure has been amended, see section IV. *infra*.

[110] Annual Report 2008, note 101 *supra*, p. 144. In 2008, 88 per cent of the applications processed or a total of 28,202 applications were declared inadmissible or struck out by Committee.

c) Other Cases

If the Committee is not unanimous or the Judge Rapporteur considers the need for a closer examination, the case is assigned to a Chamber. The Case Lawyer identifies any important or urgent cases requiring priority treatment. The same applies to any application considered suitable for a pilot judgment or any proceedings concerning a sensitive issue. With the assistance of the Case Lawyer and the Section Registrar, the Judge Rapporteur prepares a report summarizing the facts, indicating the issues at stake and making a proposal as to the procedure to be followed (inadmissibility, communication to the respondent Government).

If an application is not declared inadmissible or is struck out of the Court's list of cases, the Chamber or its President can give notice of the application to the respondent Contracting Party. In the so-called communication, the State Party is expected to submit written observations on the application and, upon receipt, to invite the applicant to submit observations in reply.[111] Typically, this is the first moment in which the parties are confronted with the idea of settling the case. After receipt of the observations and reply, the Chamber may decide to hold a hearing, which will usually concern the issues of admissibility and merits. A decision on inadmissibility is final and concludes the case. It is for the Judge Rapporteur in close co-operation with the Case Lawyer to prepare the draft decisions for consideration by the Chamber.

The first step leading towards a friendly settlement usually occurs at the stage of the communication sent to the parties. With this communication, the Registry may already make a proposal for a friendly settlement.[112] This is usually done when the case concerns an area where established case law exists (routine friendly settlement).[113] Alternatively, the Registry can include a statement in the communication indicating that the Court puts itself at the parties' disposal to conclude a friendly settlement pursuant to Article 38 (1) (b) ECHR. In this situation, the Court waits for a signal from the parties showing their willingness to enter into negotiations.

d) Joint Procedure on Admissibility and Merits

The decision to communicate an application may also follow the so-called joint examination procedure.[114] Although Article 29 (3) ECHR only foresees this procedure in exceptional circumstances, the Court's practice shows that the joint examination is rather the rule than the exception.[115] In such cases, the parties are

---

[111] Rule 54 (2) Rules of Court.

[112] Reid, K. (2008), p. 14.

[113] For the different types of settlements, see the chapter "Beyond Doctrine", section I.

[114] Article 29 (3) ECHR and Rule 54A Rules of Court.

[115] In October 2004, the Court decided to apply the principle that recourse to the joint procedure is the rule in dealing with individual applications and the separate decision on admissibility the exception. The Court took into account Article 29 ECHR, as amended by Article 9 of Protocol no 14 to the Convention for the Protection of Human Rights and Fundamental Freedoms, amending

invited to include in their observations any submissions concerning just satisfaction and proposals for a friendly settlement. This is usually done in repetitive and clone cases. There is well-established case law in the area of length of proceedings, non-enforcement of court orders, court martial proceedings, court access or property rights.

The Court has devised a variety of techniques for handling such repetitive cases. More specifically, an accelerated procedure was introduced under Article 29 (3) ECHR, a proactive approach to settle cases was applied and standard "mask" judgments were adopted. In this area, the conclusion of routine friendly settlements assisted the Court in reducing its backlog.[116] In the last decade, the Court's Registry decided to play a more active role in respect of friendly settlements.[117] While the Registry's personnel only used to act as a "postal box" for the exchange of friendly settlement proposals,[118] it now makes original proposals as soon as the case has been declared admissible, or even earlier, if the procedure under Article 29 (3) ECHR is used. This usually means that there is a clear-cut case in an area with established case law. The amount proposed is based on the so-called *tableaux* developed internally by the Registry to provide a guide for the calculation of just satisfaction under Article 41 ECHR and for the sums awarded in comparable judgments of the Court.

e) Grand Chamber Cases

A Chamber may at any stage of the proceedings relinquish jurisdiction in favour of the Grand Chamber when the case raises serious questions affecting the interpretation of the Convention, or where the Chamber might possibly arrive at a result inconsistent with previous judgments of the Court.[119] The Chamber must first inform the parties about its willingness to relinquish the case. The parties may submit reasoned objections within a period of one month. If the objection is accepted by the Chamber, the case is not relinquished to the Grand Chamber and the proceedings continue before that Chamber. At this stage, a friendly settlement can still be concluded, but it is rather rare.[120]

In exceptional circumstances, judgments handed down by a Chamber may

the control system of the Convention, CETS 194, opened for signature on 13 May 2004, and entered into force on 1 June 2010.

[116] O'Boyle, M. (2003).

[117] Ang, F./Berghmans, E. (2005), p. 91. It was impossible to trace back the actual decision taken regarding this policy change. However, the proactive role is mentioned as early as 2001 in the Report of the Evaluation Group to the Committee of Ministers on the European Court of Human Rights, 27 September 2001, EG Court (2001)1, p. 4: "The Group endorses the suggestion that the Court should continue to play a proactive role in respect of friendly settlements, with attempts to reach a settlement being pursued at an earlier stage in the proceedings."

[118] Michael O'Boyle, Deputy Registrar, information given in his interview of 2 February 2009, interview on file with the authors.

[119] Article 30 ECHR.

[120] See for example, *Varey v. United Kingdom* (Appl. No. 26662/95), Judgment (Grand Chamber–Arrangement), 21 December 2000, not reported, paras. 6 and 7.

be referred to the Grand Chamber upon request of a party to the case. Chamber judgments thus become final, if three months after the date of the judgment such a reference has not been requested, if the parties declare that they will not request a reference of the case to the Grand Chamber, or if such reference has been requested, but rejected. A panel of five Judges of the Grand Chamber accepts the request if the case raises a serious question affecting the interpretation or application of the Convention or the Protocols attached thereto, or a serious issue of general importance.[121] If the panel accepts the request for a reference, the case will be re-examined and subsequently determined by a judgment of the Grand Chamber. In the event of rejection of a referral request, the judgment becomes final on the date of the panel's meeting. In general, the possibility for referral is waived in friendly settlements.[122]

In theory, a case can still be settled between the referral to and the final decision of the Grand Chamber.[123] This occurs nonetheless quite rarely. Once the parties have reached the Grand Chamber, their wish for an authoritative judgment probably exceeds their will to settle the application. The same holds true for the Judges.[124] They eagerly look up to the Grand Chamber and have little interest in settling a case.[125]

f) Applicant's Representation

All applicants other than States, namely persons, non-governmental organizations or groups of individuals, may initially lodge an application themselves or through a representative under Article 34 ECHR.[126] The parties must be represented after the notification of the case to the Contracting Party. This is an important aspect for the settlement of cases. As soon as the applicant is represented by a lawyer, the Registry finds itself with two persons. Any procedural step and formal proposition for settling the case would usually be addressed to the legal representative.[127] However, the applicant is the person that ultimately has to be convinced and has to agree.

The Registry advises unrepresented applicants and informs them about the possibility of applying for legal aid. According to the practice of the Court, no legal representation is required for certain types of applications (e.g., in length of proceedings applications and in certain specific types of cases, such as Moldovan,

---

[121] Article 43 (2) ECHR.
[122] See for example, *Erkanli v. Turkey* (Appl. No. 37721/97), Judgment (Second Section–Friendly Settlement), 13 February 2003, not reported.
[123] Zwaak, L. (2006), p. 224.
[124] Reid, K. (2008), p. 15.
[125] Luzius Wildhaber, former President of the ECtHR, information given in his interview of 19 June 2009, interview on file with the authors.
[126] Rule 36 (1) Rules of Court.
[127] Frank Schürmann, Swiss Agent before the ECtHR, information given in his interview of 30 January 2009, reprinted in annex 1.

Russian and Ukrainian non-execution judgments, Italian eviction of tenant cases, Turkish expropriation and State Security Court cases).

g) Time Framework

Time is a decisive factor in making the choice between a normal procedure and a friendly settlement. All the interview partners confirmed that friendly settlements are to be reached much faster than a normal judgment or decision.[128] It is difficult to determine how long an average case can take. The Court's internal targets might give an indication of the length. As part of the ordinary proceedings, the Registry aims at bringing an application before a decision body for a first admissibility examination within one year from the allocation. Applications that have been communicated to the parties come back before the Court for a second examination within the year following the communication. Applications that have been declared admissible and in which no hearing was held are brought before the Court for a judgment within the year following the admissibility decision. It is clear that time targets cannot be met without exception. However, in a regular case, an applicant has to wait on average between two and three years for a judgment from the time that he has lodged his application with the Court.

Setting strict time-limits is a crucial element in the handling of friendly settlements. The experience of the Registry clearly shows that these proceedings can otherwise be misused to gain time or to unduly delay the examination of the case on the merits.[129]

h) Supervision of the Execution

The obligation to abide by a judgment may require the payment of just satisfaction, the adoption of individual measures to counter the effect of the ECHR violation, and the implementation of general measures to prevent further similar violations. The Committee's supervision of the execution of judgments covers all of these elements. Friendly settlements handed down in the form of judgments are also subject to the control of the Committee of Ministers.[130] The Committee's supervision ensures that the undertakings agreed on by the parties are implemented. Naturally, the undertakings set have to be described in specific terms, particularly when they refer to the adoption of general measures.

All interview partners emphasized that they were not aware of any execution problems in cases settled before the Court.[131] Once they have agreed to a friendly settlement, most Governments usually paid the compensation in due time. This

---

[128] For more details, see for example, Elisabet Fura, Judge at the ECtHR, information given in her interview of 12 January 2009, reprinted in annex 1.

[129] Michael O'Boyle, note 118 *supra*.

[130] Ress, G. (2005), p. 373; Zwaak, L. (2006), p. 236.

[131] Identical information concerning the old Commission and Court in Krüger, H. C./Nørgaard, C. A. (1988), p. 333; a bit more ambiguous Courell, A. M. (2006), pp. 148–149.

general statement holds true for most of the friendly settlements concluded in most cases. It is nonetheless subject to two important *caveats*. First, minor execution problems may result in delayed payments. If the friendly settlement does not provide for a default interest clause, it might be difficult to claim this before the national authorities. As friendly settlements usually mention that the financial award is made *ex gratia*, the legal obligation for the payment of default interest might be disputed.[132] Second, there are restrictions concerning the implementation of general measures. If a friendly settlement foresees general measures, the implementation is as difficult and cumbersome as if they were endorsed in an ordinary judgment. The same problems can therefore occur at the execution stage.

2. Legal Character of Friendly Settlements

Pursuant to Article 37 (1) *in fine* ECHR, the Court must evaluate whether a settlement proposed by the parties respects human rights, as guaranteed under the Convention and the Protocols. This obligation is crucial for understanding the legal nature of friendly settlements. Under the provisions of the Convention, no friendly settlement can be reached without the consent of the Court. Any agreement approved by the Court is a judicial settlement; it is not the result of an alternative dispute mechanism. Hence, the Court as a judicial body bears the final responsibility for the appropriateness of the settlement. The margin of manoeuvre, however, is wide. Article 37 (1) *in fine* ECHR only obliges the Court to "continue the examination of an application if the respect of human rights in the Convention and the protocols thereto so requires."

Although the final examination of a settlement is crucial, it is rare for the Court not to endorse a settlement proposal. In the judgments and decisions available, only a single case is reported as a clear refusal for a settlement.[133] In *Çiçek and Öztemel and 6 other cases v. Turkey*,[134] the Court did not fully endorse the friendly settlement reached at the national level. This judgment clearly shows the importance of a thorough examination of any agreement by the Court.[135] In sensitive areas, the Court sends a signal to the responding State in citing very broadly its jurisprudence.[136] We assume that more

---

[132] See section III.2. *infra*.

[133] *Ukrainian Media Group v. Ukraine* (Appl. No. 72713/01), Judgment (Former Second Section), 29 March 2005, not reported, para. 7; information about the case in Sweeney, J. A. (2005), pp. 16–17. Cf. Reid, K. (2008), p. 15, mentioning also *Tyrer v. UK* (Appl. No. 5856/72), Judgment (Chamber), 25 April 1978, Series A, Vol. 26, paras. 24–27; *Karner v. Austria* (Appl. No. 40016/98), Judgment (First Section), 24 July 2003, Reports 2003-IX, 199, paras. 25–28.

[134] *Çiçek and Öztemel and 6 other cases v. Turkey* (Appl. Nos. 74069/01; 74703/01; 76380/01; 16809/02; 25710/02; 25714/02; 30383/02), Judgment (Second Section), 3 August 2007, not yet reported, para. 24.

[135] Ibid., para. 24 et seq.

[136] See for example, *Aspichi Dehwari v. Netherlands* (Appl. No. 37014/97), Judgment (First Section–Arrangement), 27 April 2000, not reported, a case concerning an asylum seeker in the

attempts to conclude friendly settlements may have failed in the Court's practice because it refused to endorse the friendly settlement proposed and agreed by the parties. It is impossible to verify this hypothesis as long as the Court considers this fact to be confidential and does not include it in the published case file.

A friendly settlement usually involves an *ex gratia* payment. From an international law point of view, this payment is made on a voluntary basis unless there is an explicit acknowledgment of a violation in the friendly settlement. If such an acknowledgement is included in the text of the agreement, it then would imply that the payment has a binding character. The wording and the legal character of friendly settlements have to be seen, however, in a broader context both at the national and the European level. First, pursuant to Article 46 ECHR, Contracting Parties undertake to abide by the final judgment of the Court.[137] The *prima facie* voluntary character of the *ex gratia* payment is therefore altered in the European context by the fact that it is handed down in the form of a judgment by the Court. Second, friendly settlements are usually combined with a waiver of the right to bring the matter before any national court or international court or tribunal. This waiver impedes legal action at the domestic level. The only way to return to the case is to write a letter to the Court requesting the case be restored to its list.

3. Confidentiality and Disclosure

Pursuant to Article 40 ECHR, hearings before the Court are public, unless the Court exceptionally decides otherwise. Documents deposited with the Registrar are also available to the public, except when such access is forbidden by the President of the Court. As an exception to this rule, all negotiations conducted as part of the friendly settlement procedure before the Court are confidential. Indeed, Rule 33 (1) of the Rules of Court explicitly excludes from public access the documents submitted as part of the friendly settlement. Rule 62 (2) Rules

---

Netherlands allegedly ill-treated in Iran, para. 17: "In this connection, the Court points out that in several previous cases it has had occasion to rule on the responsibility under the Convention of a Contracting State where the complaint was that there existed substantial grounds for believing that the person concerned would, if expelled or extradited, face a real risk of being subjected to inhuman or degrading treatment in the country of destination (see the Soering v. the United Kingdom judgment of 7 July 1989, Series A no. 161, pp. 35–36, §§ 90–91; the Cruz Varas and Others v. Sweden judgment of 20 March 1991, Series A no. 201, p. 28, § 69; the Vilvarajah and Others v. the United Kingdom judgment of 30 October 1991, Series A no. 215, p. 36 §§ 107–08; and the Chahal v. the United Kingdom judgment of 15 November 1996, Reports of Judgments and Decisions 1996-V, p. 1859, §§ 95–97). In so doing, the Court has specified the nature and extent of the Contracting States' obligations under the Convention in that regard."

[137] See for examples, *Scoppola v. Italy (No. 2)* (Appl. No. 10249/03), Judgment (Grand Chamber), 17 September 2009, not yet reported, para. 146 et seq.; *Burdov v. Russia (No. 2)* (Appl. No. 33509/04), Judgment (First Section–Pilot Judgment), 15 January 2009, not yet reported, para. 122 et seq.

of Court further provides that the parties' arguments used in friendly settlement negotiations cannot be referred to or relied on in the contentious proceedings. The parties therefore hand in documents or observations for their case in different envelopes, depending on whether this information will be part of a friendly settlement or the ordinary procedure.

The rationale behind the confidentiality rule is that the sensitive information which was revealed during the friendly settlement negotiations should not prejudice the outcome of the ordinary proceedings. If friendly settlement negotiations fail, the ordinary proceedings are conducted independently of the information provided in that friendly settlement. At the same time, the respondent Government is also able to avoid publicity which could have been caused if the sensitive information provided had been revealed. The drawback of such a requirement is that it is difficult to determine the reasons why the Court approved or rejected a friendly settlement. This is particularly disquieting in cases involving allegations of serious human rights violations, which would have normally been resolved on the merits via ordinary proceedings.[138] In such cases, it is particularly important to provide the reasons justifying the acceptance of a friendly settlement. The confidentiality rule therefore compounds the problem of legitimacy of friendly settlements.

4. Content of Friendly Settlements

The new Court handed down its first settlement in 1999 in a case against Portugal concerning the length of civil proceedings. It followed the Commission's approach and accepted the settlement in this context.[139]

Under the regime of Protocol no 11 with the two Court levels, a new standard requirement has been regularly included in friendly settlements, namely the waiver of the right to refer the case to the Grand Chamber.[140] The choice of law and jurisdiction was rather unusual.[141] Another rather technical clause is introduced if a concrete settlement reached between the applicant and the State Agent has to be approved by the respective Government.[142]

---

[138] See the chapter "Philosophical Background", section V.

[139] *Rebocho v. Portugal* (Appl. No. 34562/97), Judgment (Fourth Section–Friendly Settlement), 30 April 1999, not reported. In fact, apart from France, Italy had the highest number of friendly settlements in the area of Article 6 (1) ECHR in the late 90s and early years of the 21st century. See also for the case managing function of friendly settlements section III.6. *infra*.

[140] See for example, *Bohunický v. Slovakia* (Appl. No. 36570/97), Judgment (Second Section–Friendly Settlement), 13 September 1999, not reported, para. 24.

[141] See for a rare exception, *Wessels-Bergervoet v. Netherlands* (Appl. No. 34462/97), Judgment (Second Section–Arrangement), 12 November 2002, not reported, para. 5: "This Agreement shall be governed by Dutch law. Any disputes arising from this Agreement shall be laid before the competent court in The Hague at first instance."

[142] *Romlin v. Sweden* (Appl. No. 48630/99), Judgment (Fourth Section–Arrangement), 15 June 2004, not reported, para. 15.

In practice, under Protocol no 11, financial awards were at the very heart of friendly settlements.[143] Nonetheless, the new Court followed the old practice and accepted a broad range of non-pecuniary measures in friendly settlements. These measures remained rather exceptional after 2003.

Following the practice of the Commission and the old Court, individual measures concerning asylum and residence permits were adopted from 1999. These included:

- the granting of residence permits,[144] of provisional residence permits on humanitarian grounds[145] or of refugee status;[146]
- the granting of a long term visa;[147]
- the delisting of the applicant from a list of fugitives.[148]

The new Court endorsed the Government's promise to amend national statutes[149] or to examine whether amendments were needed.[150] The Government's commitment was sometimes formulated in very broad and general terms.[151] Examples of concrete legislative measures include:

---

[143] Zwaak, L. (2006), p. 226. See for the financial dimension section III.5. *infra*.

[144] *Abdurrahim Incedursun v. Netherlands* (Appl. No. 33124/96), Judgment (Grand Chamber–Friendly Settlement), 22 June 1999, not reported, para. 23; *Abbas v. France* (Appl. No. 35783/97), Judgment (Third Section–Friendly Settlement), 20 July 2000, not reported, para. 18; *Aspichi Dehwari v. Netherlands*, note 136 *supra*, para. 16; *Sahli v. Belgium* (Appl. No. 38707/97), Judgment (Third Section–Friendly Settlement), 9 January 2001, not reported, para. 13; *Güler v. Germany* (Appl. No. 48967/99), Decision (Fourth Section–Arrangement), 13 September 2001, not reported [no paragraphs]; *Lotter and Lotter v. Bulgaria* (Appl. No. 39015/97), Judgment (First Section–Arrangement), 19 May 2004, not reported, para. 17; *Dinić v. Netherlands* (Appl. No. 7137/07), Decision (Third Section–Arrangement), 1 July 2008, not yet reported [no paragraphs].

[145] *Tatete v. Switzerland* (Appl. No. 41874/98), Judgment (Second Section–Arrangement), 6 July 2000, not reported, para. 20.

[146] *Esmaili v. Netherlands* (Appl. No. 23254/05), Decision (Third Section–Arrangement), 23 May 2006, not reported [no paragraphs].

[147] *Tahraoui v. France* (Appl. No. 39776/04), Decision (Fifth Section–Arrangement), 17 June 2008, not yet reported [no paragraphs].

[148] *Popov v. Russia* (Appl. No. 34310/06), Decision (First Section–Arrangement), 10 January 2008, not yet reported [no paragraphs].

[149] *Millan I Tornes v. Andorra* (Appl. No. 35052/97), Judgment (First Section–Friendly Settlement), 6 July 1999, Reports 1999-IV, 1, para. 21; *F.C. v. United Kingdom* (Appl. No. 37344/97), Decision (Third Section–Arrangement), 7 September 1999, not reported [no paragraphs]; *F.F. v. Italy* (Appl. No. 30133/96), Decision (Second Section–Arrangement), 27 January 2000, not reported [no paragraphs]; *Cornwell v. United Kingdom* (Appl. No. 36578/97), Judgment (Third Section–Friendly Settlement), 25 April 2000, not reported, para. 11; *Siglfirðingur Ehf v. Iceland* (Appl. No. 34142/96), Judgment (First Section–Friendly Settlement), 30 May 2000, not reported, para. 12; *Croke v. Ireland* (Appl. No. 33267/96), Judgment (Fourth Section–Friendly Settlement), 21 December 2000, not reported, para. 11; *M. v. United Kingdom* (Appl. No. 30357/03), Decision (Fourth Section–Friendly Settlement), 13 February 2007, not yet reported [no paragraphs].

[150] *Leppänen and Aittamäki v. Finland* (Appl. No. 30271/96), Decision (Fourth Section–Arrangement), 13 January 2000, not reported [no paragraphs]. Cf. Zwaak, L. (2006), p. 231.

[151] *Erkanlı v. Turkey* (Appl. No. 37721/97), Judgment (Second Section–Friendly Settlement), 13 February 2003, not reported, para. 21: "*Les condamnations de la Turquie prononcées par la Cour dans les affaires concernant les poursuites engagées en vertu de la législation pénale, avec des chefs d'inculpation comparables, en substance, à ceux retenus contre M. Erkanlı, font clairement apparaître que le droit et la pratique turcs doivent d'urgence être mis en conformité avec les exigences résultant de*

- new guidance in a revised Mental Health Act Code of Practice;[152]
- a legal aid scheme in civil proceedings.[153]

In contrast to previous practice, individual measures in the field of criminal law did not dominate the new Court's practice. In isolated cases, the Court endorsed individual measures, including the destruction of the applicant's criminal record.[154] However, there were no measures concerning the annulment of a penalty or the reduction of a sentence in the new Court's practice.[155]

A wider range of individual measures concerning property rights was endorsed under the new Court than in the previous years, including *inter alia*:

- the restitution of real estate;[156]
- the granting of a construction permission to the applicant;[157]
- the granting of usufruct of properties to the applicants.[158]

In different fields, various individual measures were included in friendly settlements. These included the following:

- access to the applicant's files;[159]
- tax credit abatement;[160]

l'article 10 de la Convention. L'ingérence incriminée dans le cas d'espèce en constitue une illustration supplémentaire." (available only in French); *Moldovan and Others v. Romania* (Appl. Nos. 41138/98; 64320/01), Judgment (Second Section–Friendly Settlement), 5 July 2005, not reported, para. 29; *Kabul and Others v. Turkey* (Appl. No. 24873/02), Decision (Second Section–Arrangement), 4 September 2007, not yet reported [no paragraphs]: "The Government undertake to issue appropriate instructions and adopt all necessary measures to ensure that the right to life – including the obligation to carry out effective investigations – is respected. It is noted in this connection that new legal and administrative measures have been adopted and more effective investigations have been conducted."

[152] *J.M. v. United Kingdom* (Appl. No. 47014/99), Decision (Fourth Section–Arrangement), 15 January 2002, not reported [no paragraphs].

[153] *Faulkner v. United Kingdom* (Appl. No. 30308/96), Judgment (Third Section–Arrangement), 30 November 1999, not reported, para. 27.

[154] *Brodtmann v. Germany* (Appl. No. 47389/99), Decision (Third Section–Arrangement), 16 June 2005, not reported [no paragraphs].

[155] See for the previous individual measures section II.1. *supra.*

[156] *Trome S.A. v. Spain* (Appl. No. 27781/95), Judgment (Fourth Section–Arrangement), 1 April 1999, Reports 1999-III, 1, para. 19; *Vogel v. Romania* (Appl. No. 46633/99), Decision (Second Section–Friendly Settlement), 8 April 2003, not reported [no paragraphs]; *Beneficio Cappella Paoloni v. San Marino* (Appl. No. 40786/98), Judgment (Second Section–Arrangement), 3 May 2007, not yet reported, para. 4; *Yedikule Surp Pirgiç Ermeni Hastanesi Vakfi v. Turkey* (Appl. Nos. 50147/99; 51207/99), Judgment (Second Section–Friendly Settlement), 26 June 2007, not yet reported, para. 28; *Rosival and Others v. Slovakia* (Appl. No. 17684/02), Judgment (Fourth Section–Arrangement), 23 September 2008, not yet reported, para. 18.

[157] *Orha v. Romania* (Appl. No. 1486/02), Judgment (Third Section–Arrangement), 4 November 2008, not yet reported, para. 8.

[158] *Institute of French Priests and Others v. Turkey* (Appl. No. 26308/95), Judgment (Fourth Section–Arrangement), 14 December 2000, not reported, para. 18.

[159] *Leggett v. United Kingdom* (Appl. No. 37517/97), Decision (Third Section–Arrangement), 31 August 1999, not reported [no paragraphs].

[160] *Ercolani v. San Marino* (Appl. No. 35430/97), Judgment (Second Section–Arrangement),

- statement from the Government that the Jehovah's Witnesses are not subject to secret surveillance on account of their religious beliefs and will never be subject to such surveillance in the future;[161]
- issuing a press release expressing their regret about the termination of the applicant's office;[162]
- quashing of an election decision and the publication of a press release indicating the Government's regret about the deficiencies in the election;[163]
- full and efficient enforcement of a judgment adopted by the national Supreme Court;[164]
- confidentiality regarding financial awards with the effect that the amount is not published in the Court's record.[165]

In contrast to the previous practice, the expression of regret or apologies has appeared more frequently in the new Court's practice. The forms of regret or apologies which appeared more frequently include:

- a declaration of regret about the suffering caused to the applicant;[166]
- an apology for the applicant's detention.[167]

The crux of the issue in this context is whether the Government expresses a full, clear and unambiguous acknowledgment of an infringement in a concrete case. Clearly, the nature of friendly settlements contrasts with the Government's willingness to officially acknowledge a violation. The settlement of the case by way of an *ex gratia* payment is one of the most important incentives for the Government to start negotiations. In the early 2000s, it was not so unusual to find an official

25 November 2003, not reported, para. 20.

[161] *Tsavachidis v. Greece* (Appl. No. 28802/95), Judgment (Grand Chamber–Arrangement), 21 January 1999, not reported, para. 22.

[162] *Gaulieder v. Slovakia* (Appl. No. 36909/97), Judgment (Second Section–Friendly Settlement), 18 May 2000, not reported, para. 15.

[163] *Spišák v. Slovakia* (Appl. No. 43730/98), Decision (Second Section–Arrangement), 7 December 2000, Reports 2000-XII, 493, p. 498 [no paragraphs].

[164] *Moldovahidromaş v. Moldova* (Appl. No. 30475/03), Judgment (Fourth Section–Arrangement), 13 May 2008, not yet reported, para. 10.

[165] *Croke v. Ireland*, note 149 *supra*, para. 11; *Cardoso and Johansen v. United Kingdom* (Appl. No. 47061/99), Decision (Third Section–Arrangement), 5 September 2000, not reported [no paragraphs].

[166] *Vilborg Yrsa Sigurdardóttir v. Iceland* (Appl. No. 32451/96), Judgment (First Section–Friendly Settlement), 30 May 2000, not reported, para. 12; *Lindelöf v. Sweden* (Appl. No. 22771/93), Judgment (First Section–Friendly Settlement), 20 June 2000, not reported, para. 24; *Slavgorodski v. Estonia* (Appl. No. 37043/97), Judgment (First Section–Arrangement), 12 September 2000, not reported, para. 11. For the Turkish cases, see for example, *Kinay and Kinay v. Turkey* (Appl. No. 31890/96), Judgment (Second Section–Friendly Settlement), 26 November 2002, not reported, para. 22.

[167] *Oates v. Poland* (Appl. No. 35036/97), Decision (Fourth Section–Arrangement), 7 September 2000, not reported [no paragraphs].

acknowledgment of a violation in the new Court's practice. The forms could vary and include:

- a public letter of apology acknowledging the substantive breach of Article 2 ECHR;[168]
- an acknowledgment by the Agent of the Government of a breach of the Convention.[169]

There were also some clear examples of acknowledgements of a violation. These included:

- an acknowledgement of a violation of Article 6 (1) ECHR;[170]
- an acknowledgement of a violation of Articles 8 and 14 ECHR.[171]

It is striking that most friendly settlements that contain an acknowledgement of a violation concern Turkey. In a series of settlements, the Government acknowledged, in a general statement, an ECHR violation and expressed its regret that it had occurred. The *Aydın v. Turkey* case included a standard statement which was also included in other cases. The Government mentioned that it regretted

(...) the occurrence of the actions which have led to the bringing of the present applications, in particular the disappearance of Mr Müslüm Aydın and the anguish caused to his family. It is accepted that the unrecorded deprivation of liberty and insufficient investigations into the allegations of disappearance constituted violations of Articles 2, 5 and 13 of the Convention. The Government undertake to issue appropriate instructions and adopt all necessary measures with a view to ensuring that all deprivations of liberty are fully and accurately recorded by the authorities and that effective investigations into alleged disappearances are carried out in accordance with their obligations under the Convention.[172]

---

[168] *Scott v. United Kingdom* (Appl. No. 62688/00), Decision (Fourth Section–Arrangement), 25 August 2005, not reported [no paragraphs].

[169] *Boltyonkov v. Ukraine* (Appl. No. 35113/03), Decision (Fifth Section–Arrangement), 19 June 2007, not yet reported [no paragraphs]: "I, Yuriy Zaytsev, Agent of the Government before the European Court of Human Rights, declare that the Government of Ukraine agree to acknowledge, unilaterally, a breach of Article 6 § 1 of the Convention from the non-enforcement of the domestic courts' judgment (...)." Similar also *Bogdan v. Moldova* (Appl. No. 148/05), Decision (Fourth Section–Arrangement), 16 October 2007, not yet reported [no paragraphs].

[170] *Abraham v. Serbia* (Appl. No. 33430/05), Decision (Second Section–Arrangement), 4 March 2008, not yet reported [no paragraphs]; *Đorić-Francuski v. Serbia* (Appl. No. 712/06), Decision (Second Section–Arrangement), 4 March 2008, not yet reported [no paragraphs]; *Novicov v. Moldova* (Appl. No. 507/04), Decision (Fourth Section–Arrangement), 20 May 2008, not yet reported [no paragraphs].

[171] *Greig v. United Kingdom* (Appl. No. 10567/05), Decision (Fourth Section–Arrangement), 7 October 2008, not yet reported [no paragraphs].

[172] *Aydın v. Turkey* (Appl. Nos. 28293/95; 29494/95; 30219/96), Judgment (First Section–Friendly Settlement), 10 July 2001, not reported, para. 13; similar other judgments (First Section–Friendly Settlements) of 10 July 2001: *Değer v. Turkey* (Appl. No. 24934/94), not reported, para. 14; *Avci v. Turkey* (Appl. No. 24935/94), not reported, para. 14; *Orak v. Turkey* (Appl. No. 24936/94), not reported, para. 14; *Boğa v. Turkey* (Appl. No. 24938/94), not reported, para. 14; *Doğan v. Turkey* (Appl. No. 24939/94), not reported, para. 15; *Parlak and Others v. Turkey* (Appl. Nos. 24942/94;

The pertinent, but by no means consistent, use of this formula in the Turkish cases[173] is probably due to a certain pressure that was put by the Court on the Turkish Government. In some cases, however, the Turkish Government acknowledged the ECHR violation in very general terms and omitted any reference to the specific case.[174] From the case file, it appears that in cases of serious human rights violations (particularly those concerning Articles 2 and 3 ECHR), the Court only approved friendly settlements when they referred to these two additional elements: regret and acknowledgement. It is interesting to note that the regret clause seldom appears in settlements concluded with other States, even in cases concerning allegations of serious human rights violations.[175]

In the years to come, the Court followed the approach applied in the Turkish cases and added a new standard formula regarding the supervision of execution of Turkish cases: "The Government consider that the supervision by the Committee

---

24943/94; 25125/94), not reported, para. 15; *Kizilgedik v. Turkey* (Appl. No. 24944/94), not reported, para. 14; *Boğ v. Turkey* (Appl. No. 24946/94), not reported, para. 14; *Demir v. Turkey* (Appl. No. 24990/94), not reported, para. 14; *Şenses v. Turkey* (Appl. No. 24991/94), not reported, para. 14; *Akbay v. Turkey* (Appl. No. 32598/96), Judgment (First Section–Friendly Settlement), 2 October 2001, not reported, para. 26; *Saki v. Turkey* (Appl. No. 29359/95), Judgment (First Section–Friendly Settlement), 30 October 2001, not reported, para. 12; *İ.İ., İ.Ş., K.E. and A.Ö. v. Turkey* (Appl. Nos. 30953/96; 30954/96; 30955/96; 30956/96), Judgment (First Section–Friendly Settlement), 6 November 2001, not reported, para. 23; *Acar v. Turkey* (Appl. No. 24940/94), Judgment (Second Section–Friendly Settlement), 18 December 2001, not reported, para. 13; *Karakoyun v. Turkey* (Appl. No. 51285/99), Decision (Third Section–Arrangement), 30 March 2006, not reported [no paragraphs]; *Hacioğlu and Others v. Turkey* (Appl. Nos. 7253/04; 7260/04; 7266/04; 7268/04; 7270/04; 7272/04; 14873/04; 15047/04; 15071/04; 15093/04; 15113/04), Decision (Second Section–Friendly Settlement), 4 January 2007, not yet reported [no paragraphs]; *Yağci and Others v. Turkey* (Appl. No. 5974/02), Decision (Third Section–Arrangement), 22 March 2007, not yet reported [no paragraphs].

[173] See for example, *Aruç v. Turkey* (Appl. No. 39675/98), Decision (Fourth Section–Arrangement), 6 April 2004, not reported [no paragraphs]: The applicant raised complaints under Article 3 and 5 (4) ECHR. However, the Turkish Government did not express its regret. Similar also *Kaptan v. Turkey* (Appl. No. 46749/99), Judgment (Third Section–Friendly Settlement), 22 December 2004, not reported, para. 23.

[174] See *Mehmet Özcan v. Turkey* (Appl. No. 29856/96), Judgment (Second Section–Friendly Settlement), 9 April 2002, not reported, para. 22: "*Le Gouvernement admet que le fait d'infliger des tortures, traitements ou peines inhumains ou dégradants à des détenus constitue une violation de l'article 3 de la Convention, et il s'engage à édicter les instructions appropriées et à adopter toutes les mesures nécessaires pour garantir que l'interdiction de pareilles formes de mauvais traitements – qui implique l'obligation de mener des enquêtes effectives – soit respectée à l'avenir. Le Gouvernement note que les mesures légales et administratives récemment adoptées ont permis de réduire les cas de mauvais traitements dans les circonstances du type de celles de la présente espèce et d'accroître l'effectivité des enquêtes menées.*" (available only in French).

[175] *Balasoiu v. Romania* (Appl. No. 37424/97), Judgment (Second Section–Friendly Settlement), 20 April 2004, not reported, para. 27; *Madi v. France* (Appl. No. 51294/99), Judgment (Second Section–Friendly Settlement), 27 April 2004, not reported, para. 30; *Constantini v. Romania* (Appl. No. 49145/99), Judgment (Third Section–Friendly Settlement), 17 February 2005, not reported, para. 22; *Velcea v. Romania* (Appl. No. 60957/00), Judgment (Third Section–Friendly Settlement), 22 December 2005, not reported, para. 31; *Mocanu v. Romania* (Appl. No. 56489/00), Judgment (Third Section–Friendly Settlement), 24 May 2006, not reported, para. 34; *Baciu v. Romania* (Appl. No. 21440/03), Decision (Third Section–Friendly Settlement), 6 July 2006, not reported [no paragraphs].

of Ministers of the execution of Court judgments concerning Turkey in this and similar cases is an appropriate mechanism for ensuring that improvements will continue to be made in this context. To this end, necessary co-operation in this process will continue to take place."[176] From 2005 onwards, however, Turkish friendly settlements with this extended regret clause became rarer. It is clear that the Court no longer insisted on this formula as a precondition for a friendly settlement.[177] In rare cases, this formula was copied by other Governments, namely by Romania.[178] In *Lee v. Ukraine*, for example, the Government explicitly referred to the Court's case law in acknowledging the violation of the Convention in that particular case.[179]

---

[176] *Erat and Sağlam v. Turkey* (Appl. No. 30492/96), Judgment (Fourth Section–Friendly Settlement), 26 March 2002, not reported, para. 34, concerning serious ill-treatment. Similar also *Oral and Others v. Turkey* (Appl. No. 27735/95), Judgment (First Section–Friendly Settlement), 28 March 2002, not reported, para. 16; *Z.Y. v. Turkey* (Appl. No. 27532/95), Judgment (Second Section–Friendly Settlement), 9 April 2002, not reported, para. 19; *Özkur and Göksungur v. Turkey* (Appl. No. 37088/97), Judgment (Second Section–Friendly Settlement), 4 March 2003, not reported, para. 21; *Ateş v. Turkey* (Appl. No. 28292/95), Judgment (Second Section–Friendly Settlement), 22 April 2003, not reported, para. 18; *Şahmo v. Turkey* (Appl. No. 37415/97), Judgment (Fourth Section–Friendly Settlement), 22 June 2004, not reported, para. 27; *Temel v. Turkey* (Appl. No. 37047/97), Judgment (Second Section–Friendly Settlement), 13 July 2004, not reported, para. 59; *Memiş v. Turkey* (Appl. No. 42593/98), Judgment (Second Section–Arrangement), 21 February 2006, not reported, para. 18.

[177] *Yücetürk v. Turkey* (Appl. No. 76089/01), Decision (Third Section–Arrangement), 4 October 2005, not reported [no paragraphs]; *Arslan and Arslan v. Turkey* (Appl. No. 57908/00), Judgment (Fourth Section–Friendly Settlement), 10 January 2006, not reported, para. 18; *Berk v. Turkey* (Appl. No. 41973/98), Judgment (Third Section–Friendly Settlement), 20 April 2006, not reported, para. 8; *Yazici v. Turkey* (Appl. No. 73033/01), Decision (First Section–Arrangement), 11 July 2006, not reported [no paragraphs]; *Okatan v. Turkey* (Appl. No. 40996/98), Judgment (Third Section–Friendly Settlement), 13 July 2006, not reported [no paragraphs]; *Tekmek v. Turkey* (Appl. No. 50035/99), Decision (Second Section–Arrangement), 28 November 2006, not reported [no paragraphs]; *Kölge v. Turkey* (Appl. No. 20227/02), Decision (Second Section–Arrangement), 21 November 2006, not reported [no paragraphs]; *Kabul and Others v. Turkey* (Appl. No. 24873/02), Decision (Second Section–Arrangement), 4 September 2007, not reported [no paragraphs]; *Içen and Içen v. Turkey* (Appl. No. 10268/02), Decision (Second Section–Arrangement), 6 May 2008, not yet reported [no paragraphs]; *Çardakçi and Others v. Turkey* (Appl. No. 39224/98), Judgment (Fourth Section–Arrangement), 23 January 2007, not yet reported, para. 14; *Salman v. Turkey* (Appl. No. 63745/00), Decision (Fourth Section–Arrangement), 3 April 2007, not yet reported [no paragraphs]; *Pektaş and Others v. Turkey* (Appl. No. 73722/01), Decision (Second Section–Arrangement), 4 December 2007, not yet reported [no paragraphs]; *Kaya v. Turkey* (Appl. No. 20981/03), Decision (Second Section–Arrangement), 13 May 2008, not yet reported [no paragraphs].

[178] *Notar v. Romania* (Appl. No. 42860/98), Judgment (Second Section–Friendly Settlement), 20 April 2004, not reported, para. 49; *Moldovan and Others v. Romania* (Appl. Nos. 41138/98; 64320/01), Judgment (Second Section–Friendly Settlement), 5 July 2005, not reported, para. 29: "The Government sincerely regret the failure of the criminal investigation to clarify fully the circumstances which led to the destruction of the applicants' homes and possessions, which left them living in improper conditions thus obliging a number of them to leave their village, and rendered difficult the applicants' possibility of filing a civil action. It also regrets the length of the civil proceedings before the domestic courts and certain remarks made by some authorities as to the applicants' Roma origin."

[179] *Lee v. Ukraine* (Appl. No. 7697/02), Decision (Fifth Section–Arrangement), 6 November 2006, not reported [no paragraphs]: "It is further accepted by the Government that: - the applicant's complaints under Article 3 of the Convention about the conditions of his detention (the size of cell

It is interesting to note that quite some time before *Broniowski v. Poland*,[180] namely in 2001, the Court endorsed some general measures in a friendly settlement. In *Dimitrov, Savov and Vishanov v. Bulgaria*,[181] for example, the Parties agreed that:

(…) all criminal proceedings and judicial sentences in Bulgaria of Bulgaria citizens since 1991 (especially but not limited to … Dian Dimitrov, Krasimir Savov and Atanas Vishanov) for refusing military service by virtue of their individual conscientious objection but who were willing at the same time to perform alternative civilian service shall be dismissed and all penalties and/or disabilities heretofore imposed in these cases shall be eliminated as if there was never a conviction for a violation of the law, thus the Council of Ministers of the republic of Bulgaria undertakes the responsibility to introduce draft legislation before the National Assembly for a total amnesty for these cases (…).[182]

5. Financial Dimension

Usually, the parties agree on a certain amount of *ex gratia* payment for the damage suffered and on a certain sum for the legal costs. This was sometimes, but not regularly, combined with a tax exemption.[183] A default interest clause in case of a delayed payment has become a standard element to include in friendly settlements concerning areas of established case law.[184] This is probably due to the fact that these friendly settlements are drafted and proposed by the Registry, which usually includes a default interest clause. If no default interest clause is included, this might cause problems during the execution process as some States do not generally agree to pay the default interest in general (in the sense of general principle of law recognized by civilized nations under Article 38 (1) (c) ICJ Statute).

---

and the number of persons in it, the bedding and hygienic conditions, ventilation, nutrition, daily walks, etc.) raise an issue similar to the one in which the Court has found a violation of Article 3 in the case of *Nevmerzhitsky v. Ukraine* (…)."

[180] *Broniowski v. Poland* (Appl. No. 31443/96), Judgment (Grand Chamber–Pilot Judgment), 22 June 2004, Reports 2004-V, 1; *Broniowski v. Poland* (Appl. No. 31443/96), Judgment (Grand Chamber–Friendly Settlement), 28 September 2005, Reports 2005-IX, 1.

[181] See for example, *Dimitrov, Savov and Vishanov v. Bulgaria* (Appl. Nos. 37358/97; 37988/97; 39565/98), Decision (Fourth Section–Arrangement), 10 April 2001, not reported.

[182] Ibid., [no paragraphs]. See also as to a similar situation in Turkey Serkan Cengiz, lawyer in private practice, information given in his interview of 30 March 2009, reprinted in annex 1.

[183] See for examples, *Klavdianos v. Greece* (Appl. No. 38841/97), Judgment (Third Section–Arrangement), 17 October 2000, not reported, para. 8; *Özgür Kiliç v. Turkey* (Appl. No. 42591/98), Judgment (Second Section–Arrangement), 22 July 2003, not reported, para. 17; *Notar v. Romania*, note 178 *supra*, para. 49; *Arslan and Arslan v. Turkey*, note 177 *supra*, para. 18.

[184] *Sünnetçi v. Turkey* (Appl. No. 28632/95), Judgment (Second Section–Arrangement), 22 July 2003, not reported, para. 22; *Pokorny v. Austria* (Appl. No. 57080/00), Judgment (Fourth Section–Friendly Settlement), 16 December 2003, not reported, para. 12; *Petrini v. Italy* (Appl. Nos. 66292/01; 66299/01), Judgment (First Section–Arrangement), 22 April 2004, not reported, para. 22; *Steno Monit v. Italy* (Appl. No. 63833/00), Judgment (First Section–Arrangement), 27 May 2004, not reported, para. 21.

The published case files do not reveal the extent of the Registry's involvement in determining the exact amount of financial award.[185]

The compensation amounts granted in friendly settlements naturally tend to vary in accordance with the gravity of the human rights violation. They also differ from case to case and from country to country. In general, the amounts tend to be modest, an aspect of which applicants are often unaware. Applicants who bring a case in an area with settled case law (e.g., lengthy proceedings, pre-trial detention, non-execution of final national decisions, etc.) with the hope of making money quickly are effectively deluding themselves. On an exceptional basis, the amount of compensation granted was spectacular in cases concerning mostly, but not exclusively,[186] Articles 2 and 3 ECHR.[187]

The financial dimension of friendly settlements becomes more apparent when it is analysed from a more general, not individual, point of view. Turkey, for

[185] For an exception, see for example, *J.M. v. United Kingdom* (Appl. No. 41518/98), Decision (Fourth Section–Arrangement), 28 September 2000, Reports 2000-X, 561, p. 567 [no paragraphs]: "The Court further notes that the parties have been unable to reach agreement as to the amount of reasonable legal costs to be paid as part of the settlement. The Court has had regard to the fact that the application did not reach beyond the stage of communication to the respondent Government and that most of the work in the file before the Court involved initial correspondence and the preparation and presentation of a nine-page application, with a limited number of supporting documents. It is therefore not satisfied that the fees claimed of GBP 16,813 may be regarded as necessarily incurred in relation to the application or as being reasonable as to quantum. The Court has given regard also to the amounts of fees claimed and awarded in other United Kingdom cases before the Court which reached the stage of a final judgment on the merits, after an oral hearing (…)."

[186] *Hattatoğlu v. Turkey* (Appl. No. 37094/97), Judgment (Third Section–Friendly Settlement), 26 June 2003, not reported, para. 15: 92,000 EUR for two applicants (Article 1 Protocol no 1); *Trygve Hegnar and Periscopus AS v. Norway* (Appl. No. 38638/02), Decision (Third Section–Arrangement), 14 October 2004, not reported [no paragraphs]: 1,993,098.20 NOK (Article 10 ECHR); *Zu Leiningen v. Germany* (Appl. No. 59624/00), Decision (Third Section–Arrangement), 17 November 2005, Reports 2005-XIII, 183, p. 191 [no paragraphs]: 2,607,588 EUR as lump sum plus 3,374,604 EUR (Article 6, 8, 12 and 14 ECHR and Article 1 Protocol no 1); *Maurice v. France* (Appl. No. 11810/03), Judgment (Grand Chamber–Arrangement), 21 June 2006, Reports 2006-IX, 33, para. 33: 2,488,113.27 EUR (Article 41 ECHR, Article 6 (1), 8, 13 and 14 ECHR and Article 1 Protocol no 1); *Draon v. France* (Appl. No. 1513/03), Judgment (Grand Chamber–Arrangement), 21 June 2006, Reports 2006-IX, 5, para. 32: 2,440,279.14 EUR (Article 41 ECHR, Article 6 (1), 8, 13 and 14 ECHR and Article 1 Protocol no 1); *Singh and Others v. United Kingdom* (Appl. No. 60148/00), Judgment (Fourth Section–Arrangement), 8 June 2006, not reported, para. 16: 42,475 GBP (Article 8 and 14 ECHR); *Pla and Puncernau v. Andorra* (Appl. No. 69498/01), Judgment (Fourth Section–Arrangement), 10 October 2006, not reported, para. 14: 970,000 EUR (Article 8 and 14 ECHR); *Uluğkay v. Turkey* (Appl. No. 9782/02), Decision (Third Section–Arrangement), 8 February 2007, not yet reported [no paragraphs]: 700,000 EUR (Article 6 (1) ECHR and Article 1 Protocol no 1); *Cojocaru v. Romania* (Appl. No. 39184/03), Decision (Third Section–Friendly Settlement), 18 October 2007, not yet reported [no paragraphs]: 40,000 EUR (Article 6 (1) ECHR and Article 1 Protocol no 1); *Rugină v. Romania* (Appl. No. 21863/04), Decision (Third Section–Friendly Settlement), 23 October 2007, not yet reported [no paragraphs]: 51,000 EUR (Article 6 (1) ECHR, Article 1 Protocol no 1 and Protocol no 12); *Dănilă v. Romania* (Appl. No. 28220/03), Decision (Third Section–Friendly Settlement), 23 October 2007, not yet reported [no paragraphs]: 75,000 EUR (Article 6 (1) ECHR and Article 1 Protocol no 1); *Rudeanu v. Romania* (Appl. No. 21428/03), Decision (Third Section–Arrangement), 2 September 2008, not yet reported [no paragraphs]: 225,000 EUR (Article 3, 6 (1) and 17 ECHR).

[187] *Adali v. Turkey* (Appl. No. 31137/96), *Yalçin v. Turkey* (Appl. No. 31152/96) and *Soğukpinar*

example, agreed in 2001 to pay a total amount of 5,000,000 EUR in compensation (this includes the compensation amount for pecuniary loss, non-pecuniary damage or legal costs and expenses, and is not adjusted to inflation). From 1999 to 2008, Turkey spent in total nearly 9,000,000 EUR (included compensation for pecuniary loss, non-pecuniary damage or legal costs and expenses, not adjusted to inflation) in friendly settlements concerning 463 applicants. These numbers clearly indicate that friendly settlements can help to resolve structural problems on a temporary basis.[188] It is difficult to deny that in these areas the Court is nothing more than a claims tribunal facilitating large numbers of financial settlements. In this context, friendly settlements are only legitimate if the State Party clearly indicates that it is capable and willing to resolve the underlying problem. In our view, it is a mistaken strategy to keep on endorsing friendly settlements in a certain area without noticing an improvement in the underlying system (for example, in the area of lengthy proceedings in Italian cases). Such friendly settlements may give the individual applicant some satisfaction. However, in this context, they merely represent window dressing and not a clear improvement in the general human rights situation.

6. Case Managing Function

Although mass friendly settlements came at a later stage, there has been a clear tendency since 1999 on the part of the new Court to merge cases together.[189]

---

v. Turkey (Appl. No. 31153/96), all judgments (Third Section–Friendly Settlements), 12 December 2002, not reported, each: 55,000 GBP (Article 2 ECHR); *Şen v. Turkey* (Appl. No. 31154/96), Judgment (Third Section–Friendly Settlement), 12 December 2002, not reported, para. 15: 70,000 GBP (Article 2 ECHR); *Binbay v. Turkey* (Appl. No. 24922/94), Judgment (First Section–Arrangement), 21 October 2004, not reported, para. 18: 45,000 EUR (Article 2, 3, 5, 8 and 13 ECHR); *Karakoç v. Turkey* (Appl. No. 28294/95), Judgment (Third Section–Friendly Settlement), 2 November 2004, not reported, para. 16: 48,000 EUR (Article 3, 5, 6, 8, 13, 14 and 18 ECHR and Article 1 Protocol no 1); *Notar v. Romania*, note 178 *supra*, para. 49: 40,000 EUR (Article 3, 5 and 13 ECHR); *Madi v. France*, note 175 *supra*, para. 30: 99,091 EUR (Article 3 and 6 (1) ECHR); *Cruz da Silva Coelho v. Portugal* (Appl. No. 9388/02), Judgment (Second Section–Friendly Settlement), 13 December 2005, not reported, para. 11: 75,000 EUR (Article 2 ECHR); *Mocanu v. Romania* (Appl. No. 56489/00), Judgment (Third Section–Friendly Settlement), 24 May 2006, not reported, para. 34: 17,000 EUR (Article 3, 8 and 13 ECHR); *Baciu v. Romania* (Appl. No. 21440/03), Decision (Third Section–Friendly Settlement), 6 July 2006, not reported, [no paragraphs]: 25,000 EUR (Article 3 ECHR).

[188] See also the figures in section III.6. *infra*.

[189] So the Court decided on 5 October 1999, 11 applications against Italy concerning the length of criminal proceedings with a total amount of financial awards of 270,000,000 ITL and 15,183 €; on 19 October 1999, five applications against Italy concerning the length of criminal proceedings with a total amount of financial awards of 115,000,000 ITL; on 2 November 1999, six cases with a total amount of financial awards of 177,000,000 ITL; on 14 December 1999, four cases (Second Section only) with a total amount of financial awards of 80,000,000 ITL. See also the similar practice of the Commission in 1999 against France: On 22 April 1999, 16 applications against France concerning the length of proceedings with a total amount of financial awards of 475,000 FF; on 3 June 1999, 18 applications against France with a total amount of financial awards of 540,000 FF; on 9 September 1999, 22 applications against France with a total amount of financial awards

Within the new Court, the Registry's so-called proactive approach became visible.[190] From the new millennium onwards, the Court resolved various cases, especially length of proceedings cases concerning, *inter alia,* Italy,[191] on the basis of a standardized case management strategy. This approach became quite evident in the year 2001. In 29 admissibility decisions, the Court accepted the settlement of a total of 249 applications against Turkey. The applicants all came from the same district in Turkey and claimed that their houses and shops were destroyed as a result of the random and disproportionate gunfire of the security forces in the course of clashes between the latter and PKK militants.[192] The new dimension of this case management function of friendly settlements also became apparent in a different area. Thirty decisions, adopted on 23 October 2003, settled the claims of 637 applicants regarding expropriations to build a highway. The total amount of compensation paid by Turkey amounted to 1,959,515 EUR.[193]

In addition, the effective handling of applications became relevant in cases concerning other countries, such as Slovenia, Ukraine or Romania.[194] In 2007, the Court started resolving cases on a large scale basis following a pilot judgment. In 38 decisions, the Court endorsed friendly settlements between the Polish Government and several applicants who were in a similar position to Broniowski with a total amount of 4,851,515 PLN (corresponding to 1,355,174 EUR at that

of 660,000 FF and on 25 October 1999, three applications against France with a total amount of financial awards of 100,000 FF.

[190]   See for example, *Carrozza v. Italy* (Appl. No. 43598/98), Judgment (Second Section–Friendly Settlement), 19 October 1999, not reported, para. 6: "On 31 August 1999, after an exchange of correspondence, the Section Registrar proposed to the parties to reach a friendly settlement within the meaning of Article 38 § 1 (b) of the Convention." This became a standard in the years to come. See for example, *Piccinini v. Italy (No. 2)* (Appl. No. 28936/95), Judgment (Second Section–Friendly Settlement), 11 April 2000, not reported, para. 3.

[191]   On 5 April 2000, the Court accepted ten friendly settlements concerning the length of proceedings, on 11 April two friendly settlements, on 28 April four friendly settlements, on 6 July one friendly settlement, on 27 July five friendly settlements, on 28 September two friendly settlements, on 5 October one friendly settlement, on 17 October two friendly settlements, on 30 November one friendly settlement, on 19 December two friendly settlements all concerning the length of proceedings; and last but not least, on 22 June 2000 122 applications.

[192]   27 admissibility decisions of 22 March 2001 and two admissibility decisions of 14 June 2001. See also *Göktaş and Others v. Turkey* (Appl. No. 31787/96), Judgment (First Section–Arrangement), 25 September 2001, not reported, in which the cases of 14 applicants were settled; *Değirmenci and Others v. Turkey* (Appl. No. 31879/96), Judgment (Second Section–Friendly Settlement), 23 September 2003, not reported, in which the cases of 37 applicants were settled.

[193]   See for example, *Ateş v. Turkey* (Appl. No. 42144/98), Decision (Third Section–Friendly Settlement), 23 October 2003, not reported. For other examples of mass friendly settlements see 51 decisions all adopted by the Court on 13 May 2004 concerning complaints under Article 1 Protocol no 1, for example, *Kılıç and Kılıç v. Turkey* (Appl. No. 42715/98), Decision (Third Section–Arrangement), 13 May 2004, not reported.

[194]   See 18 decisions all adopted on 21 October 2004 concerning Article 6 (1) and 13 ECHR against Slovenia, for example, *Salkič v. Slovenia* (Appl. No. 76508/01), Decision (Third Section–Arrangement), 21 October 2004, not reported. 29 decisions adopted in 2008 concerning Article 6 (1) ECHR and Article 1 Protocol no 1, all adopted in 2008, for example, *Groza and Others v. Romania* (Appl. No. 28139/04), Decision (Third Section–Arrangement), 10 January 2008, not yet reported.

time).[195] Interestingly, the Court struck out on the same date three applications where the applicants did not accept the Government's offer.[196] These decisions demonstrate that the applicants must carefully choose their tactic during the negotiation process. Following a pilot judgment procedure, when the Court accepts that the general national measures are adequate, the margin of manoeuvre in the negotiations phase becomes very limited and the Court will no longer intervene.

The year 2001 is of special interest in the Turkish cases for two reasons. First, the number of friendly settlements started to increase[197] and, second, the Court accepted for the very first time a unilateral declaration.[198]

7. Critical Areas

While most friendly settlements concerned areas with established case law, the Court also endorsed friendly settlements in areas with unclear and disputed human rights situations. A good example of this is the *Singh and Others v. United Kingdom* case[199] concerning an Indian couple who adopted a child from India. This child could not join its adoptive parents, as the UK authorities did not accept the adoption. The applicants raised claims under Articles 8 and 14 ECHR. Another critical case where the Court could have expressed itself more authoritatively is the *Dömel v. Germany* case,[200] where allegations of violations of Article 1 Protocol no 1 were made by several hundred persons in Germany.

The new Court continued to endorse friendly settlements even in situations where it seemed quite clear that the national law did not yet comply with the Convention requirements. This holds for some Turkish cases where the Court accepted friendly settlements on the basis of the Government's general declaration to bring national law in line with the Convention requirements.[201] It was not

---

[195] See for example, *Wolkenberg and Others v. Poland* (Appl. No. 50003/99), Decision (Fourth Section–Arrangement), 4 December 2007, not yet reported, all decisions are dated either of 4 or of 11 December 2007. As in one decision the financial award is not mentioned, the precise total amount is not available, *Caliński v. Poland* (Appl. No. 4744/03), Decision (Fourth Section–Arrangement), 11 December 2007, not yet reported.

[196] Three strike out decisions (Fourth Section–Arrangement) of 11 December 2007, *Stankiewicz v. Poland* (Appl. No. 25217/02), not yet reported; *Szymańska-Baier v. Poland* (Appl. No. 12935/03), not yet reported; *Antoszczuk and Others v. Poland* (Appl. No. 15230/04), not yet reported.

[197] In 2001, the Court accepted a total of 81 friendly settlements and a total of four arrangements against Turkey. While in 2000, the Court accepted a total of four friendly settlements and a total of eight arrangements against Turkey.

[198] *Akman v. Turkey* (Appl. No. 37453/97), Judgment (First Section–Unilateral Declaration), 26 June 2001, Reports 2001-VI, 223. Cf. Ang, F./Berghmans, E. (2005), p. 98; Myjer, E. (2007), p. 318 et seq.; Reid, K. (2008), pp. 15–16; Rozakis, C. L. (2007), p. 1003; Zwaak, L. (2006), p. 233 et seq.

[199] *Singh and Others v. United Kingdom*, note 186 *supra*.

[200] *Dömel v. Germany* (Appl. No. 31828/03), Decision (Fifth Section–Arrangement), 9 May 2007, not yet reported.

[201] *Altan v. Turkey* (Appl. No. 32985/96), Judgment (First Section–Arrangement), 14 May 2002,

only in Turkish cases that the Court contented itself with a reference to a similar, previously-decided case under review by the Council of Europe and endorsed a proposal for a friendly settlement.[202]

8. Form of Settlements

In general, the Court can hand down a case in the form of a judgment or decision. A judgment contains the Court's authoritative answer to the question whether the Convention has been violated or not. All other judicial findings are handed down in the form of a decision (e.g., admissibility of an application, ordering

---

Reports 2002-III, 341, para. 18: "The Court's rulings against Turkey in cases involving prosecutions under Article 312 of the Penal Code or under the provisions of the Prevention of Terrorism Act clearly show that Turkish law and practice urgently need to be brought into line with the Convention's requirements under Article 10 of the Convention. This is also reflected in the interference underlying the facts of the present case. The Government undertake to this end to implement all necessary reform of domestic law and practice in this area, as already outlined in the National Programme of 24 March 2001." *Erdogan v. Turkey* (Appl. No. 26337/95), Judgment (Third Section–Friendly Settlement), 20 June 2002, not reported, para. 18: "It is accepted that such acts and failures (sc. the unjustified force by the police) constituted a violation of Articles 2 and 3 of the Convention and the Government undertake to issue appropriate instructions and adopt all necessary measures to ensure that the right to life and the prohibition of ill-treatment – including the obligation to carry out effective investigations as also required by Articles 2 and 13 – are respected in the future. It is noted in this connection that new legal and administrative measures have been adopted which have resulted in a reduction in the occurrence of deaths and ill-treatment of detainees in circumstances similar to those of the instant application and in more effective investigations being carried out." *Kaplan v. Turkey* (Appl. No. 38578/97), Judgment (Third Section–Friendly Settlement), 10 October 2002, not reported, para. 26: "It is accepted that the recourse to ill-treatment, as in the circumstances of the present case, and the failure to conduct effective investigations constituted a violation of Article 3 of the Convention. The Government undertake to issue appropriate instructions and adopt all necessary measures to ensure that the prohibition of such actions – including the obligation to carry out effective investigations as required by Articles 3 and 13 – is respected. It is noted in this connection that new legal and administrative measures have been adopted which have resulted in, among other things, more effective investigations into cases of ill-treatment in circumstances similar to those of the instant application."

[202] *M.S. v. Bulgaria* (Appl. No. 40061/98), Judgment (First Section–Arrangement), 4 July 2002, not reported, para. 15: "The Court observes in this regard that neither the agreement nor the Government's decision approving it make any reference to relevant amendments in domestic law which, as established in Varbanov cited above, does not provide sufficient safeguards against arbitrariness. Having regard, however, to the fact that the execution of the Varbanov judgment – which concerned issues almost identical to those in the present case – is currently under review by the Committee of Ministers of the Council of Europe in accordance with Article 46 § 2 of the Convention, the Court is satisfied that the settlement is based on respect for human rights as defined in the Convention or its Protocols." *Demir v. Turkey* (Appl. No. 22280/93), Judgment (First Section–Friendly Settlement), 5 December 2002, not reported, para. 16: "The Government consider that the supervision by the Committee of Ministers of the Council of Europe of the execution of Court judgments concerning Turkey in this and similar cases is an appropriate mechanism for ensuring that improvements will continue to be made in this context. To this end, necessary co-operation in this process will continue to take place." Similar also *Yalçin v. Turkey* (Appl. No. 31152/96), Judgment (Third Section–Friendly Settlement), 12 December 2002, not reported, para. 15; *Soğukpinar v. Turkey* (Appl. No. 31153/96), Judgment (Third Section–Friendly Settlement), 12 December 2002, not reported, para. 15; *Şen v. Turkey* (Appl. No. 31154/96), Judgment (Third Section–Friendly Settlement), 12 December 2002, not reported, para. 15.

interim measures, etc.). Although Article 39 ECHR clearly indicates that friendly settlements are concluded by way of a decision, the actual practice shows a more colourful picture.

The majority of cases that the Court settled under Protocol no 11 were endorsed in the form of a judgment striking out the application.[203] In the judgments, the Court provides substantive information about the settlement reached and often examines whether human rights standards included in its previous case law have been respected.[204] However, the parties did sometimes conclude a friendly settlement before the Court could pronounce itself on the admissibility question.[205] The case files also suggest that in some instances the Registry was not very much involved during the negotiations process and that the initiative rather came from the Government's side.[206] In these circumstances, the Court took note of the agreement and struck the case out in a decision. The same applied when the parties agreed to withdraw their application.[207] On a regular basis, the Court nonetheless examined whether human rights were respected in these cases and included the content of the settlement reached by the parties in its decision. However, the Court's practice is still not completely uniform. For instance, in *Halil v. Cyprus*,[208] the Court noted that: "On 3 November 1999 the Government informed the Court that at a meeting of the parties on 9 October 1999 a friendly settlement had been reached 'in full and final satisfaction of all the applicant's claims set out in the application inclusive of all other claims relating to all the applicant's properties situated in Paphos in respect of which he had not as yet filed an application with the Court.'"[209] It was subsequently noted that respect for human rights, as defined in the Convention, does not require any further examination of the application. It goes without saying that this statement can hardly be verified on the basis of the information published in the decision.[210] In several

---

[203] Courell, A. M. (2006), p. 67; Zwaak, L. (2006), pp. 225–226, 236.

[204] See for examples, *Jaffredou v. France* (Appl. No. 39843/98), Judgment (Third Section–Friendly Settlement), 19 Mai 1999, not reported, para. 28; *Abdurrahim Incedursun v. Netherlands* (Appl. No. 33124/96), Judgment (Grand Chamber–Friendly Settlement), 22 June 1999, not reported, para. 27.

[205] *Leggett v. United Kingdom* (Appl. No. 37517/97), Decision (Third Section–Arrangement), 31 August 1999, not reported [no paragraphs].

[206] *J. T. v. United Kingdom* (Appl. No. 26494/95), Judgment (Fourth Section–Arrangement), 30 March 2000, not reported [no paragraphs]: "By letter dated 11 March 1999, the Government indicated that they were pursuing a friendly settlement of the case and that they had put proposals in this respect to the applicant's representative."

[207] *F.C. v. United Kingdom* (Appl. No. 37344/97), Decision (Third Section–Arrangement), 7 September 1999, not reported [no paragraphs].

[208] *Halil v. Cyprus* (Appl. No. 33981/96), Decision (Third Section–Arrangement), 7 December 1999, not reported.

[209] Ibid., [no paragraphs]. Similar also *Schisas v. Cyprus* (Appl. No. 62078/00), Decision (First Section–Arrangement), 25 October 2005, not reported [no paragraphs].

[210] Similar also *Amnesty International (United Kingdom) v. United Kingdom* (Appl. No. 38383/97), Decision (Third Section–Arrangement), 18 January 2000, not reported [no paragraphs]: "By a letter dated 13 December 1999, the applicant's representatives informed the Court that the applicant had concluded a settlement with the United Kingdom Government and did not wish to pursue the

Russian cases, the information available regarding the settlements concluded is very limited.[211]

Follow-up friendly settlements are usually handed down in the form of a judgment.[212]

According to Article 37 ECHR, the Court may decide to strike an application out of the list at any time during the proceedings. The Court can strike a case out when the applicant no longer intends to pursue his application, when the matter has been resolved, or when the examination of the application is no longer justified. If the matter is resolved through friendly settlement before the communication phase, the application is struck out by a decision. If the parties settle after the application has been declared admissible, the Court adopts the settlement in the form of a strike out judgment. These types of judgments are nonetheless much shorter than the ones that are handed down in other cases, although the text includes the following elements:

application (Article 37 § 1 (a) of the Convention). In accordance with Article 37 § 1 *in fine,* the Court finds no special circumstances regarding respect for human rights as defined in the Convention which require the continuation of the examination of the application." *Kastrati v. Bulgaria* (Appl. No. 41348/98), Decision (Fourth Section–Arrangement), 30 November 2000, not reported [no paragraphs]: "By letter of 2 November 2000 the Government's agent informed the Court that on 30 October 2000 the parties had reached a friendly settlement. She enclosed its text, signed by her and the applicant's lawyer. The document stated, *inter alia,* that the Government would disseminate information about the case and would adopt a methodology permitting to identify officials responsible for human rights violations. The document further stated that the applicant would withdraw his application and that the parties put an end to the dispute." *Kurier Zeitungsverlag und Druckerei GmbH v. Austria* (Appl. No. 48481/99), Decision (Third Section–Arrangement), 20 March 2001, not reported; *Blakemore and 41 Others v. United Kingdom* (Appl. Nos. 10471/0; 10467/05; 10474/05; 10478/05; 10480/05; 10483/05; 10541/05; 10546/05; 10550/05; 10553–54/05; 10556/05; 10558/05; 10565–66/05; 10568/05; 10572/05; 10573/05; 10575–76/05; 10579/05; 10581/05; 10583–85/05; 10589/05; 10591/05; 10593/05; 10595–97/05; 10602/05; 10607/05; 10609/05; 10611–13/05; 10616/05; 10619/05; 10622–23/05; 16517/05), Decision (Fourth Section–Friendly Settlement), 11 December 2007, not yet reported.

[211] *Rogalev v. Russia* (Appl. No. 55941/00), Decision (Third Section–Arrangement), 3 March 2005, not reported [no paragraphs]: "As follows from the text of the friendly settlement [which is not reprinted], the applicant agreed to withdraw his application pending before the Court provided that within three months after the striking-out of the application by the Court from its list of cases, the authorities would pay him a compensation for the non-pecuniary damage caused by the lengthy non-enforcement of the court judgment in his favour. Pursuant to the agreement, the payment of this compensation would constitute a final settlement of the case." (text inserted by the authors); similar also *Starshova and Starshov v. Russia* (Appl. No. 8333/05), Decision (First Section–Arrangement), 8 September 2005, not reported; *Shpynov v. Russia* (Appl. No. 21940/03), Decision (First Section–Arrangement), 23 May 2006, not reported; *Oganov v. Russia* (Appl. No. 53826/00), Decision (First Section–Arrangement), 23 May 2006, not reported; *Pyatko and Others v. Russia* (Appl. No. 38374/02), Decision (First Section–Arrangement), 14 September 2006, not reported; *Shvetsova v. Russia* (Appl. No. 18967/04), Decision (First Section–Arrangement), 8 February 2007, not yet reported [no paragraphs]: "In December 2006 the applicant informed the Court that she and the Government had reached an agreement related to the issue of the non-enforcement of the above judgment. In view of this she was no longer interested in pursuing her application before the Court."

[212] See for example, *Miragall v. Spain* (Appl. Nos. 38366/97; 38688/97; 40777/98; 40843/98; 41015/98; 41400/98; 41446/98; 41484/98; 41487/98 and 41509/98), Judgment (Fourth Section–Arrangement), 25 May 2000, Reports 2000-I, 275.

- the various stages of the friendly settlement negotiations;
- a brief outline of the facts;
- the friendly settlement declaration signed by the parties, including the amount of money agreed upon and the statement that the case has been finally settled;
- the Court's standard formula that it is satisfied that the settlement is based on respect of human rights as defined in the Convention and its Additional Protocols (Article 37 *in fine* ECHR).

Since 2003, friendly settlements have been adopted following a procedure whereby the Court jointly examined the admissibility and the merits of the case.[213] From 2005 onwards, this procedure was followed on a regular basis by the Court.[214] As soon as numerous cases in areas concerning established case law were settled, there was an expectation on the part of the Governments that such agreements would be adopted by way of a strike out decision since they had been reached prior to the admissibility phase. Further, it was considered that it might not always be appropriate to declare such cases admissible.[215] This might explain why the Court indicated in the text of the decision that the examination under Article 29 (3) ECHR had been discontinued and proceeded to a strike out.[216]

9. Restoration to the Court's List of Cases

According to Article 37 (2) ECHR, the "Court may decide to restore an application to its list of cases if it considers that the circumstances justify such course." This might occur in cases in which the Government does not implement the settlement previously agreed by the parties and thereafter endorsed by the Court. A good example of such a failure is demonstrated in the case of *Katić v. Serbia*.[217] The applicants, two handicapped Serbian nationals, had agreed in a friendly settlement on a pecuniary award of 6,000 EUR *ex gratia* from the Serbian Government. The Court struck the case out of its list on the basis of Article 29 (3) ECHR.[218] However, the applicants subsequently informed the Court about the

---

[213] Article 29 (3) ECHR; see for examples, *Andrzejewska v. Poland* (Appl. No. 15153/02), Decision (Fourth Section–Arrangement), 18 November 2003, not reported; *Vefa v. Turkey* (Appl. No. 31139/96), Decision (Fourth Section–Arrangement), 2 December 2003, not reported.

[214] See for examples, *Üstün and Others v. Turkey* (Appl. No. 44056/98), Decision (Second Section–Arrangement), 22 February 2005, not reported; *Sisák v. Slovakia* (Appl. No. 73532/01), Decision (Fourth Section–Arrangement), 1 March 2005, not reported; *Kanoš v. Slovakia* (Appl. No. 67037/01), Decision (Fourth Section–Arrangement), 15 March 2005, not reported; *Mosgöller & Partner Engineering GmbH v. Austria* (Appl. No. 640/03), Decision (First Section–Arrangement), 16 June 2005, not reported.

[215] O'Boyle, M. (2003).

[216] For the resolution of the problem under Protocol no 14, see section V. *infra.*

[217] *Katić v. Serbia* (Appl. No. 13920/04), Decision (Second Section), 7 July 2009, not yet reported.

[218] *Katić v. Serbia* (Appl. No. 13920/04), Decision (Second Section–Arrangement), 4 March 2008, not yet reported.

difficulties with the implementation of the settlement. In particular, the special guardian appointed to manage the spending of the financial award was inactive. As the Serbian Government failed to respond to this allegation, the Court decided to restore the case to its list.[219]

Restoration of an application to the list is possible after a unilateral declaration as well.[220] The case of *Aleksentseva and Others v. Russia* illustrates this sensitive issue.[221] The applicants were clean-up workers of the Chernobyl nuclear accident site or dependants of deceased workers. They had obtained final judgments against the local social security offices and the latter were ordered to pay certain amounts to the applicants. However, the judgments were not enforced at the national level. Before the Court, the Russian Government acknowledged the violation of the Convention (Article 6 (1) ECHR and Article 1 Protocol no 1), provided appropriate redress and expressed their readiness to pay specifically indicated additional amounts to cover any damages and costs to the applicants. The Court decided that it was no longer justified in continuing the examination of the applications according to Article 37 (1) c ECHR.[222] The social security payment was made much later. Although the Russian Government thereafter contested the Court's decision to restore the case to its list, the Court did so and held that there was a violation of Article 6 (1) ECHR. It is worth mentioning that the final award that the Court granted was considerably higher than the amount previously offered in the unilateral declaration by the Russian Government.[223]

Astonishingly, the Court very rarely decides to restore cases to its list.[224] This might be due to the fact that friendly settlements are in general well-implemented. However, we expect that the ratio of restored cases will rise once the Court starts using friendly settlements and unilateral declarations more frequently in cases concerning countries with systemic problems.

---

[219] At the time of writing (March 2010) the judgment on the merits was still pending.

[220] *Toğcu v. Turkey* (Appl. No. 27601/95), Judgment (Second Section–Unilateral Declaration), 9 April 2002, not reported; *Toğcu v. Turkey* (Appl. No. 27601/95), Judgment (Second Section), 31 May 2005, not reported.

[221] *Aleksentseva and Others v. Russia* (Appl. Nos. 75025–26/01; 75028–29/01; 75036/01; 75031/01; 75033–34/01; 8192/02; 5314/02; 77049/01; 76386/01; 77051–53/01; 3999/02; 5384/02; 5388/02; 5419/02), Judgment (First Section), 17 January 2008, not yet reported.

[222] *Aleksentseva and 28 Others v. Russia* (Appl. Nos. 75025–38/01; 75136/01; 76386/01; 76542/01; 76736/01; 77049/01; 77051–53/01; 3999/02; 5314/02; 5384/02; 5388/02; 5419/02; 8190/02; 8192/02), Decision (First Section–Unilateral Declaration), 4 September 2003, not reported.

[223] The Russian Government had offered to pay the amount of 1,500 EUR or 3,000 EUR depending on the period when the judgment remained unenforced, whereas the Court granted the applicants pecuniary or alternatively non-pecuniary damage between 2,300 and 5,200 EUR, see *Aleksentseva and Others v. Russia*, note 221 *supra*, paras. 34–35.

[224] Indeed, the two cases cited (notes 217 and 221 *supra*) were the only instances that we could find in the Court's database. See also Elisabet Fura, note 128 *supra*: "This Court has found in some rare cases that the Government, the administration or the public authorities have threatened applicants to withdraw their complaint. Of course, if they can do that, they can also threaten to settle. I would therefore not exclude it, but I have not seen it myself."

IV. After Protocol No 14[bis]

Protocol no 14[bis] [225] did alter the procedure for two types of applications, namely in clearly inadmissible cases and in well-founded cases with established case law. While in the former category friendly settlements are rather rare, they are quite common in the latter. In practice, the concrete steps for concluding a friendly settlement under Protocol no 14[bis] will not be changed significantly, as the initiative and proposal come from the Registry under the so-called proactive approach.

V. After Protocol No 14

A twist in the Court's reform history explains the fact that Protocol no 14[bis] entered into force before Protocol no 14. Protocol no 14 did not dramatically alter the functioning and the procedure of friendly settlements.[226] It emphasized, however, that the Court should be at all times at the disposal of the parties for the negotiation of a friendly settlement.[227] The confidential nature of the negotiations was preserved under Protocol no 14.[228]

As seen above, the Court uses both decisions and judgments to close the proceedings in friendly settlement cases.[229] From the point of view of the Government, friendly settlements approved by a judgment have the disadvantage of attracting as much public attention as normal proceedings.[230] This can, of course, constitute a general obstacle to the conclusion of friendly settlements. This argument is nonetheless misleading. The information provided about friendly settlements is usually more or less the same and does not depend on the

---

[225] Protocol no 14[bis] to the Convention for the Protection of Human Rights and Fundamental Freedoms, CETS 204, was open for signature on 27 May 2009. It required only three ratifications and it entered into force on 1 October 2009.

[226] Ang, F./Berghmans, E. (2005), p. 90; Caflisch, L. (2006), p. 411; Courell, A. M. (2006), p. 126; Egli, P. (2007), p. 14. See for the general importance of Protocol no 14 section I. *supra.*

[227] Ang, F./Berghmans, E. (2005), p. 91; Courell, A. M. (2006), p. 82; Zwaak, L. (2006), p. 222.

[228] Article 15 of Protocol no 14, which amends Article 39 ECHR reads:

"Article 39 – Friendly settlements

1. At any stage of the proceedings, the Court may place itself at the disposal of the parties concerned with a view to securing a friendly settlement of the matter on the basis of respect for human rights as defined in the Convention and the Protocols thereto.

2. Proceedings conducted under paragraph 1 shall be confidential.

3. If a friendly settlement is effected, the Court shall strike the case out of its list by means of a decision which shall be confined to a brief statement of the facts and of the solution reached.

4. This decision shall be transmitted to the Committee of Ministers, which shall supervise the execution of the terms of the friendly settlement as set out in the decision." (reprinted in annex 3).

[229] See section III.8. *supra.*

[230] Michael O'Boyle, note 118 *supra.*

form in which they are handed down. The descriptions, facts and the agreements reached, which appear in the HUDOC database, are equally short in both kinds of friendly settlements. The possibilities for the public to obtain more information about a certain friendly settlement are limited. Nonetheless, the fact that friendly settlements do not appear in the Court's statistics as a violation of the Convention can be decisive for the State concerned. Hence, friendly settlements do not attract as much media attention as ordinary judgments, in particular those in which the Court found an ECHR violation.

The form used to approve friendly settlements plays an important role in the control of the execution of friendly settlements. The Committee of Ministers is only competent to supervise friendly settlements adopted in the form of a judgment. In this regard, Protocol no 14 resolved the dilemma in an unorthodox manner by stipulating that friendly settlements adopted as decisions would be transmitted to the Committee of Ministers, which shall supervise their execution.[231] From the wording of the new Article 39 ECHR, it seems unclear whether all friendly settlements – routine friendly settlements, real friendly settlements, follow-up friendly settlements on just satisfaction and pilot friendly settlements – will be handled in this manner.[232] It does nonetheless appear appropriate to use judgments in pilot friendly settlements.

[231] See Article 39 (4) ECHR, as amended by Article 15 of Protocol no 14, note 228 *supra*. Cf. Zwaak, L. (2006), p. 223.
[232] See for the various categories of friendly settlements the chapter "Beyond Doctrine", section I.

3

Beyond Doctrine – The Strasbourg Realities

In the field of friendly settlements, a considerable gap exists between the law in theory and the law in practice. It is almost impossible to grasp the present function and meaning of friendly settlements in the Court's daily life simply on the basis of the legal material. In this research, we therefore decided to gather information from the different stakeholders. We carried out 28 interviews with Judges, State Agents, the Registry's personnel and human rights lawyers, and these form the basis for this chapter. We tried to look beyond the legal doctrine by distinguishing various types of friendly settlements with different functions. The various categories of friendly settlements illustrate the diversity of the instrument, although the legal framework remains the same for all types.

The question why the number of friendly settlements differs considerably among the various Contracting States cannot only be answered from a purely legal point of view. States' policy in pursuing friendly settlements, and the Court's trust in the State Party concerned, play a predominant role. An explanation as to the existence of these differences undoubtedly lies beyond legal doctrine.

During the interviews at the Court, we became aware of the crucial role that the Registry plays in applying friendly settlements. It is mainly due to the Registry's proactive attitude that the number of friendly settlements increased considerably in recent years. The Registry, however, is not a monolithic bloc, but consists of several Sections headed by different personalities. We witnessed that the Court as a whole lacks a uniform or unique attitude towards friendly settlements.

Finally, a crucial feature of any alternative dispute settlement is the negotiation process and this, therefore, is the focus of the last section of this chapter. Surprisingly, in a large number of friendly settlements the parties will not negotiate the agreement at all, at least not in a traditional sense.

I. Typology

1. Arrangements, Friendly Settlements and Withdrawals

From a legal perspective, the various phases during which friendly settlements can be concluded, the different forms of decisions and the legal framework play a predominant role.[1] However, other aspects matter much more in the Court's day-to-day activities. A crucial aspect is whether the application falls into an area where the Court already has well-established case law. Furthermore, applications can be settled on the national or on the European level, with or without the Court's assistance. Friendly settlements can follow a judgment where the Court finds a violation yet does not decide the financial issue. Finally, friendly settlements can be limited to a single applicant or a small group of applicants or can have implications on a large group of persons in defining general measures. These factors are decisive for different categories of friendly settlements which are governed by the same legal framework but fulfil different purposes.

First, it is important to distinguish between "arrangements" (*arrangements*) and "friendly settlements" (*règlements amiables*). The former term was exclusively applied for an alternative solution mechanism on the national level, whereas the latter was reserved for judgments or decisions based on Articles 38 and 39 ECHR. This study focuses on cases that were settled before the Court. However, the Parties can also agree to resolve the dispute without the Court's assistance. Occasionally, the mere threat of an application can prompt the Government to offer negotiations. Sometimes the seemingly everlasting proceedings tire the parties and they decide to resolve the dispute by asking the Court to strike the case out of its list.[2] Thus, the distinction between both categories is based on the extent of the Court's involvement in the negotiations of the settlement. While the Court is not very much involved in the negotiation of arrangements, it plays an active role in friendly settlements.

Although the distinction between arrangements and friendly settlements seems to be clear, in practice it might be more complicated to distinguish the two types of instruments. From a purely formal point of view, a settlement always requires a decision or a judgment handed down by the Court. The distinction between arrangements on the national level and friendly settlements, however, gets blurred if the applicant decides to withdraw the application after having reached an arrangement with the Government. In these situations, the Registry is typically not involved in the negotiations. The Court can strike out such cases only on the assumption that further examination is not required out of respect for human rights.[3] The Court will then strike out the case in the form of a decision. However, withdrawing the application in these circumstances has much the same function as a friendly settlement: the parties agree to a primarily financial solution of the matter.

The arrangements can be subdivided into the following categories: mass arrangements (*arrangements de masse*), routine arrangements (*arrangements de*

---

[1] See for more details, the chapter "Legal Framework and Practice", section III.

[2] See for an early case *Kurtz and Seltmann v. Germany* (Appl. No. 2707/66), Decision (Commission–Arrangement), 4 April 1967, Y.B. 10, 320, strike out decision because the parties found an extrajudicial solution to the case.

[3] Article 37 (2) ECHR.

routine), simple arrangements (*arrangements simples*) and follow-up arrangements (*arrangements de suivi*). Mirroring these categories, the friendly settlements also include routine friendly settlements (*règlements amiables de routine*), follow-up settlements (*règlements amiables de suivi*), pilot friendly settlements (*règlements amiables pilotes*) and real friendly settlements (*règlements amiables réels*). Similar functions are therefore performed by routine arrangements and friendly settlements, follow-up arrangements and friendly settlements as well as mass arrangements and pilot friendly settlements. These various categories of analogical friendly settlements and arrangements are analysed as part of the next section. The simple arrangements and real friendly settlements will be analysed separately due to the intrinsic differences that exist between them.

The simple arrangements appear as basic strike outs, withdrawals based on Council of Europe resolutions (including general and individual measures), withdrawals as a condition of settlement, withdrawals on the basis of previous case law, simple withdrawals and withdrawals including general and individual measures. In these cases, the scope of the Court's intervention manifested itself in an ascending order. The strike outs left the least room for manoeuvre for the Court whereas the withdrawals including general and individual measures seem to have given it the most discretion.

As part of the strike outs, the Court did not mention the will of the parties and did not seem to rely on it to any greater extent.[4] The parties also often mentioned in the text that they renounced all claims and did not request a hearing before the Grand Chamber. In some cases, there was no response on behalf of the applicants and the Court struck the case out of the list due to a lack of interest or unknown intention (lack of response).[5] At times, the Court also assumed that the parties' implicit intention was not to request a hearing before the Grand Chamber.[6]

In simple withdrawals, the applicant often mentioned that he, or she, wished to withdraw the case following the arrangement.[7] In most cases, the text of the

---

[4] See for examples, *K. v. Austria* (Appl. No. 16002/90), Judgment (Chamber–Arrangement), 2 June 1993, Series A, Vol. 255-B; *Poláková and Machová v. Slovak Republic* (Appl. No. 30903/96), Decision (Commission–Arrangement), 3 December 1997, not reported; *Wilson v. United Kingdom* (Appl. No. 30535/96), Decision (Commission–Arrangement), 4 March 1998, not reported; *Watson v. United Kingdom* (Appl. No. 41379/98), Decision (Third Section–Arrangement), 10 May 2001, not reported; *Güler v. Germany* (Appl. No. 48967/99), Decision (Fourth Section–Arrangement), 13 September 2001, not reported; *Lewandowska v. Poland* (Appl. No. 55204/00), Decision (Fourth Section–Arrangement), 27 November 2001, not reported; *Virdi v. United Kingdom* (Appl. No. 58851/00), Decision (Fourth Section–Arrangement), 8 October 2002, not reported.

[5] See for example, *M.R. and C.S. v. Italy* (Appl. No. 42286/98), Decision (First Section–Arrangement), 17 October 2002, not reported.

[6] *Kósa v. Hungary* (Appl. No. 43352/98), Judgment (Second Section–Arrangement), 1 October 2002, not reported; *Bódiné Bencze v. Hungary* (Appl. No. 42373/98), Judgment (Second Section–Arrangement), 1 October 2002, not reported.

[7] See for examples, *Ayadi v. France* (Appl. No. 18000/91), Report (Commission–Arrangement), 1 September 1993, not reported; *O'Brien v. United Kingdom* (Appl. No. 20121/92), Decision (Commission–Arrangement), 8 September 1993, not reported; *G.T. v. Netherlands* (Appl. No. 15416/89), Report (Commission–Arrangement), 19 January 1994, not reported; *Holzinger v. Austria* (Appl.

settlement reproduced in the judgment or decision mentioned that the claimant abandoned all other claims based on the application and would not request a hearing before the Grand Chamber.[8] In cases where the withdrawal was a condition for the arrangement, the parties sometimes mentioned this explicitly in their pleadings which were reproduced by the Court.[9] In an important number of cases, the withdrawal requirement was also included as part of the text of the settlement mentioned by the Court.[10] In some cases, the Court took note of the withdrawal and mentioned that it saw no additional public policy reason, given that there was established case law.[11] In other cases, legislation had been passed and this was an important factor for the Court.[12] Sometimes withdrawals

No. 20204/92), Decision (Commission–Arrangement), 13 April 1994, not reported; *Bozovic v. Austria* (Appl. No. 21684/93), Decision (Commission–Arrangement), 29 June 1994, not reported; *De Vos v. Belgium* (Appl. No. 20597/92), Decision (Commission–Arrangement), 5 July 1994, not reported; *Friedl v. Austria* (Appl. No. 15225/89), Judgment (Chamber–Arrangement), 31 January 1995, Series A, Vol. 305-B; *Todescato v. Italy* (Appl. No. 24307/94), Decision (Commission–Arrangement), 11 April 1995, not reported; *Kurier Zeitungsverlag und Druckerei GmbH v. Austria* (Appl. No. 48481/99), Decision (Third Section–Arrangement), 20 March 2001, not reported.

[8] See for examples, *Friedl v. Austria,* ibid.; *Aggiato v. Italy* (Appl. No. 36822/97), Judgment (Second Section–Arrangement), 29 February 2000, not reported; *Pitsillos v. Cyprus* (Appl. No. 41854/98), Judgment (Third Section–Arrangement), 28 March 2000, not reported.

[9] See for examples, *Crook and National Union of Journalists v. United Kingdom* (Appl. No. 11552/85), Decision (Commission–Arrangement), 15 July 1988, D.R. 56, 148; *Lamguindaz v. United Kingdom* (Appl. No. 16152/90), Judgment (Chamber–Arrangement), 23 June 1993, Series A, Vol. 258-C; *Colman v. United Kingdom* (Appl. No. 16632/90), Judgment (Chamber–Arrangement), 28 June 1993, Series A, Vol. 258-D; *Zeidler, Strauss and Puhm v. Austria* (Appl. Nos. 17755/91, 17756/91; 17757/91), Decision (Commission–Arrangement), 7 December 1994, not reported; *Marlhens v. France* (Appl. No. 22862/93), Judgment (Chamber–Arrangement), 24 May 1995, Series A, Vol. 317-A; *Fouquet v. France* (Appl. No. 20398/92), Judgment (Chamber–Arrangement), 31 January 1996, Reports 1996-I, 19.

[10] See for examples, *Hurtado v. Switzerland* (Appl. No. 17549/90), Judgment (Chamber–Arrangement), 28 January 1994, Series A, Vol. 280-A; *Sätterlund v. Sweden* (Appl. No. 30157/96), Decision (Commission–Arrangement), 9 July 1997, not reported; *Sur v. Turkey* (Appl. No. 21592/93), Judgment (Chamber–Arrangement), 3 October 1997, Reports 1997-VI, 2034; *S.B. and Others v. Italy* (Appl. No. 62976/00), Decision (Second Section–Arrangement), 17 May 2001, not reported; *Maria Castelli v. Italy* (Appl. No. 30920/96), Judgment (Second Section–Arrangement), 31 May 2001, not reported; *Colangelo v. Italy* (Appl. No. 29671/96), Judgment (Second Section–Arrangement), 31 May 2001, not reported; *Z.E. and Others v. Turkey* (Appl. No. 35980/97), Judgment (Second Section–Arrangement), 7 June 2001, not reported.

[11] *Demai v. France* (Appl. No. 22904/93), Judgment (Chamber–Arrangement), 28 October 1994, Series A, Vol. 289-C; *Tsavachidis v. Greece* (Appl. No. 28802/95), Judgment (Grand Chamber–Arrangement), 21 January 1999, not reported; *Trome S.A. v. Spain* (Appl. No. 27781/95), Judgment (Fourth Section–Arrangement), 1 April 1999, Reports 1999-III, 1; *Nepomuceno Mora and Others v. Portugal* (Appl. No. 38780/97), Decision (Fourth Section–Arrangement), 21 September 1999, not reported; *Amorim Gomes v. Portugal* (Appl. No. 40311/98), Decision (Fourth Section–Arrangement), 21 September 1999, not reported; *Aspichi Dehwari v. Netherlands* (Appl. No. 37014/97), Judgment (First Section–Arrangement), 27 April 2000, not reported; *Morris v. United Kingdom* (Appl. No. 31701/96), Decision (Fourth Section–Arrangement), 27 November 2001, not reported (the change in legislation also played a role); *A. v. Italy* (Appl. No. 40453/98), Judgment (First Section–Arrangement), 9 October 2003, not reported; *Sartorelli v. Italy* (Appl. No. 42357/98), Judgment (First Section–Arrangement), 9 October 2003, not reported; *Rocca v. Italy* (Appl. No. 59452/00), Judgment (First Section–Arrangement), 27 November 2003, not reported.

[12] *Wiener Stadtische Wechselseitige Versicherungsanstalt v. Austria* (Appl. No. 2076/63), Decision (Commission–Arrangement), 30 May 1967, Y.B. 10, 136; *N.V. Televizier v. Netherlands* (Appl. No.

contained general and individual measures included in the text of the settlement.[13] Also, certain arrangements including general and individual measures were grounded in Council of Europe resolutions.[14]

In addition to the above mentioned examples, it is noteworthy that there are cases where the withdrawal may seem to be clearly implied from a practical and procedural point of view but not from the applicant's perspective. In fact, the applicant could consider the case as being settled as between the parties without necessarily thinking that it was fully withdrawn. In some of these cases, the applicant mentioned that he renounced to all claims,[15] that he waived his right to just satisfaction, that he was not interested in pursuing the case further and that he would not request a hearing before the Grand Chamber. In all these instances, the intention of the applicant as to the withdrawal is not explicitly spelled out.

The function of friendly settlements varies in accordance to the different stages of a case's progression between the last national authority and the European level. Sometimes, the national authorities settle a case or a certain category of cases without the involvement of the Registry. They may even settle before the cases are lodged in Strasbourg. This is typical in situations where new case law has been established by the Court; this triggers similar applications because in the meantime domestic law has not yet been amended. In order to avoid new applications in the transitional phase, the Government, on its own initiative, wants to settle the case or even a whole series of cases.[16] This form of settlement agreed without the help of the Registry (before the case has been registered) can be called an "arrangement outside proceedings" (*arrangement hors procédures*).

2690/65), Report (Commission–Arrangement), 3 October 1968, Y.B. 11, 782; *K. v. Austria*, note 4 *supra*; *Crouch v. United Kingdom* (Appl. No. 39472/98), Decision (Third Section–Arrangement), 18 September 2001, not reported; *Selim v. Cyprus* (Appl. No. 47293/99), Judgment (Fourth Section–Arrangement), 16 July 2002, Reports 2002-VI, 179.

[13] *Muyldermans v. Belgium* (Appl. No. 12217/86), Judgment (Chamber–Arrangement), 23 October 1991, Series A, Vol. 214-A; *Crossland v. United Kingdom* (Appl. No. 36120/97), Judgment (Third Section–Arrangement), 9 November 1999, not reported; *Faulkner v. United Kingdom* (Appl. No. 30308/96), Judgment (Third Section–Arrangement), 30 November 1999, not reported; *F.F. v. Italy* (Appl. No. 30133/96), Decision (Second Section–Arrangement), 27 January 2000, not reported; *J.T. v. United Kingdom* (Appl. No. 26494/95), Judgment (Fourth Section–Arrangement), 30 March 2000, not reported; *Dimitrov, Savov and Vishanov v. Bulgaria* (Appl. Nos. 37358/97; 37988/97; 39565/98), Decision (Fourth Section–Arrangement), 10 April 2001, not reported; *Ali Erol v. Turkey* (Appl. No. 35076/97), Judgment (First Section–Arrangement), 20 June 2002, not reported; *Özkan Kiliç v. Turkey* (Appl. Nos. 27209/95; 27211/95), Judgment (Second Section–Arrangement), 26 November 2002, not reported; *Külekçi and Others v. Turkey* (Appl. No. 39330/98), Decision (First Section–Arrangement), 12 December 2002, not reported; *Yurtseven and Others v. Turkey* (Appl. No. 31730/96), Judgment (First Section–Arrangement), 18 December 2003, not reported; *Aruç v. Turkey* (Appl. No. 39675/98), Decision (Fourth Section–Arrangement), 6 April 2004, not reported.

[14] See for example, *Sürek v. Turkey (No. 5)* (Appl. Nos. 26976/95; 28305/95; 28307/95), Judgment (Second Section–Arrangement), 16 July 2002, not reported.

[15] See for example, *C.Z. v. Austria* (Appl. No. 21874/93), Decision (Commission–Arrangement), 2 March 1994, not reported.

[16] See for the Swiss practice Frank Schürmann, Swiss Agent before the ECtHR, information given in his interview of 30 January 2009, reprinted in annex 1.

In this area, friendly settlements and arrangements fulfil the function of providing transitional justice.[17] A good example of this is the case *Hegnar and Periscopus AS v. Norway* that reached the ECtHR, but was finally settled. The Government explicitly referred to the Court's case law, admitting that the national decision could raise concerns under Article 10 ECHR.[18] Other examples of such friendly settlements include an application which concerned the Widowed Mother's Allowance and Widow's Payment scheme in the UK. The Court held that this scheme was discriminatory in 2002.[19] Between 2002 and 2008, the Court endorsed over 100 applications with an agreement concerning the same matter. The total amount of financial awards added up to approximately 900,000 GBP.[20]

The transitional function of friendly settlements also became apparent in a series of cases concerning Slovenia. In 2007, the Act on the Protection of the Right to a Trial without Undue Delay became operational, indicating in the transitional rules a solution for the cases pending prior to the implementation of the Act. On the basis of this legislative provision, the Government was prepared to acknowledge the violation of Article 6 (1) ECHR and to pay just satisfaction.[21]

---

[17] Cf. Allen, T. (2007), pp. 1–46; for the general discussion on transitional justice, see Dyzenhaus, D. (2001), pp. 345–369; Posner, E. A./Vermeule, A. (2004), pp. 761–825; Teitel, R. G. (2000); Teitel, R. G. (2003), pp. 893–906.

[18] *Hegnar and Periscopus AS v. Norway* (Appl. No. 38638/02), Decision (Third Section–Arrangement), 14 October 2004, not reported [no paragraphs]: "In light of the present day state of the law as expounded in a number of decisions by the European Court of Human Rights since 1999, the Government of Norway recognizes that the impugned judgment of 4 January 1999 by Eidsivating High Court, as upheld by the Supreme Court's Appeal Committee in its decision 18 November 1999, raises concerns under Article 10 of the European Convention on Human Rights. Taking into consideration also that Norwegian courts – following the European Court of Human Rights' judgments in 1999 and 2000 in the cases of *Bladet Tromsø vs. Norway, Johnsen and Nilsen vs. Norway* and *Bergens Tidende vs. Norway* – have adjusted their practice in this field of law significantly, the Norwegian Government does not consider it fruitful to defend the state of law which prevailed in 1999. Consequently, the Norwegian Government has agreed to cover the pecuniary losses sustained by the applicants on account of the impugned decisions, including legal costs and applicable interest. According to a specification provided by the applicants, their losses amount to NOK 1,993,098.20. The Government agrees to pay that amount and applicable interest by 1 June 2004." The situation was similar in *Oliver and Britten v. United Kingdom* (Appl. Nos. 61604/00; 68452/01), Judgment (Fourth Section–Arrangement), 25 April 2006, not reported, paras. 7 and 8.

[19] *Willis v. United Kingdom* (Appl. No. 36042/97), Judgment (Fourth Section), 11 June 2002, Reports 2002-IV, 311.

[20] See for examples, *Fielding v. United Kingdom* (Appl. No. 36940/97), Judgment (Second Section–Arrangement), 29 January 2002, not reported; *Atkinson and Others v. United Kingdom* (Appl. Nos. 63587/00, 28034/02; 30478/02), Decision (Fourth Section–Arrangement), 26 September 2006, not reported; *McErlane and Others v. United Kingdom* (Appl. Nos. 67777/01; 68429/01; 68430/01), Decision (Fourth Section–Arrangement), 3 May 2007, not yet reported; *Arkwell and Others v. United Kingdom* (Appl. No. 47289/99), Judgment (Fourth Section–Arrangement), 25 September 2007, not yet reported; *Robson v. United Kingdom* (Appl. No. 7112/06), Decision (Fourth Section–Arrangement), 9 September 2008, not yet reported.

[21] See for examples, *Zagožen and Suhoveršnik and 4 Others v. Slovenia* (Appl. Nos. 4497/03; 5177/03; 5584/03; 10880/03; 14191/03), Decision (Third Section–Arrangement), 4 January 2008,

2. Routine Friendly Settlements, Routine Arrangements and Unilateral Declarations

Once a case reaches the European level, the question whether the matter falls into an area with established case law – such as in cases concerning lengthy proceedings, pre-trial detention and non-execution of judgments – is decisive for the future destiny of an application. In such situations, the Registry usually sends to the parties a letter with a complete draft for a friendly settlement, indicating that the Court puts itself at their disposal for a settlement.[22] For such settlements, the term "routine friendly settlements" (*règlements amiables de routine*) was used in the study. The Registry's draft contains a concrete proposal for the financial award. The proposal is usually done in written form and communicated to the parties independently of their intention to settle the case. No real negotiations then take place. At this stage, the information given to the applicant by the Registry and by his, or her, lawyer plays a central role. The question whether the applicant should insist on an ordinary proceeding or accept the Registry's proposal for the settlement can not easily be answered. The advantages and drawbacks have to be considered carefully.

In such situations, various – although not all – Sections have a recurring practice of proposing slightly higher amounts of compensation (approximately 10 per cent of the award that could be received in ordinary proceedings).[23] This increase is meant to be an incentive for the applicant to agree to the settlement despite the lack of a finding of violation.[24] It has to be noted that the proposed amount of money, slightly higher than in a judgment, is usually reduced if the applicant does not wish to settle and the respondent State is prepared to terminate the case via a unilateral declaration. However, we found no evidence of the opposite phenomenon; if the Registry's proposal for a settlement failed because the State Party refused to settle, the final amount in a judgment based on Article 41 ECHR was not – as one could have expected – increased.

The case of *Alfatli and Others v. Turkey*[25] illustrates this mechanism. The application originated from sixteen Turkish nationals complaining that the criminal

---

not yet reported; *Golob and 5 Others v. Slovenia* (Appl. Nos. 2589/03; 2590/03; 3051/03; 3882/03; 10405/03; 14197/03), Decision (Third Section–Arrangement), 4 March 2008, not yet reported; *Leber and 5 Others v. Slovenia* (Appl. Nos. 17520/03; 18425/03; 21523/03; 22641/03; 31198/03; 33936/03), Decision (Third Section–Arrangement), 11 March 2008, not yet reported.

[22] Courell, A. M. (2006), pp. 131–132; Reid, K. (2008), p. 14. For the so called pro-active approach of the Registry, see section III. *infra.*

[23] For the divergent approaches among the various Court Sections, see section III. *infra.*

[24] Only in cases against Turkey was the acknowledgment of the violation of the Convention in cases of serious breaches (for example, Article 2 and 3 ECHR) frequently a precondition for the friendly settlement, see the chapter "Legal Framework and Practice", section III.4.

[25] *Alfatli and Others v. Turkey* (Appl. No. 32984/96), Judgment (Third Section–Friendly Settlement), 2 October 2003, not reported.

proceedings brought against them were not determined within a reasonable time, as required by Article 6 (1) ECHR. Additionally, some applicants complained that their right to a fair hearing under Article 6 (1) ECHR was breached as they were tried by the Martial Law Court, which lacked the required independence and impartiality. All applicants but one agreed to settle the case. In the friendly settlement, the Turkish Government was willing to pay a total sum of 222,650 EUR. The fifteen applicants were divided into four different groups. Applicants in each group received 16,500 EUR, 14,500 EUR, 14,636 EUR or 15,325 EUR on the basis of the duration of criminal proceedings before the national authorities. As part of the friendly settlement, every applicant received on average 14,843 EUR.

Mahmut Memduh Uyan, who had not agreed to settle the case, alleged the same ECHR breaches (length of proceedings and right to an impartial and independent court) before the Court. Violations were found with respect to both complaints. Under Article 41 ECHR, the applicant claimed an amount between 20,000 and 30,000 EUR.[26] Finally, the Court held that the Turkish Government had to pay a total amount of 13,000 EUR, including 11,000 EUR in respect of non-pecuniary damages and 2,000 EUR in respect of costs and expenses.

It is difficult to determine to which of the four groups Mahmut Memduh Uyan would have belonged if he had been willing to settle the case. However, the numbers clearly show that he was not better off financially with the final judgment. From a psychological perspective, at least, he had the satisfaction that the Court acknowledged that there was an ECHR violation in his case. In financial terms, however, it appears that he could have obtained more in a friendly settlement than in ordinary proceedings.[27] Applicants and their lawyers therefore have to consider this mechanism carefully before rejecting the proposal for a routine friendly settlement.

In routine friendly settlements, the State Agent sometimes wants to reduce the proposed just satisfaction amount. In routine cases, where the Government is likely to lose on the basis of existing case law and where there are numerous judgments confirming the compensation level, such a resistance only significantly complicates matters. "Where a dispute arises about the amount to be awarded, the reality for the Registry is that it is much easier to go to the judgment in the case than to make an effort to resolve the differences between the parties."[28] In fact, counter-proposals will – in most cases – signal the end of the settlement process and the case will revert to a normal procedure. It is the Court's clear position that handing down an ordinary judgment or decision is the most effective

---

[26] *Alfatli and Others v. Turkey* (as regards the applicant Mahmut Memduh Uyan) (Appl. No. 32984/96), Judgment (Third Section), 30 October 2003, not reported, para. 48.

[27] For a more comprehensive analysis of the financial awards granted in Turkish cases see the chapter "Analysis of the Court's Practice", section II.

[28] O'Boyle, M. (2003).

and quickest way to terminate a case if the first proposal for a settlement is disputed by one of the parties.

Against this background, the question arises whether a routine friendly settlement can be considered as a real settlement. In this context, neither of the parties takes the initiative to settle the case and no negotiations take place. What is more, the settlement is generally closed when parties cannot agree on the financial award. In these circumstances, the use of the term "settlement" is a misnomer. Functionally, routine friendly settlements are best understood as *fast track judgments or decisions* in certain areas with established case law. The parties' role is very much limited to an agreement on an accelerated termination of the case, but no more than that. The Registry offers them a proposal and they can take it or leave it. This rationale of the fast track procedure becomes even more convincing in a situation where the applicant is considered to unreasonably withhold his consent to the proposed friendly settlement. The Polish State Agent clearly stated: "From time to time, the applicants refuse the proposed amounts. In such situations, I use unilateral declarations."[29]

Following the judgments in *Akman v. Turkey*[30] and *Acar v. Turkey*[31], it became quite clear that the Court prefers to switch directly from the routine friendly settlement to a fast track judgment or decision acknowledging a violation of the Convention against the applicant's will. The statistics show that in recent years the use of unilateral declarations has become a routine procedure.[32] It is now a well-established practice between some State Agents and the Court. While in 2006 only three unilateral declarations had been issued, this number increased to 47 in 2007 and to 78 in 2008.[33] On the basis of these statistics, it becomes all the more apparent that the Court might be too lenient in striking cases from its docket.[34] In some cases, the Court accepted a unilateral declaration based on a questionable offer from the respondent Government.[35]

Although friendly settlements and unilateral declarations might be seen as fulfilling the same function, namely allowing the Court to strike out a case

---

[29] Jakub Wołasiewicz, Polish Agent before the ECtHR, information given in his interview of 29 January 2009, reprinted in annex 1. In the same sense also Lech Garlicki, Judge at the ECtHR, information given in his interview of 2 February 2002, interview on file with the authors.

[30] *Akman v. Turkey* (Appl. No. 37453/97), Judgment (First Section–Unilateral Declaration), 26 June 2001, Reports 2001-VI, 223. It is, however, noteworthy that the Turkish Government acknowledged the violation of the Convention only *in abstracto* and not in the individual case.

[31] *Tahsin Acar v. Turkey* (Appl. No. 26307/95), Judgment (Grand Chamber), 6 May 2003, Reports 2003-VI, 1.

[32] See the statistics in annex 2, "Table II/1. Statistics 1998–2008". Myjer, E. (2007), p. 318 et seq.; Rozakis, C. L., (2007), p. 1003 et seq.; Zwaak, L. (2006), pp. 233–236.

[33] See the statistics in annex 2, "Table II/1. Statistics 1998–2008".

[34] Ang, F./Berghmans, E. (2005), p. 96 et seq.; Koopmans, S. M. G. (2008), p. 195 et seq.; Sardaro, P. (2003), p. 620.

[35] *T.A. v. Turkey* (Appl. No. 26307/95), Judgment (Second Section–Unilateral Declaration), 9 April 2002, not reported; *Toğcu v. Turkey* (Appl. No. 27601/95), Judgment (Second Section–Unilateral Declaration), 9 April 2002, not reported.

that does not raise new legal questions on the basis of existing case law, the two instruments are legally very distinct. While the negotiations leading to a friendly settlement are confidential, the Government's offer to issue a unilateral declaration forms part of the public procedure before the Court. Friendly settlements always require the parties' consent, whereas the termination of a case with a unilateral declaration will usually be triggered by the applicant's rejection of the offer made by the Government during the friendly settlement negotiations. The Court's final task is to examine whether a friendly settlement respects human rights, as guaranteed in the Convention and its Protocols. However, if the Court is confronted with a unilateral declaration, it has an unfettered discretion to accept or to reject the proposals made.[36] A friendly settlement does not normally include an acknowledgment of a violation, whereas this is usually a condition for issuing a unilateral declaration.[37] While a friendly settlement usually excludes the possibility of challenging the matter before the Grand Chamber, this is allowed when a case has been struck out on the basis of a unilateral declaration. The termination of a case by a friendly settlement does not automatically give the opportunity to re-open the national proceedings. This is an important point, and has to be considered carefully. In cases concerning long pre-trial detention or violations of procedural rights, this waiver might be a disadvantage in countries where the national law provides for a possibility to re-open the case before the national authorities. National legislation progressively foresees such a possibility in criminal, civil and even administrative matters.[38] One has to bear all these differences in mind when considering the alternative between a friendly settlement and a unilateral declaration.

Routine arrangements concern similar areas to routine friendly settlements, as well as other areas where the Court has firmly established case law. The intervention of the Court and the Commission in these cases appears to have been minimal. There were numerous repetitive Italian cases concerning the applicant's inability to recover possession of their apartment and the duration of eviction

---

[36] Rozakis, C. L. (2007), p. 1011.

[37] See the Court's cryptic formula in *Tahsin Acar v. Turkey*, note 31 *supra*, para. 84: "The Court accepts that a full admission of liability in respect of an applicant's allegations under the Convention cannot be regarded as a condition *sine qua non* for the Court's being prepared to strike an application out on the basis of a unilateral declaration by a respondent Government." *Estate of Nitschke v. Sweden* (Appl. No. 6301/05), Judgment (Third Section), 27 September 2007, not yet reported, para. 39: "Moreover, even in respect of this one complaint, the Government have neither admitted that there has been a violation of the Convention nor regretted the inconvenience caused to the applicant by the duration of the proceedings. Instead, the Government have simply referred to their observations where they have left it for the Court to decide. Furthermore, although the Court considers that the sum offered by the Government to the applicant is very reasonable, it observes that it is proposed to be paid ex gratia. Having regard to what have been stated above and the facts of the present case, the Court finds that the unilateral declaration does not offer satisfactory redress to the applicant and that, consequently, the Government have failed to submit a statement offering a sufficient basis for finding that respect for human rights as defined in the Convention does not require the Court to continue its examination of the case (…)."

[38] See for the reference, Keller, H./Stone Sweet, A. (2008), p. 704.

proceedings.[39] Another important cluster of cases originated from expropriation of property for the construction of a highway in Turkey.[40] As with friendly settlements, arrangements also concern lengthy proceedings, pre-trial detention, and non-execution of judgments. These arrangements play a similar role to the friendly settlements in that they allow the Court to strike out a case that does not raise new legal questions on the basis of existing case law. In this context, the Court's task is facilitated as the parties settle at the domestic level and request their case to be struck out of the list without additional intervention. The Court then rubber stamps this settlement indicating that respect for human rights does not require an examination of the case.[41] The Court also frequently indicates that it has already considered certain issues in previous case law and that there is no need to re-examine it in the case at hand.[42]

3. Scarcity of Real Friendly Settlements

In a small group of cases, the parties agree to settle the application. The initiative might come from the parties themselves or from the Registry. Such "real friendly settlements" (*règlements amiables réels*) are the result of a negotiation process assisted by the Registry or conducted only by the parties. In areas where there is no established case law – that is in fields other than lengthy proceedings, pre-trial detention, non-execution of judgments – the Registry may sometimes suggest a first draft for the settlement.[43] However, this does not happen on a regular basis and the settlement does not follow a concrete predefined scheme. In these situations, real negotiations between the parties take place. These friendly settlements are therefore referred to as non-paper settlements in the Court's internal jargon as opposed to routine friendly settlements, which generally involve a written

[39] See for examples, *S.A. and D.D.L. v. Italy* (Appl. No. 30973/96), Judgment (Second Section–Arrangement), 12 April 2001, not reported; *Tarducci v. Italy* (Appl. No. 31460/96), Judgment (Second Section–Arrangement), 19 April 2001, not reported; *D.L. and M.A. v. Italy* (Appl. No. 31926/96), Judgment (Second Section–Arrangement), 19 April 2001, not reported; *L.M.G. v. Italy* (Appl. No. 32655/96), Judgment (Second Section–Arrangement), 19 April 2001, not reported.
[40] See for examples, *Ergüne and Others v. Turkey* (Appl. No. 42838/98), Decision (Third Section–Arrangement), 7 November 2002, not reported; *Gülhan and Others v. Turkey* (Appl. No. 42839/98), Decision (Third Section–Arrangement), 7 November 2002, not reported; *Karci and Others v. Turkey* (Appl. No. 42841/98), Decision (Third Section–Arrangement), 7 November 2002, not reported; *Bağatur and Others v. Turkey* (Appl. No. 42847/98), Decision (Third Section–Arrangement), 7 November 2002, not reported; *Kara and Others v. Turkey* (Appl. No. 42849/98), Decision (Third Section–Arrangement), 7 November 2002, not reported.
[41] See for examples, *Popescu v. Romania* (Appl. No. 3831/04), Decision (Third Section–Arrangement), 10 January 2008, not yet reported; *Pavel v. Romania* (Appl. No. 28709/04), Decision (Third Section–Arrangement), 10 January 2008, not yet reported; *Marian v. Romania* (Appl. No. 42239/04), Decision (Third Section–Arrangement), 10 January 2008, not yet reported.
[42] See for examples, *Brocco v. Italy* (Appl. No. 68074/01), Judgment (Third Section–Arrangement), 7 April 2005, not reported; *Enrico Cecere v. Italy* (Appl. No. 70585/01), Judgment (Third Section–Arrangement), 24 November 2005, not reported.
[43] Courell, A. M. (2006), pp. 131–132.

procedure. In sheer numbers, the large majority of friendly settlements concluded before the Court in the recent years belong to the category of routine friendly settlements. There are, however, important real friendly settlements,[44] including pilot friendly settlements, which form a separate sub-group in this category.[45]

4. Follow-up Friendly Settlements

Friendly settlements also play a major role in situations where the Court has already found a violation of the Convention and has adjourned the applicant's claim for compensation and costs on grounds that this claim could not be decided at that time. Normally, the Court would only set a time limit for the handing in of written observations or of the draft settlement. Under these circumstances, the parties generally come – with or without the Registry's assistance – to a friendly settlement.[46] They may in fact settle more easily, given that the violation of the Convention is not in question and usually only the financial award remains to be negotiated. The Court then strikes the case out of its list in the form of a judgment. We call this category of friendly settlements "follow-up friendly settlements" (*règlements amiables de suivi*).

A good example of a follow-up settlement is the *Zeman v. Austria* case, where a detailed description of the agreement is provided in the version available on HUDOC.[47] Recent follow-up friendly settlements seem to indicate that the parties now tend to agree on considerably higher financial awards.[48]

5. Pilot Judgments, Pilot Friendly Settlements, Pilot Arrangements and Mass Arrangements

In the second half of the 90s, the Court was increasingly faced with a large number of identical applications stemming from a structural problem in a particular

---

[44] See for examples, *Cagirga v. Turkey* (Appl. No. 21895/93), Report (Commission–Friendly Settlement), 7 July 1995, D.R. 82-B, 20; *Isiyok v. Turkey* (Appl. No. 22309/93), Report (Commission–Friendly Settlement), 31 October 1997, D.R. 91-A, 5; *Dömel v. Germany* (Appl. No. 31828/03), Decision (Fifth Section–Arrangement), 9 May 2007, not yet reported.

[45] See section I.5. *infra.*

[46] See for examples, *Von Hannover v. Germany* (Appl. No. 59320/00), Judgment (Third Section–Arrangement), 28 July 2005, not reported; *Zeman v. Austria* (Appl. No. 23960/02), Judgment (First Section–Arrangement), 10 January 2008, not yet reported.

[47] *Zeman v. Austria*, ibid., para. 6.

[48] *Eugenia Michaelidou Developments Ltd and Michael Tymvios v. Turkey* (Appl. No. 16163/90), Judgment (Fourth Section–Arrangement), 22 April 2008, not yet reported, para. 13: 1,000,000 U.S.D.; *Morea v. Italy* (Appl. No. 69269/01), Judgment (Second Section–Arrangement), 29 April 2008, not yet reported, para. 7: 250,000 EUR; *Kolona v. Cyprus* (Appl. No. 28025/03), Judgment (First Section–Arrangement), 2 October 2008, not yet reported, para. 7: 218,326.28 EUR (pecuniary and non-pecuniary damage and costs and expenses), 13,800 EUR (legal costs); *Gianazza v. Italy* (Appl. No. 69878/01), Judgment (Second Section–Arrangement), 14 October 2008, not yet reported, para. 8: 355,000 EUR.

Contracting State[49] concerning the well-known categories of excessive length of proceedings and the lack of an effective remedy. It was not until the *Bottazzi v. Italy*[50] case that the Court started noting an accumulation of identical breaches resulting from a lack of sufficient remedy at the national level. Subsequently, in one day, the Court accepted 120 friendly settlements in invalidity cases against Italy concerning Article 6 (1) ECHR, with a total amount of 1,696 million ITL for non-pecuniary damage and 120 million ITL for legal costs.[51] Against this background, the assumption becomes plausible that the Italian Government may have been more eager to offer financial awards than to introduce the necessary reforms. At that time, the Court did not yet spell out any general measures. In *Kudła v. Poland*,[52] the Court began to stress that there must be a national remedy under Articles 6 and 13 ECHR to tackle the problem at the national level. It was then recognized that the Committee of Ministers was responsible for finding the solution to the underlying problem.[53]

Following the accession of the Central and Eastern European States, the number of applications rose exponentially and the case law concerning structural problems also dramatically expanded. The Court was increasingly faced with severe human rights issues of a systemic character, including overcrowding in detention facilities, delayed or inadequate compensation for expropriation, the chronic non-execution of final judicial decisions, to mention only a few. In 2004, the Committee of Ministers invited the Court to tackle this problem with a new instrument.[54] The Committee of Ministers encouraged the Court to assist States in finding appropriate solutions whenever a finding of a violation of the Convention stemmed from an underlying problem that could give rise to numerous applications. In the same year, the Court used this new instrument in

---

[49] However, the phenomenon of systemic problems appeared much earlier, see for example, *Ireland v. United Kingdom* (Appl. No. 5310/71), Judgment (Plenary), 18 January 1978, Series A, Vol. 25, para. 159: "A practice incompatible with the Convention consists of an accumulation of identical or analogous breaches which are sufficiently numerous and inter-connected to amount not merely to isolated incidents or exceptions but to a pattern or system; a practice does not of itself constitute a violation separate from such breaches."

[50] *Bottazzi v. Italy* (Appl. No. 34884/97), Judgment (Grand Chamber), 28 July 1999, Reports 1999-V, 1, para. 22: "The frequency with which violations are found shows that there is an accumulation of identical breaches which are sufficiently numerous to amount not merely to isolated incidents. Such breaches reflect a continuing situation that has not yet been remedied and in respect of which litigants have no domestic remedy."

[51] For the rise in Italian cases, see the statistics in annex 2, "Table II/2. Statistics per Country 1998–2008: Friendly Settlements" and "Table II/3. Statistics per Country 1998–2008: Arrangements". The amounts of compensation were calculated on the basis of statistics collected for this study, not published in this volume, on file with the authors.

[52] *Kudła v. Poland* (Appl. No. 30210/96), Judgment (Grand Chamber), 26 October 2000, Reports 2000-XI, 197.

[53] Wildhaber, L. (2009), p. 69.

[54] Resolution Res(2004)3 on judgments revealing an underlying systemic problem, Committee of Ministers, 12 May 2004.

Broniowski v. Poland.[55] The *Broniowski* case concerned a compensation scheme for Polish citizens displaced after World War II from the regions located east of the Bug River. The term "pilot judgment" does not appear in the text of this Grand Chamber judgment. However, it is generally agreed that this instrument must be considered as a new type of judgment.[56]

The former President of the Court, Luzius Wildhaber, defined the main characteristics of the pilot judgments in eight points:[57]

1. A finding by the Grand Chamber that a systemic problem in a Contracting State affects an entire class of individuals in their enjoyment of the Convention's rights;[58]

2. A finding that these deficiencies may give rise to numerous subsequent applications;

3. A recognition that general measures are necessary;

4. An acknowledgement that such measures should have retroactive effect;

5. A decision to adjourn the consideration of all pending applications deriving from the same systemic problem;

6. A decision reinforcing the obligation to take legal and administrative measures in the operative part of the judgment;

7. A decision reserving the question of just satisfaction in the sense of Article 41 ECHR;

8. Communication of the Court's approach in the case to the Committee of Ministers and the periodic provision of the further developments in the case to the Committee of Ministers, the Parliamentary Assembly and the Council of Europe's Human Rights Commissioner.

The main issues in pilot friendly settlements concern Article 41 ECHR and general measures. In this sense, pilot judgments differ greatly from routine friendly settlements and follow-up friendly settlements, as they do not only concern the individual applicant and they require the Government to propose general measures.[59] Pilot friendly settlements presuppose a principal judgment in which the

[55] *Broniowski v. Poland* (Appl. No. 31443/96), Judgment (Grand Chamber–Pilot Judgment), 22 June 2004, Reports 2004-V, 1; *Broniowski v. Poland* (Appl. No. 31443/96), Judgment (Grand Chamber–Friendly Settlement), 28 September 2005, Reports 2005-IX, 1.

[56] Garlicki, L. (2007), p. 177; Gattini, A. (2007), p. 276 et seq.; Jackson, J. L. (2006), p. 759 et seq.; Paraskeva, C. (2007), [no page numbers]; Sadurski, W. (2009), p. 397 et seq.; Wildhaber, L. (2009), p. 70; Wołąsiewicz, J. (2008), p. 94 et seq.; Zagrebelsky, V. (2007), p. 521 et seq.

[57] Wildhaber, L. (2009), p. 71.

[58] However, in *Burdov v. Russia (No. 2)* (Appl. No. 33509/04), Judgment (First Section–Pilot Judgment), 15 January 2009, not yet reported, the Court made it clear that pilot judgments have not necessarily to be decided by the Grand Chamber.

[59] See the wording in the pilot friendly settlement in *Broniowski v. Poland*, note 55 *supra*, para. 31: "The terms of the following settlement are intended to take into account (...) not only the interests of the individual applicant (...), but also the interests and prejudice of complainants in similar

Court determines the national room for manoeuvre. "In the *Broniowski* case, we would not have accepted a friendly settlement before a judgment."[60]

The dimension of pilot friendly settlements becomes apparent if one considers the follow-up process both on the national and the European level. In November 2005, following the friendly settlement concluded in the *Broniowski* case and the entry into force of the Law of 8 July 2005 on the realization of the right to compensation for property left beyond the present borders of the Polish State, Government delegates visited the Court's Registry and inspected the case files of all "Bug River" cases. The purpose of the Government's mission was to select a group of applicants in respect of whom, on account of their age, health or difficult personal situation, the Government was prepared to secure the accelerated implementation of their right to compensation, as defined by the July 2005 Act.

By a letter of 16 February 2006, the Government supplied the Court with the names of 50 applicants to be included in the so-called "accelerated payment procedure". On 14 June 2006, the Government submitted a document setting out a "plan of action" for the payment of compensation. This document also clarified the requirements and formalities that had to be satisfied in order to receive payment pursuant to the relevant provisions of the July 2005 Act. The Act introduced a ceiling of 20 per cent of the original property's current value on compensation recoverable by the Bug River claimants. The persons who were not satisfied with this solution brought proceedings to Strasbourg, but got no relief.[61] This was followed by 246 strike out decisions in 2008.[62] The Court held that the procedures under the July 2005 Act had provided the applicants and other Bug River claimants with relief at the domestic level, which made its further examination of their applications and of other similar applications no longer justified.[63] These cases could be called follow-up arrangements, as they were concluded on the domestic level without the intervention of the Court. From a functional

---

applications pending before the Court or liable to be lodged with it; the obligation of the Polish Government under Article 46 of the Convention, in executing the principal judgment, to take not only individual measures of redress (...) but also general measures covering other Bug River claimants (...)." Similar the wording of the pilot friendly settlement in *Hutten-Czapska v. Poland* (Appl. No. 35014/97), Judgment (Grand Chamber–Friendly Settlement), 28 April 2008, not yet reported.

[60] Christos Rozakis, Vice-President of the ECtHR, citation from his interview of 2 February 2009, interview on file with the authors.

[61] *Wolkenberg and Others v. Poland* (Appl. No. 50003/99), Decision (Fourth Section–Arrangement), 4 December 2007, not yet reported, on the same date the Court struck out 40 applications on the same ground.

[62] See for example, *Zawadzka and Others v. Poland* (Appl. No. 10476/02), Decision (Fourth Section–Arrangement), 15 January 2008, not yet reported.

[63] In some cases, the applicants decided to pursue the case before the Court, see *Stankiewicz v. Poland* (Appl. No. 25217/02), Decision (Fourth Section–Arrangement), 11 December 2007, not yet reported; *Szymańska-Baier v. Poland* (Appl. No. 12935/03), Decision (Fourth Section–Arrangement), 11 December 2007, not yet reported; *Antoszczuk and Others v. Poland* (Appl. No. 15230/04), Decision (Fourth Section–Arrangement), 11 December 2007, not yet reported. However, the Court struck them out of its list of cases on the basis of previous case law.

point of view, however, they appear to be analogical to the pilot friendly settlement concluded following the pilot judgment.

6. Interstate Friendly Settlements

The purpose of settling interstate cases is the same as in individual cases. The parties want to avoid an authoritative judgment which could result in much publicity and media attention. However, interstate friendly settlements differ in two important ways from individual cases. First, the parties negotiate on a more balanced basis and, second, the scarce amount of interstate friendly settlements demonstrates that they do not play an important role in the Court's case law.[64] The latter is undoubtedly due to the fact that interstate applications are rarely used in general. The Contracting States are reluctant to expose each other to a procedure that is by its nature undiplomatic and that might impair the relations with another country.

The only interstate case settled by means of a friendly settlement under the Commission was an application brought by Denmark, France, the Netherlands, Norway and Sweden against Turkey regarding alleged serious violations of the Convention by Turkey's then military Government.[65] The Commission played an active role in this settlement procedure. The final settlement was based on proposals made by the parties and sanctioned by the Commission. Turkey promised, *inter alia*, that such breaches would not occur in the future, that the Turkish authorities would provide continued information to the Commission on human rights issues, and that they would progressively lift martial law and facilitate amnesty. This settlement was highly politicized and its outcome has been criticized for not requiring enough from the Turkish Government. Clearly, the settlement did not adequately address the human rights violations dating from the moment of the application. However, a tacit condition of this settlement was that Turkey would accept the right of individual application.[66] In fact, as one of the last to join the Council of Europe, Turkey shortly after recognized the right to individual petition.[67] Overall, the result of the friendly settlement procedure in the case was certainly of much greater importance than a judgment stating that Turkey had violated the Convention.

---

[64] Janis, M. W./Kay, R. S./Bradley, A. W. (2008), p. 56. See for interstate friendly settlements, *France, Norway, Denmark, Sweden, Netherlands v. Turkey* (Appl. Nos. 9940–9944/82), Report (Commission–Friendly Settlement), 7 December 1985, D.R. 44, 31; *Denmark v. Turkey* (Appl. No. 34382/97), Judgment (First Section–Friendly Settlement), 5 April 2000, Reports 2000-IV, 1.

[65] *France, Norway, Denmark, Sweden, Netherlands v. Turkey*, ibid.

[66] Koopmans, S. M. G. (2008), p. 191.

[67] On 28 January 1987, Turkey deposited its declaration concerning Article 25 of the ECHR in force at the time. Further declarations concerning Article 25 and also Article 46 of the ECHR in force at the time were made in the 90s. See *Loizidou v. Turkey* (Appl. No. 15318/89), Judgment (Grand Chamber), 23 March 1995, Series A, Vol. 310, para. 15 et seq.

Under the new Court, Denmark lodged an application against Turkey in 1997. The Danish Government asked the Strasbourg bodies to examine the treatment of a Danish citizen, Mr Kemal Koç, by the Turkish authorities. He was allegedly ill-treated and tortured while he was in custody in Turkey. In 2000, the Court accepted the friendly settlement reached by the parties.[68] This friendly settlement is particularly interesting because it includes a statement of regret on part of the Turkish Government acknowledging occasional and individual cases of torture and ill-treatment as well as a commitment to pay a substantial sum in settlements and to provide certain human right projects. The case was resolved bilaterally with occasional drafting advice from the Registry.[69]

II. States' Policy, Interests and Trust

The statistics collected demonstrate that there has been a gradual increase in friendly settlements, arrangements and unilateral declarations over the years.[70] In 1998, there were only 55 friendly settlements and arrangements and no unilateral declarations. In 2002, this number increased to 302 friendly settlements/arrangements and to three unilateral declarations. In 2008, this number increased once more to 670 friendly settlements and arrangements and to 78 unilateral declarations. Friendly settlements and arrangements represented in 2008 43.4 per cent of the judgments handed down that year. Overall, this ratio has generally increased in the recent years. The greatest group of beneficiaries of the system are Turkey, Italy and Poland. These three countries have consistently concluded the most friendly settlements and arrangements over the longest period of time. The rationale behind this phenomenon could be due to the fact that all three countries have had important systemic problems. In Poland, the large number of applications can be accounted for by the great number of applicants who have lost faith in the domestic mechanism and are eager to bring cases to Strasbourg.

Friendly settlements are to a large degree dependent on the willingness of the State Party to settle. This may explain why Russia concludes fairly few friendly settlements although it has recently generated the largest amount of applications before the Court.[71] For Switzerland, the rate of friendly settlements is also rather low. While the Swiss Government is not fundamentally opposed to friendly settlements, it primarily tries to uphold domestic decisions, in particular those of

---

[68] *Denmark v. Turkey*, note 64 *supra*.
[69] Koopmans, S. M. G. (2008), p. 197.
[70] See the statistics in annex 2, "Table II/1. Statistics 1998–2008".
[71] See for some examples, *Taykov v. Russia* (Appl. No. 48498/99), Decision (First Section–Arrangement), 28 March 2000, not reported [no paragraphs]; *Solovyev v. Russia* (Appl. No. 52339/99), Decision (Second Section–Arrangement), 11 October 2001, not reported [no paragraphs]; *Bochkov v. Russia* (Appl. No. 58826/00), Decision (Second Section–Arrangement), 10 February 2004, not reported [no paragraphs].

the Federal Supreme Court. It ultimately tries to defend the national law that is the basis for the national decision.[72] This policy contrasts sharply with the Italian, Turkish or Polish approaches. For various reasons, these countries have a higher rate of friendly settlements.

As regards Italy, numerous cases concerned lengthy proceedings and prolonged inability to recover possession of property. In most cases, Article 6 ECHR and/ or Article 1 Protocol no 1 were mentioned as the grounds of the complaint. In some repetitive cases, however, no legal basis was indicated.[73] The cases already mentioned concerned property owners who decided to terminate leases on the expiry of their term and asked the tenant to vacate the premises. Attempts at recovering the property had proven unsuccessful as the statutory provisions in force did not entitle the applicant to police assistance. These cases were concentrated on a short span of several years (from 2000 to 2003) and the caseload appears to have been generated by a defective domestic remedy system.

The Turkish commitment in concluding friendly settlements is remarkable both in terms of the numbers of cases settled and in the wide range of areas in which friendly settlements are reached. The Turkish Government is keen on settling cases concerning Articles 2 and 3 ECHR.[74]

One of the most innovative and creative approaches towards friendly settlements was shown by the Polish Government. In addition to having settled an important number of repetitive cases, Poland has also had some pilot friendly settlements.[75] It could be argued that Poland has the "friendliest approach" towards friendly settlements.

A Contracting State might want to settle a case for various reasons.[76] Financial matters do not play a decisive role. It is rather exceptional for a Contracting State to be financially better off by concluding a friendly settlement than undergoing normal proceedings.[77] However, the total costs of receiving a judgment in Strasbourg are much higher in ordinary proceedings than in friendly settlements. As regards routine friendly settlements, the benefit for the Government is that the State Agent is not required to hand in written submissions to the applicant's complaints or to finance the translation of the Court's documents. A Contracting State might also be interested in concluding real friendly settlements in order to avoid media attention and to resolve a dispute fairly swiftly. Further, another important motive is that friendly settlements are not included as part of the Court's

[72] Frank Schürmann, note 16 *supra*.
[73] See for example, *Maria Castelli v. Italy* (Appl. No. 30920/96), Judgment (Second Section–Arrangement), 31 May 2001, not reported.
[74] See for more details, the chapter "Analysis of the Court's Practice", section II.
[75] *Broniowski v. Poland* (Appl. No. 31443/96), Judgment (Grand Chamber–Friendly Settlement), 28 September 2005, Reports 2005-IX, 1; *Hutten-Czapska v. Poland* (Appl. No. 35014/97), Judgment (Grand Chamber–Friendly Settlement), 28 April 2008, not yet reported.
[76] Cabral Barreto, I. (1999), p. 39; Courell, A. M. (2006), pp. 137–139; Dollé, S. (1998), p. 244; Zwaak, L. (2006), p. 223.
[77] However, see for the Polish practice Jakub Wołasiewicz, note 29 *supra*.

statistics concerning the violations of the Convention. Occasionally, uncertainty about the facts might also motivate a Government to settle.

The attitude of a Contracting State towards friendly settlements is dependent on several factors. If alternative dispute settlement mechanisms are not available or used at the domestic level, the Government could be reluctant to resort to them in the European context. The Government involved does not always consist of a single monolithic bloc; there can be divergent attitudes towards friendly settlements across the Ministries and complicated budget questions might arise.[78] Finally, in federal States, the co-operation with the *Länder* (or *Cantons* or *States*) might constitute an additional obstacle.[79] The State Agent's decision to accept the Court's invitation to settle clearly depends on the circumstances of the case. A Government might prefer to follow the Court's ordinary procedure in order to obtain an authoritative judgment on the compatibility of the national legislation with the Convention. In other words, the Government may wish to defend the national position before the Court and use the application as a test case.[80]

To resolve a dispute with a friendly settlement rather than an authoritative judgment is ultimately also a question of trust. The Court would only endorse an agreement reached by the parties if it can count on the fact that the settlement will be properly implemented. Confidence in the partnership is particularly solid as part of the pilot friendly settlement procedure. The Court will only endorse the pilot friendly settlement if it is convinced that the State Party is willing and able to tackle the underlying problem by implementing the general measures agreed upon. This might also explain why this instrument has been used so rarely.

III. The Registry's Proactive Approach

Together with the communication of the case, the Court also signals to the parties that it is at their disposal if they wish to settle the case. This invitation to settle

---

[78] In federal States, the amount awarded in the friendly settlement may be jointly paid by the *Länder/Cantons/States* and the federal Government. This situation raises complicated questions, especially if there is no clear legal basis for distribution of competences. See for example, the case *I.O. v. Switzerland* (Appl. No. 21529/93), Judgment (Second Section–Friendly Settlement), 8 March 2001, not reported; Frank Schürmann, note 16 *supra*.

[79] Claudia Westerdiek, Section Registrar, information given in her interview of 14 January 2009, interview on file with the authors; Almut Wittling-Vogel, German Agent before the ECtHR, information given in her interview of 28 January 2009, interview on file with the authors. In Germany, the co-operation with the *Länder* used to be a problem. In the more recent years, the co-operation is well established, see also *Gesetz zur Lastentragung im Bund-Länder-Verhältnis bei Verletzung von supranationalen oder völkerrechtlichen Verpflichtungen* (*Lastentragungsgesetz, LastG*; The Act on the Financial Consequences for the German Federation and the *Länder* of the Violation of Supranational and International Obligations) of 5 September 2006 (BGBl. I S. 2098, 2105), entered into force on 12 September 2006.

[80] Frank Schürmann, note 16 *supra*: *"Il ne faut pas oublier que tout règlement amiable met en question, en quelque sorte, le bien-fondé de l'arrêt national."* Almut Wittling-Vogel, ibid.

is issued on a recurrent basis. Normally, the Registry would only continue on this track after receiving from the parties a positive answer for a settlement or a very first proposal for a settlement. The parties have to hand in documents or observations for the case in different envelopes, depending on whether this information will be part of a friendly settlement or the ordinary procedure.[81] This distinction is essential because the former, unlike the latter, is confidential.

For several years now, the Court has followed a so-called proactive approach towards the settlement of cases. In areas of established case law, the Case Lawyer sends a proposal for the settlement of the case together with the communication. This proposal is written in the name of the Registry and will be approved by the Judge Rapporteur if the parties agree. A precondition for this approval is that the case does not give rise to new legal questions. This means that the application has to be a clear cut case that does not develop the Court's jurisprudence.[82]

The proactive approach plays a major role in the practice of friendly settlements. The Registry defines the financial awards that the applicant can, and must, expect from the very beginning. The Court has developed a standard for defining the financial award in cases concerning lengthy proceedings in particular. Internally, the Court applies the so-called *tableaux* for each country in which the amount for just satisfaction is defined in accordance with the nature (civil, criminal or administrative) and the length of the proceedings. The *tableaux* also take into account the different living conditions and costs in the various Contracting States.

There are important differences in the amount for just satisfaction granted in routine friendly settlement cases across the five Sections of the Court. Together with the communication of the case to the parties, some Sections propose a sum that is slightly higher (approximately 10–20 per cent) than the one that would be granted as part of ordinary proceedings. The rationale of this practice is to create an incentive for the applicant to settle the case in spite of the lack of acknowledgement of a violation of the Convention. The applicant is then compensated for this lack. Other Sections propose at that stage a slightly lower amount (approximately 10–20 per cent) of compensation than in ordinary proceedings. This practice is usually justified by the fact that the applicant will receive the award much sooner than in ordinary proceedings. For the Government, the difference in amounts of compensation constitutes a financial incentive to settle the case. Both schools of thought are equally valid and it is difficult for the Court to develop a uniform practice in this matter. During the interviews, the Registry's personnel was sometimes unaware of the fact that there were divergences between the different Sections. In this regard, better communication and more consistency are certainly needed.

---

[81] See the Practice Direction – Written Pleadings, paras. 16 and 17, in annex 3.
[82] Claudia Westerdiek, note 79 *supra*.

Several State Agents are fully aware of the fact that the Registry pursues a policy aimed at settling repetitive cases in areas of established case law rather than terminating the applications through the ordinary procedure. The Registry's proactive approach is considered to be effective.[83] However, there are some demurrals when the State Agent is confronted with a concrete proposal for a friendly settlement and has not yet had the opportunity to state the Government's position. The criticism is based on the fact that the Registry would act exclusively on the basis of the documents received from the applicant.[84] It goes without saying that the State Party must be heard before a concrete amount of money is proposed by the Court.

The Registry's approach has been further developed in recent years. During a meeting held in Warsaw in 2008, the Polish Government and a delegation of the Registry agreed that friendly settlements will be used on a regular basis in a number of areas.[85] Such an informal agreement paves the way towards the systematic use of friendly settlements with a particular country in certain fields. It presupposes a mutual trust between the Registry and the country concerned.

IV. Written Procedures and Negotiations

The published case files reveal little about the negotiation stage given that the negotiations are confidential. Several interview partners stressed that the negotiations could be difficult for two main reasons. First, the applicant may want to have his, or her, case decided by the Court in order to "win" against the national authorities. Second, he or she may have higher expectations in terms of the financial award.[86]

Sometimes, the Court hints between the lines that there might have been difficulties in the negotiation process or in the execution of the friendly settlement.[87]

---

[83] Frank Schürmann, note 16 *supra*; Almut Wittling-Vogel, note 79 *supra*; Jakub Wołasiewicz, note 29 *supra*.

[84] Almut Wittling-Vogel, note 79 *supra*.

[85] Jakub Wołasiewicz, note 29 *supra*; confirmed by Lech Garlicki, note 29 *supra*.

[86] See for example, Frank Schürmann, note 16 *supra*; Reid, K. (2008), p. 15.

[87] See for a telling example, *Prokudin v. Russia* (Appl. No. 24408/02), Decision (Third Section–Arrangement), 7 December 2006, not reported [no paragraphs]: "On 28 February 2006 the applicant submitted his observations. He asked the Court to disregard his written declaration of 30 November 2005 because the Kemerovo Regional administration had intimidated him with the view to securing the friendly settlement. Moreover, the applicant averred that he expected to receive a bigger award than the one paid under the friendly settlement if the Court establishes a violation of his rights due to the lengthy non-enforcement of the judgment of 1 June 2001. (...) Under the friendly settlement the Kemerovo Regional Administration had paid the applicant RUR 1,000 (approximately EUR 30) in compensation for inflation losses during the period of the non-enforcement of the judgment award. The Administration had also undertaken to pay for medical treatment and holidays of the applicant's daughter twice a year. The Government provided the Court with copies of financial documents confirming the payment and the Administration's undertaking. (...) The Court observes that it has already on a number of occasions examined similar factual background and legal issues as

A good example of this is a Turkish property case where the Cyprus Government intervened as a third party:

The Court also notes that the applicant and the Government have made submissions concerning measures allegedly taken by the Government of Cyprus, an intervening party, against the applicant in the context of bankruptcy proceedings. Given the delay in the disposal of this case, which the Court regrets, it cannot justify any further adjournment. To the extent therefore that any allegations are made of interferences with property or other rights under the Convention and its Protocols, these would fall to be examined rather in an application against the respondent Government alleged to be responsible for any violations of the provisions of the Convention or its Protocols and having due regard to the requirements of Articles 34 and 35 of the Convention. Further, insofar as the Court has received submissions from the Official Receiver, Ministry of Commerce, Tourism and Industry in the Republic of Cyprus drawing attention to the applicant's bankruptcy and questioning his ability to enter into any settlement or receive any compensation, it would only remark that the applicant's status as a bankrupt may be of relevance on a domestic level but does not affect the present application which was introduced validly under former Article 25 of the Convention and to which no objection was taken by the intervening Government concerning any lack of standing by the applicant to pursue his property claims.[88]

The question whether the applicant was bankrupt was not entirely insignificant in this case, as the Turkish Government agreed to pay the sum of 1,000,000 USD.

It is seldom apparent from the published decision that the applicant was undecided as to whether he should accept a proposed settlement due to practical

---

in the present case and decided to strike applications out of its lists of cases under Article 37 § 1 (see *Lipatova v. Russia* (dec.), no. 14827/03, 19 October 2006, and *Yaurov and Others v. Russia* (dec.), no. 33492/04, 16 November 2006). The Court does not see any reason to depart from its findings in the present case. The Court takes note of the settlement reached between the parties. Furthermore, it observes that the applicant did not contest the authenticity of the agreement and the declaration of 30 November 2005. The Court also sees no reason to conclude that the applicant signed the agreement against his will. He had almost a month (between the first meeting with the representatives of the Regional Administration and signing of the settlement) for thinking over and negotiating the terms of the agreement. Accordingly, the Court does not find any ground to doubt the validity of the settlement reached by the parties and, thus, it considers that the matter was resolved at the domestic level (see *Yaurov and Others*, cited above). The Court further reiterates that in cases in which it is possible to eliminate the effects of an alleged violation and the Government declare their readiness to do so, the intended redress is more likely to be regarded as appropriate for the purposes of striking out the application, the Court, as always, retaining its power to restore the application to its list as provided in Article 37 § 2 of the Convention and Rule 44 § 5 of the Rules of Court (see *Tahsin Acar v. Turkey* [GC], no. 26307/95, § 76 *in fine*, ECHR 2004-III)."

[88] *Eugenia Michaelidou Developments Ltd and Michael Tymvios v. Turkey* (Appl. No. 16163/90), Judgment (Fourth Section–Arrangement), 22 April 2008, not yet reported, para. 16.

implementation difficulties. However, in *Paritchi v. Moldova*,[89] *Leonov v. Russia*[90] and *Podbolotova v. Russia*,[91] the applicants wanted to retract their agreement to withdraw the applications. In *Ogloblin v. Russia*, the Court summarized its practice in the following:

The Court recalls that in the recent cases (…) it made recourse to Article 37 § 1 (c) in the situations where the applicants first settled their cases at the domestic level but then disagreed to regard their case settled and insisted on the examination of their applications. The Court sees no reason to depart from this practice in the present case. It considers that, in the circumstances of the case, it is no longer justified to continue the examination of the application. The Court takes note of the settlement reached between the parties,

---

[89] *Paritchi v. Moldova* (Appl. No. 54396/00), Decision (Fourth Section–Arrangement), 1 March 2005, not reported [no paragraphs]: "By letters of 3 November 2003 and 5 May 2004 the applicant confirmed that she had signed the agreement of 7 October 2003 and that she had received the money provided for therein. At the same time she informed the Court that she did not intend to withdraw her application since she considered that the Government should also compensate her for the non-pecuniary damage suffered. (…) The Court notes that the applicant has agreed to settle her claims on the basis of payment of MDL 205,362 and signed an agreement in this respect, under advice from her lawyer. However later she refused to abide by the terms of the agreement whereby she undertook to withdraw her application from the Court. In these circumstances, the Court considers that it is no longer justified to continue the examination of the application under Article 37 § 1 (c) of the Convention."

[90] *Leonov v. Russia* (Appl. No. 16606/02), Decision (First Section–Arrangement), 10 November 2005, not reported [no paragraphs]: "By a letter of 13 July 2004 the Government informed the Court that on 12 April 2004 the applicant had accepted to withdraw the application on the condition that he should be paid RUR 103,444.50 (~3,000 euros) in respect of the damage sustained. They also submitted a copy of the agreement to that effect and the District Court decision of 12 April 2004 validating the settlement. By a letter dated 12 April 2004 the applicant confirmed that the case had been settled and requested the Court to strike his application out of its list accordingly. On 3 January 2005 the Court received the applicant's letter in which he confirmed the validity of the friendly settlement of 12 April 2004 but retracted his request of strike-out with reference to an unsatisfactory outcome of a fresh set of civil proceedings against the authority." The Court, nonetheless, endorsed the friendly settlement: "The Court takes note of the friendly settlement reached between the parties. As regards the applicant's request of 3 January 2005, the Court notes that it refers essentially to a fresh sets (sic) of proceedings instituted by the applicant against the authority and has no bearing on the fact that the present case has been settled. This being so, the Court is satisfied that the settlement is based on respect for human rights as defined in the Convention and its Protocols and finds no public policy reasons to justify a continued examination of the application (Article 37 § 1 in fine of the Convention). Accordingly, Article 29 § 3 of the Convention should no longer apply to the case and it should be struck out of the list."

[91] *Podbolotova v. Russia* (Appl. No. 26091/02), Decision (First Section–Arrangement), 24 November 2005, not reported [no paragraphs]: "On 14 January 2005 the applicant submitted her reply, in which she confirmed the payment to her of the sum due under the friendly settlement agreement. The applicant then informed the Court that on 21 December 2004 she had obtained a writ of execution in respect of a new judgment in her favour against the State delivered on 7 December 2004, and that the bailiffs had allegedly refused to enforce that judgment in view of the lack of funds. By reference to this refusal, the applicant disagreed to regard her case settled and insisted on the examination of her application." The Court, nonetheless, endorsed the friendly settlement: "The Court takes note of the friendly settlement reached between the parties, the authenticity of the respective agreement submitted by the Government on 2 December 2004 having not been contested by the applicant. As regards the applicant's request of 14 January 2005, the Court notes that it refers essentially to a new set of civil proceedings brought by the applicant against the welfare authority and has no bearing on the fact that the present case has been settled."

the authenticity of the respective agreement having not been contested by the applicant. Against this background, the Court is satisfied that the settlement in the present case is based on respect for human rights as defined in the Convention and its Protocols and finds no reasons of a general character, as defined in Article 37 § 1 *in fine*, which would require the examination of the application by virtue of that Article.[92]

Strikingly, there were numerous cases in which Russian applicants did not react to the Court's request to confirm the friendly settlement after having agreed to settle with the Government.[93]

From the interviews and the practice of the Registry, it becomes clear that there are no negotiations in the large majority of friendly settlements. In all routine friendly settlements, the Case Lawyer sends a written proposal for a settlement together with the communication. Generally, the parties should take this proposal as a signal from the Court that there could be a finding of an ECHR violation and that they have the choice to take, or leave, the draft friendly settlement. This is a purely written procedure. The Registry's personnel rarely calls the parties and gives them additional information about the general advantages of terminating a case via a settlement. The decision as to whether such contact is initiated depends greatly on the character and personality of the Registry staff involved. At any rate, this is not foreseen as a standard course of action in routine friendly settlements. In fact, any attempt to discuss the amount of financial awards in routine friendly settlements can foreclose a settlement before the Court. In this situation, the Registry pursues a general policy of switching to ordinary proceedings. In terms of time and effort, it is easier for the Registry to go straight to an ordinary procedure without bargaining over the financial awards proposed. It has become common to terminate a case with a unilateral declaration when there is resistance on part of the applicant. This is not unproblematic. The Court is under a legal obligation to promote friendly settlements which require, by their very nature, negotiation of the content. Vice-President Rozakis and Judge Villiger argue vigorously in favour of negotiating friendly settlements.[94]

---

[92] *Ogloblin v. Russia* (Appl. No. 30028/02), Decision (First Section–Arrangement), 23 November 2006, not reported.

[93] *Gapicheva v. Russia* (Appl. No. 34746/04), Decision (First Section–Arrangement), 2 March 2006, not reported; *Agibalova and Others v. Russia* (Appl. No. 26724/03), Decision (First Section–Arrangement), 13 April 2006, not reported; *Sharomova v. Russia* (Appl. No. 34750/04), Decision (First Section–Arrangement), 23 May 2006, not reported; *Oganov v. Russia* (Appl. No. 53826/00), Decision (First Section–Arrangement), 23 May 2006, not reported; *Revina v. Russia* (Appl. No. 32150/03), Decision (First Section–Arrangement), 9 November 2006, not reported; *Samoylenko v. Russia* (Appl. No. 7366/04), Decision (First Section–Arrangement), 8 November 2007, not yet reported.

[94] Rozakis, C. L. (2007), p. 1011: "It goes without saying that, as happens in all procedural steps before the Court, applicants are notified of the proposal through its communication to them, and are able to react by submitting observations on its contents." Villiger M. E. (2009), p. 97: "[T]here must always be the possibility of negotiating friendly settlements between the parties even if this looks like a waste of time."

In two types of friendly settlements, however, negotiations play a central role. Negotiations are indispensable as part of real friendly settlements (namely in areas in which no established case law exists) and in pilot friendly settlements. There is no standard agreed upon for the negotiations in those two types of friendly settlements. Nonetheless, interviews with persons who have a long standing experience with negotiations revealed that there are several common traits in the practice of the Court. As a matter of principle, Judges are never involved in friendly settlement negotiations.[95] In fact, negotiations are considered to be incompatible by their very nature with the impartiality of Judges.[96] In general, the Court is represented by one or two persons from the Registry and the Case Lawyer who is familiar with the case, knows the national law and speaks the language. Usually, the negotiations take place in the country concerned and, ideally, in a neutral place.[97]

A precondition for such a mission is a clear signal from both parties that they are willing to settle the case. Before travelling to the country, the Registry prepares a draft of the settlement. On the spot, the Registry delegates hold informal talks with both sides in order to evaluate the differences between the parties' positions and whether it is possible to narrow them down. As part of the negotiations of general measures included in a pilot friendly settlement, it is particularly crucial to have a common understanding of the Court's pilot judgment. The negotiations are more difficult in these situations given that the Registry's representatives have in mind the public interest involved in a pilot friendly settlement. It is not only the resolution of the individual problem which is at stake, but also the systemic violation of the Convention.

Against this background, it becomes clear that this type of friendly settlement aims not only at resolving *ex bono et aequo* but also at remedying a systemic human rights violation. All the actors involved then play different roles and have different interests. This renders the negotiations very difficult, as all actors have to switch from one role to the other. An important conflict arises for the applicant's lawyer.[98] He is first, and foremost, his client's legal representative. His main duty is to settle the case in the best interest of his client. In addition, he has a central interest in the issues at stake. Further, he probably has a professional interest, given that several hundred other potential applicants are affected by the same

---

[95] Lech Garlicki, note 29 *supra*.

[96] Elisabet Fura, Judge at the ECtHR, information given in her interview of 12 January 2009, re-printed in annex 1.

[97] For the negotiations in the pilot friendly settlement after *Broniowski v. Poland* (Appl. No. 31443/96), Judgment (Grand Chamber–Friendly Settlement), 28 September 2005, Reports 2005-IX, 1, para. 6 and *Hutten-Czapska v. Poland* (Appl. No. 35014/97), Judgment (Grand Chamber–Friendly Settlement), 28 April 2008, not yet reported, para. 6, the parties chose the Warsaw office of the European Council headed by Hanna Machińska. See also Wojciech Hermeliński, former lawyer in private practice, currently Judge at the Polish Constitutional Tribunal, information given in his interview of 30 January 2009, interview on file with the authors. The Polish Government financed an interpreter for those who did not speak Polish.

[98] Stefan von Raumer, lawyer in private practice, information given in his interview of 4 March 2009, interview on file with the authors. Wojciech Hermeliński, ibid.

friendly settlement. Naturally, these persons could also become new clients. In addition, the situation of the applicant is also quite difficult. Fate – or the Court's Registry – has not only selected this very person to represent the others in the pilot judgment, but also as an individual whose name will go down in history. The flipside of the coin is that this person has to bear in mind that he, or she, stands for a whole group of persons whose rights have been equally violated. It is needless to say that these actors' divergent interests render the negotiations extremely delicate.

4

Philosophical Background

Friendly settlements in the area of human rights raise fundamental questions. They seem particularly problematic in the context of severe human rights violations. At first glance, financial compensation appears inappropriate where serious human rights violations such as murder or torture are at issue. One is instinctively seized by a feeling of unease when States settle such disputes by payment.

Friendly settlements involve the risk of pay-off by the State Parties concerned. Without full investigation and effective improvement of the legal situation, the problem may be resolved on a purely material basis. At the far end of this development looms a monetarization of human rights, with human rights violations standing for little more than an occasion for earning, or paying money, respectively. A court ruling, by contrast, has broad effects like the public recognition of the alleged damage done by the State and, if that State is found in breach, an authoritative ascertainment thereof. Furthermore, human rights could become by the practice of friendly settlements the object of negotiations and thereby lose their imperative character. The European Court of Human Rights, for its part, may increasingly turn into a forum for negotiations, neglecting its genuine function of authoritative definition and protection of human rights.

The instinctive discontent surrounding the issue of friendly settlements prompts the question of their ethical legitimacy, particularly with respect to violations of Articles 2 and 3 ECHR. One should not only consider friendly settlements under legal, but also under moral aspects. In this chapter, we seek to evaluate friendly settlements in human rights cases from an ethical perspective. By "ethics" and "ethical", we understand the reflection on the moral quality of acts and incidents. "Ethics" and "morality" are closely related concepts, but one should be clear about their respective fields of reference. Whereas "morality" refers to individuals' beliefs about right or wrong conduct, "ethics" denotes the reflection on the theoretical and philosophical aspects of the moral domain. While "morality" is used descriptively in its reference to factual norms, "ethics" refers to the mental acts of reasoning and deliberation about these norms.[1] The complex term "legitimacy" may be understood as a sociological concept, linked up with factual acceptance and compliance, or be employed in its normative sense. In the present context, we use "legitimacy" in this latter sense, meaning the accordance with ethical principles. These ethical principles transcend the ambit of legal norms

---

[1] Cf. Gensler, H. J./Spurgin, E. W. (2008), pp. 89–90; Post, St. G. (2004), pp. 795–841.

which define a minimum standard of co-operative action. Morals and ethics concern wider aspects of living. Therefore, an act may be legal, but not necessarily legitimate from an ethical angle.[2]

I. Human Rights and Ethics

One could venture to dispute the importance of ethical considerations in a legal context. In domestic relations, we are familiar with the distinction between law and ethics. Law is justified on its own terms. In the international realm, however, the situation is more complicated. Ethical and legal categories are intrinsically linked in this area. International human rights protection is not only a legal, but also a moral responsibility. Since international law lacks the backbone of institutionalized coercive power for authoritative rule enforcement, comparable to that which guarantees respect for the law within the nation-state, the effectiveness of international legal rules depends heavily on the voluntary compliance of States. Given the scarcity of coercive authority, compliance is elicited either by a calculation of a State's self-interest, or is motivated by an internal sense of moral obligation.[3] Put differently, in view of the deficiency of international law's enforcement procedures, human rights claims basically remain moral ones. Moreover, international law is in general ethically more questionable than the domestic law of democratic States. It is based on the consent of democratic as well as non-democratic, albeit legally recognized, States. We cannot generally presume that what their representatives agree on is also correct from an ethical standpoint. There is no global *demos* which could serve as legitimizing subject as within the States. It follows from the above that in the international arena, moral considerations with regard to human rights are more salient than in the domestic context.

Compared to the global level, however, a more effective system of human rights enforcement exists in Europe. A success story with regard to the protection of human rights was written with the adoption of the European Convention on Human Rights, which has evolved into the most effective human rights regime in the world. With the entry into force of Protocol no 11 to the Convention, for the first time in legal history, an international treaty granted individuals not only substantive human rights, but also the procedural entitlement to institute international proceedings against a State for allegedly violating such rights. However, since the judgments of the European Court of Human Rights are declaratory, their implementation remains with the Contracting Parties. Furthermore, being an international agreement, the Convention machinery is necessarily shaped by State interests. The friendly settlement procedure provided in the ECHR illustrates this point in that States thereby have the opportunity to save their

---

[2] Cf. Becker, L. C./Becker, C. B. (2001), pp. 960–963.
[3] Hurd, I. (1999), p. 387.

face. At the same time, the *raison d'être* of the Court is precisely to provide a watertight safety net for human rights protection at the European level. Thus, underlying the friendly settlement procedure is a fundamental tension between two main strands that pervade the contemporary system of international law: On the one hand, international law today gives importance to the individual and the protection of human rights;[4] on the other hand, international law is – still – a coordinated system of States, respecting the basic principles of sovereign equality and non-intervention.[5]

The issue of friendly settlements concerning human rights cases serves in part as an instance of the pervasive problem of reconciling these two strands of international law. From the perspective of full and exclusive individual rights protection, an unrestricted enforcement of fundamental rights would be adequate; from the perspective of the States' interests. However, the possibility of avoiding external interventions and dealing autonomously with the problem is absolutely necessary. We have to balance these two conflicting aims.

II. Philosophical Foundations

The ethical assessment of friendly settlements before the European Court of Human Rights is connected with fundamental moral and philosophical questions. Given the variance of stances towards philosophical problems, the evaluation is determined by respective choices for one or another philosophical doctrine. A core distinction in moral philosophy is the one between consequentialism and deontology.[6]

1. Consequentialism and Deontology

Consequentialism is a moral theory which holds that the moral rightness of an act is determined by the consequences of that act. Accordingly, a morally right act is one that maximizes the general good. The paradigmatic case of consequentialist moral thinking is utilitarianism, which originated in late 18th century Britain, but has had a lasting influence down to present times.[7] In contrast to deontology,

---

[4] Brownlie, I. (2008), pp. 553–585 (with references to decisions and literature); Partsch, K. J. (1995), pp. 957–962.

[5] Fassbender, B./Bleckmann, A. (2002), pp. 68–91; Warbrick, C. (1994), pp. 204–229; for the vast discussion on sovereignty in general, see for example, Camilleri, J. A./Falk, J. (1992); Chayes, A./Handler Chayes, A. (1995); Gottlieb, G. (1993); MacCormick, N. (1999); Sassen, S. (1996); Schreuer, Ch. (1993), pp. 447–471; Slaughter, A.-M. (1995), p. 534 et seq.

[6] The most prominent representative of deontological ethics is Kantianism.

[7] As a school of thought, utilitarianism originated with Jeremy Bentham who advanced the ethical principle that an action is right if it produces the greatest good for the greatest number of people, cf. Bentham, J. (1789/1970), p. 11 et seq. John Stuart Mill revised the concept, claiming a connection between utility and justice, Mill, J. St. (2003), p. 217 et seq.

consequentialism denies that moral rightness depends on anything other than consequences, particularly "inner" circumstances such as motives.[8]

In contrast to consequentialism, deontological theories are non-teleological.[9] Deontology denotes that acts are inherently good or evil. What makes an act right is, from a deontological perspective, its conformity with a moral norm.[10] According to Kant, moral normativity is essentially embodied in the *Categorical Imperative:* "Act only in accordance with that maxim through which you can at the same time will that it become a universal law."[11] An act which does not correspond to this rule is morally false, even if its consequences were positive.

It is not possible to resolve the conflict between consequentialism and deontology.[12] Both moral theories have a long-lasting tradition and for both one can raise good reasons. However, one has to be aware of these fundamentally different moral approaches, their impact and one's own standpoint towards them when finding a reflected judgment in special contexts such as the one of friendly settlements concerning human rights disputes.

2. Deontology's Affinity to Rights

Deontology and consequentialism have a different affinity to rights. The idea of inherent and unalienable human rights is primarily rooted in the deontological tradition. From this point of view, human rights should always be respected, regardless of any considerations of utility, and remain unaffected by the social dynamics. Leading theorists conceived human rights as natural rights, being valid independently of social appreciation. John Locke, the most important founder of human rights theory, declared human rights to be owned by human beings even before entering into civil society.[13] Subsequently, Kant spoke about the original right of liberty.[14]

The tension between these ideas and utilitarian reasoning is obvious. From the utilitarian perspective, it would be legitimate to curtail rights if the effects as a whole were positive for society. Therefore, utilitarian calculation stands in contrast to unconditional rights claims. Rights as well as justice have traditionally been a contentious issue for utilitarians.[15] While utilitarianism has traditionally dominated the moral thinking of the Anglo-American world, deontologist ethics

---

[8] See for an overview, Pettit, P. (1991), pp. 42–55; Goodin, R. E. (1991), pp. 241–248; Hooker, B. (2000), pp. 183–204; Frey, R. G. (2000), pp. 165–182; Sinnott-Armstrong, W. (2009).

[9] Rawls, J. (1999), p. 26.

[10] See Davis, N. (1991), pp. 205–218; O'Neill, O. (1991), pp. 175–185; Kamm, F. M. (2000), pp. 205–226; Hill Jr., T. E. (2000), pp. 227–246; Alexander, L./Moore, M. (2009).

[11] Kant, I. (1785/2002), p. 37.

[12] This conflict requires a far more detailed ethical discussion than is possible here.

[13] Locke, J. (1690/1960), para. 87.

[14] Kant, I. (1797/1968), p. 237.

[15] Cf. Lyons, D. (1977), pp. 114–115; Hart, H. L. A. (1983), pp. 198–222; Henkin, L. (1990), p. 1.

have successively gained ground in Anglo-American philosophy, and criticism of utilitarianism has arisen. The greatest impact among the critiques is to be credited to John Rawls' *Theory of Justice*, with its claim that "[u]tilitarianism does not take seriously the distinction between persons".[16] Dworkin's rights theory was likewise of great importance, also rejecting utilitarian maxims.[17]

Although human rights may be justified from a utilitarian standpoint,[18] it proves to be more difficult than on the basis of deontological premises. In a human rights context – like ours – core values of deontology must therefore play a prominent role.

3. Philosophical Approaches and Friendly Settlements

Fundamental ethical assumptions, whether utilitarian or deontological, determine the ethical assessment of friendly settlements. Consequentialists examine whether the consequences of friendly settlements before the European Court of Human Rights may be qualified as good. We can appraise these consequences only approximately. At first sight, some positive effects are apparent: Settlements relieve the Court from examining a case in detail and adjudicating on it. Furthermore, consequences are also positive from the perspective of the Contracting State concerned. The State pre-empts a potential defeat before the Court and consequent displeasing media attention. Moreover, the State Agent may reduce the required efforts. Likewise, the applicant profits from friendly settlements: He, or she, obtains financial compensation and averts a situation of uncertainty.

The consequences for human rights protection in general are more difficult to evaluate. The pressure on States to improve the human rights situation could be declining when many cases are settled. However, these concerns are based on the perspective of rights. As mentioned above, utilitarianism and consequentialism are basically not focused on rights, but on the greater good.[19] The question therefore is whether a possible impairment of legal compliance affects the general welfare adversely. In a speculative manner, we may assume that negative effects will ensue in this respect. The risk of harm inflicted by the State on its own citizens may increase with the practice of friendly settlements. Therefore, it is worth noting that friendly settlements can have negative consequences in the abstract.

---

[16] Rawls, J. (1999), p. 24.

[17] Dworkin, R. (1987), p. 191: "If citizens have a moral right of free speech, the governments would do wrong to repeal the First Amendment that guarantees it, even if they were persuaded that the majority would be better off if speech were curtailed." See also p. 203: "But these are utilitarian arguments in favour of starting one place rather than another, and such arguments are ruled out by the concept of rights."

[18] Lyons, D. (1977), pp. 113–129; Pettit, P. (1988), pp. 42–55; compare Nozick's considerations about utilitarianism of rights: Nozick (1974), pp. 28–30.

[19] For the complex issue of the greater good in consequentialism, compare Sinnott-Armstrong (2009), para. 3.

Although consequentialists may be wary of friendly settlements as an institutionalized practice, their approach will, overall, take a rather favourable view of friendly settlements. On the one hand, preferences of the Court, the States and the applicants are fulfilled. Possible negative consequences, on the other hand, are of a more general and speculative character. In sum, the consequences of friendly settlements are likely to be advantageous.

Deontology proceeds differently: An act is considered rightful in so far as it conforms to a moral norm. Accordingly, the question is whether the action corresponds to universally-acceptable rules. In this regard, individual rights are crucial. It is morally wrong to violate certain fundamental rights, since no one can reasonably approve the creation or sustaining of a social order in which basic interests are disregarded. A corresponding practice is not generally acceptable and therefore morally illegitimate. Consequently, most deontologists call for a sanctions system with respect to the violation of rights. Deontology has an affinity to retributivism, which is a theory requiring that guilty offenders be punished. The link between deontology and retributivism is not a necessary one.[20] However, retributivist claims correspond to deontological principles in demanding the punishment of the guilty independently of the consequences.

Thus, deontological ethics basically calls for a categorical validity of rights as well as the prosecution of their violation. From this perspective, scepticism towards friendly settlements concerning human rights cases is indicated. Although human rights remain valid when cases are settled, their enforcement is impaired. States can avoid the negative consequences of abuses by finding individual solutions. Payments do not amount to an extraordinary financial burden. Thus, the authority of human rights appears to be impaired. Other problems relate to the core values of deontology, such as justice and equality. When individual applicants and the representatives of States settle a case, the situation between the negotiating parties is unbalanced. The experience, resources and influence of the parties are different. The Governments are in a much more favourable position in this respect. Therefore, fairness is not *a priori* guaranteed.

All factors considered, deontological ethics emphasizes the problematic sides of friendly settlements in the area of human rights. The categorical claim to duly sanction human rights violations pits deontological ethics against the use of friendly settlements.

4. Different Evaluation

As an interim result, we note that the approaches of consequentialism and deontology differ on the question of the ethical quality of friendly settlements. The

---

[20] For the concept of consequentialist retributivism, see Moore, M. (1997), p. 156 et seq.; about the relation between deontological moralities and retributivism Alexander, L./Moore, M. (2009), para. 6; for an overview on newer theories of punishment and criminal law Duff, A./Garland, D. (1994).

consequentialist perspective tends to an affirmative view, whereas the deontological position is more sceptical.

Since deontology has an affinity to rights, deontological reasoning may appear more adequate to human rights questions. However, such a conclusion would be quite restrictive. Moreover, it would require a fundamental discourse about the preferences of deontology, which would go beyond the scope of this study. Therefore, we have to find another way to answer our questions. It is nevertheless important to note that a single ethical answer to the problem does not exist. We should not seek indisputable, but rather well-founded, solutions to the question as to when friendly settlements are legitimate.

III. Conflict of Interests

The problem of friendly settlements before the European Court of Human Rights is ethically complex. One has to develop the assessment from the bottom to the top, step by step. Different actors, with divergent interests, are involved in friendly settlements. The consideration of these interests may be a good starting point. The structure of the interests underlying the problem needs to be clarified. Afterwards, the located interests need to be reflected under normative aspects.

1. Individual Interests

a) The Court

The European Court of Human Rights has a vital interest in promoting friendly settlements,[21] particularly, for they allow the Court to dispose of cases more speedily and thus contribute to alleviating its workload crisis.[22] Enhancing the Court's efficiency is pivotal for the very future of the Court. Friendly settlements seem particularly appropriate with regard to routine, well-founded cases which are not of any added value to the Court's jurisprudence.[23]

Friendly settlements, however, do not necessarily promote effectiveness. In difficult cases, the time and effort that the Court's Registry invests into reaching a settlement can be similar to that of an ordinary proceeding.[24] Furthermore, it is

---

[21] The discussion of the interests of the Court must be taken in an institutional sense. The interests of each of the Judges may be different from these.

[22] Courell, A. M. (2006), pp. 142–144.

[23] Cf. Explanatory Report to Protocol no 14 to the Convention for the Protection of Human Rights and Fundamental Freedoms, para. 93, available at: <http://conventions.coe.int/Treaty/EN/Reports/Html/194.htm> (last visited 15 April 2010): "Friendly settlements are therefore encouraged, and may prove particularly useful in repetitive cases, and other cases where questions of principle or changes in domestic law are not involved."

[24] Elisabet Fura, Judge at the ECtHR, information given in her interview of 12 January 2009, reprinted in annex 1.

also a basic interest of the Court to ensure that justice is done. The Court seeks to adjudicate cases and pronounce judgments. Therefore, the judges are somewhat sceptical about friendly settlements, having an affinity to conventional judgments.[25] Under the constraints of a tremendous caseload, however, and as a result of the expansion of the system, the procedure of friendly settlements has gained an important role in case management, enabling the ECtHR to effectively perform its judicial function. Therefore, the Section Registrars, in particular, facilitate the conclusion of friendly settlements.[26]

b) Applicants

The mere fact that an applicant consents to resolve a case by way of a friendly settlement indicates that the latter serves his, or her, interests. Friendly settlements are, on the one hand, a means to quickly end a state of legal insecurity, save time and costs and obtain compensation.[27] Furthermore, settlements allow individuals a greater participation compared with judicial proceedings.[28] On the other hand, the individual applicant may have an interest in an authoritative judgment. The absence of a public acknowledgement that a violation has taken place may keep the applicant from settling the case, particularly where grave violations of the Convention are at issue. However, at least the possibility of settling cases is advantageous for the applicants.

c) Contracting States

The advantages of a settlement for the States are obvious. Through reaching a friendly settlement, States pre-empt adverse publicity which is usually triggered by a negative verdict of the Court. The Contracting State concerned avoids a binding judgment establishing that a particular rule or practice violates human rights. Thereby, the Contracting State gains room to manoeuvre. Furthermore, the Contracting State's representatives are involved in a substantive dialogue about the human rights situation and possibilities to improve it. At the same time, financial compensation connected with a settlement is affordable for the State in comparison to a possibly higher just satisfaction award combined with a finding of a violation. Public funding makes such compensation more affordable. In a nutshell, the option of friendly settlements broadly corresponds to the interests of the State.[29]

As an interim conclusion, it can be noted that the interests of the directly concerned parties are mainly promoting friendly settlements. Particularly the

---

[25] See Elisabet Fura, ibid., who considers negotiating incompatible with the judge's impartiality.

[26] See for the Registry's so-called proactive approach towards friendly settlements, the chapter "Beyond Doctrine", section III.

[27] For a partly falsification of these basic assumptions, see the chapter "Analysis of the Court's Practice", sections II.1. and IV.

[28] Courell, A. M. (2006), p. 139.

[29] Cf. ibid., pp. 137–139.

Contracting States, but also the Court and the applicants, have an interest in settling cases. Apart from these specific considerations, however, general interests also have to be taken into account.

2. General Interests

The general interests are more ambiguous than the individual ones. The interest in an efficiently and effectively functioning system of rights protection supports the case for friendly settlements. Other interests, however, concern the development and the guiding function of law and rather militate against friendly settlements.

a) Functioning of the System

The efficiency of the institutions concerned is not only in the interest of the parties involved, but also in the basic interest of human rights and at the very heart of their protection in general. There is a basic interest in a well-functioning human rights system and, in particular, in the success of the ECtHR.[30] From this perspective, friendly settlements are helpful. The admission and promotion of friendly settlements is an instrument to keep the system working properly.

The decisive variable in this respect is the workload of the Court. Were there only a few cases to adjudge, full judicial review would be adequate. Under heavy caseload conditions, however, alternative means are imperative. In view of the overriding goal of the efficient functioning of the system, certain practices can be viewed as legitimate and even necessary, which may seem sub-optimal from an ideal perspective.

Apart from efficiency, friendly settlements promote the general acceptance of the jurisdiction of the ECtHR. They do not acknowledge winners and losers. No inequality between the parties is created when cases are settled. Co-operative dispute resolution gives rise to common satisfaction. Particularly, the concerns of the applicants are respected, and their specific hardships become part of a common solution. For these reasons, the solution is sustainable and the chances of a successful implementation are better.

b) Development of Law

The development of the law by case law is of eminent importance. From a general perspective, the individual case is a reason to define and enforce law standards. This aspect of jurisdiction is affected by the increase of friendly settlements due to the absence of a detailed judicial evaluation. Agreements which can be resolved according to established case law are not problematic. However, new relevant

---

[30] A well-functioning Court does not only contribute to the protection of human rights on the European level, but renders also the domestic legal system and Government more trustworthy, assuring citizens that their Government merits obedience, etc.

problems call for a detailed juridical investigation and interpretation. A policy of encouraging settlements could result in the underproduction of opinions and precedents.[31]

Apart from resolving specific conflicts, adjudication plays an important role by defining human rights standards and thereby providing essential guidance. Decisions handed down by judges determine which behaviour is regarded as acceptable and which is not. They give a specific meaning to public values embodied in abstract texts. Cases with a potential leading function should therefore not be settled.[32] It is the task of the Court to decide disputes of high general relevance.[33] Accordingly, most of the cases in which friendly settlements are reached concern repetitive cases.[34] The guiding function of these cases for society is of lesser importance and it should not impede settlements.

3. Outcome

Considering the interests involved on the whole, individual and public interests obviously diverge: While individual interests are supportive of friendly settlements, public interests are ambivalent. There is a common interest in an efficient, well-functioning system which supports the use of friendly settlements, whereas the common interests in law finding and development are rather opposed to them. All in all, however, the structure of interests demonstrates the inclination to be favourably disposed to settlements.

Additional aspects must be taken into account, particularly the concerns regarding settlements from an ethical perspective. Although purely interest-based ethics exist,[35] ethics usually transcend the realm of interests. In our context, particularly, the aspect of justice is crucial. One could try to interpret these ethical aspects, especially the aim of justice, as public interests. This attempt appears to be slightly artificial, however, and would not correspond to the very idea of justice. In the following section, justice is therefore discussed separately from interests.

---

[31] Coleman, J./Silver, Ch. (1987), pp. 116–117.

[32] Cf. Elisabet Fura, note 24 *supra*.

[33] Former President of the Court Luzius Wildhaber forcefully argued in favour of the Court's "constitutional" mission. In his view, the way forward for the Court was to determine issues on public policy grounds in order to "concentrate its efforts on decisions of 'principle', decisions which create jurisprudence." See Wildhaber, L. (2002), p. 164.

[34] Ang, F./Berghmans, E. (2005), p. 92.

[35] The most prominent example is Gauthier, D. (1986).

IV. Concerns of Justice

Settling cases, particularly with regard to severe human rights violations, is suspected of being unjust for two main reasons. First, justice demands that severe wrongdoing should be followed by negative consequences. A violation of fundamental human rights should have its appropriate response. This is a duty of fairness towards the affected individual(s). But also justice between States calls for a clear denunciation of breaches of the Convention, and those Contracting States which fulfil their obligations would be disadvantaged if the non-compliance of other States remained without serious consequences. Rich States could buy off their non-compliance with the Convention, while others sought to comply, which would be unfair. Second, the conditions under which the agreement is reached may be unjust. The State and the applicant have a basically unequal position, since the State has far more power and resources than the applicant.

1. Necessity of Sanctions

In the field of international human rights protection, public notification of violations is a central option in sanctioning. It should be emphasized that the latter term is not to be understood in the sense used in domestic criminal law. Apparently, a State cannot, and should not, be condemned like a criminal in domestic law.[36] The judgments of the ECtHR have, nevertheless, an authoritative character and findings of violations evoke adverse publicity. Therefore, States try to avoid an authoritative Court judgment by settling. In this respect, friendly settlements raise questions. Even severe infringements have no serious consequences for the State concerned when cases are settled. A clear and authoritative declaration of violations does not take place. Instead the problem remains hidden on grounds of confidentiality, as a precondition of settlements.

The nature of the specific violation is crucial in this respect. Particularly with regard to severe offences, settlements seem inappropriate. Massive human rights violations demand an investigation and finding by an independent authority, i.e. the Court. For the sake of comparison, it is worthwhile to take a look at the situation within States since there are different procedures regarding the various sorts of legal problems and violations. Breaches of commercial law or family law are dealt with before other fora than criminal cases. Possibilities of sanctioning differ depending on the nature of the respective conflict. Actions which are considered to be criminal have far more serious consequences than other illegal acts. Criminal actions ask for condemnation and punishment, whereas others such as in civil law can be resolved by means of compensation and restitution.[37]

---

[36] Cf. Courell, A. M. (2006), p. 299.
[37] Cf. Shelton, D. (2005), p. 12: "Certain human rights violations are deemed so serious that society labels them criminal. Punishment of these offences does not constitute restitution to the

2. Balance of Power

Justice requirements are relevant with regard to the legitimization of friendly settlements in another way – the parties of settlements have to be in an equal, or at least similar, negotiating position in order to reach a legitimate agreement. A settlement which was actually determined by only one party could not be regarded as just. Serious problems arise in this respect and the unbalanced situation is apparent, especially in cases that individuals bring forward to Strasbourg. The individual applicant and Government Agents are, as mentioned above,[38] usually not on a par with one another. The Government is in a much more favourable position in terms of influence, experience and resources,[39] and this imbalance must not lead to a legal disadvantage. The autonomous representation of interests by the applicant has to be secured. However, a certain imbalance is acceptable – settlements, for example, between companies and individual plaintiffs in private law matters are also characterized by such inequalities. What has to be secured is the free and informed decision-making of the applicant in order to agree to settle a case. The applicant must not be put under pressure and should know about the relevant consequences and circumstances.

3. Efficiency versus Justice

One may reduce the core problem we are dealing with to an antagonism between efficiency and justice. Friendly settlements are legitimate especially under the aspects of efficiency. Although not every friendly settlement serves to promote the Court's efficiency, their overall effect is very likely to be positive. By contrast, settlements are problematic particularly with regard to justice.[40] Aspects of efficiency have become increasingly important for law in recent times and the economic analysis of law particularly focuses on these aspects. This discipline is centred on the effects of law and assesses which existing legal rules are economically efficient and what should be born in mind when setting economically efficient norms.[41] Thereby, negotiations play an important role.[42] Negotiated solutions between parties are usually more efficient than proceedings before courts.[43] In this respect, friendly settlements are basically regarded as positive.

---

victim (…), but imposes a penalty on the perpetrator and restraints to avoid a repetition of the offence."

[38] See section II.3. *supra.*

[39] Ang, F./Berghmans, E. (2005), p. 95; Coleman, J./Silver, Ch. (1987), p. 110; De Schutter, O. (2000), pp. 234–237; Fiss, O. (1984), pp. 1076–1078; Standaert, P. E. (1999), p. 529 et seq.

[40] Cf. Sardaro, P. (2003), p. 613: "Efficiency, however, does not necessarily coincide with justice."

[41] Posner, R. A. (2007); Cooter, R./Ulen, T. (2008); Marciano, A. (2009); Mathis, K. (2009); Miceli, T. J. (2009); Wittman, D. A. (2003).

[42] Mathis, K. (2009), p. 55 et seq.

[43] Polinsky, A. M./Rubinfeld, D. L. (1988), p. 109: "Settlements clearly are superior to trials if one's goal is to minimize transaction costs."

From the perspective of justice, however, substantial criticism has been levelled against friendly settlements. For instance, Owen Fiss has formulated an important critique concerning settlements, paying special attention to justice.[44] As he points out, the purpose of adjudication should not be reduced to the resolution of disputes between parties. According to him, the public officials are neither supposed to maximize the ends of private parties, nor to simply secure peace, but rather to explicate and enforce the values embodied in authoritative statutes. This duty is, in his eyes, not discharged when the parties settle: "Parties might settle while leaving justice undone."[45] Other authors also stress that justice must not be sacrificed on grounds of efficiency. Jules Coleman and Charles Silver point out that this possibly takes place when cases are settled. With regard to justice, they prefer it when persons who make valid allegations receive full compensation whereas those who advance false arguments are denied such benefits. Ascertaining whether the submitted claims are valid can be best handled through adjudication. Indeed, the correlation between vindication at trial and the actual validity of a claim is high. Therefore, justice requires (costly) litigation.[46] Coleman and Silver have other reservations regarding settlements. They consider that bargaining may be unfair, as agreements could be contrary to public policy, and third party effects and interests could be neglected.[47]

Clearly, a tension exists between the aims of justice and efficiency. This state of affairs had already been observed in the context of the antagonism between consequentialism, which, amongst other things, strives for efficiency, and deontology, which focuses on justice. A similar relationship exists with regard to interests, which tend to be supportive of settlements, and ethical concerns, centred on the value of justice. Thus, the antagonism between efficiency versus justice appears to be a crucial aspect of the legitimacy of friendly settlements before the European Court of Human Rights.

In respect of the connection between human rights and deontological reasoning, one may grant priority to justice. However, the criteria of efficiency deserve some attention, especially for the proper functioning of the Court.[48] Accordingly, we have to strike a balance between the basic demands of efficiency and justice.[49]

---

[44] Fiss, O. (1984), pp. 1073–1090.
[45] Ibid., p. 1085.
[46] Coleman, J./Silver, Ch. (1987), pp. 106–108.
[47] Ibid., pp. 109 et seq.
[48] Section III.2. *supra.*
[49] Mathis, K. (2009), p. 201.

V. Finding the Balance

The aforementioned tensions do not allow a categorical affirmation or rejection of friendly settlements. Rather, conciliative solutions have to be found which take into account all important aspects. Thereby, a line may be drawn between an abstract and a specific level.

1. Abstract Level

a) Formal Conditions

First of all, some formal conditions can be established for friendly settlements to be legitimate. The process of negotiations leading to settlements has to meet certain requirements. The general requirement is fairness.

At the time of the settlement, the applicant shall be (1) free in his, or her, decision-making and (2) informed as much as possible about the circumstances and consequences of his, or her, decision. Regarding the first point, this means that no pressure can be exerted on the applicant in order to obtain his consent to an agreement. Neither the State nor the Court's administration must announce negative consequences in cases where an agreement is rejected. If an agreement does not result, the procedure before the ECtHR has to take its usual course without disadvantages for the non-co-operating party. Regarding the second point, the parties must have the required cognitive ability for making decisions. Particular regard should be given to the deficiencies of the applicants in comparison with the State and its representatives, in terms of knowledge and experience, and the applicants should be compensated as much as possible. The applicants have to be fully informed about the prospects and options of acting. It is particularly unacceptable to manipulatively induce parties to agree to friendly settlements by downplaying their chances of success before the Court. Truth and transparency are both indispensable and essential. Overall, the settlements must correspond to the free and informed will of the parties. Particularly concerning individual applicants, these requirements may imply efforts on the part of the Court and the Court should adopt adequate measures to achieve this.[50]

b) Conditions on the Merits

Beside formal aspects, content-related questions are also important for the legitimacy of friendly settlements. Settlements are not appropriate for every legal problem. Insofar as applicants have not been injured in their physical or mental integrity, friendly settlements are usually unproblematic. Financial and other disadvantages (like loss of time and opportunities, etc.) can be financially

---

[50]   De Schutter, O. (2000), p. 259; Zwaak, L. (2006), p. 225.

compensated. The situation is different with physical injuries, especially regarding violations in the context of Articles 2 und 3 ECHR.

An agreement may be inappropriate for the adjudication of these specific violations, since an official investigation and findings might be necessary. One has not, however, to assume a categorical illegitimacy of friendly settlements with regard to these cases.[51] Instead, special justification is required regarding settlements in the area of Articles 2 and 3 ECHR.

Friendly settlements concerning the right to life and the prohibition of torture may be regarded as initially suspect. Serious concerns oppose friendly settling in such cases. However, other aspects improve the legitimacy of friendly settlements on such issues and may compensate for the drawbacks. The following aspects are particularly relevant:

- A settlement may be appropriate if the facts are so unclear that the application could probably not be proved, yet some evidence of a violation is apparent.

- Friendly settlements become more acceptable when the Court is so heavily overburdened that its functionality is endangered.

- The nature of the violation plays an important role. If the case in question is not about planned violations, but rather about unintended consequences, settling becomes more legitimate.

- The existence of previous case law is crucial. If settlements can be oriented towards it, they are more adequate.

- Friendly settlements become more legitimate if they are combined with substantial legal improvements in the field of human rights.

Furthermore, additional conditions with regard to the content of the agreement itself should be taken into account. The compensation which is foreseen in the agreement must be in due proportion to the damage that the parties suffered.

Altogether, these various aspects can legitimize friendly settlements. At least implicitly, a justification is required for all friendly settlements concerning serious human rights violations. It would also be desirable to include an explicit justification in the official publication. The Court could include, for instance, a passage where it would clarify why the friendly settlement is, in its view, an adequate way to resolve the conflict and why it is preferable to an ordinary judgment.[52]

---

[51] As the Inter-American Court of Human Rights does: *Velásquez Rodriguez Case (Preliminary Objections)*, Inter-Am. Ct. H. R. (Ser. C.) No. 1 (1994), 26 June 1989, para. 43. Cf. Staendart, P. E. (1999), p. 524 et seq.

[52] Occasionally, the Court commented on the appropriateness of a friendly settlement agreement. One example concerns an interstate conflict, the case *Denmark v. Turkey* (Appl. No. 34382/97), Judgment (First Section–Friendly Settlement), 5 April 2000, Reports 2000-IV, 1, which is discussed in the chapter "Beyond Doctrine", section I.6. There, the Court writes (paras. 23–24): "The Court takes note of the friendly settlement reached between the parties. It observes that the above agreement, *inter alia*, makes provision for the payment of a sum of money to the applicant Government, includes a statement of regret by the respondent Government concerning the occurrence of

2. Specific Level

With regard to the legitimacy of friendly settlements before the European Court of Human Rights, limits are set to an abstract consideration. The specific circumstances of the particular case play an important role. Therefore, a careful examination of each particular case is indispensable. In doing so, the many aspects mentioned above have to be considered; even new aspects, which cannot be anticipated in an abstract way, may play a role. The different aspects carry special weight depending on the specific circumstances. For instance, the problem of a heavy caseload may be so urgent that efficiency aspects are predominant. Furthermore, investigation problems may seem insurmountable in the case concerned and may therefore be crucial for settling the case. The meaning of some aspects does not become fully clear unless the particular situation is considered. The requirement of free will, for example, has to be interpreted with regard to the individual persons concerned with their individual backgrounds.

A balancing of the different interests as well as the ethical values is indispensable. A *Güterabwägung* has to take place, i.e. a harmonization of the different fundamental values. The fundamental conflict between efficiency and justice cannot be resolved once and for all. Instead, an agreement between the differing forces has to be reached. Thereby, every case has to be carefully examined by considering the ethical validity of a – possible – friendly settlement.

3. Concrete Examples

With regard to particular cases, the considerations mentioned previously need to be further specified. Most friendly settlements concern problems which do not raise grave ethical problems, like the length of proceedings under Article 6 (1) ECHR or property cases under Article 1 Protocol no 1.[53] These cases are generally well-suited for settlement.[54] Other cases are, however, ethically problematic. This is especially the case with Turkey which has settled many cases in very sensitive

---

occasional and individual cases of torture and ill-treatment in Turkey, emphasises, with reference to Turkey's continued participation in the Council of Europe's police-training project, the importance of the training of Turkish police officers and in addition provides for the establishment of a new bilateral project in this area. Furthermore it has been decided to establish a continuous Danish-Turkish political dialogue which will also focus on human rights issues and within which individual cases may be raised. The Court also observes the changes to the legal and administrative framework which have been introduced in Turkey in response to instances of torture and ill-treatment as well as the respondent Government's undertaking to make further improvements in the field of human rights – especially concerning the occurrence of incidents of torture and ill-treatment – and to continue their co-operation with international human rights bodies, in particular the Committee for the Prevention of Torture."

[53] See the chapter "Analysis of the Court's Practice", section I.

[54] Cf. Elisabet Fura, note 24 *supra*.

areas, such as ill-treatment in custody,[55] police violence,[56] or even instances of loss of life.[57]

---

[55] *Çavuşoğlu v. Turkey* (Appl. No. 32983/96), Judgment (Third Section–Friendly Settlement), 6 March 2001, not reported; *Kaplan v. Turkey* (Appl. No. 24932/94), Judgment (Second Section–Friendly Settlement), 26 February 2002, not reported; *Z.Y. v. Turkey* (Appl. No. 27532/95), Judgment (Second Section–Friendly Settlement), 9 April 2002, not reported; *Mehmet Özcan v. Turkey* (Appl. No. 29856/96), Judgment (Second Section–Friendly Settlement), 9 April 2002, not reported; *Yıldız v. Turkey* (Appl. No. 32979/96), Judgment (Fourth Section–Friendly Settlement), 16 July 2002, not reported; *Aydın v. Turkey* (Appl. No. 29289/95), Judgment (Second Section–Friendly Settlement), 16 July 2002, not reported; *Benzan v. Croatia* (Appl. No. 62912/00), Judgment (First Section–Friendly Settlement), 8 November 2002, not reported; *P.K. v. Poland* (Appl. No. 37774/97), Judgment (First Section–Arrangement), 6 November 2003, not reported; *Yücetürk v. Turkey* (Appl. No. 76089/01), Decision (Third Section–Arrangement), 4 October 2005, not reported; *Yazici v. Turkey* (Appl. No. 73033/01), Decision (First Section–Arrangement), 11 July 2006, not reported; *Lee v. Ukraine* (Appl. No. 7697/02), Decision (Fifth Section–Arrangement), 6 November 2006, not reported; *Kölge v. Turkey* (Appl. No. 20227/02), Decision (Second Section–Arrangement), 21 November 2006, not reported; *Tekmek v. Turkey* (Appl. No. 50035/99), Decision (Second Section–Arrangement), 28 November 2006, not reported; *Acar v. Turkey* (Appl. No. 74941/01), Decision (Third Section–Arrangement), 30 August 2007, not reported; *Lipcan v. Moldova* (Appl. No. 32737/03), Decision (Fourth Section–Arrangement), 9 October 2007, not yet reported; *Talankovs v. Latvia* (Appl. No. 5001/04), Decision (Third Section–Arrangement), 4 January 2008, not yet reported; *Rudeanu v. Romania* (Appl. No. 21428/03), Decision (Third Section–Arrangement), 2 September 2008, not yet reported.

[56] *Özbey v. Turkey* (Appl. No. 31883/96), Judgment (First Section–Friendly Settlement), 31 January 2002, not reported; *H.D. v. Poland* (Appl. No. 33310/96), Judgment (Fourth Section–Friendly Settlement), 20 June 2002, not reported; *Ramazan Sari v. Turkey* (Appl. No. 41926/98), Judgment (First Section–Arrangement), 31 July 2003, not reported; *Bozkurt v. Turkey* (Appl. No. 35851/97), Judgment (First Section–Arrangement), 31 March 2005, not reported; *Abid v. France* (Appl. No. 3541/05), Decision (Third Section–Arrangement), 5 July 2007, not yet reported; *Sumak v. Turkey* (Appl. No. 29735/03), Decision (Third Section–Arrangement), 11 October 2007, not yet reported; *Bojagić v. Croatia* (Appl. No. 37421/04), Decision (First Section–Arrangement), 23 October 2007, not reported.

[57] *Cantürk v. Turkey* (Appl. No. 30779/96), Decision (Second Section–Friendly Settlement), 22 March 2001, not reported; *Canpolat v. Turkey* (Appl. Nos. 28506/95; 30780/96), Decision (Second Section–Friendly Settlement), 22 March 2001, not reported; *Kiraç v. Turkey* (Appl. No. 30844/96), Decision (Second Section–Friendly Settlement), 22 March 2001, not reported; *Oral and Others v. Turkey* (Appl. No. 27735/95), Judgment (First Section–Friendly Settlement), 28 March 2002, not reported; *Siddik Yasa v. Turkey* (Appl. No. 22281/93), Judgment (First Section–Friendly Settlement), 27 June 2002, not reported; *Yakar v. Turkey* (Appl. No. 36189/97), Judgment (Fourth Section–Friendly Settlement), 26 November 2002, not reported; *Adali v. Turkey* (Appl. No. 31137/96), Judgment (Third Section–Friendly Settlement), 12 December 2002, not reported; *Yalçin v. Turkey* (Appl. No. 31152/96), Judgment (Third Section–Friendly Settlement), 12 December 2002, not reported; *Soğukpinar v. Turkey* (Appl. No. 31153/96), Judgment (Third Section–Friendly Settlement), 12 December 2002, not reported; *Şen v. Turkey* (Appl. No. 31154/96), Judgment (Third Section–Friendly Settlement), 12 December 2002, not reported; *Yaman v. Turkey* (Appl. No. 37049/97), Judgment (First Section–Arrangement), 22 May 2003, not reported; *Oğraş and Others v. Turkey* (Appl. No. 39978/98), Judgment (Fourth Section–Arrangement), 28 October 2003, not reported; *Memiş v. Turkey* (Appl. No. 42593/98), Judgment (Second Section–Arrangement), 21 February 2006, not reported; *Karakoyun v. Turkey* (Appl. No. 51285/99), Decision (Third Section–Arrangement), 30 March 2006, not reported; *Çardakçi and Others v. Turkey* (Appl. No. 39224/98), Judgment (Fourth Section–Arrangement), 23 January 2007, not yet reported; *Kabul and Others v. Turkey* (Appl. No. 24873/02), Decision (Second Section–Arrangement), 4 September 2007, not yet reported; *Pektaş and Others v. Turkey* (Appl. No. 73722/01), Decision (Second Section–Arrangement), 4 December 2007, not yet reported.

Under certain conditions, settlements in these areas can be legitimate. The facts may be hard to prove, the applicant may be in desperate need, or there may be other reasons the parties are willing to close the matter. In any case, a detailed consideration of such settlements by the Court is necessary. Particularly, the free and informed will of the applicant and the fairness of the agreement must be secured. Only solid justifications can legitimize settlements concerning degrading and inhuman treatment or the killing of innocent persons.

The problems are even more obvious with respect to cases of torture, and settlements have also been concluded with respect to such allegations.[58] The incidents in question are often of a grave nature:

- In *Erat and Sağlam v. Turkey*, the applicant alleged that she was physically and psychologically tortured while in custody. On the first day of her custody, according to her statements, she was taken to a dark room and stripped naked. She was subjected to sexual harassment and subjected to electric shocks through her nipples, sexual organs, fingers and toes. She was, as she complained, strung up by her arms in the form of torture known as "Palestinian hanging" and was again subjected to electronic shocks. She was not allowed to go to the toilet and was not given food and drink. Furthermore, she was threatened and beaten.[59]

- In *Süleyman Kaplan v. Turkey*, the applicant alleged to have been beaten, hung by his arms, given electric shocks to his body, and threatened with death during his interrogation by police officers.[60]

- In *N.Ö. v. Turkey*, the allegations are equally severe. The applicant complained that her husband was stripped naked and strung up by his arms using the form of torture known as "Palestinian hanging", that the police officers fastened a

---

[58] *Gelgeç and Özdemir v. Turkey* (Appl. No. 27700/95), Judgment (Second Section–Friendly Settlement), 1 March 2001, not reported; *Erat and Sağlam v. Turkey* (Appl. No. 30492/96), Judgment (Fourth Section–Friendly Settlement), 26 March 2002, not reported; *Önder v. Turkey* (Appl. No. 31136/96), Judgment (Third Section–Friendly Settlement), 25 July 2002, not reported; *Süleyman Kaplan v. Turkey* (Appl. No. 38578/97), Judgment (Third Section–Friendly Settlement), 10 October 2002, not reported; *N.Ö. v. Turkey* (Appl. No. 33234/96), Judgment (First Section–Friendly Settlement), 17 October 2002, not reported; *Keçeci v. Turkey* (Appl. No. 38588/97), Judgment (Fourth Section–Friendly Settlement), 26 November 2002, not reported; *Özgür Kiliç v. Turkey* (Appl. No. 42591/98), Judgment (Second Section–Arrangement), 22 July 2003, not reported; *Sünnetçi v. Turkey* (Appl. No. 28632/95), Judgment (Second Section–Arrangement), 22 July 2003, not reported; *Aruç v. Turkey* (Appl. No. 39675/98), Decision (Fourth Section–Arrangement), 6 April 2004, not reported; *Salman v. Turkey* (Appl. No. 63745/00), Decision (Fourth Section–Arrangement), 3 April 2007, not yet reported; *Trybus v. Poland* (Appl. No. 31503/03), Decision (Fourth Section–Arrangement), 15 May 2007, not yet reported; *Kaya v. Turkey* (Appl. No. 20981/03), Decision (Second Section–Arrangement), 13 May 2008, not yet reported; *İçen and İçen v. Turkey* (Appl. No. 10268/02), Decision (Second Section–Arrangement), 6 May 2008, not yet reported.

[59] *Erat and Sağlam v. Turkey*, ibid., para. 8.

[60] *Süleyman Kaplan v. Turkey*, note 58 *supra*, para. 8.

rope to his genitals and pulled on it, and that electric shocks were administered to his body.[61]

- In *Keçeci v. Turkey*, similar incidents were in dispute. According to the applicant, the police officers beat and hit him on the head with a nailed stick, squeezed his testicles, kept him in a cold room and did not allow him to go to the toilet. Furthermore, the applicant complained that the police officers sexually harassed his wife and attempted to rape her in his presence.[62]

Settlements concerning such cases are highly problematic. Financial compensation could hardly be adequate with regard to such severe human rights violations. The value of justice is sorely affected when intense human suffering remains without serious consequences for the offenders. The reasons justifying a settlement in such cases would need to be very strong. Normally, they would not measure up to the required legitimacy level. As a general rule, torture cases are therefore not suitable for settlements. Problems of this type call for investigation and adjudication.

VI. The Specific Case of Unilateral Declarations

A special problem concerning the justification of friendly settlements raises the question whether settlements should include an acknowledgment that the respective State committed a breach of the Convention. This problem appears to be even more acute with regard to unilateral declarations. Under unilateral declarations, proceedings can be concluded against the will of the applicant if the State concerned accepts its responsibility and offers appropriate compensation.[63]

1. Acceptance of Unilateral Declarations

In recent years, the ECtHR has increasingly accepted unilateral declarations. Unilateral declaration were even accepted with respect to Articles 2 and 3 ECHR, namely in Turkish cases. These declarations regularly contain an acknowledgment of the violation, which is, however, phrased in relatively abstract terms. The wording used in *Akman v. Turkey* serves as a model for other cases: "The Government regrets the occurrence of individual cases of death resulting from the use of excessive force as in the circumstances of Murat Akman's death notwithstanding existing Turkish legislation and the resolve of the Government to prevent such actions."[64]

---

[61] *N.Ö. v. Turkey*, note 58 *supra*, para. 12.

[62] *Keçeci v. Turkey*, note 58 *supra*, para. 9.

[63] See Ang, F./Berghmans, E. (2005), pp. 98–104; Myjer, E. (2007), pp. 318–327; Rozakis, C. L. (2007), pp. 1003–1014; Zwaak, L. (2006), pp. 233–235.

[64] *Akman v. Turkey* (Appl. No. 37453/97), Judgment (First Section–Unilateral Declaration), 26 June 2001, Reports 2001-VI, 223, para. 24. Continued as follows: "It is accepted that the use

Recently, more unilateral declarations have been rejected. In general, the reason for rejection was that the Court did not regard the compensation offered as appropriate.[65] In *Tahsin Acar v. Turkey*, the responsibility admitted by the Government was not sufficient. The Court noted that:

The Court accepts that a full admission of liability in respect of an applicant's allegations under the Convention cannot be regarded as a condition *sine qua non* for the Court's being prepared to strike an application out on the basis of a unilateral declaration by a respondent Government. However, in cases concerning persons who have disappeared or have been killed by unknown perpetrators and where there is *prima facie* evidence in the case-file supporting allegations that the domestic investigation fell short of what is necessary under the Convention, a unilateral declaration should at the very least contain an admission to that effect, combined with an undertaking by the respondent Government to conduct, under the supervision of the Committee of Ministers in the context of the latter's duties under Article 46 § 2 of the Convention, an investigation that is in full compliance with the requirements of the Convention as defined by the Court in previous similar cases.[66]

The practice concerning unilateral declarations has had its impact on the configuration of friendly settlements. For a long time, settlements have not included acknowledgments of infringement, but often a statement that the settlement would not amount to an evaluation of the allegation's validity.[67] Since *Akman v. Turkey*, however, most Turkish settlements concerning similar violations embodied a clause of acknowledgement of the respective violation. The phrases vary in detail,

of excessive or disproportionate force resulting in death constitutes a violation of Article 2 of the Convention and the Government undertakes to issue appropriate instructions and adopt all necessary measures to ensure that the right to life – including the obligation to carry out effective investigations – is respected in the future." Cf. *Toğcu v. Turkey* (Appl. No. 27601/95), Judgment (Second Section–Unilateral Declaration), 9 April 2002, not reported, para. 30; *T.A. v. Turkey*, (Appl. No. 26307/95), Judgment (Second Section–Unilateral Declaration), 9 April 2002, not reported, para. 58.

  [65] *Melnic v. Moldova* (Appl. No. 6923/03), Judgment (Fourth Section), 14 November 2006, not reported; *Venera-Nord-Vest Borta A.G. v. Moldova* (Appl. No. 31535/03), Judgment (Fourth Section), 13 February 2007, not yet reported; *Wawrzynowicz v. Poland* (Appl. No. 73192/01), Judgment (Fourth Section), 17 July 2007, not yet reported; *Estate of Nitschke v. Sweden* (Appl. No. 6301/05), Judgment (Third Section), 27 September 2007, not yet reported; *Tur v. Poland* (Appl. No. 21695/05), Judgment (Fourth Section), 23 October 2007, not yet reported; *Krawczak v. Poland* (Appl. No. 40387/06), Judgment (Fourth Section), 8 April 2008, not yet reported; *Pohlen v. Slovenia* (Appl. No. 28457/03), Decision (Third Section), 3 June 2008, not yet reported; *Carević v. Slovenia* (Appl. No. 17314/03), Decision (Third Section), 3 June 2008, not yet reported; *Sadura v. Poland* (Appl. No. 35382/06), Judgment (Fourth Section), 1 July 2008, not yet reported; *Figiel v. Poland (No. 1)* (Appl. No. 38190/05), Judgment (Fourth Section), 17 July 2008, not yet reported; *Zając v. Poland* (Appl. No. 19817/04), Judgment (Fourth Section), 29 July 2008, not yet reported; *Krzysztof Kaniewski v. Poland* (Appl. No. 49788/06), Judgment (Fourth Section), 30 September 2008, not yet reported; *Śliwa v. Poland* (Appl. No. 10265/06), Judgment (Fourth Section), 2 December 2008, not reported.

  [66] *Tahsin Acar v. Turkey* (Appl. No. 26307/95), Judgment (Grand Chamber), 6 May 2003, Reports 2003-VI, 1, para. 84.

  [67] See for example, *Gündüz and Others v. Turkey* (Appl. No. 31249/96), Judgment (First Section–Friendly Settlement), 14 November 2000, not reported, para. 14.

according to the circumstances of the case, but have the same basic form: The Government expresses its regret and accepts in general terms that a certain treatment constitutes a violation of the Convention. However, since 2005, Turkish friendly settlements with this regret clause have become rarer.[68]

2. Ethical Evaluation

Friendly settlements correspond to the free will of the parties. Therefore, they do not necessarily require an element such as the unilateral acknowledgment of violations. On the contrary, their very sense and function is often to avoid a public acknowledgment. It is at the parties' discretion to decide whether a public statement shall be part of the settlement and, if so, which form it shall have. However, the situation is different with regard to unilateral declarations. The argument of free will as an important element of legitimization is lacking in these cases. The applicant prefers to continue the proceedings, but they are concluded against his, or her, will. Thus, a deficit in terms of legitimacy emerges and must be compensated for by other legitimizing elements.

The unilateral acknowledgment of having violated the rules of the ECHR is crucial in this regard. Through the publicly announced acceptance of responsibility, the outcome of the case can have a similar effect to a Court decision. The State does, somehow, judge itself and anticipating a finding of violation, the State declares itself responsible for the violations. To a certain extent, this unilateral concession is capable of compensating for the absence of the applicant's agreement. In order to have this effect, however, the declaration of the State has to be unambiguous and precise. Its precision and clarity must be comparable to a judgment of the Court, which it is, in a certain manner, replacing. General phrases of regret are not sufficient. The unilateral declaration has to include a clear explanation about what had happened and an unambiguous statement about the State's responsibility.[69] Otherwise, the termination of the case is not legitimate with respect to the applicant's demand for an independent, objective judgment.[70]

Unilateral declarations may be appropriate with regard to purely repetitive cases, in which only financial interests are involved. Generally, however, the instrument should be cautiously used. Although they may be nearly identical in content, a unilateral act can never be equated with a judgment handed down by an independent authority. The unilateral act has a voluntary character and allows the State to autonomously define what is said. Moreover, if the applicant wants to continue the proceedings, obtaining a favourable outcome following an ordinary procedure appears obviously possible to him or her. The Court should

---

[68] See the chapter "Legal Framework and Practice", section III.4.
[69] Courell, A. M. (2006), pp. 268, 318; Zwaak, L. (2006), p. 235.
[70] Cf. Ang, F./Berghmans, E. (2005), pp. 101–102.

therefore hear the case.[71] Generally, the European Court of Human Rights has to acknowledge its responsibility to protect human rights and to implement the rules of the Convention.

VII. Considering Specific Cases

In assessing the legitimacy of friendly settlements, fundamental differences have become apparent. An inherent conflict of values underlies the problem, namely a clash between efficiency and justice. On the one hand, friendly settlements provide the Court with a tool for a more expeditious processing of cases. In a time when an ever-increasing caseload threatens the very survival of the Court, gains in the Court's efficiency are more than welcome. On the other hand, friendly settlements come with serious drawbacks. The absence of a thorough judicial scrutiny, as well as of an authoritative finding of an alleged Convention violation, appear, on the face of it, to undermine the authority of human rights, particularly in cases involving breaches of Articles 2 and 3 ECHR.

Furthermore, different interests collide with respect to friendly settlements. Generally, friendly settlements cater to the interests of the respondent States and the applicants involved. General interests, however, are somewhat opposed to the settlement of cases. While the general interest in the functioning of the system favours settlements, interests in the development of law and the authoritative enforcement of human rights are rather opposed to them. Being basically factual, this conflict of interests does not have the same ethical importance as the conflict of values. It underscores, however, the complexity of the problem and the necessity of finding balanced solutions.

It would almost border on squaring a circle if one wanted to definitively resolve the basic conflict of efficiency and justice. The question of the ethical legitimacy of friendly settlements does not concern an *a priori* clear right, or a yes or no answer, since it must be contextualized. The assessment can ultimately only be undertaken on a case-by-case basis. On the whole, settlements seem especially appropriate in repetitive, routine cases where the Court's case law is clear. Against this, settlements are *prima facie* doubtful where violations of Articles 2 and 3

---

[71] Cf. critical remarks of Judges Costa and Loucaides in *Toğcu v. Turkey*, note 64 *supra* [no paragraphs]; *T.A. v. Turkey*, note 64 *supra*, Judge Loucaides dissenting: "However, the Government do not accept any responsibility for the violation complained of and do not undertake to carry out any investigation in respect of the disappearance of the applicant's son, which was the subject-matter of the application (...) I fear that the solution adopted may encourage a practice by States – especially those facing serious or numerous applications – of 'buying off' complaints for violations of human rights through the payment of *ex gratia* compensation, without admitting any responsibility and without any adverse publicity (...). This practice will inevitably undermine the effectiveness of the judicial system of condemning publicly violations of human rights through legally binding judgments and, as a consequence, it will reduce substantially the required pressure on those Governments that are violating human rights."

ECHR are at issue. Settlements in this area call for a special justification which should be part of the official declaration of their acceptance by the Court. As a general rule, the more serious the violations in question are, the stronger the justification has to be.

Due to a lack of clear borderlines on the merits, the legitimacy of friendly settlements strongly depends on the correctness of the procedure. It is essential that the will of the applicant to settle is free and based on comprehensive knowledge. It is the task of the Court to guarantee the compliance with these principles. Friendly settlements whose formally correct development is doubtful shall not be accepted.

Generally, one needs to strike a balance between the conflicting interests. No single aspect is decisive and crucial in itself. Depending on the specific situation and the particular case, the ethical legitimacy of friendly settlements varies and the concrete circumstances need to be carefully considered. Ultimately, only an individual evaluation in each and every case can form the basis for an ethical assessment.

5

Analysis of the Court's Practice
in Selected Areas

The ECtHR's jurisprudence relating to friendly settlements sometimes lacks uniformity and is difficult to classify into precisely circumscribed categories. In order to be understood properly, it often needs to be seen against the background of the political situation in a given country, the systemic nature of the alleged violations, or the circumstances of the individual case. In an attempt to provide a useful insight into the practice, this chapter examines different countries, different ECHR areas and different procedures used by the Court. The samples to be studied were selected on the basis of a thorough analysis of the Court's case law and the interviews were conducted with the most relevant actors. The objective of this multi-levelled analysis is to uncover some of the most relevant and complex features of friendly settlements. The practice of two countries, Turkey and Poland, under three different provisions, Articles 2, 3 and 6 (1) ECHR, is considered on the basis of the statistics collected for this study. This chapter also examines whether the premise "more money faster", often associated with friendly settlements, really holds.

The choice of countries for this part was based on the number and the nature of friendly settlements concluded by the respective Contracting States. Poland and Turkey featured among those Contracting States which generate the highest numbers of judgments and findings of violations in Strasbourg. They have also concluded the most friendly settlements and arrangements at a very consistent rate over the years.[1] Both States have grappled in the past with certain systemic human rights problems. Settlements under Articles 2 and 3 ECHR represent a substantial part of the applications lodged against Turkey. This country is also an interesting Contracting Party to evaluate, as – unlike other countries – it has accepted serious ECHR violations as part of friendly settlements. Further, the Turkish cases gave an opportunity to the Court to develop the new instrument of unilateral declaration to alleviate its heavy work load. Poland has settled most of its cases under Article 6 ECHR, and this research will, thus, focus on this area. As a result of its communist past, Poland has also brought new human rights

---

[1] For the difference between friendly settlements and arrangements, see the chapter "Beyond Doctrine", section I.1.

issues to Strasbourg which had not been touched upon before by its Western counterparts.

Settlements under Articles 2 and 3 ECHR provide a useful sample for a detailed study. They are a challenging test case for the practice itself, given the difficult moral questions that they implicate. The appropriateness of this sample stems from the fact that it represents a circumscribed set of cases. Further, it forms part of the core human rights guarantees enshrined in the ECHR. In this area, there are various ethical obstacles for the conclusion of friendly settlements. Despite this, certain Contracting States have settled many more cases under Articles 2 and 3 ECHR than under other provisions. Thus, these settlements represent some of the most difficult, and most serious, aspects of the procedure. In contrast to this, Article 6 ECHR provides a different analytical basis, as it relates to a guarantee which has a much less substantive and much more procedural content. It is also an area where Contracting States have massively concluded friendly settlements. It is characterized by clone and repetitive cases, which could be seen as being particularly well suited for friendly settlements. Finally, Article 6 (1) ECHR cases constitute established case law where the result is often clearly known in advance. In these cases, we have focused on civil proceedings and we have excluded criminal proceedings. It was considered that they had to be separated, as they implicated different interests and policies.

The statistics collected for this study cover the period of activity of the new Court: the overall statistics and the statistics per country (friendly settlements and arrangements) encompass the period between 1 November 1998 and 1 January 2009, whereas the statistics relating specifically to Turkey and Poland encompass the period between 1 January 1999 and 1 January 2009. The country-specific statistics are intended to compare the level of compensation and the duration of proceedings in judgments, friendly settlements and unilateral declarations. The sample chosen for this purpose was thought to be representative of a gradual progression in the amount of friendly settlements, arrangements and judgments. Articles 2, 3 and 6 ECHR were chosen in an attempt to demonstrate the various advantages and disadvantages of using friendly settlements and arrangements instead of unilateral declarations and standard proceedings in very different ECHR areas. The Court's judgments and decisions were both taken into account, while the Commission's Reports and rejected unilateral declarations were excluded. In all cases, the number of recipients was used instead of the number of applicants in the case. This approach was thought to be more reliable as it filtered out technical inheritance issues.

We included the three categories of awards, namely pecuniary, non-pecuniary, as well as costs and expenses. The Court, however, sometimes provided a single amount for pecuniary and non-pecuniary damages. As it was not possible to find the respective sum for each type of award, this amount was divided in two in order to be able to provide pecuniary and non-pecuniary averages. By dividing these types of awards, it was possible to define more precisely the exact amount of money that was granted for the alleged violation or the violation found by the Court. Thus, issues which were not directly related to the financial value of the violation were filtered out.

While most awards granted by the ECtHR were in Euros, some were also in Turkish Liras, UK Pounds Sterling, Polish Złoty, Danish Krones and US Dollars. In order to harmonize these amounts, we converted these currencies into Euros. The yearly average exchange rate was used. This approach appeared to be more accurate than using the daily rates, as the amount was not usually paid out on the date of the judgment, but rather six months later (and there could also be delays in enforcement). To make things simpler, we took into account the yearly exchange rate. We then calculated the average of compensation per recipient and per year. Given that we compared these amounts on a yearly basis, we considered that it was not necessary to calculate the inflation rate as the variation would not be significant. In parts where we commented on the overall statistics and on their evolution, we had to take inflation into account in order to reflect the changes in prices over the years. For this purpose, we applied a mathematical formula that we developed in consultation with a financial expert.[2]

I. General Overview of the Statistics

1. Case Analysis

a) Rise in the Number of Friendly Settlements

Despite views to the contrary,[3] the continued relevance of friendly settlements has reaffirmed itself over the years and is clearly reflected in the overall statistics collected for this study. As the years progressed, the amount of friendly settlements and arrangements steadily increased.[4] From 2007 to 2008, the number of friendly settlements and arrangements has nearly doubled, dissipating any doubts as to the importance of their role. This increase in friendly settlements and arrangements is closely related to the ECtHR's expanding caseload.[5] In this context, it is nonetheless important to note that, while the number of applications has increased, the number of friendly settlements and arrangements has continued

---

[2] The inflation rates in percentages for the period between 1998 and 2008 were: 1.1 per cent (1998); 1.1 per cent (1999); 2.1 per cent (2000); 2.3 per cent (2001); 2.2 per cent (2002); 2.1 per cent (2003); 2.1 per cent (2004); 2.2 per cent (2005); 2.2 per cent (2006); 2.1 per cent (2007); 3.3 per cent (2008), see <http://epp.eurostat.ec.europa.eu/tgm/table.do?tab=table&language=en&pcode =tsieb060&tableSelection=1&footnotes=yes&labeling=labels&plugin=1> (last visited 20 March 2010). See also the explanatory note in annex 2, "I. Statistics – Explanatory Note".

[3] See Weber, G. S. (2007); Courell, A. M. (2006), pp. 68–73.

[4] See the statistics in annex 2, "Table II/1. Statistics 1998–2008".

[5] This statement finds less support in the statistics that were collected in Turkish and Polish cases.

to rise at a much faster pace. This trend demonstrates that friendly settlements and arrangements have started playing a greater role in the Court's workload, and they now represent a greater proportion of the case law in comparison to the earlier years. This is due to a change in policy used by the ECtHR and to the type of cases that have flooded the Court's docket in the recent years. In fact, the Court has been more proactive in its approach to friendly settlements and has encouraged Contracting States to settle.[6] Moreover, repetitive cases which do not add anything new to the Court's jurisprudence now tend to be handled via friendly settlements or arrangements. Many of these cases have recently made it to Strasbourg and this could explain the rise in friendly settlements. Further, when the new Court came into being, it was faced with an increasing caseload and a large amount of straightforward cases which it may have wanted to process quickly. This may have also given rise to an increase in friendly settlements. Finally, there were in total almost two and a half times more arrangements than friendly settlements. This great difference in amount could be due in part to the fact that Contracting States – concerned with their sovereignty – still prefer to handle issues domestically and seek the Court's intervention only when necessary.

Turkey and Poland have made the greatest and the most consistent use of both friendly settlements and arrangements over the years. Most of these cases concerned Articles 2 and 3 ECHR. An important number of complaints also concerned expropriation of property under Article 1 Protocol no 1.[7] The highest amount of arrangements per year appeared in 2008 and it was generated by Polish cases. This number of arrangements can be explained in part on the basis of the pilot judgment handed down in *Broniowski v. Poland*.[8] Indeed, the *Broniowski* case generated a significant number of pilot arrangements, which contributed substantially to the dramatic increase of arrangements in the recent years.

b) Unilateral Declarations

An important parallel development to settlements that needs to be highlighted is the increase in unilateral declarations made by the Contracting States. While the number of applications has risen in the recent years, the number of unilateral declarations – similarly to friendly settlements and arrangements – grew at

---

[6] For the proactive approach, see the chapter "Beyond Doctrine", section III.

[7] See for examples, *Önsöz v. Turkey* (Appl. No. 73676/01), Decision (Third Section–Friendly Settlement), 21 November 2002, not reported; *Akbaş v. Turkey* (Appl. No. 42744/98), Decision (Third Section–Friendly Settlement), 21 November 2002, not reported; *Türkoğlu and Turan v. Turkey* (Appl. No. 42745/98), Decision (Third Section–Friendly Settlement), 21 November 2002, not reported; *Aydın v. Turkey* (Appl. No. 42747/98), Decision (Third Section–Friendly Settlement), 21 November 2002, not reported; *Doğan v. Turkey* (Appl. No. 73675/01), Decision (Third Section–Friendly Settlement), 21 November 2002, not reported; *Ayan v. Turkey* (Appl. No. 73789/01), Decision (Third Section–Friendly Settlement), 21 November 2002, not reported.

[8] *Broniowski v. Poland* (Appl. No. 31443/96), Judgment (Grand Chamber–Pilot Judgment), 22 June 2004, Reports 2004-V, 1; *Broniowski v. Poland* (Appl. No. 31443/96), Judgment (Grand Chamber–Friendly Settlement), 28 September 2005, Reports 2005-IX, 1.

a much faster pace. Overall, Poland and the United Kingdom have made the greatest use of this instrument. Until 2006, there were only a few unilateral declarations per year. However, their number has risen exponentially from 2006 to 2007 and it has nearly doubled from 2007 to 2008. During these last two years, most unilateral declarations concerned Article 6 (1) ECHR cases which appeared to add little to the existing jurisprudence. In 2007, the United Kingdom and Poland made the greatest amount of declarations, with 36 per cent and 23 per cent respectively of all unilateral declarations made. Slovenia was the third greatest beneficiary of unilateral declarations that year with 21 per cent. In 2008, the Polish unilateral declarations represented almost half of all unilateral declarations made by all Contracting States that year. Germany did not make a substantial amount of unilateral declarations, but it has been consistent in using them in length cases. The remaining countries made several unilateral declarations, but there was no consistent trend in their practice.

2. Country-Specific Problems

a) Notorious Italian Cases

The examination of the case law revealed that Italy was the third most important beneficiary of friendly settlements and arrangements before the ECtHR. In addition, Italy generated the greatest amount of friendly settlements per year in 2000. This important inflow of cases was due to a systemic problem at the domestic level which gave rise to an important amount of repetitive or clone cases. There were few arrangements that year, but this has changed over time. This trend emerged prior to the implementation of important legislative reforms at the domestic level. Most of the complaints which appeared before the ECtHR related to the length of civil proceedings. In this context, many cases concerned the recognition of a right to an invalidity pension[9] and the right to assistance for a person at home.[10] These cases did not add anything new to the Court's existing

---

[9] See for examples, *A.S. v. Italy* (Appl. No. 43077/98), Judgment (Second Section–Friendly Settlement), 22 June 2000, not reported; *Ascierto v. Italy* (Appl. No. 40363/98), Judgment (Second Section–Friendly Settlement), 22 June 2000, not reported; *Fusco v. Italy* (Appl. No. 43049/98), Judgment (Second Section–Friendly Settlement), 22 June 2000, not reported; *Ciaramella v. Italy* (Appl. No. 43035/98), Judgment (Second Section–Friendly Settlement), 22 June 2000, not reported; *D'Adonna v. Italy* (Appl. No. 43031/98), Judgment (Second Section–Friendly Settlement), 22 June 2000, not reported; *Bello v. Italy* (Appl. No. 43063/98), Judgment (Second Section–Friendly Settlement), 22 June 2000, not reported.

[10] See for examples, *C.B. v. Italy* (Appl. No. 43094/98), Judgment (Second Section–Friendly Settlement), 22 June 2000, not reported; *Circelli v. Italy* (Appl. No. 43107/98), Judgment (Second Section–Friendly Settlement), 22 June 2000, not reported; *G.A. v. Italy* (Appl. No. 43096/98), Judgment (Second Section–Friendly Settlement), 22 June 2000, not reported; *G.P. v. Italy* (Appl. No. 43093/98), Judgment (Second Section–Friendly Settlement), 22 June 2000, not reported; *Galietti v. Italy* (Appl. No. 43104/98), Judgment (Second Section–Friendly Settlement), 22 June 2000, not reported; *Lombardi and 7 Others v. Italy* (Appl. No. 43103/98), Judgment (Second Section–Friendly Settlement), 22 June 2000, not reported.

jurisprudence. It was clearly mentioned in the text of the decisions that the Section Registrar proposed the parties to settle. The Court thus actively intervened to stop the inflow of similar cases.

Italy has breached the ECHR on a regular basis in cases dealing with excessive length of domestic proceedings. Significantly, the Committee of Ministers had found that the situation was inadequate and could represent a danger for a democratic State based on the rule of law.[11] In response to this, Italy adopted a number of measures to remedy this problem, including the *Pinto* Law.[12] The *Pinto* Law was issued by the Italian Parliament in 2001 and it put into place a domestic remedy which allowed applicants to obtain compensation in the case of excessively lengthy proceedings. It is possible that the *Pinto* Law has stemmed to some extent the inflow of applications by the repatriation of cases before the Italian courts. It has, however, also generated a fair share of additional problems. The first decisions handed down following the entry into force of the *Pinto* Law revealed that the interpretation of domestic and Strasbourg judges differed considerably.[13] The domestic interpretation of Article 6 (1) ECHR has generated additional complaints before the ECtHR.[14] The *Pinto* Law did not resolve the dilemmas which it was initially meant to remedy. Its enactment has therefore played a minor role in stemming the flow of lengthy Italian proceedings cases to Strasbourg.

b) Lengthy Proceedings in German Cases

A less known aspect of the settlement practice in Strasbourg is the situation of German cases. Eighty per cent of these concerned the length of proceedings under Article 6 (1) ECHR. Apart from a few rare exceptions, all of them were arrangements[15] and unilateral declarations.[16] The highest number appeared in 2007 and

[11] See for examples, *Di Mauro v. Italy* (Appl. No. 34256/96), Judgment (Grand Chamber), 28 July 1999, Reports 1999-V, 31; *Bottazzi v. Italy* (Appl. No. 34884/97), Judgment (Grand Chamber), 28 July 1999, Reports 1999-V, 1; *Ferrari v. Italy* (Appl. No. 33440/96), Judgment (Grand Chamber), 28 July 1999, not reported.

[12] Law No. 89 of 24 March 2001, in *Gazzetta Ufficiale*, 3 April 2001, No. 78; Candela Soriano, M. (2008), p. 426.

[13] Ibid., p. 427; Mirate (2007), p. 425.

[14] Candela Soriano, M. (2008), ibid.

[15] See for examples, *Grimm v. Germany* (Appl. No. 27696/05), Decision (Fifth Section–Arrangement), 13 March 2007, not yet reported; *Kozlowski v. Germany* (Appl. No. 23462/03), Decision (Fifth Section–Arrangement), 15 May 2007, not yet reported; *Beau v. Germany* (Appl. No. 16996/03), Decision (Fifth Section–Arrangement), 11 September 2007, not yet reported; *Krächan v. Germany* (Appl. No. 39644/03), Decision (Fifth Section–Arrangement), 27 November 2007, not yet reported; *Löhr v. Germany* (Appl. No. 10465/05), Decision (Fifth Section–Arrangement), 4 December 2007, not yet reported.

[16] See for examples, *Oleksiw v. Germany* (Appl. No. 31384/02), Decision (Fifth Section–Unilateral Declaration), 11 September 2007, not yet reported; *Parry v. Germany* (Appl. No. 24378/02), Decision (Fifth Section–Unilateral Declaration), 16 October 2007, not yet reported; *Hassdenteufel v. Germany* (Appl. No. 21214/03), Decision (Fifth Section–Unilateral Declaration), 6 November 2007, not yet reported; *Talewski v. Germany* (Appl. No. 16308/05), Decision (Fifth Section–

this figure slightly decreased in 2008. Despite this small downturn, the German length of proceedings arrangements are generally on the rise. The German Government developed a standard approach over the years. It was no longer considered appropriate to defend length of proceedings cases in Strasbourg, especially if years had passed since the first instance decision. Instead, the Government asked the Registry to make a proposal as part of a friendly settlement. The applicants accepted these proposals in most cases. When they refused, the Government then proceeded with a unilateral declaration. In these declarations, the Government accepted that there had been a violation and paid 90 per cent of the amount proposed by the Registry. The rationale behind this practice was that when the applicant obtained a declaration of violation he, or she, was then entitled to less money.[17] The Government usually informed the Court in a letter about the points which could have made the length of proceedings understandable or justifiable. The Government assumed that the level of compensation depended on whether the duration of proceedings could be justifiable or whether the applicant could be responsible for the delay. Since then, this practice has been discontinued for reasons on which we can only speculate. One way to explain this development is that the Court is no longer willing to accept such declarations. It is yet to be seen whether more German length of proceedings arrangements will appear in the future.

c) Critical Areas in Russian Cases

A surprising aspect of the friendly settlement and arrangement practice is also revealed by the Russian cases. In spite of Russia's long-standing reluctance to co-operate with Strasbourg, it has nonetheless been willing to settle a certain amount of cases via arrangements. The number of arrangements concluded by Russia remains, however, insignificant in comparison with the massive amount of applications originating from this country. Russia mostly concluded arrangements in cases concerning Article 6 (1) ECHR and Article 1 Protocol no 1 regarding the non-enforcement or delayed enforcement of a domestic judgment.[18] It remains to be seen whether this trend will replicate itself in the upcoming cases.

Unilateral Declaration), 6 November 2007, not yet reported; *Guttschuss v. Germany* (Appl. No. 771/04), Decision (Fifth Section–Unilateral Declaration), 8 January 2008, not yet reported; *Zingraf v. Germany* (Appl. No. 27156/05), Decision (Fifth Section–Unilateral Declaration), 12 February 2008, not yet reported.

[17] Almut Wittling-Vogel, German Agent before the ECtHR, information given in her interview of 28 January 2009, interview on file with the authors.

[18] See for examples, *Sevostyanov v. Russia* (Appl. No. 76736/01), Judgment (First Section–Arrangement), 12 April 2007, not yet reported; *Dremlyugin v. Russia* (Appl. No. 75136/01), Judgment (First Section–Arrangement), 12 April 2007, not yet reported; *Gaydukov v. Russia* (Appl. No. 75038/01), Judgment (First Section–Arrangement), 12 April 2007, not yet reported; *Grechko v. Russia* (Appl. No. 75037/01), Judgment (First Section–Arrangement), 12 April 2007, not yet reported; *Shishlov v. Russia* (Appl. No. 75035/01), Judgment (First Section–Arrangement), 12 April 2007, not yet reported.

A rather worrisome development in the Russian context was the adoption by the Court of an arrangement concluded in the *Samoylenko* case.[19] The decision mentions that the Government informed the Court in a letter that it had settled the case with the applicant and that he no longer intended to pursue his application. The Court then invited the applicant to submit his observations or to confirm his wish to withdraw the application. The applicant did not reply and was informed once more that the failure to submit observations might result in a strike out of the application. There was no response on the part of the applicant despite indications that he had received the letter. The Court inferred from this lack of reply that the applicant did not intend to pursue his application. It therefore appears curious that this lack of reaction was rubber-stamped by the endorsement of the arrangement. The Court was much more critical of the Russian Government's attempts to have cases struck out on the basis of unilateral declarations. It has regularly found that the Russian Government "(...) failed to submit any formal statement capable (...) offering a sufficient basis for finding that respect for human rights as defined in the Convention does not require the Court to continue its examination of the case (...)".[20] Despite an increasing use of unilateral declarations, the Court nonetheless stays on guard when it comes to the frequent use of this instrument by certain countries.

d) *Transitional Solutions in Swedish and UK Cases*

Established democracies with good human rights records have also used friendly settlements and arrangements in order to remedy transitional problems in the legal order. The statistics collected revealed that Sweden has concluded a number of arrangements in cases relating to length of proceedings before domestic tax authorities.[21] These were complex questions of a rather technical nature and would not

---

[19] *Samoylenko v. Russia* (Appl. No. 7366/04), Decision (First Section–Arrangement), 8 November 2007, not yet reported.

[20] See for examples, *Kukalo v. Russia* (Appl. No. 63995/00), Judgment (First Section), 3 November 2005, not reported, para. 43; *Levin v. Russia* (Appl. No. 33264/02), Judgment (First Section), 2 February 2006, not reported, para. 19; Nikolayev v. Russia (Appl. No. 37927/02), Judgment (Third Section), 2 March 2006, not reported, para. 34; *Fedotova v. Russia* (Appl. No. 73225/01), Judgment (First Section), 13 April 2006, not reported, para. 28; *Alekhina and Others v. Russia* (Appl. No. 22519/02), Judgment (First Section), 13 April 2006, not reported, para. 20; *Blagovestnyy v. Russia* (Appl. No. 72558/01), Judgment (Second Section), 4 July 2006, not reported, para. 25; *Terekhova v. Russia* (Appl. No. 21425/04), Judgment (Fifth Section), 13 July 2006, not reported, para. 14; *Shamina v. Russia* (Appl. No. 70501/01), Judgment (Fifth Section), 13 July 2006, not reported, para. 12; *Polupanova v. Russia* (Appl. No. 21447/04), Judgment (Fifth Section), 13 July 2006, not reported, para. 11.

[21] See for examples, *Manasson v. Sweden* (Appl. No. 41265/98), Judgment (Fourth Section–Friendly Settlement), 20 July 2004, not reported; *Karlsson v. Sweden* (Appl. No. 68721/01), Decision (Second Section–Arrangement), 4 October 2005, not reported; *Grill v. Sweden* (Appl. No. 38503/02), Decision (Second Section–Arrangement), 22 November 2005, not reported; *Korva v. Sweden* (Appl. No. 27818/04), Decision (Second Section–Arrangement), 9 May 2006, not reported; *Mathiasson v. Sweden* (Appl. No. 6161/04), Decision (Second Section–Arrangement), 9 May 2006, not reported; *Danielsson v. Sweden* (Appl. No. 38458/04), Decision (Second Section–Arrangement), 12 September 2006, not reported; *Josefsson v. Sweden* (Appl. No. 38477/04), Decision (Second

have contributed greatly to the jurisprudence of the Court. A number of these cases were repetitive and have been awarded the same amount of compensation. They were eventually remedied at this domestic level through the enactment of required legislation. This change in the domestic situation is also reflected in the statistics collected; the number of arrangements reached the highest point in 2006 and then suddenly decreased.[22] Arrangements therefore contributed to the resolution of the problem.

A similar solution to a transitional problem was used by the United Kingdom with regard to legislation concerning widows' benefits. Under domestic law, only widows were entitled to benefits when their husbands died, as these were only aimed at women. The applicants claimed that the domestic legislation infringed Articles 8 and 14 ECHR. This legislation has generated a significant number of applications to Strasbourg. As of 9 April 2001, a new law entered into force allowing both widows and widowers whose spouses died on, or after, that date to claim benefits. The number of arrangements concerning this legislation has more than doubled from 2007 and 2008 as a result of an increase in applications.[23] The Government agreed to settle all claims made by widowers arising out of the legislation applicable prior to April 2001. In this manner, the Government handled a transitional problem in its domestic legislation via arrangements.

II. Turkish Settlement Practice under Articles 2 and 3 ECHR

1. Overview

Articles 2 and 3 ECHR settlements concluded by Turkey represent an important sample to study, as they are challenging and indicative of the difficulties that pervade the practice of friendly settlements.[24] Concluding friendly settlements in cases relating to the right to life, and prevention of torture and ill-treatment,

---

Section–Arrangement), 12 September 2006, not reported; *Kotsidis v. Sweden* (Appl. No. 9933/03), Decision (Third Section–Arrangement), 20 February 2007, not yet reported.

[22] See the statistics in annex 2, "Table II/3. Statistics per Country 1998–2008: Arrangements".

[23] See for examples, *Rathfelder v. United Kingdom* (Appl. No. 63507/00), Judgment (Fourth Section–Arrangement), 9 January 2007, not yet reported; *Gamble v. United Kingdom* (Appl. No. 68056/01), Judgment (Fourth Section–Arrangement), 9 January 2007, not yet reported; *Crew v. United Kingdom* (Appl. No. 61928/00), Judgment (Fourth Section–Arrangement), 9 January 2007, not yet reported; *Beard v. United Kingdom* (Appl. No. 27951/02), Decision (Fourth Section–Arrangement), 24 June 2008, not yet reported; *Bilby v. United Kingdom* (Appl. No. 76944/01), Decision (Fourth Section–Arrangement), 24 June 2008, not yet reported; *Heron v. United Kingdom* (Appl. No. 66181/01), Decision (Fourth Section–Arrangement), 24 June 2008, not yet reported; *Worsley v. United Kingdom* (Appl. No. 71758/01), Decision (Fourth Section–Arrangement), 24 June 2008, not yet reported; *Nugent v. United Kingdom* (Appl. No. 77423/01), Decision (Fourth Section–Arrangement), 24 June 2008, not yet reported.

[24] For a detailed review of the implementation of the ECHR in Turkey, see Kaboğlu, I. O./Koutnatzis, S.-I.(2008).

could be viewed as disquieting.[25] Terminating a case without the finding of a violation, and without the provision of general measures, in an area with systemic violations may not improve the human rights situation in a given country. It is an area where justice, policy issues, financial questions and closure often come into play and may render it difficult for the parties and the Court to strike the right balance.

The statistics collected demonstrate that the arrangements and friendly settlements concerning Articles 2 and 3 ECHR represent 17.5 per cent of all friendly settlements and arrangements concluded by Turkey during the period considered (1998 to 2008).[26] At the same time, the judgments under Articles 2 and 3 ECHR correspond to 11 per cent of all judgments handed down against Turkey. The first friendly settlements concerning Article 2 ECHR and Articles 2 and 3 ECHR combined were concluded in 2001. The first friendly settlements under Article 3 ECHR were reached in 2000. There were in total 55 more judgments than friendly settlements and arrangements. Initially, the number of friendly settlements and arrangements was low, but it gradually increased over time. The total number of recipients was slightly higher in judgments than in friendly settlements and arrangements. In addition, the Turkish Government paid out almost two million Euros more in judgments than in friendly settlements; a recipient received on average approximately 3,000 EUR more in judgments than in friendly settlements and arrangements; and the average duration of proceedings lasted about a year longer in judgments than in friendly settlements and arrangements.

Another important phenomenon to take into account in this context is the rise in unilateral declarations. The Government made five unilateral declarations and one of them was rejected. As part of these declarations, the Turkish Government paid out approximately half a million Euros between the years 1998 to 2008. On average, applicants could obtain about six times more money in a unilateral declaration than in a friendly settlement and in a judgment. The negotiations leading towards a unilateral declaration lasted almost the same time as in friendly settlements, but they were about a year shorter than in ordinary proceedings. The number of unilateral declarations made is not very high and can be viewed as a circumstantial rather than as a consistent trend.

The prevailing assumption regarding the advantages which friendly settlements might have over ordinary proceedings appears to be partly disproved by these statistics. It was initially considered that applicants could obtain more money within a shorter time frame in a friendly settlement than in ordinary proceedings. Some Court Sections seem to support this rationale in the settlement negotiations. As the amount of compensation is not established by the Court, the parties

---

[25] For the philosophical questions concerning friendly settlements, see the chapter "Philosophical Background".

[26] See the statistics in annex 2, "Table II/2. Statistics per Country 1998–2008: Friendly Settlements", "Table II/3. Statistics per Country 1998–2008: Arrangements" and "Table X/2. Average Length of Negotiations".

can agree on a sum which is higher than the one granted in similar cases. The higher amount of compensation could then be an incentive for applicants to settle. Applicants would also be able to obtain compensation quicker and the Government would avoid a possibly shameful violation. Although logical and sensible, this initial premise has only proven to be true in part. As mentioned above, the average recipient was able to receive more money in judgments than in friendly settlements or arrangements. It was nonetheless correct to assume that the ordinary proceedings would last longer than the conclusion of friendly settlements or arrangements.

While for some, less fortunate, applicants it may have been worth waiting another year for this amount of money, others – as well as the lawyers advising them – may question whether it is worth the risk and the additional waiting. If applicants are less concerned about the finding of violation, judgments and friendly settlements may both be viable options giving rise to similar advantages. Applicants can obtain up to 3,000 EUR more in a judgment, but this may take another year and the outcome of the proceedings remains uncertain. If applicants are primarily motivated by the moral aspect of the complaint and seek a finding of violation, then the choice between a friendly settlement and a judgment is much clearer. In this situation, friendly settlements have even fewer advantages than for claimants concerned with closure. The advantages which friendly settlements and arrangements seemed to offer initially are therefore overshadowed by trends that can be seen in these general statistics. The analysis of settlements under specific Articles depicts a more subtle picture of the advantages and disadvantages that can be drawn from friendly settlements.

2. Article 2 ECHR Cases

Settlements and judgement under Article 2 ECHR concerned the substantive and the procedural aspect of this provision, namely deaths and disappearances as well as the lack of effective investigation. Overall, there were four times more judgments than friendly settlements and fifteen times more judgments than arrangements concerning the right to life. The statistics indicate that Turkey settled at a rate of 21.7 per cent in cases concerning Article 2 ECHR.[27] As with most cases, the procedure in Article 2 ECHR was written and no oral negotiations as such took place. The proceedings were conducted through the intermediary of the Court.

The ordinary proceedings took about a year longer than friendly settlements and about two years longer than unilateral declarations. Further, the difference

---

[27] See Weber, G. S. (2007), where the settlement rate was initially used as an indicator in statistical analysis of the friendly settlements. We took into account arrangements, friendly settlements, judgments and accepted unilateral declarations. We left out, however, rejected unilateral declarations.

between the amount of compensation that could be obtained in a friendly settlement and a judgment was insignificant; an applicant could obtain at most 14 EUR more in a judgment. There was nonetheless a very important difference in the amount that could be obtained in a judgment, a unilateral declaration and an arrangement. These indications should be analysed carefully as there were only four unilateral declarations and four arrangements. Turkey paid out almost two and a half times more in judgments than in arrangements and almost 26 times more in unilateral declarations than in arrangements.

Between the years 2004 and 2006, there was a general increase in the number of judgments finding a violation of Article 2 ECHR, with 14 in 2004, 18 in 2005 and 13 in 2006. Otherwise, there were only a few judgments per year. In general, there have been fewer findings of violations under Article 2 ECHR since 2006. The highest amount of friendly settlements concluded per year appeared in 2002. This number started to decrease significantly after 2005. This could indicate the Turkish Government's discontentment with the Court's practice resulting in a more cautious approach towards friendly settlements. The greatest number of unilateral declarations was made in 2002 and the greatest number of arrangements emerged in 2007. In fact, the number of arrangements seems to have increased in the recent years, but it remains to be seen how this trend will evolve. There is no growing tendency in the use of unilateral declarations under Article 2 ECHR.

Turkey has paved the way towards the Court's acceptance of unilateral declarations in cases concerning severe human rights violations. The first unilateral declaration was made in *Akman v. Turkey*,[28] an Article 2 ECHR case where the applicant's son was shot by the security forces. Shortly after, additional unilateral declarations followed in *Haran v. Turkey*[29] and *Toğcu v. Turkey*,[30] both Articles 2 and 3 ECHR cases which concerned the disappearance of the applicants' sons. Although negotiations had been conducted in these cases, they failed because the parties were not able to agree on a friendly settlement. The Government then submitted a unilateral proposal seeking a strike out on the basis of Article 37 ECHR, which was opposed by the parties. The text of the statement mentioned that the Government regretted the events and accepted that unrecorded deprivations of liberty, insufficient investigations into allegations of disappearance, excessive or disproportionate force resulting in death and unjustified use of force resulting in death constitute a violation of Article 2 ECHR. The cases were not

---

[28] *Akman v. Turkey* (Appl. No. 37453/97), Judgment (First Section–Unilateral Declaration), 26 June 2001, Reports 2001-VI, 223.
[29] *Haran v. Turkey* (Appl. No. 25754/94), Judgment (Fourth Section–Unilateral Declaration), 26 March 2002, not reported.
[30] *Toğcu v. Turkey* (Appl. No. 27601/95), Judgment (Second Section–Unilateral Declaration), 9 April 2002, not reported. See also Leach, P. (2005), p. 79. It should be noted, however, that the *Toğcu* case was restored to the list. See *Toğcu v. Turkey* (Appl. No. 27601/95), Judgment (Second Section), 31 May 2005, not reported.

resolved, but the Chamber decided nevertheless to strike them out of its lists. This disquieting development was limited when the *Tahsin Acar* case reached the Grand Chamber.[31] In its reasoning, the Court laid down important principles for the strike out of cases, which seems to have halted a potential flow of unilateral declarations under Articles 2 and 3 ECHR in Turkish cases.[32] There have only been four Article 2 ECHR unilateral declarations, and it therefore cannot be claimed that they constitute a consistent practice. The Court is careful in accepting such declarations with regard to grave human rights violations underlined by systemic problems. In those cases, ordinary proceedings or friendly settlements recognizing the violation still prevail.

While there are in general no findings of violation in friendly settlements and arrangements, the Turkish Government was asked by the Court to accept in a certain form the violations that it had allegedly perpetrated. The first Article 2 friendly settlement as well as the first regret regarding a disappearance and the acceptance that unrecorded deprivation of liberty and insufficient investigation constituted a violation of Article 2 ECHR appeared in 2001.[33] These statements are tremendously important, but they do not allow a case to be re-opened at the domestic level; this can only be done following a judgment finding a violation.[34] They can be interpreted as acknowledgements of violations, but they are most likely merely apologies. They were mostly made in repetitive cases and they have also included some general measures.[35]

A survey of the case law reveals that Turkey is one of the only countries to have accepted such serious violations as part of the friendly settlements that it concluded. The Court usually has to arrange fact-finding missions in hard cases, where the alleged events are difficult to prove. In such situations, there is consistent case law demonstrating that the Court shifts the burden of proof to the State.[36] The Turkish Government could thus have expected that it would have the burden of proof and that it could lose these cases. This may have constituted an important incentive to settle. At that time, the Court may have lacked confidence in the Turkish legal system and it therefore required the authorities to

---

[31] *Tahsin Acar v. Turkey* (Appl. No. 26307/95), Judgment (Grand Chamber), 6 May 2003, Reports 2003-VI, 1.

[32] Philip Leach, Professor of Law and lawyer in private practice, information given in his interview of 9 July 2009, interview on file with the authors.

[33] *İ.İ., İ.Ş., K.E. and A.Ö. v. Turkey* (Appl. Nos. 30953/96; 30954/96; 30955/96; 30956/96), Judgment (First Section–Friendly Settlement), 6 November 2001, not reported.

[34] Serkan Cengiz, lawyer in private practice, information given in his interview of 30 March 2009, reprinted in annex 1.

[35] For more information, see the chapter "Legal Framework and Practice", section III.4.

[36] See for examples, *McCann and Others v. United Kingdom* (Appl. No. 18984/91), Judgment (Grand Chamber), 27 September 1995, Series A, Vol. 324; *Kaya v. Turkey* (Appl. No. 22729/93), Judgment (Chamber), 19 February 1998, Reports 1998-I, 297; *Osman v. United Kingdom* (Appl. No. 23452/94), Judgment (Grand Chamber), 28 October 1998, Reports 1998-VIII, 3124; *Kılıç v. Turkey* (Appl. No. 22492/93), Judgment (Grand Chamber), 28 March 2000, Reports 2000-III, 75.

acknowledge the violations. Further, the Court may have wanted to come up with an approach that appealed to the applicant and which looked appropriate. It is possible that the Court was seeking a concession on the part of a State which had been repeatedly found responsible for numerous ECHR violations. Finally, it is also possible that the Court wanted to compensate, for ethical reasons, the endorsement of a friendly settlement in such a sensitive area with an explicit acknowledgment of a violation.

Overall, it is not more financially advantageous for applicants to seek a judgment instead of a friendly settlement in Article 2 ECHR cases, as the sums paid out are similar. Ordinary proceedings can nevertheless take considerably longer than the conclusion of a friendly settlement. Most applicants in these circumstances are less concerned about the financial award and the duration of the proceedings. They want to find out what happened to their loved ones and who is responsible.[37] In many of the disappearance cases, there is no information as to whether the person is dead or alive. It could therefore be in their interest to wait a year longer in order to obtain a finding of violation than to settle. In this manner, applicants would also not foreclose the possibility of re-opening the case at the domestic level. It is therefore generally disadvantageous for applicants to conclude friendly settlements in cases concerning Article 2 ECHR. This is not the case, however, for the less numerous applicants who would only wish to terminate the case. A friendly settlement could also be advisable in a situation where a person has little financial resources, where the case is weak and where there is no need to re-open proceedings at the domestic level.

On the Government's side, it is naturally more beneficial to seek friendly settlements in Article 2 ECHR cases. Pursuant to the case law, the Government pays out almost the same amount of money in judgments and in friendly settlements, and the financial aspect is therefore not an incentive for it to settle. The most important interest in settling is to avoid findings of Article 2 ECHR violations, which are particularly severe and shameful. The Government is also willing to settle as this precludes an eventual re-opening of the case at the domestic level.

In this context, the role of the Court as a guardian of the ECHR comes vigorously into question. Settling cases concerning allegations of Article 2 ECHR violations is a disconcerting development for the protection of human rights. In many of the cases settled, the applicants were unable to find out what happened to their loved ones or who was responsible for their disappearance. In exchange for a sum of money and a vague statement of regret, the matter was closed and the case was struck out from the Court's list. The Court is certainly under enormous pressure to filter out repetitive cases such as these which do not develop or contribute to its case law. In this situation, it often plays a case managing role rather than a more substantive function aimed at the protection of human rights. This is an unfortunate state of affairs for situations such as these, which involve

---

[37] Philip Leach, note 32 *supra*.

deep-rooted systemic problems. It needs to be underlined, however, that there are still substantially more judgments than friendly settlements and arrangements in Article 2 ECHR cases. Finally, it is reassuring that no significant rise in Article 2 ECHR friendly settlements and arrangements has been noted in the recent years.

3. Article 3 ECHR Cases

Friendly settlements and arrangements under Article 3 ECHR concerned both torture and ill-treatment. Overall, the difference between the number of judgments and friendly settlements in Article 3 ECHR cases was not radical, which allowed for a balanced comparison between both types of instruments. There were, however, six times more judgments than arrangements. According to the statistics, Turkey settled at a rate of 50.2 per cent in Article 3 ECHR case, which is almost 30 per cent higher than in Article 2 ECHR cases. The first friendly settlement concluded by Turkey appeared in 1992 and it concerned Article 3 ECHR.[38] The applicants complained that they were subjected to ill-treatment during custody in violation of this provision. The friendly settlement that they concluded contained a clause regarding the financial award and the waiver of further claims. There was no mention of regret and no acceptance of the violations. The content of friendly settlements has nonetheless evolved over time and additional measures were later included in them.

As with Article 2 ECHR, friendly settlements and arrangements under Article 3 ECHR consisted of written proceedings and the parties did not effectively negotiate. However, exceptionally, negotiations took place in the *Denmark v. Turkey* case,[39] which marked an important shifting point in Article 3 ECHR settlements. This interstate case required negotiations to reach a compromise solution between two Contracting States. The friendly settlement mentioned that the Government regretted the case of torture and ill-treatment. In the following cases, the Government stated that it regretted and accepted Article 3 ECHR violations. Following this case, friendly settlements and arrangements started including formulas where the Government either expressed its regret and/or agreed that a breach of the ECHR had occurred. A comprehensive statement including both the regret and acceptance appeared for the first time in the *Değer* case,[40] where the applicant

---

[38] *Hazar, Hazar and Açik v. Turkey* (Appl. Nos. 16311/90; 16312/90; 16313/90), Report (Commission–Friendly Settlement), 10 December 1992, D.R. 73, 111.

[39] *Denmark v. Turkey* (Appl. No. 34382/97), Judgment (First Section–Friendly Settlement), 5 April 2000, Reports 2000-IV, 1. See also the chapter "Beyond Doctrine", section I.6.

[40] *Değer v. Turkey* (Appl. No. 24934/94), Judgment (First Section–Friendly Settlement), 10 July 2001, not reported. For additional examples, see also *Avci v. Turkey* (Appl. No. 24935/94), Judgment (First Section–Friendly Settlement), 10 July 2001, not reported; *Orak v. Turkey* (Appl. No. 24936/94), Judgment (First Section–Friendly Settlement), 10 July 2001, not reported; *Boğa v. Turkey* (Appl. No. 24938/94), Judgment (First Section–Friendly Settlement), 10 July 2001, not reported; *Doğan v. Turkey* (Appl. No. 24939/94), Judgment (First Section–Friendly Settlement), 10 July 2001,

alleged *inter alia* that he was ill-treated in custody. These statements were often made in repetitive cases which underlined a systemic problem. It is questionable whether friendly settlements were the best solution to handle this situation and whether ordinary proceedings would not have been more beneficial in the long run for the improvement of the human rights situation.

The first cluster of Turkish cases which appeared in 2001 seems to have given rise to mass friendly settlements. The applicants complained that their homes and shops were destroyed as a result of the random and disproportionate gunfire of the security forces in the course of clashes between these forces and Kurdistan Workers' Party (PKK) militants in Lice. They invoked Articles 3, 5, 6, 13, 14, 17 and 18 ECHR and Article 1 Protocol no 1.[41] The text of the friendly settlements did not appear in the decisions. It is noteworthy that these settlements were handed down in the form of admissibility decisions and not judgments. Their enforcement thus did not fall under the competence of the Committee of Ministers. The parties agreed to withdraw the applications on the proposal of the Registry in exchange of compensation. The Court struck the cases out of the list. No regret or acceptance of the violations was included in the friendly settlements. Friendly settlements were thus chosen here as a solution to a temporary problem.

The highest number of judgments finding a violation of Article 3 ECHR appeared between the years 2004 and 2006, ranging from 12 to 27. The number of judgments then decreased in 2007 and 2008. The highest number of friendly settlements emerged between 2001 and 2003, ranging between eight and 48. These tendencies show a similar trend to Article 2 ECHR judgments and friendly settlements. There was no general increase over the years in the number of arrangements concluded under Article 3 ECHR; they ranged from one to three between the years 2001 to 2008. Further, the number of judgments, friendly settlements, arrangements and unilateral declarations in Article 3 ECHR cases did not increase in the recent years. This could be due to the fact that fewer of these cases now reach Strasbourg, as the human rights situation in Turkey has generally improved.

---

not reported; *Parlak and Others v. Turkey* (Appl. Nos. 24942/94; 24943/94; 25125/94), Judgment (First Section–Friendly Settlement), 10 July 2001, not reported; *Kizilgedik v. Turkey* (Appl. No. 24944/94), Judgment (First Section–Friendly Settlement), 10 July 2001, not reported.

[41] See for examples, *Korkusuz, Suiçmez, Canpolat, Karaman, Bayhan, Delidere and Orakçi v. Turkey* (Appl. Nos. 30763–30772/96), Decision (Second Section–Friendly Settlement), 22 March 2001, not reported; *Can, Can, Güneş, Menteşe, Kasap, Akgök, Kasap, Daimi, Tosun and Tanriverdi v. Turkey* (Appl. Nos. 30662–30667/96; 30669/96; 30670/96; 30672/96; 30673/96), Decision (Second Section–Friendly Settlement), 22 March 2001, not reported; *Gündan, Karadag, Can, Canpolat, Şaşmaz, Şaşmaz, Izgi and Tasdemir v. Turkey* (Appl. Nos. 30674–30677/96; 30679/96; 30680/96; 30682–30685/96), Decision (Second Section–Friendly Settlement), 22 March 2001, not reported; *Şaşmaz, Karadağ, Özsucu, Vuran, Yülçin and Taşkaya v. Turkey* (Appl. Nos. 30652–30661/96), Decision (Second Section–Friendly Settlement), 22 March 2001, not reported; *Dakman, Özsucu, Bilal, Aytek, Hocaoğlu, Öztürk and Ersancan v. Turkey* (Appl. Nos. 30741–30743/96; 30745/96; 30747–30752/96), Decision (Second Section–Friendly Settlement), 22 March 2001, not reported.

Recipients obtained on average about 2,000 EUR more in friendly settlements than in judgments and about 4,000 EUR more in friendly settlements than in arrangements. The Court's intervention could – albeit circumstantially – have played a decisive role in the level of compensation granted. The ordinary proceedings in Article 3 ECHR cases lasted almost a year longer than friendly settlement negotiations concerning the same provision. Further, arrangements took almost half a year less than friendly settlements. The parties can therefore spare themselves much time in settling rather than seeking a judgment. The proceedings are also quicker when the Court did not intervene and the parties concluded an arrangement. It is thus more advantageous for an applicant to obtain a friendly settlement rather than a judgment in Article 3 ECHR cases, as he, or she, can obtain more money in much less time. Given that in cases under Article 3 ECHR, evidence is frequently missing and the facts are disputed, the conclusion of a friendly settlement often remains a suitable solution.

The clear disadvantage for applicants, however, is that these settlements do not allow for the re-opening of a case due to the lack of a finding of violation. In certain cases, this fact could constitute an important reason for claimants to seek judgments. This could be a solution worth considering for applicants who seek closure, who do not want or cannot afford to retain a lawyer for a longer period of time, and who may not need to re-open a case in the near future. Ordinary proceedings would be more appropriate for applicants who have sufficient financial resources, who are mostly motivated by a desire to obtain justice and who can afford to wait longer.

The Government may also benefit from settlements concluded under Article 3 ECHR. Unlike in Article 2 ECHR cases, the Government has traditionally paid more in Article 3 ECHR friendly settlements than in regular judgments. This additional amount may, however, be viewed by the Government as a price worth paying for the previously-mentioned advantages, such as the avoidance of publicity and the quicker resolution of the dispute. Due to the repetitiveness of the cases, it may be more practical for the Government to settle rather than to take part in lengthy proceedings each time. From the Court's perspective, it is crucial to handle these repetitive cases quickly in order to move on to more complex issues which develop the case law. It is, nonetheless, disquieting for the protection of human rights that severe human rights violations which originate from a systemic problem are handled rapidly without a thorough examination and without the possibility of finding a violation. Such an approach may not be able to remedy the underlying problem in the long run.

4. Article 2 and Article 3 ECHR Cases

Settlements under Articles 2 and 3 ECHR combined constitute another important sample to study given that they regroup two fundamental ECHR guarantees. As with the two categories of cases analysed above, the judgments outnumbered the friendly settlements and arrangements concluded: There were overall 11 friendly settlements, seven arrangements, 31 judgments and one rejected unilateral declaration. These numbers were lower than in Article 2 ECHR and in Article 3 ECHR cases. Articles 2 and 3 ECHR cases therefore represent a smaller sample to study. Turkey has settled at a rate of 36 per cent, which is higher than in Article 2 ECHR cases but lower than in Article 3 ECHR cases.

In Articles 2 and 3 ECHR cases, Turkey has spent almost five times more in total in judgments than in friendly settlements and ten times more in judgments than in arrangements. The amounts granted in friendly settlements and judgments differed to some extent: Applicants could obtain over 2,000 EUR more in friendly settlements than in judgments. There was, however, a bigger difference between judgments and arrangements, in that an applicant could obtain about 7,000 EUR more in judgments than in arrangements. Further, friendly settlement proceedings took two years less than ordinary proceedings, but they lasted about half a year longer than arrangement proceedings. The highest number of judgments concerning Articles 2 and 3 ECHR was handed down in 2000, 2005 and 2008. These judgments emerged at approximately the same time as Article 2 ECHR judgments and Article 3 ECHR judgments. All friendly settlements were concluded between the years 2001 and 2003, and ranged from three to five cases per year. This time period also coincides with the years where most Article 2 ECHR friendly settlements and Article 3 ECHR friendly settlements were concluded. There were no similar trends with regard to arrangements and unilateral declarations. The highest number of arrangements emerged in 2003 and the only unilateral declaration was also accepted the same year. Thus, many of these serious human rights cases were considered by the Court at approximately the same time.

The first statement of regret and acceptance of a violation in Articles 2 and 3 ECHR cases was made in *Aydın v. Turkey*[42] with regard to an alleged violation of Article 2 ECHR. Similar statements followed in three cases decided in 2002,[43] where the Government regretted and accepted violations of both Articles 2 and 3 ECHR or only of Article 2 ECHR. In 2003, the Government expressed its regret and accepted violations under Articles 2 and 3 ECHR in three subsequent cases.[44] The same year four arrangements were concluded, where the Government also acknowledged either a violation of Article 2 ECHR or violations of Articles 2

---

[42] *Aydın v. Turkey* (Appl. Nos. 28293/95; 29494/95; 30219/96), Judgment (First Section–Friendly Settlement), 10 July 2001, not reported.

[43] *Erdoğan v. Turkey* (Appl. No. 26337/95), Judgment (Third Section–Friendly Settlement), 20 June 2002, not reported; *N.Ö. v. Turkey* (Appl. No. 33234/96), Judgment (First Section–Friendly Settlement), 17 October 2002, not reported; *Demir v. Turkey* (Appl. No. 22280/93), Judgment (First Section–Friendly Settlement), 5 December 2002, not reported.

[44] *H.K. and Others v. Turkey* (Appl. No. 29864/96), Judgment (Second Section–Friendly Settlement), 14 January 2003, not reported; *Macir v. Turkey* (Appl. No. 28516/95), Judgment (Second Section–Friendly Settlement), 22 April 2003, not reported; *Başak and Others v. Turkey* (Appl. No. 29875/96), Judgment (Third Section–Friendly Settlement), 16 October 2003, not reported.

and 3 ECHR.[45] In 2004 and 2006, two additional arrangements followed where the Government either expressed only its regret[46] or expressed its regret and accepted, *inter alia,* violations of Article 3 ECHR.[47] The Government did not make similar statements in other cases.

From a financial point of view, there is a small difference between friendly settlements and judgments in Articles 2 and 3 ECHR cases; applicants can obtain approximately 2,000 EUR more in friendly settlements than in judgments. The applicant therefore has no distinctive financial advantage to draw from a friendly settlement and the incentive to settle is reduced. A clear difference exists between the amounts that could be obtained in judgments and arrangements. The intervention of the Registry could therefore make a difference in this context. The statistics show clearly that it is more beneficial to seek a judgment rather than an arrangement, as the applicant can obtain over 7,000 EUR more in the former than in the latter.[48] Despite this he, or she, could have to wait up to two years longer for a judgment. This may be worthwhile for those applicants with sufficient resources seeking a finding of violation and not wanting to foreclose the possibility of re-opening their case at the domestic level. However, claimants seeking closure, claimants with little financial means or claimants who cannot wait longer will not draw greater advantages from a judgment. In these instances, friendly settlements offer a more practical solution to terminating a case.

From the perspective of the Government, the difference in amount between judgments and friendly settlements is not significant in itself, but it may become important if mass settlements start appearing. There is no distinct financial incentive on part of the Government to settle in isolated Articles 2 and 3 ECHR cases. The most important advantage remains the fact that it will avoid publicity and the fact that the case will not be re-opened at the domestic level. Ordinary proceedings can also last up to two years longer and this requires additional resources. These elements may be sufficient in themselves to prompt the Government to conclude a friendly settlement rather than to wait for a judgment. In addition, it appears that the Government granted a substantially smaller sum of money in arrangements than in judgments. This may constitute an additional incentive on part of the Government not to seek out judgments, but also to

---

[45]   *Yaman v. Turkey* (Appl. No. 37049/97), Judgment (First Section–Arrangement), 22 May 2003, not reported; *Oğraş and Others v. Turkey* (Appl. No. 39978/98), Judgment (Fourth Section–Arrangement), 28 October 2003, not reported; *Hanim Tosun v. Turkey* (Appl. No. 31731/96), Judgment (First Section–Arrangement), 6 November 2003, not reported; *Yurtseven and Others v. Turkey* (Appl. No. 31730/96), Judgment (First Section–Arrangement), 18 December 2003, not reported.

[46]   *Karakoyun v. Turkey* (Appl. No. 51285/99), Decision (Third Section–Arrangement), 30 March 2006, not reported.

[47]   *Binbay v. Turkey* (Appl. No. 24922/94), Judgment (First Section–Arrangement), 21 October 2004, not reported.

[48]   See the statistics in annex 2, "Table X/4. Damages Paid by Turkey in Arrangements: Articles 2 and 3 ECHR" and "Table XII/3. Damages Paid by Turkey in Judgments: Articles 2 and 3 ECHR".

circumvent the intervention on the part of the Court and to conclude an arrangement at the domestic level.

From the point of view of the Court, it is advantageous in terms of time to settle repetitive cases which do not advance its jurisprudence. It needs to be emphasized, however, that – in comparison to Article 2 ECHR cases and Article 3 ECHR cases – few cases concerning both Articles 2 and 3 ECHR emerged. They were thus not as time- and resource-consuming as the cases which concerned only one of these provisions. It is clear that the same rationale as in repetitive cases should not be applied here. Given the severity of allegations involved, it may be more appropriate and not impracticable to conduct ordinary proceedings in these types of cases. Finally, the protection and advancement of human rights may benefit more from judgments than friendly settlements in cases generated by deep-rooted systemic problems.

III. Polish Settlement Practice under Article 6 (1) ECHR

Poland is an important beneficiary of the ECHR mechanism and generates a fair share of the Court's workload. The number of cases originating from Poland has dramatically increased over the last decade. This trend could be explained in part by the fact that the ECHR has become very popular in Poland and that applicants have become much more aware of the advantages that can be drawn from the Strasbourg proceedings. Unlike Turkey, there have been few complaints against Poland raising very serious human rights violations, such as torture or killings. An important component of the Polish case law concerns excessive length of proceedings under Article 6 (1) ECHR. This study focuses on civil proceedings and excludes criminal proceedings. The Polish cases concerning this provision are repetitive and they concern an area where there is established case law.

The statistics collected for this study demonstrate that friendly settlements under Article 6 (1) ECHR represent 86.4 per cent of all friendly settlements, and that arrangements under Article 6 (1) ECHR stand for 23 per cent of all arrangements.[49] There is also a significant amount of unilateral declarations made by Poland as part of these proceedings. Finally, the settlement rate in Article 6 (1) ECHR cases was 37 per cent, which is lower than the Turkish settlement rate in Article 3 ECHR cases, but comparable to the Turkish settlement rate in Articles 2 and 3 ECHR cases. It therefore appears that the interest in settling cases related to procedural and substantive provisions is comparable. The nature of the violation does not appear to affect the parties' readiness to seek a judgment or a friendly

---

[49] See the statistics in annex 2, "Table II/2. Statistics per Country 1998–2008: Friendly Settlements", "Table II/3. Statistics per Country 1998–2008: Arrangements", "Table IV/2. Average Length of Negotiations" and "Table VI/2. Average Length of Negotiations".

settlement. The decisive factor is rather the willingness to settle, especially on the part of the Government.

Poland has become widely known for its case law on lengthy proceedings. Many changes following the 1989 reforms led to the expansion of the domestic courts' jurisdiction and to a corresponding increase in their workload.[50] The high number of cases relating to lengthy proceedings was also generated by a malfunction of the domestic judicial system, which has not been operating very efficiently. The increase in applications before the ECtHR was mostly due to a general mistrust in the judiciary at the domestic level. Proceedings lasted excessively long and access to courts as well as their independence and impartiality were generally deficient. Nonetheless, such an improvement requires a substantial investment in human resources, technical facilities and general infrastructure in order to render the judiciary more efficient.[51] Applicants therefore looked to the ECtHR for potential relief. It has been pointed out that Article 6 ECHR cases could have been over-represented in the Polish case law.[52] Further, given that Polish applicants were often unrepresented, it was easier for them to conclude that proceedings have lasted longer than necessary rather than to base their arguments on more complex procedural or substantive grounds.[53]

Contracting States must ensure that their judicial systems respect all the requirements of the Convention. In handing down its judgment in the *Kudła* case,[54] the Court reminded the parties that it was their responsibility to provide a national remedy when an individual's rights were violated under the ECHR. An applicant must be able to rely on a domestic remedy in cases of lengthy proceedings. This follows from the principle of subsidiarity, which makes Contracting States responsible for ensuring the efficient protection of human rights.[55] The *Kudła* judgment[56] initiated a trend in setting up domestic remedies to prevent lengthy domestic proceedings. In Poland, a new Act on Complaints About a Breach of Right to Trial Within a Reasonable Time entered into force on 17 September 2004.[57] Modelled on the Italian *Pinto* Law, the 2004 Act provided a remedy to parties seeking a declaration that their right to have the case heard within a reasonable time has been breached. In addition, the complainant could seek compensation as well as an order from the court to take specific measures to speed

---

[50] Dembour, M.-B./Krzyżanowska-Mierzewska, M. (2004), p. 519; Krzyżanowska-Mierzewska, M. (2008), pp. 555–559.

[51] Keller, H. (2005), p. 324.

[52] Dembour, M.-B./Krzyżanowska-Mierzewska, M. (2004), p. 520.

[53] Ibid.

[54] *Kudła v. Poland* (Appl. No. 30210/96), Judgment (Grand Chamber), 26 October 2000, Reports 2000-XI, 197.

[55] Dembour, M.-B./Krzyżanowska-Mierzewska, M. (2004), p. 519.

[56] *Kudła v. Poland*, note 54 *supra*.

[57] *Ustawa z dnia 17 czerwca 2004 r. o skardze na naruszenie prawa strony do rozpoznania sprawy w postępowaniu sądowym bez nieuzasadnionej zwłoki* (the Act on Complaints About a Breach of Right to Trial Within a Reasonable Time), *Dziennik Ustaw* 04.179.1843; Krzyżanowska-Mierzewska, M. (2008), p. 556.

up proceedings.[58] Following the adoption of this Act, the length complaints seem to have been repatriated to Poland. Further, the ECtHR found that the remedies introduced by the Act are capable of preventing the alleged violations of the right to have a case heard within a reasonable time and providing adequate redress by way of compensation for any violation which had already occurred.[59] In the last three or four years, several difficulties have arisen from the application of the law and it appeared that the 2004 Act did not adequately remedy the problem of length of judicial proceedings.[60]

The Government decided to amend the 2004 Act with the new Act Amending the Act on Complaints About a Breach of Right to Trial Within a Reasonable Time, which entered into force on 1 May 2009.[61] At the same time, the Government convened with the Registry that the Government Agent could terminate all new complaints dealing with the former 2004 Act with a friendly settlement.[62] In these instances, friendly settlements have played a transitional function by facilitating the transition between the old and the new system. The 2009 Act applies to both the length of judicial proceedings and preparatory proceedings carried out, or supervised, by the prosecutor. It renders it mandatory for the domestic courts to issue an order upon the request of the complainant to undertake certain measures within a specified period of time (unless it is unnecessary). The amount of compensation was also increased from a maximum of 10,000 PLN to an amount between 2,000 PLN and 20,000 PLN.

The highest number of judgments was observed in 2004 and there was a general increase in judgments between the years 2003 and 2006. From 2006 onwards, the number of judgments drastically decreased. Interestingly, all the friendly settlements concluded appeared around the same period, namely in 2003 and 2004. There were no friendly settlements before or after these dates. As regards arrangements, their number was higher than usual in 2003 and it then decreased. In 2006, it started once more to increase. These trends therefore indicate that arrangements could be an alternative to judgments, which are no longer sought under Article 6 (1) ECHR. This could be due in part to the fact that the

---

[58] Ibid.

[59] Ibid, p. 557. See *Kudła v. Poland*, note 54 *supra*, paras. 158–159; *Krasuski v. Poland* (Appl. No. 61444/00), Judgment (Fourth Section), 14 June 2005, Reports 2005-V, 1, para. 66; *Charzyński v. Poland* (Appl. No. 15212/03), Decision (Fourth Section), 1 March 2005, Reports 2005-V, 323. See, however, the Court's position with regard to cases that have come to an end more than three years before the entry into force of the 2004 Act. In these instances the remedy provided cannot be used and renders the procedure ineffective. *Ratajczyk v. Poland* (Appl. No. 11215/02), Decision (Fourth Section), 31 May 2005, Reports 2005-VIII, 379.

[60] Krzyżanowska-Mierzewska, M. (2008), pp. 557–558.

[61] *Ustawa z dnia 20 lutgego 2009 r. o zmianie ustawy o skardze na naruszenie prawa strony do rozpoznania sprawy w postępowaniu sądowym bez nieuzasadnionej zwłoki* (the Act amending the Act on Complaints About a Breach of Right to Trial Within a Reasonable Time), *Dziennik Ustaw* 2009.61.498.

[62] Jakub Wołąsiewicz, Polish Agent before the ECtHR, information given in his interview of 29 January 2009, reprinted in annex 1.

Polish Government engaged in a dialogue with the Court.[63] The Registrars visited Poland and met the Minister of Justice and other Government delegates. They discussed the possibility of concluding more settlements in certain groups of cases, which included the length of proceedings cases. Finally, it is important to note that this increase was only reflected in the arrangements and not in friendly settlements.[64] There was thus an attempt to settle more cases at the domestic level without the intervention of the Court.

As of 2006, there was a marked rise in arrangements concluded following domestic proceedings under the 2004 Act. In general, the ECtHR provided very little information in its short decisions about the domestic proceedings. Some information was, nonetheless, available regarding the findings of the domestic courts. Thus, arrangements had been concluded in cases where:

- the domestic courts rejected the complaints considering that they had been terminated with an earlier judgment;[65]

- the domestic courts found that the 2004 Act did not apply to the proceedings at hand;[66]

- the applicant obtained compensation in proceedings under the 2004 Act;[67]

- the complaint was dismissed on the grounds that there had not been any undue delay when the 2004 Act came into force;[68]

- the domestic court held that there was undue delay, but did not grant compensation on grounds that it was caused by the judge in charge of the case;[69]

[63] Ibid.
[64] For the distinction between friendly settlements and arrangements, see the chapter "Beyond Doctrine", section I.1.
[65] *Mączyński v. Poland* (Appl. No. 1084/02), Decision (Fourth Section–Arrangement), 7 February 2006, not reported.
[66] *Zielonkiewicz v. Poland* (Appl. No. 25656/05), Decision (Fourth Section–Arrangement), 19 September 2006, not reported; *Kos v. Poland* (Appl. No. 36240/03), Decision (Fourth Section–Arrangement), 26 June 2007, not yet reported; *Pawłowska v. Poland* (Appl. No. 37991/04), Decision (Fourth Section–Arrangement), 10 June 2008, not yet reported.
[67] *Wiśniewski v. Poland* (Appl. No. 64205/01), Decision (Fourth Section–Arrangement), 17 October 2006, not reported; *Szymanowicz v. Poland* (Appl. No. 16658/04), Decision (Fourth Section–Arrangement), 20 March 2007, not reported; *Wróblewski v. Poland* (Appl. No. 9359/03), Decision (Fourth Section–Arrangement), 12 April 2007, not yet reported; *Witer v. Poland* (Appl. No. 39814/03), Decision (Fourth Section–Arrangement), 18 September 2007, not yet reported; *Franosz and Franosz v. Poland* (Appl. No. 17992/03), Decision (Fourth Section–Arrangement), 2 October 2007, not yet reported; *Kuberski v. Poland* (Appl. No. 33099/03), Decision (Fourth Section–Arrangement), 2 October 2007, not yet reported; *Marchel v. Poland* (Appl. No. 31119/02), Decision (Fourth Section–Arrangement), 13 November 2007, not yet reported; *Lisiecki v. Poland* (Appl. No. 18034/05), Decision (Fourth Section–Arrangement), 6 May 2008, not yet reported; *Markieta v. Poland* (Appl. No. 49718/06), Decision (Fourth Section–Arrangement), 21 October 2008, not yet reported; *Remesz v. Poland* (Appl. No. 32224/04), Decision (Fourth Section–Arrangement), 9 December 2008, not yet reported.
[68] *Skórzybót v. Poland* (Appl. No. 3858/05), Decision (Fourth Section–Arrangement), 21 November 2006, not reported.
[69] *Strzelecki v. Poland* (Appl. No. 23051/05), Decision (Fourth Section–Arrangement),

- the domestic court held that there was undue delay, but did not grant compensation on grounds that the applicant did not demonstrate that he had suffered any damage;[70]

- the domestic court held that there was undue delay, but did not grant compensation on grounds that the applicant had not done anything to accelerate the proceedings;[71]

- the domestic court held that there was undue delay, but did not grant compensation and did not provide any specific reasons for this decision;[72]

- the domestic court did not find that there were any undue delays;[73] or

- the domestic court held that the sole finding of undue delay was sufficient just satisfaction.[74]

These arrangements demonstrate that the Court has effectively short circuited a great part of the ordinary proceedings in Polish length cases. Despite this, the flow of cases has not been completely stemmed, as numerous applications concerning the 2004 Act came to Strasbourg and were terminated by way of arrangements. This important caseload has uncovered a malfunction in the proceedings under the 2004 Act.

The increase in arrangements as of 2006 was accompanied by a rise in unilateral

12 December 2006, not reported; *Bąk v. Poland* (Appl. No. 21092/04), Decision (Fourth Section–Arrangement), 16 October 2007, not yet reported; *Ciechanowski v. Poland* (Appl. No. 2863/06), Decision (Fourth Section–Arrangement), 16 September 2008, not yet reported.

[70] *Sarnowski v. Poland* (Appl. No. 3879/05), Decision (Fourth Section–Arrangement), 12 December 2006, not reported.

[71] *Lendzion v. Poland* (Appl. No. 41587/05), Decision (Fourth Section–Arrangement), 30 January 2007, not yet reported.

[72] *Broszczakowska v. Poland* (Appl. No. 18262/05), Decision (Fourth Section–Arrangement), 13 March 2007, not reported.

[73] *Matkowska v. Poland* (Appl. No. 18410/06), Decision (Fourth Section–Arrangement), 19 June 2007, not yet reported; *Walder v. Poland* (Appl. No. 45032/06), Decision (Fourth Section–Arrangement), 26 June 2007, not yet reported; *Falkowski v. Poland* (Appl. No. 32743/06), Decision (Fourth Section–Arrangement), 23 October 2007, not yet reported; *Militowska v. Poland* (Appl. No. 10002/05), Decision (Fourth Section–Arrangement), 11 December 2007, not yet reported; *Piekarczyk v. Poland* (Appl. No. 47727/06), Decision (Fourth Section–Arrangement), 29 January 2008, not yet reported; *Laskowski v. Poland* (Appl. No. 17220/03), Decision (Fourth Section–Arrangement), 12 February 2008, not yet reported; *Kornacki v. Poland* (Appl. No. 2967/05), Decision (Fourth Section–Arrangement), 27 March 2008, not yet reported; *Antkowiak v. Poland* (Appl. No. 14056/06), Decision (Fourth Section–Arrangement), 22 April 2008, not yet reported; *Wiktor v. Poland* (Appl. No. 42178/05), Decision (Fourth Section–Arrangement), 10 June 2008, not yet reported; *Bieńkowski and Bieńkowska v. Poland* (Appl. No. 39010/05), Decision (Fourth Section–Arrangement), 17 June 2008, not yet reported; *Śliwa v. Poland* (Appl. No. 6738/07), Decision (Fourth Section–Arrangement), 1 July 2008, not yet reported; *Czemarnik-Noga v. Poland* (Appl. No. 21905/06), Decision (Fourth Section–Arrangement), 2 September 2008, not yet reported; *Makowska v. Poland* (Appl. No. 34762/06), Decision (Fourth Section–Arrangement), 16 September 2008, not yet reported; *Woźniak v. Poland* (Appl. No. 10511/07), Decision (Fourth Section–Arrangement), 14 October 2008, not yet reported; *Małagocki v. Poland* (Appl. No. 53122/07), Decision (Fourth Section–Arrangement), 21 October 2008, not yet reported.

[74] *Stanek v. Poland* (Appl. No. 16244/03), Decision (Fourth Section–Arrangement), 6 November 2007, not yet reported.

declarations. These unilateral declarations revealed further problems concerning the 2004 Act. In some cases, the applicants complained that the 2004 Act was inefficient in terms of providing redress and expediting the proceedings.[75] The ECtHR also rejected unilateral declarations on the basis that the 2004 Act was either inapplicable or ineffective.[76] Further, the Government acknowledged in some unilateral declarations that the 2004 Act failed to provide redress to the applicant's length of proceedings complaint and that the applicant was denied an effective remedy, as required under Article 13 ECHR.[77] The Polish Government was also prepared to recognize that the applicant's right of access to a court, in the sense of Article 6 (1) ECHR, in proceedings under the 2004 Act was unduly restricted.[78] In addition, the Government agreed that the applicant could claim to be a victim of a violation of Article 6 (1) ECHR.[79] It is important to note that the Court rejected 28.2 per cent of all unilateral declarations proposed by the Government. As a ground for its decision, the Court often mentioned that, in spite of the Government's acceptance to acknowledge the undue delay and the fact that the remedy was inefficient, it had not offered adequate compensation.[80] The Court is therefore critical of the Polish remedies against lengthy proceedings and has gone at great lengths to state this clearly as part of its reasoning. The cases relating to the 2004 Act have not yet been completely stemmed and it is yet to be seen whether the 2009 Act will improve the situation.

Overall, there were one and a half times more judgments than friendly settlements and arrangements. There were also 1.6 times more recipients in judgments than in friendly settlements and arrangements. In sheer numbers, Poland thus

[75] *Waza v. Poland* (Appl. No. 11602/02), Decision (Fourth Section–Unilateral Declaration), 26 June 2007, not yet reported; *Figiel v. Poland* (Appl. No. 10281/03), Decision (Fourth Section–Unilateral Declaration), 8 July 2008, not yet reported.

[76] *Wawrzynowicz v. Poland* (Appl. No. 73192/01), Judgment (Fourth Section), 17 July 2007, not yet reported, para. 37; *Tur v. Poland* (Appl. No. 21695/05), Judgment (Fourth Section), 23 October 2007, not yet reported, para. 40; *Kyzioł v. Poland* (Appl. No. 24203/05), Judgment (Fourth Section), 12 February 2008, not yet reported, para. 17.

[77] *M.M. v. Poland* (Appl. No. 37850/03), Decision (Fourth Section–Unilateral Declaration), 4 January 2008, not yet reported; *Modłkowska v. Poland* (Appl. No. 6420/02), Decision (Fourth Section–Unilateral Declaration), 29 January 2008, not yet reported; *Arvaniti v. Poland* (Appl. No. 20797/06), Decision (Fourth Section–Unilateral Declaration), 18 March 2008, not yet reported; *Seweryn v. Poland* (Appl. No. 38620/06), Decision (Fourth Section–Unilateral Declaration), 13 May 2008, not yet reported; *Kwaśnik v. Poland* (Appl. No. 6480/04), Decision (Fourth Section–Unilateral Declaration), 20 May 2008, not yet reported; *Sakowski and Sakowska v. Poland* (Appl. No. 5201/06), Decision (Fourth Section–Unilateral Declaration), 10 June 2008, not yet reported; *Figiel v. Poland*, note 75 *supra*.

[78] *Nowiński v. Poland* (Appl. No. 14883/04), Decision (Fourth Section–Unilateral Declaration), 7 October 2008, not yet reported.

[79] *Galusiewicz v. Poland* (Appl. No. 8651/04), Decision (Fourth Section–Unilateral Declaration), 9 December 2008, not yet reported.

[80] *Wawrzynowicz v. Poland*, note 76 *supra*, para. 38; *Tur v. Poland*, note 76 *supra*, para. 41; *Kyzioł v. Poland*, note 76 *supra*, para. 18; *Sadura v. Poland* (Appl. No. 35382/06), Judgment (Fourth Section), 1 July 2008, not yet reported, para. 30; *Zając v. Poland* (Appl. No. 19817/04), Judgment (Fourth Section), 29 July 2008, not yet reported, para. 65; *Śliwa v. Poland* (Appl. No. 10265/06), Judgment (Fourth Section), 2 December 2008, not yet reported, para. 27.

paid out in total 17 times more money in judgments than in friendly settlements and almost three times more in judgments than in arrangements. There were few friendly settlements and the number of arrangements was six times higher than the number of friendly settlements. The cost of this structural problem was tremendous, as the Polish Government paid out 1,637,297 EUR in friendly settlements, arrangements, judgments and unilateral declarations during the period considered.[81] These overall statistics demonstrate that ordinary proceedings have played a predominant role in the Court's case law relating to Article 6 (1) ECHR cases. This situation is about to change, as the Polish Government has now embraced a change of policy in Strasbourg proceedings by settling more cases than before and by trying to avoid judgments. Given that this trend only appeared as of 2006, it is not yet sufficiently reflected in the overall statistics.

There is a clear financial incentive for the Government to conclude a friendly settlement or an arrangement in an Article 6 (1) ECHR case. According to the statistics collected, an applicant could obtain up to 1,500 EUR more in a judgment than in a friendly settlement or an arrangement. As the Government had numerous lengthy proceedings cases, it was therefore clearly financially advantageous to settle. This sum of money would not constitute, however, a sufficient financial incentive for the applicants to seek a judgment instead of a friendly settlement. It is important to note, however, that applicants who claimed compensation domestically under the 2004 Act and then filed an application with the ECtHR were able to obtain a higher amount.[82] Indeed, the maximum amount that could be claimed under the 2004 Act was 10,000 PLN (2,489 EUR), which was lower than the average amount that was granted by the ECtHR in ordinary proceedings, friendly settlements, arrangements and unilateral declarations under Article 6 (1) ECHR. This amount has now been increased to 20,000 PLN (4,978 EUR) under the 2009 Act, which is higher than the amounts granted on average by the Court in Article 6 (1) ECHR cases.[83] Thus, the general interest of applicants to initiate proceedings in Strasbourg is not as clear as it was previously.

The proceedings in Article 6 (1) ECHR cases lasted almost a year longer in judgments than in friendly settlements and arrangements. Applicants seeking closure may therefore be more willing to settle than to seek a judgment as these

---

[81] This amount rises to 1,772,440 EUR when the actual rate for 2008 is taken into account. See the statistics in annex 2, "Table IV/3. Damages Paid by Poland in Friendly Settlements and Arrangements: Article 6 (1) ECHR (Length of Civil Proceedings)", "Table VI/3. Damages Paid by Poland in Judgments: Article 6 (1) ECHR (Length of Civil Proceedings)" and "Table VIII/3. Damages Paid by Poland in Unilateral Declarations: Article 6 (1) ECHR (Length of Civil Proceedings)".

[82] Jakub Wołąsiewicz, note 62 *supra*.

[83] In ordinary proceedings, the average was 4,609 EUR, whereas it amounted to 3,339 EUR in friendly settlements and to 3,096 EUR in arrangements. The average in unilateral declarations was 3,484 EUR. See the statistics in annex 2, "Table IV/3. Damages Paid by Poland in Friendly Settlements and Arrangements: Article 6 (1) ECHR (Length of Civil Proceedings)", "Table VI/3. Damages Paid by Poland in Judgments: Article 6 (1) ECHR (Length of Civil Proceedings)" and "Table VIII/3. Damages Paid by Poland in Unilateral Declarations: Article 6 (1) ECHR (Length of Civil Proceedings)".

proceedings are quicker. Further, the financial advantage that could be obtained in a judgment may not be viewed as sufficiently important to justify the additional waiting. In all likelihood, many of the applicants complaining about the length of proceedings are tired of the duration and are more willing to settle in order to terminate the case. This rationale is also reflected in the statistics which demonstrate that there were fewer judgments concerning Article 6 (1) ECHR in the last two years in comparison to the previous years. Indeed, both the Government and the applicants appear to have favoured friendly settlements over ordinary proceedings in recent Article 6 (1) ECHR cases dealing with the 2004 Act. It remains to be seen whether this trend will maintain itself in the future.

IV. A Multitude of Factors

The general conclusions formulated in this part are mostly tentative, as we only collected information on Turkish and Polish cases under Articles 2, 3 and 6 (1) ECHR. Undeniably, much more work has to be done as part of future research. This chapter nonetheless dares to make certain statements regarding the general tendencies which were observed in the areas selected. The review of Turkish and Polish cases does not reveal any unified trend in the Court's treatment of friendly settlements. Although Poland and Turkey have very different historical, political and economic backgrounds, they are also marked by substantial similarities in the context of the Strasbourg proceedings; they experienced systemic human rights problems; they both generated one of the highest numbers of judgments and findings of violations; they concluded the highest number of settlements at a very consistent rate; and they gave the Court the opportunity to develop new instruments to alleviate its heavy case load. The potential for drawing interesting conclusions was therefore very important as part of the sample chosen. Any far-reaching statements regarding the Court's segmented and fragmented approach to friendly settlements are nevertheless difficult to assert. It can only be determined with some degree of certainty that the initial assumption whereby an applicant can obtain more money faster in a friendly settlement only applies in part. Beyond this finding, the conclusion of friendly settlements before the ECtHR depends on a multitude of factors that cannot be easily explained.

The analysis of the friendly settlement practice in selected areas reveals that various interests need to be taken into consideration as part of the Strasbourg proceedings. The main interests are those of the parties, the Court and human rights protection, both individually and generally. A balancing act giving some consideration to all of them should then be performed before the appropriate instrument for the resolution of a dispute is chosen. The analysis of the friendly settlement practice underlines that the general interests of human rights protection and of the individual applicant do not always coincide with the interest of the Court, which has been overwhelmed in the recent years by an expanding case load. As the Court is unable to adequately fulfil its function as the ECHR guardian, it has to seek more practical or pragmatic solutions.

The balancing of interests also occurs at the level of the parties. The applicants usually seek compensation, justice or closure. Their motivations have to be viewed on a case by case basis. It cannot be assumed, for instance, that considerations of justice prevail in Articles 2 and 3 ECHR friendly settlements and that closure and compensation dominate in Article 6 (1) ECHR friendly settlements. Each applicant has different means and needs, which have an important bearing on the type of proceedings that he, or she, will choose. The respondent Governments also encounter complex questions which require careful consideration. In settling, the respondent Governments are mostly interested in avoiding findings of violations and lengthy, costly proceedings. At the same time, they are also aware that a potential friendly settlement may sometimes circumvent a malfunction that will resurface in future cases. They are thus also interested in finding a solution to inadequacies in the domestic legal system and not only in postponing the problem.

The statistics collected for this study reveal that the parties are willing to settle both procedural and substantive matters at similar levels. A concrete example of this affirmation is the fact that the settlement rate in Articles 2 and 3 ECHR cases and Article 6 (1) ECHR cases was approximately the same. These types of cases differ greatly in character and they involve different interests. Similarities in settlement rates could have been merely coincidental. A more plausible explanation, however, seems to be that generally Contracting States and applicants are willing to settle all types of cases. In other words, there was no proof confirming that the seriousness or the nature of the allegations of human rights violations have influenced the settlement level.[84] It does not seem that the repetitiveness of cases was a relevant factor in this particular situation: While Article 6 (1) ECHR cases were clearly repetitive, the same cannot be said about Articles 2 and 3 ECHR cases. This aspect should not, however, be easily dismissed as a potential influence on the settlement level. It can be argued with some degree of certainty that different Governments can settle at the same rate in different categories of cases. This trend in the friendly settlement practice therefore reinforces the view that friendly settlements can be concluded with respect to all ECHR provisions.

Quite significantly, the highest settlement rate appeared in Article 3 ECHR cases and the lowest in Article 2 ECHR cases. This state of affairs further confirms our finding that the nature or seriousness of the alleged violation does significantly influence the settlement rates. While both Article 2 ECHR and Article 3 ECHR cases concern very serious human rights violations, their level of settlement was dramatically different. Other factors therefore seem to have played an important

---

[84] However, the Polish State Agent made it clear in his interview that he would be reluctant to settle cases under Articles 2 and 3 ECHR. Jakub Wołąsiewicz, note 62 *supra*.

role in this context. It cannot be excluded that the repetitive nature of Article 3 ECHR cases may have been a relevant factor in this situation. The respondent Government may have wanted to resolve these recurring cases quickly. Another important factor was the opposing interest of the parties involved. In fact, when the parties have very different motivations, it becomes much more difficult to conclude a friendly settlement. In Article 2 ECHR cases, the Government's and the applicant's interests are likely to clash the most and this fact may account for the lower settlement level. In Article 3 ECHR cases, the parties' interests are less opposed and more difficult to categorize. This may explain why the parties have reached more friendly settlements in these areas.

Two additional factors also had an important impact on the number of friendly settlements and arrangements concluded, namely the willingness of the Government to settle and the trust that the Court manifested in the capabilities of the respective Government. This was especially apparent in the arrangements which followed the *Broniowski* case,[85] where the Polish Government co-operated with the Court and where the Court in return trusted that it would carry out the required reforms. It could also be observed in Turkish friendly settlements, where the Government actively co-operated with the Court, acknowledged an important number of violations and carried out an considerable number of reforms. This approach on part of the Turkish Government may have injected more trust in the working relationship with the Court, which eventually gave rise to an increase in Turkish friendly settlements.

Most importantly, the statistics collected refute, at least in part, the initial view that friendly settlements offer the applicant the prospect of obtaining a higher level of compensation more quickly than ordinary proceedings. The financial advantages of friendly settlements only appeared very clearly in areas concerning Article 3 ECHR. In all remaining areas, the amounts of compensation that could be obtained in friendly settlements and arrangements were either not substantially higher, or actually lower, than in ordinary proceedings. As the content of friendly settlements mostly includes money and therefore concerns, to a greater extent, financial interests it is to be vigorously questioned whether applicants are offered a sufficient incentive to settle. The question arises whether, and how, friendly settlements or arrangements are meant to serve the interests of the individual applicant. Recent trends indicate that the individual, who was originally at the heart of the Court's pre-occupations, may have been left somewhere behind amidst other more pressing issues relating to the good functioning of the Court. The increasing use of unilateral declarations is an important reflection of this changing reality.

---

[85] *Broniowski v. Poland* (Appl. No. 31443/96), Judgment (Grand Chamber–Pilot Judgment), 22 June 2004, Reports 2004-V, 1; *Broniowski v. Poland* (Appl. No. 31443/96), Judgment (Grand Chamber–Friendly Settlement), 28 September 2005, Reports 2005-IX, 1.

One aspect of the initial assumption therefore still holds in that friendly settlements proceedings are quicker than ordinary proceedings. The difference in length ranges from approximately half a year up to two years as regards both friendly settlements and arrangements. Under certain specific circumstances, such a variation can be detrimental to the parties involved and may lead them to choose friendly settlements over judgments. The initial premise should thus be reformulated: Friendly settlements take less time than ordinary proceedings, but they do not usually generate higher amounts of compensation. On the balance of advantages that can be gained by the parties, friendly settlements are in general less advantageous for the individual applicant than for the respondent Government. While the Government avoids a finding of violation, shameful publicity, and obtains a result faster, the individual applicant can only effectively count on shortening the proceedings. The remaining advantages are mostly circumstantial and do not appear as a constant in the Court's case law. It is therefore doubtful whether friendly settlements can take into account the best interests of the individual applicant who seeks justice and compensation. This may be the case in certain isolated situations, but it is not an assumption that can be readily made and generalized in the context of the Court's practice.

The increased use of friendly settlements remains a worrisome trend indicating that speedier justice sometimes impinges on the more meaningful and substantive adjudication of alleged human rights violations. It further reflects the changing realities of the ECtHR and its gradual distancing from the needs of the individual applicant. This question is rooted in a more basic issue, namely the role that the Court should play in the adjudication of ECHR complaints. Should it pay more heed to the needs of the individual applicant or to the reinforcement of its own regime? Recent trends concerning friendly settlements in Strasbourg mostly reinforce the latter role. The place that friendly settlements occupy in the practice of the Court should therefore be carefully re-evaluated. While settlements are an important tool in the reduction of the caseload, they will not effectively replace the benefits that could be gained from less cosmetic, and more far-reaching, institutional reforms. Due to the difficulties that friendly settlements can engender for the individual applicant, they should be taken as one of the many components of an effective strategy aimed at ensuring the good functioning of the Court.

6

Future of Friendly Settlements

Alternative dispute resolution is an intriguing phenomenon for the protection of human rights. For us, it was a tempting motive for embarking on the research for this book. We expected friendly settlements to play an interesting, albeit somewhat minor role for the European Court of Human Rights. Our basic assumption was that the Judges would in some exceptional cases sit together with the parties to find an individual compromise. Our thoughts were inspired by alternative dispute mechanisms in other fields (e.g., in international business law or national civil law). We expected that the main aim of friendly settlements was to find a solution for both sides that would be more suitable than the one provided by an authoritative judgment. During the course of our study, we had to revise our original – admittedly slightly naïve – conception of friendly settlements before the Court. Much to our surprise, we found that Judges were hardly involved in friendly settlements apart from the final endorsement and that, for the most part, friendly settlements did not involve negotiations between the parties.

Over the last 10 years, the Court and its Registry have made use of friendly settlements in a most creative way which has thus far gone essentially unnoticed by the public. To wit, friendly settlements have partly assumed, beyond their original conception, the function of a fast-track procedure. This new development has to be seen against the background of an ever-growing caseload of alarming dimensions and relatively minimal legal parameters for settlements in the Convention. This has prompted the Court to innovatively devise friendly settlements as a means for reducing its caseload through the speedier handling of cases. Although credit should be given to the Court's good intentions, such re-conceptualization of friendly settlements has proven problematic, not least because it went beyond the four cornerstones of the rules on friendly settlements agreed in the Convention and the Rules of Court.

Friendly settlements before the Court still represent uncharted territory for scholars. Until now, little has been published on friendly settlements before the European Court of Human Rights and even less has been done with regard to the most recent developments. The experience with the new use of friendly settlements is still too fresh for a conclusive analysis. Nevertheless, our research allows us to formulate several *caveats* and reform proposals. In the present chapter, we build upon our previous findings in order to draw some legal, philosophical and practical conclusions for the years to come. One should bear in mind that friendly settlements are subject to the overall dynamics affecting the development of the Court.

I. Understanding, Potential and Limits

In referring to friendly settlements, we understand the term in its original sense, which is that the Court endorses the closure of human rights cases on a primarily financial basis after obtaining the full and informed consent of the parties. According to Article 38 ECHR, the Court has to ensure in each friendly settlement the respect for human rights as defined in the Convention and the Protocols. This understanding implies by its very nature that the parties have a genuine choice between a friendly settlement and an ordinary procedure. Thus, it would be inconceivable for the Registry's personnel to signal to the applicant an automatic loss of advantages if he, or she, dares negotiating the possible content of a friendly settlement. Friendly settlements might significantly speed up the proceedings at the Court. They have the potential to reduce the time required for the processing of cases. Yet, to reduce their function to a mere fast-track procedure for clear-cut cases would be an oversimplification. Finally, the judicial nature of friendly settlements must be emphasized. Defining the content of a friendly settlement is not at the disposal of the parties, as the Court needs to endorse the agreement authoritatively confirming its compatibility with the human rights standards in the Convention and the Protocols.

Friendly settlements bear a great potential. They fulfil manifold functions, and may prove to be promising tools, depending on the form of the agreement and the stage at which the parties choose to settle a case.[1] Settlement proceedings, however, have their inherent limits. Friendly settlements cannot resolve the Court's basic problem of backlog or change the Court's very mission as an international judicial body for the protection *and* promotion of human rights. And last but not least, nobody would want to equate the ECtHR with a claims tribunal facilitating large numbers of money settlements originating from a country with systemic deficiencies.[2]

On a theoretical level, friendly settlements can be used in all areas of human rights violations. While we would not limit them only to certain areas, we assume that a routine friendly settlement (*règlement amiable de routine*) in a field of established case law, a pilot friendly settlement (*règlement amiable de pilote*) tackling a systemic problem and a real friendly settlement (*règlement amiable réel*)

---

[1] See for the various possibilities of friendly settlements, the charts in annex 4.

[2] Elisabet Fura, Judge at the ECtHR, information given in her interview of 12 January 2009, reprinted in annex 1; Serkan Cengiz, lawyer in private practice, information given in his interview of 30 March 2009, reprinted in annex 1: "My (sc. Turkish) clients tend to regard the ECtHR mainly as a Court which can remedy all of their losses, including their pecuniary and non-pecuniary ones. They generally see the Court as a compensation court, but it clearly is not a court of this type."

in torture cases would have to be dealt with differently, both procedurally and substantially.

II. Basic Assumptions Partially Refuted

A commonly-held belief concerning friendly settlements is that they are more beneficial than ordinary proceedings because they allow the applicants to obtain more money faster. As the amount is not determined by the Court, there are *a priori* no limits set on the amount of compensation on which the parties can agree. This popular assumption holds true only in part in the selected areas examined as part of this study.[3] The financial advantages of friendly settlements appeared very clearly in Article 3 ECHR cases. However, in all remaining cases that we examined, the amounts of compensation that could be obtained in friendly settlements and arrangements were either not substantially higher, or actually lower, than in ordinary proceedings. The financial incentive for applicants to settle was not as important as initially envisaged. Applicants should be warned about this aspect of friendly settlements and not delude themselves that the determination of the compensation amount by the parties automatically entails more money. In cases where there is existing case law, the amount agreed by the parties will rarely exceed the amount predetermined by the Court in previous comparable cases.

One aspect of the initial assumption does still hold in Articles 2, 3 and 6 (1) ECHR cases; as expected, friendly settlements are quicker than ordinary proceedings. Indeed, the duration of ordinary proceedings can be shortened by up to two years in Articles 2 and 3 ECHR cases. Such an important variation could constitute a sufficient motive for the parties to conclude a friendly settlement. The time factor therefore constitutes the main incentive for the individual applicants to settle.

Although we did not collect the statistical data for all cases in all areas, our material allows to draw a number of general assumptions: Friendly settlements take less time than ordinary proceedings, but they do not generally entail higher amounts of compensation. The initial premise is therefore partially refuted and should be reformulated.

III. Professionalizing the Handling

Given the scarce legal basis in the Convention for settling cases, the Court's Registry is its own master in applying and developing friendly settlements. It is mainly due to the Registry's proactive approach that the use of friendly settlements

---

[3] See the chapter "Analysis of the Court's Practice", section II.1. and IV.

has increased over the last 10 years.[4] The Registry's personnel in the various Sections of the Court developed standards of good practice. Thanks to our interview partners, we had the chance to learn about these standards although we have never been present during the confidential negotiations or conclusion of a friendly settlement. In certain areas such as the pilot friendly settlements, the development of standards is still at a nascent stage, whereas for the routine friendly settlements, for example, the procedural steps are well-established and applied on a regular basis.

We noticed during our interviews that the Registry as a whole is well aware of how delicate friendly settlements are in principle.[5] Sometimes, however, we could not help thinking that the heavy workload of the Court had a negative impact on the use of friendly settlements. The temptation to dispose of a case fairly easily via a friendly settlement might weigh more heavily in certain circumstances than the concern for a thorough scrutiny of the procedure and the outcome of a concrete friendly settlement. As critical observers from the outside, we suggest some improvements in the handling of friendly settlements. Our proposals cover a wide variety of suggestions. They run the gamut from purely practical matters to ethical considerations.

1. Information for Applicants, their Lawyers and State Agents

An average lawyer in Europe knows little about the Convention in general and nearly nothing about the possibility of settling a case before the Court in particular. This information gap can easily be filled. Information about the advantages and drawbacks of a settlement in comparison to an ordinary judicial procedure could be compiled and made available on the Court's website. The very functions of the settlement procedure need to be clearly expounded to a broader public. In more general terms, it would be essential to explain to the potential applicants the limited function of the Court (compared with all the national authorities), the involvement of a new counterpart (no longer a State official, but the State Agent taking a fresh look at the case from a European perspective) and the involvement of the Registry as an *éminence grise* that determines the fate of a potential settlement. This information should take into account that the average applicant is usually not prepared to settle the case when he, or she, arrives before the ECtHR. In fact, he or she might be completely unfamiliar with alternative dispute resolution because this is not known in his or her country of origin or residence. Although

---

[4] See the statistics in annex 2, "Table II/1. Statistics 1998–2008".

[5] See also the statement by Judge Fura, note 2 *supra*: "I think that these cases (sc. property cases) are much better suited for friendly settlements than for judgments. One of the reasons for this is that we have become some kind of a real estate agency. (...) The Court should not become a money machine."

there are certain countries where mediation procedures are well-established, it remains an unusual way to settle human rights cases in Europe.

Moreover, an applicant who fought before all the national authorities for his, or her, rights is not psychologically prepared to settle the case. His, or her, main objective is to finally obtain justice before the Court. It goes without saying that the information provided by the Court in such a sensitive situation has to be both instructive and persuasive if its aim is to increase the number of friendly settlements.

Several interview partners pointed to a specific and widespread problem for the settlement of cases: The applicants often have unrealistic ideas about the amount of the financial award that they can receive from the Court.[6] In this regard, more concrete information about the practice of the Court is needed. It would be most helpful to put together some standard cases in areas with established case law and to indicate the probable amount of financial awards. Of course, such information has to be prepared for each individual country, as the various factors (e.g., living costs, devaluation of money, etc.) diverge so drastically in the different Contracting States.

As a matter of fact, the successful adoption of a friendly settlement depends largely on the parties. It is nearly impossible to work on the applicants' intention for settling a case, as this target group is too large. By contrast, the circle of possible lawyers is more restricted. It would thus be sensible to make the information on friendly settlements more accessible to human rights lawyers coming to Strasbourg. The smallest group involved in friendly settlement is composed of the State Agents. We suppose that this target group would also be best served by receiving more substantive information about the possibility of settling cases. There was an important difference in knowledge and experience among the several State Agents who we interviewed.

2. Time

For the applicant, the clear advantage of a routine friendly settlement is the acceleration of the proceedings. He, or she, will obtain a financial award much quicker than in a normal procedure. The difference in time may amount up to

---

[6] An illustrative example for this wide-spread phenomenon is *Akimova v. Azerbaijan* (Appl. No. 19853/03), Judgment (First Section–Friendly Settlement), 9 October 2008, not yet reported, para. 3: "Under Article 41 of the Convention the applicant sought, in the absence of restitution of the property in question, compensation in the principal amount of 51,525 United States dollars (USD) which, according to her, constituted the market value of her apartment at the date of submission of her just satisfaction claim, to be increased by 1.3 per cent for each month from the date of submission of her just satisfaction claim until the date of the Court's decision on just satisfaction. She also sought USD 30,000 in respect of non-pecuniary damage." In the settlement, the applicant agreed finally on a financial award of 10,000 AZN (pecuniary and non-pecuniary damage as well as costs and expenses ~ 12,070 USD). Claudia Westerdiek, Section Registrar, information given in her interview of 14 January 2009, interview on file with the authors.

two years in Articles 2 and 3 ECHR cases. Strict time limits should be established by the Court and Registry in order to encourage the applicants to use the friendly settlement procedure in areas of established case law.[7] It is also worth considering speeding up by all possible means the proceedings in paper settlements.[8]

In all other types of friendly settlements, however, time plays a slightly different role. Negotiations are by their very nature time-consuming. If need be, it might be advisable to grant the applicant some weeks' time to reconsider a concrete offer. Obviously, the length of the respite should not make it possible for the parties – particularly the State Parties – to misuse their decision-making time to playing a waiting game. The Registry, thus, has the difficult task of speeding up as much as possible routine friendly settlements. For the other types of friendly settlements, a careful balance has to be struck between the efficiency of the proceedings and the risk of failing to conclude a friendly settlement.

3. Form

The distinction between decision and judgment stems from a time where the Court examined the questions of admissibility and merits separately. However, nowadays when the so-called joint procedure is the rule rather than the exception, the distinction between decision and judgment has lost most of its legitimacy. In the area of friendly settlements, the form chosen is particularly confusing: Although the Court strikes the cases out of its list, it occasionally does so in the form of a judgment. This confusing practice should be abandoned. A good solution is provided in Protocol no 14, which states that friendly settlements should be handed down in the form of a decision whose execution is to be supervised by the Committee of Ministers.

In the Court's practice, there is no clear distinction between applications that have been settled in the sense of Article 38 ECHR and applications in which the applicants, upon an agreement with the Government, are willing to withdraw the case on the basis of Article 37 ECHR. In both situations, the Court has to ensure that human rights are respected.[9] However, in several cases in which the applicant agreed to withdraw the application, we had doubts whether the Court indeed lived up to a full examination of the human rights affected.[10] Therefore,

---

[7] See also Serkan Cengiz, note 2 *supra*, who considers that the conclusion of friendly settlements loses its attractiveness because of *inter alia* its length.

[8] Jakub Wołasiewicz, Polish Agent before the ECtHR, information given in his interview of 29 January 2009, reprinted in annex 1. Similar also Elisabet Fura, note 2 *supra*: "If we could process applications more quickly, then friendly settlements could also be handled more rapidly."

[9] Article 37 (1) in fine ECHR and Article 38 (1) (b) ECHR.

[10] See for examples, *Rogalev v. Russia* (Appl. No. 55941/00), Decision (Third Section–Arrangement), 3 March 2005, not reported; *Starshova and Starshov v. Russia* (Appl. No. 8333/05), Decision (First Section–Arrangement), 8 September 2005, not reported; *Shpynov v. Russia* (Appl. No. 21940/03), Decision (First Section–Arrangement), 23 May 2006, not reported; *Oganov v. Russia* (Appl. No. 53826/00), Decision (First Section–Arrangement), 23 May 2006, not reported; *Pyatko*

we would encourage the Court to draw a clear distinction between cases that have been settled and classical cases of withdrawals in the sense of strike out decisions. The Court should in this respect define distinct criteria when a purely national arrangement is merely a reason for the applicant to withdraw the application and when the Court understands the settlement as a friendly settlement in the sense of Article 38 ECHR. The arrangements following the *Broniowski* pilot friendly settlement[11] show how closely those two issues are correlated. From a purely technical standpoint, the follow-up arrangements were concluded on the national level. However, the Court co-operated in defining 50 persons for whom the accelerated payment was justified and examined in depth whether the Polish law and practice fulfilled the criteria set out in the *Broniowski* pilot judgment on the merits and the pilot friendly settlement.[12]

4. Professional Training and Manual

Friendly settlements are special proceedings that need to be conducted by people with particular personalities. In real negotiations, much depends on the personality and character of the mediator. It would certainly be ideal if their experience in settlements could be gathered and passed over to other personnel.

At one point, the Court considered the possibility of setting up a friendly settlement unit. This idea, however, was quickly abandoned.[13] It is obvious that the practice prevailing in the recent years presupposes the involvement of a Case Lawyer. This person has to be familiar with the law and the language of the country concerned. As friendly settlements negotiations are often likely to switch to a normal procedure, it is quite reasonable that the person most involved in the application should be a Case Lawyer. Human resources are used most efficiently when the person who prepares the draft of a settlement is also responsible for drafting the judgment. As a general rule, this is appropriate for both routine and real friendly settlements. However, in situations where real negotiations have to be conducted via the mediation of the Registry, a centralized unit of specially trained persons would be most welcome. It would also be wise to provide some vocational training in alternative dispute resolution for senior Registry personnel

---

and Others v. Russia (Appl. No. 38374/02), Decision (First Section–Arrangement), 14 September 2006, not reported; *Shvetsova v. Russia* (Appl. No. 18967/04), Decision (First Section–Arrangement), 8 February 2007, not yet reported. See for other cases the chapter "Legal Framework and Practice", section III.7.

[11] *Broniowski v. Poland* (Appl. No. 31443/96), Judgment (Grand Chamber–Friendly Settlement), 28 September 2005, Reports 2005-IX, 1.

[12] *Wolkenberg and Others v. Poland* (Appl. No. 50003/99), Decision (Fourth Section–Arrangement), 4 December 2007, not yet reported, paras. 13 and 60 et seq.; *Witkowska-Toboła v. Poland* (Appl. No. 11208/02), Decision (Fourth Section–Arrangement), 4 December 2007, not yet reported, paras. 17 and 62 et seq.

[13] Judge Fura, note 2 *supra*; Michael O'Boyle, Deputy Registrar, information given in his interview of 2 February 2009, interview on file with the authors.

interested in this kind of activities. Having at least one specialized and trained person in all of the five Sections of the Court would not be a mere luxury. In fact, such a specialized unit would combine the need for effective and professional handling of friendly settlements very handily.

The specialized unit should elaborate a manual for friendly settlements. Most importantly, this manual should serve as a code of conduct aimed at handling friendly settlement professionally, effectively and coherently. If real negotiations are to take place, all cases are different. Here, the undisputed advantage of friendly settlements comes into play, namely the possibility of finding a solution on an individual basis. However, some uniformity in settling cases is indispensable. The proposed manual should cover practical matters, such as the most important steps for preparing the negotiations, organizing the negotiations in a neutral place, handling confidentiality, coping with difficult phases in the negotiations or setting strict time limits. Also, a coherent policy setting the amount of financial awards in repetitive cases should be defined. Finally, various ethical questions should be covered in such a publication. Undoubtedly, the Registry's self-perception as mediator, the guarantee of equal arms during the negotiations, the inclusion of general measures in pilot friendly settlements and the respect of human rights should also be included.

Last but not least, the professional handling of real friendly settlements requires knowledge, human resources and time. Seen against this background, the general overburdening of the Court remains an urgent concern, which real friendly settlements cannot be expected to relieve. This statement contrasts clearly with the widespread attitude of the Registry's personnel dealing mostly with routine friendly settlement. The justification for the broad use of routine friendly settlement in repetitive cases is precisely to speed up the pending proceedings and to alleviate the Court's overburdening. This argumentation obviously does not hold true for the time consuming real friendly settlement, nor for pilot friendly settlements.

5. Sword of Damocles: Unilateral Declarations

Proceedings in which the parties start negotiating an agreement for a friendly settlement come increasingly to an abrupt end via a unilateral declaration.[14] As a parallel development to friendly settlements, the practice in Strasbourg has been marked by a rise in unilateral declarations made by the Contracting States. While the number of applications has risen in the recent years, the number of unilateral declarations – similarly to friendly settlements and arrangements – grew at a much faster pace.[15] Overall, Poland and the United Kingdom have made the greatest use of this instrument. The other countries made several unilateral

---

[14] See the statistics in annex 2, "Table II/1. Statistics 1998–2008".
[15] See the chapter "Analysis of the Court's Practice", section I.1.b.

declarations per year. Until 2006, there were only several unilateral declarations per year. However, their number rose exponentially from 2006 to 2007 and it has nearly doubled from 2007 to 2008. During these last two years, most unilateral declarations concerned Article 6 (1) ECHR cases which appeared to add little to the existing jurisprudence.

The interplay between friendly settlements and unilateral declarations should be better known by the applicants. Most applicants are not aware of the fact that in routine friendly settlements the Registry does not allow, in practice, any negotiations in areas of established case law. On the contrary, a request for reconsideration of the proposed amount of financial award that is comparable to the outcome of a normal procedure usually leads to the end of the friendly settlement proceedings.[16] Once a State Party is prepared to acknowledge a particular violation of the Convention, the Court then terminates the case with a unilateral declaration. Seen from the Court's perspective, such cases do not add anything to the existing case law. Thus, the quick disposition of a case via a unilateral declaration in which the applicant receives the amount deemed appropriate by the Court under the given circumstances and which the State Party is prepared to pay in acknowledgement of the Convention violation is in the very interests of all stakeholders. This assumption, however, is simplistic and does not take into account the manifold interests that might motivate an applicant to challenge the State Agent's offer in his, or her, case.

The Court made it clear that the explicit acknowledgement of a particular breach of the Convention is not a *conditio sine qua non* for the acceptance of a unilateral declaration.[17] In most cases struck out on the basis of a unilateral declaration, the State Party, however, did acknowledge the violation of the Convention.[18] The situation was different in the Turkish cases, in which the Government

---

[16] For a critique of this practice, see the chapter "Beyond Doctrine", section I.2.

[17] *Tahsin Acar v. Turkey* (Appl. No. 26307/95), Judgment (Grand Chamber), 6 May 2003, Reports 2003-VI, 1, para. 84: "The Court accepts that a full admission of liability in respect of an applicant's allegations under the Convention cannot be regarded as a condition *sine qua non* for the Court's being prepared to strike an application out on the basis of a unilateral declaration by a respondent Government."

[18] See for examples, *Guttschuss v. Germany* (Appl. No. 771/04), Decision (Fifth Section–Unilateral Declaration), 8 January 2008, not yet reported; *Modłkowska v. Poland* (Appl. No. 6420/02), Decision (Fourth Section–Unilateral Declaration), 29 January 2008, not yet reported; *Orlowski v. Germany* (Appl. No. 35000/05), Decision (Fifth Section–Unilateral Declaration), 1 April 2008, not yet reported; *Ševčíková v. Slovakia* (Appl. No. 1928/04), Decision (Fourth Section–Unilateral Declaration), 1 April 2008, not yet reported; *Hryniewicki v. Poland* (Appl. No. 18779/02), Decision (Fourth Section–Unilateral Declaration), 22 April 2008, not yet reported; *Seweryn v. Poland* (Appl. No. 38620/06), Decision (Fourth Section–Unilateral Declaration), 13 May 2008, not yet reported; *Lück v. Germany* (Appl. No. 58364/00), Judgment (Fifth Section–Unilateral Declaration), 15 May 2008, not yet reported; *Kwaśnik v. Poland* (Appl. No. 6480/04), Decision (Fourth Section–Unilateral Declaration), 20 May 2008, not yet reported; *Marković v. Serbia* (Appl. No. 27919/05), Decision (Second Section–Unilateral Declaration), 10 June 2008, not yet reported.

regularly acknowledged a violation in general terms but not explicitly with respect to the individual case.[19]

The fact that the financial award in this situation would at best be the same, but is in many instances reduced, is essential for the applicant. When the applicant receives the Registry's proposal for a settlement he, or she, has to consider carefully the next step with the help of legal counsel. If the applicant wishes to bargain over the proposed amount of money, he runs the risk that the Registry will switch the proceedings in the case from the friendly settlement to the ordinary track terminated by a unilateral declaration. For the applicant, disposing a case via a friendly settlement could potentially mean that he, or she, might receive a slightly higher amount of compensation in less time. The disadvantage is, however, that the financial award is usually made *ex gratia*, i.e. the State Party does not acknowledge any violation of the Convention and the applicant has no right to re-open the case at the national level.[20] In this situation, good advice is hard to come by.

6. Special Care and Reasoning in Sensitive Cases

Friendly settlements as provided in the Convention are not an instrument of purely alternative dispute resolution. They are conceived as a judicial solution to a human rights case. As such, each and every friendly settlement is a delicate matter requiring the approval of the Court. In other words, the Court rubber-stamps, in each settlement, the agreement reached by the parties. By doing so, the agreement transcends the realm of privacy and confidentiality and becomes an official matter. Eventually, the Court declares the compatibility of the friendly settlement with the protection of human rights as covered in the Convention and the Protocols.

Human rights violations allow for graduation in terms of gravity. Also, cases of human rights violations are more or less sensitive, depending not only on the type of the human right concerned, but also on the larger political context surrounding a case. Without wanting to create a hierarchy of different human rights guarantees, it is probably a matter of common sense that a torture case has a greater weight than a lengthy proceedings matter. Consequently, it is more problematic to settle a case dealing with Articles 2 or 3 ECHR than with Article 6 (1) ECHR. Friendly settlements concerning the right to life and the prohibition

---

[19] *Akman v. Turkey* (Appl. No. 37453/97), Judgment (First Section–Unilateral Declaration), 26 June 2001, Reports 2001-VI, 223; *Haran v. Turkey* (Appl. No. 25754/94), Judgment (Fourth Section–Unilateral Declaration), 26 March 2002, not reported. See, however, Serkan Cengiz, note 2 *supra*, who qualifies the formulation used by the Turkish Government as pure apologies not giving the applicant the possibility to re-open the case on the national level.

[20] See for examples concerning the situation in Turkey, Cengiz, note 2 *supra*. See also Frank Schürmann, Swiss Agent before the ECtHR, information given in his interview of 30 January 2009, reprinted in annex 1.

of torture might be regarded as initially suspicious. We do not want to go as far as excluding such cases from the possibility of settling. However, friendly settlements concerning the right to life and the prohibition of torture need special care procedurally and substantively. For the sake of legitimacy, it is advisable that the Court makes its reasoning more apparent in the text of the published friendly settlement. Without infringing the confidentiality of friendly settlements, it should be possible to provide grounds for finding that a friendly settlement is more appropriate than an authoritative judgment in the case of an applicant who has been allegedly ill-treated or tortured.

We recommend that the Court formulates a self-binding internal rule where the justification for friendly settlements of such a sensitive nature is spelled out. The public will find these types of settlements legitimate only once the Court's motives for terminating such sensitive cases via friendly settlements become clear.

IV. Distribution of Tasks

At present, the distribution of tasks among the Judges and the Registry is simple: The Registry has the lead role in settling the case, whereas the Judges are not involved in the negotiations.[21] "A Judge cannot negotiate with the Government."[22] Most Judges argue that negotiating would affect by its very nature their impartiality. Hence, the Court's task is limited to endorsing friendly settlements either in the form of a decision or of a judgment. This underlying assumption is not compelling. Indeed, national judges are regularly involved in friendly settlement negotiations in social security cases. In this situation, it is not considered that they lose their impartiality and independence when the friendly settlement fails.[23]

The prevailing division of tasks between the Registry and the Judges does not fully take into account the fact that the Judges bear the final responsibility for the case independently, whether it is closed by a friendly settlement or an ordinary procedure. It is especially necessary to consider carefully the delicate question of whether a case in an area with no established case law can be settled or rather needs to be clarified through an authoritative judgment. This is clearly the Judges'

---

[21] However, some Judges would clearly be in favour of a more active role in the friendly settlement procedure, so for example, Christos Rozakis, Vice-President of the ECtHR, information given in his interview of 2 February 2009, interview on file with the authors.

[22] Lech Garlicki, Judge at the ECtHR, information given in his interview of 2 February 2009, interview on file with the authors. Judges usually are more interested in giving a judgment, in particular in the Grand Chamber, as to endorse a friendly settlement which is normally not widely perceived in the public. See Luzius Wildhaber, Former President of the ECtHR, information given in his interview of 19 June 2009, interview on file with the authors.

[23] For instance, Article 6 (1) ECHR is not violated when a judge takes part in conciliation proceedings prior to the decision and notifies the applicant about the possible outcome of the case. See *Jensen v. Denmark* (Appl. No. 14063/88), Decision (Commission), 7 January 1991, D.R. 68, 182.

responsibility. In other words, it is probably not enough for the Judges to give the Registry a *carte blanche* in all friendly settlement cases. All doubtful cases have to be submitted to the Judge Rapporteur.

For real friendly settlements, i.e. in areas in which no established case law exists, the distribution of tasks among the Judges and the Registry on the one hand and the parties on the other, is not absolutely clear. As a standard formula, the Registry invites the parties in the so-called communication of the case to consider a settlement. It might happen that this routine invitation by itself triggers a negotiation process among the parties without the further engagement of the Registry.[24] In these situations, much depends on the personality of the State Agent and the applicant's attorney. If they are inclined to settle, if they have strong motives for settling and if they are willing to make concessions, the chances for concluding a friendly settlement are good. However, the main work has to be done by the parties. As the Court is very busy, the Registry is only able to intervene as a mediator in exceptional circumstances. Obviously, real friendly settlements could be increased by providing the Registry with more resources.

At first glance, the distribution of powers between the bodies on the European and national level is well-defined. It is the Registry that leads the negotiation and the Court that endorses the friendly settlement. Finally, the implementation is monitored by the Committee of Ministers. Apart from the fact that the national State Agent has to agree, a friendly settlement in the sense of the Convention is a purely European matter. Functionally, however, arrangements concluded by the applicant and a State representative without the involvement of the Court's Registry serve the same purpose as friendly settlements endorsed by the Court. In particular, if these arrangements follow a pilot friendly settlement, the Court should not lose sight of them completely.

In most situations, follow-up friendly settlements concerning solely Article 41 ECHR issues are least problematic. Upon a Court judgment declaring a violation of the Convention, the parties should regularly envisage settling the case. If ever possible, the Court should refer the purely financial matter to the national level and to the parties. This would underpin the subsidiary role of the Convention's control mechanism by relieving the Court of tasks which could be carried out more effectively by national authority, and the parties would have the chance to find an individual agreement – a classical win-win situation for all stakeholders.

Against this background, one might ask whether the Council of Europe should become more actively involved in promoting friendly settlements at the national level. While alternative dispute resolution or mediation are broadly used in some countries, they are not applied in the area of human rights. We strongly suggest

---

[24] See for example, *Dömel v. Germany* (Appl. No. 31828/03), Decision (Fifth Section–Arrangement), 9 May 2007, not yet reported. In this case, the applicant's lawyer and the State Agent negotiated on their own and handed in the settlement reached, information given by Stefan von Raumer, lawyer in private practice, information given in his interview of 4 March 2009, interview on file with the authors.

that this field should not be left completely to the national authorities. Once the applicants have reached the Court, they are already beyond the stage of friendly settlements. More specifically, they want the Court to be involved in their cases as a new and impartial actor. Generally at this stage, trust in the national authorities is largely lacking from the applicants' side. Therefore, the involvement of a European mediator – be it through the Registry or a member of the Council of Europe Bureau (as for instance established in Warsaw) – would greatly facilitate the negotiations in friendly settlements. The closing of human rights disputes at the national level via friendly settlements would be particularly suitable in areas with established case law.

V. Confidentiality and Disclosure

The confidential nature of settlements can be an important motive for the parties to choose this way of terminating a case. It is particularly interesting for a Contracting Party to settle the case given that this procedure does not create a lot of publicity against the Government. However, as important as confidentiality might be for any kind of negotiations, the danger inherent in such a procedure is obvious. From the outside of the Court, it has become nearly impossible to trace the friendly settlements procedure. Publicly available information has become scarcer in recent years. While in the 1980s and the 1990s the information provided about the negotiations was quite extensive,[25] it is much more limited in the recent friendly settlements.[26] One can hardly determine whether the initiative for settling the case came originally from the parties or from the Registry. It is equally difficult to find out whether the first proposal was made by the Registry or the parties. It would be particularly useful to know the reasons for which the applicants rejected a friendly settlement in cases where the negotiations failed and where the Government made a unilateral declaration.[27] In addition, the Court does not spell out the reasons for its refusal to accede to a friendly settlement in order to preserve the confidential nature of the negotiations.[28] This practice makes

---

[25] See for example, *Weeks v. United Kingdom* (Appl. No. 9787/82), Judgment (Plenary–Arrangement), 5 October 1988, Series A, Vol. 145-A.

[26] See for a typical settlement *Arslan and Arslan v. Turkey* (Appl. No. 57908/00), Judgment (Fourth Section–Friendly Settlement), 10 January 2006, not reported; *İçen and İçen v. Turkey* (Appl. No. 10268/02), Decision (Second Section–Arrangement), 6 May 2008, not yet reported.

[27] See for examples, *Tahsin Acar v. Turkey* (Appl. No. 26307/95), Judgment (Grand Chamber), 6 May 2003, Reports 2003-VI, 1, para. 6; *Alfatli and Others v. Turkey* (as regards Mahmut Memduh Uyan) (Appl. No. 32984/96), Judgment (Third Section), 30 October 2003, not reported, para. 12.

[28] See the standard formula in *Ukrainian Media Group v. Ukraine* (Appl. No. 72713/01), Judgment (Former Second Section), 29 March 2005, not reported, para. 7: "On 5 October 2004 the Court decided to dispense with a hearing in the case and to reject the settlement proposed by the parties, as it considered that respect for human rights, as defined in the Convention, required the further examination of the case, pursuant to Articles 37 § 1 *in fine* and 38 § 1(b) of the Convention."

it difficult to determine the exact criteria for the rejection of a friendly settlement. Clearly, the demands of public interest and confidentiality conflict sharply. However, it is only when this information is made available to the outside world that the public can have a certain control over the use of friendly settlements. The more friendly settlements are concluded, the more such a control becomes vital. The legitimacy of friendly settlements depends much on transparency and on the control by civil society.

As part of the interviews conducted, we enquired whether the confidential nature of negotiations could constitute a problem once these failed. None of the interviewees found that this state of affairs could be challenging and they had not encountered any situations where such a question presented itself. This could be due in part to the fact that too few friendly settlements had been concluded by a given country and the problem had not yet arisen.[29] The question of confidentiality plays a smaller role in routine friendly settlements, such as length of proceedings cases. In these cases, real negotiations are rarely conducted and all procedures are generally written. As part of this process, little information is provided and the Government can reuse the same arguments in ordinary proceedings when the friendly settlement negotiations fail. The only confidential aspect remains that the Government acknowledges that there could have been a friendly settlement.

The question of confidentiality becomes more compelling in the context of real friendly settlements. These settlements involve oral negotiations, often assisted by the Registry, in areas where there is no established case law. The Registry sometimes proposes a first draft for the settlement and the procedure is not written. As part of such settlements, the parties may reveal sensitive information. Such a state of affairs could therefore be problematic if the negotiations fail and the parties decide to seek a judgment. However, the number of real settlements is much smaller than the number of routine friendly settlements. Indeed, the latter have dominated the Court's docket and represent the greater part of the settlements concluded in the recent last years. As a result of this development, the question of confidentiality therefore plays a smaller role than one would have expected in the context of friendly settlements.

VI. New Competences for Old and New Actors

The smallest group of persons from outside of the Court involved in settling cases consists of the State Agents. It would make most sense to provide this target group with substantive information about the function of friendly settlements and to grant them more powers. The former is obviously the Court's task. The latter would be in the hands of the Contracting States. It would be most welcomed

---

[29] See for example, Frank Schürmann, note 20 *supra*.

if the State Agent and the Government on the one side, and the Court and the Registry on the other side, could agree on the areas where friendly settlements could be used as a transitional measure to resolve a broader problem. Such an understanding depends on the willingness and capability of a given State Party to tackle the underlying problem. This has occurred with respect to Poland,[30] and could also be sued in the case of Romania, which accounts for a large amount of applications caused by a structural problem. Further, it could also be used with regard to Bulgaria, which experiences difficulties in implementing the Strasbourg cases into the domestic legal system. Even more, it would be helpful if State Agents could regularly conclude a friendly settlement up to a certain amount of compensation in these areas without requiring the special consent of the Government.[31] This would speed up the negotiations considerably.

If a case deals with a systemic problem that the Court identifies in a pilot judgment followed by a pilot friendly settlement, the question of the actors involved is more problematic for two reasons. First, pilot friendly settlements have a tremendous influence on the fate of other applications pending before the Court. Although the specific pilot friendly settlement is only legally binding for the applicant involved, the other applicants are in a similar situation and are influenced indirectly by the agreement concluded. Second, the content of the settlement is not limited to individuals, but also includes also general measures. In respect of the latter, the Court exceeds, in strict terms, its competencies. The implementation of a judgment at the national level clearly falls under the competence of the Committee of Ministers. Hence, it may be worthwhile to consider involving a representative of the Committee of Ministers in the negotiation process.

VII. Friendly Settlements in the Future Court

Today, the Court is in a serious predicament. The docket is ever growing with no prospect for improvement. Although the entry into force of Protocol no 14 is meant to have some alleviating effect, this might be compensated for by other developments that will undoubtedly increase the number of applications lodged in Strasbourg, such as the accession of the European Union to the Convention and the entry into force of Protocol no 12. The question of the reform of the Court is as old as the Court itself, and Protocol no 14 is certainly not the end, but rather the beginning of this reform process.

We have argued that friendly settlements cannot resolve the Court's basic problem. However, the various types of friendly settlements offer the opportunity to tackle a wide variety of problems affecting the Contracting States and should

---

[30] See for Poland Jakub Wołasiewicz, note 8 *supra*.

[31] Such a proposal was made by Claudia Westerdiek, note 6 *supra*. See for the Polish practice Wołasiewicz, note 8 *supra*.

therefore be understood as one of the many instruments at the Court's disposal. We recommend that the future Court takes advantage of the flexible nature of friendly settlements.

The *caveats* expressed in the sections above should not overshadow the fact that the Court's recent practice is both promising and inspiring. Thus far, however, the Court has not yet tapped the full potential of friendly settlements. Our research offers only a tentative analysis of the first decade of the new Court's practice (1998–2008) and outlines the limits of certain developments. A broader experience with friendly settlements and future research in this area will certainly improve the appraisal of friendly settlements in the years to come. There is still much to be done, practically and academically.

PART II

ANNEXES

1

Interviews

I. Interview with Elisabet Fura

Respondent: Elisabet Fura, Judge at the ECtHR
Interviewer: Helen Keller
Assistant: Maya Sigron
Date: 12 January 2009
Time: 16:00–17:10
Interview time: 1:04 hrs
Place: Office of Judge Fura at the ECtHR, Strasbourg

ELISABET FURA: My name is Elisabet Fura. I was born on 28 March 1954. I have a law degree from the University of Stockholm. Prior to my appointment to the European Court of Human Rights, I was a lawyer in private practice. Initially, my career was oriented towards becoming a lawyer. It took five years in Sweden in those days before you could be admitted to the Bar. I worked for the same law firm all the way through and I eventually became a partner. Before that, I worked two and a half years as a junior judge in the District Court. I became involved on a voluntary basis with the Bar Association and I was elected to the Board of the Stockholm District. I also became a member of the Bar Council. Later, I occupied the position of Vice-President and President of the National Bar. I was also active at the international level because the Bar Associations in Europe have a group, a sort of policy-making body, working in Brussels, the Council of the Bars and Law Societies of the European Union (CCBE; *Conseil des Barreaux de l'Union européenne*). I represented the Swedish Bar before this organization for a number of years. Previously, I was also involved in an international organization for young lawyers.

HELEN KELLER: As part of your long career and education, did you have any special training in alternative dispute resolution?

FURA: No, not really. There was no training at the university level because the concept of alternative dispute resolution hardly existed at the time. Of course, arbitration existed and this has been – you could almost say – a national sport.

We like to say that we are good at arbitration. The Chamber of Commerce in Stockholm, for instance, has a certain reputation for this. I think that we had some courses as a part of the procedural law course. As a practicing lawyer, I acquired quite a lot of experience litigating in arbitration proceedings and also in settling cases. This occurred practically on a daily basis. I have had a little less experience as an arbitrator. One of my fields of expertise as a practicing lawyer was insolvency law. As an insolvency practitioner, it is very often more important to reach an acceptable result quickly than to obtain the right outcome. In this field, a lawyer could get a certain feel for mediation and friendly settlements. We also had a lot of educational programmes at the Bar Association and we adopted (during my time especially) a rule making it compulsory for the Bar members to do a certain amount of training per year. For instance, one of the courses set up for that purpose was alternative dispute resolution/friendly settlements, the art of negotiation. I was very much involved in alternative dispute resolution, but more on a practical basis than as part of formal education.

KELLER: You mentioned that you were here since 2003. Were you in touch with friendly settlements at the Court?

FURA: Yes and no. I do not have any hands-on experience because I think that, as a Judge, I should stay away as a matter of principle from friendly settlements. This is nonetheless unfortunate. We do quite a lot of friendly settlements in Swedish cases or applications against Sweden. I think that settling cases in this way is not completely uncontroversial in my country. There have been some allegations that the Swedish Government is much too willing to settle.

Some found that the Government gets out through the back door and that it does not have to show that there had been a violation. A smaller circle then finds out about the violation and this suits the Government. I do not quite see it like that, but I think that it is more appropriate to settle within a reasonable time than to wait for so many years for a final judgment. While this is not so critical in Swedish cases, we do have a backlog here. In Swedish cases, it takes normally three to four years from the filing of an application until the day of the judgment. However, I still think that, if there is a case with no new legal issue and a clear outcome, then it is more appropriate to conclude a settlement than to undergo the ordinary proceedings.

KELLER: Do you have any influence on the conclusion of settlements?

FURA: Yes, I think that I have. I can indicate to a lawyer working on a case that it is particularly well-suited for a settlement or *vice versa*.

KELLER: From your experience, what do you think makes the parties want to conclude a settlement rather than to obtain a judgment?

FURA: Before they come here, there has normally been a certain amount of litigation at the domestic level. The initiative to conclude a friendly settlement very seldom comes from the applicant. Usually, it comes from the Court or the Government. However, the applicants are willing to settle for various reasons. I think the main motive is that they can put an end to these proceedings. They also have the satisfaction that the Government in a way accepts that a violation may have occurred. Our friendly settlements normally imply that. The Government expresses its regret about the events and pays an amount of money as damages. It may not formally acknowledge, but in a certain sense it accepts at least by implication that a violation has occurred. From my experience, it is not only about the sum of money that can be obtained but rather about obtaining some form of closure representing recognition of the violation which they have suffered.

KELLER: Are there any specific grounds or reasons for the Government to conclude a settlement?

FURA: Yes. I think that, in a normal settlement, it would be more efficient for the Government to settle because it costs more in terms of time and resources – I suppose – to deal with the case than to pay out the money immediately. It could be that, if it is a sensitive case or a case that has attracted a lot of media attention, it would be better to settle than to have an ongoing dispute in Strasbourg and the fanfare leading to a judgment. However, the information about the settlement is public in Sweden and people can find out. Nonetheless, there will be normally less media attention regarding a settlement.

KELLER: Do you think that, at the end of the day, the expectations of both parties taking part in a normal friendly settlement are fulfilled?

FURA: Yes, I would say so. The expectations might be different on either side, but I think that, as an applicant or an applicant's lawyer, it is possible to know in advance the content of a settlement. This puts an end to the dispute and the applicant gets his, or her, money. For the Government, this also marks an end in the proceedings and it can then move on to other cases or tasks.

KELLER: Let us discuss the procedure. This is probably a question for the personnel from the Registry. However, it would be interesting to know your point of view regarding some of these questions. For example, how much work does a settlement involve in comparison to normal proceedings?

FURA: Sometimes, it can be just as much work or even more work to settle a case. It depends on the parties of course. If both parties understand the procedures, then it goes quicker. Normally, we would expect the Government to be familiar with the proceedings, to know what will happen and to know how things are done. However, if the applicant is unassisted or is assisted by a lawyer who is not so familiar with the proceedings, then more work is required from the Registry personnel. Most Swedish lawyers are not familiar with the proceedings, as they are not experts in the area of human rights.

KELLER: Are all the negotiations held at the Court?

FURA: No.

KELLER: Does it only occur exceptionally?

FURA: Yes, I think that it occurs on an exceptional basis. This happened many years ago and I think that, unfortunately, the Court does not have the resources anymore to conduct those kinds of negotiations. However, I would not exclude it. I mean there could still be these kinds of settlements. I suppose that it would have to be really important cases. These are important cases because they deal with a large amount of applications or relate to a new issue that is important to one or several countries. I think that negotiations aimed at reaching a friendly settlement are in some cases similar to therapy, which is more important than the actual sum of money obtained.

KELLER: Do the applicants come before the Court?

FURA: No, they do not come before the Court.

KELLER: Do they hand in their documents?

FURA: Yes.

KELLER: This process has a kind of psychological value.

FURA: I think so, absolutely.

KELLER: Do you have any experience with difficult parties, either from the side of the applicant or of the Government Agent?

FURA: When it comes to a friendly settlement?

KELLER: Yes.

FURA: Yes, both. We sometimes have difficult lawyers on the applicant's side, but we can handle this via unilateral declarations.

I also experienced difficulties with Governments. In one of these cases, it seemed that the Government – it was not the Swedish one – had no previous experience in settling a case. Once we finally reached a friendly settlement, it was explained to me that this Government Agent had problems at home because there was no specific procedure implementing the friendly settlement. I mean there was no account from where the money would be debited. Afterwards, the Government Agent explained to me: "Well you see, if I have a judgment in which my Government is found to be in violation of a certain article and requires it to pay three thousand euros, then I give it to the Minister of Finance or to the

Minister of Justice who hands it over to the Minister of Finance and then the money is paid out." However, it was explained to me that they did not know who was responsible for the payment of a friendly settlement. I think that these kinds of problems happen once and then they are resolved or not. In this case, it was resolved and I am not aware whether it recurred in relation to that particular Government. However, as you know, we change the composition of the Sections on a regular basis. I am no longer in the same Section with this country and I am no longer aware of what is happening.

KELLER: This is probably more of a technical issue. Let us say that there is a line for friendly settlement in the budget. In countries with a friendly settlement tradition, the Government is probably more willing to settle.

FURA: Yes, absolutely. I am sure that it works like that.

KELLER: In the former Communist bloc countries, it might be difficult.

FURA: Yes, it was one of those countries. However, I think that it is too easy to say that there is a difference of mentality. I think that it is rather a lack of experience and maybe also a lack of trust.

KELLER: It is a wholly different approach to law.

FURA: Yes, exactly, it is a different approach. It needs to be explained to the authorities of these countries – at least in the beginning – why it would be advantageous for them to settle. Then, if it does not work, maybe you have to be a bit tougher and push for settlements. It is of course a different approach to law and you do not change approaches that quickly.

KELLER: This is especially the case with lawyers.

FURA: We become conservative through our education.

KELLER: Let us turn to confidentiality. Did you have any difficulties with the confidentiality of friendly settlements?

FURA: I have not encountered them myself and I have not heard of anyone who has had difficulties.

KELLER: You already mentioned that sometimes the parties are inexperienced and that they might not be well-represented. How do you handle that?

FURA: I do not know because I do not handle these issues. This is done by the Registry. I would assume that they have to be careful. The Government Agent can also be inexperienced. He, or she, is sometimes new. If he, or she, has been around for a while, then it can work. However, if the applicant is not represented, then you have to be very careful not to force him, or her, into something that he, or she, does not want. I suppose that sensitivity is something that you learn by working as a lawyer in the Registry. You can not push too hard and you must try to help out. You are not supposed to take sides. It is a delicate balancing act for the lawyer who is doing this.

KELLER: Did you ever encounter a situation where an applicant was threatened or intimidated?

FURA: No, I have not seen it in any case in which I was involved.

KELLER: Do you think that it could happen?

FURA: Yes, I think that it could happen. This Court has found in some rare cases that the Government, the administration or the public authorities have threatened applicants to withdraw their complaint. Of course, if they can do that, they can also threaten to settle. I would therefore not exclude it but I have not seen it myself.

KELLER: We already touched upon the issue of unsuccessful negotiations. Are there cases where the negotiations were interrupted because the applicant was not satisfied?

FURA: No, not as part of my personal experience, but I would assume it happens all the time when the end result is a unilateral declaration. I suppose that, normally, it transpires quite early on if the applicant is unwilling to discuss a friendly settlement. You could also come across an applicant – which is not infrequent here – who says that it is a matter of principle and that he, or she, wishes to bring the case before the Court to obtain a judgment. The applicant may not even want to have a conversation and may just want his, or her, rights established and confirmed. Then, it is more difficult to persuade such an applicant that he, or she, should be happy, or not happy, but satisfied with a friendly settlement. However, that is simply not what they want. Then, of course, the proceedings should not be dragged on if that is the wish of the applicant. The applicant can find out or may be informed about the time lapse if we tell him or her: "Okay, if you settle, you get your money now, but if you go all the way to the judgment, then maybe you will have to wait another two or three years." You can say that this is a threat. I do not think that it is. It is just practical information. Then, maybe the applicant will say: "Okay, I will settle." However, if it is really a matter of principle, then he, or she, will not settle.

KELLER: A matter of principle could thus be a hard case for a friendly settlement. How would this situation be approached if the Government behaved in a similar manner? Let us say that the Government thinks that it is an important case, it does not want to settle, and it wants to let the Court decide on the merits.

FURA: Yes, I have seen that too. The Government insisted on a judgment because it wanted the reasoning. It did not merely want a decision indicating a "violation" or "no violation", but rather a decision on a certain issue. The Government wanted the reasoning and did not want to settle. I have heard the Government saying that the case was not appropriate for a friendly settlement.

KELLER: What is the condition for the Court to decide unilaterally?

FURA: For me, it is very important that no new issues are involved. Should it go to a judgment, it will follow clearly established case law. It is always possible to argue – and the applicant will always do so – that the case at hand is different from all the others. However, it is our job to identify those cases, to indicate that there is no new issue, and to determine that there is clearly established case law. For instance, there is well-established case law both in terms of substance and damages in cases dealing with the length of proceedings. You can use the tables established internally and say: "For so many years and so many levels, this is what you get." I think that, if the parties obstruct a friendly settlement, then the Court should be tougher and say: "Now it is enough. It is not the best use of the Court's resources to continue these negotiations and to give a full judgment. We can terminate this case via a unilateral declaration." In a unilateral declaration, we would normally require the Government to explicitly acknowledge the violation.

KELLER: Would you say that the need to have the parties agree on the facts is another precondition for a unilateral declaration?

FURA: Of course. It is much easier when they agree on the facts. I would not rule out a unilateral declaration in a case where the facts are contested. Of course, the length of proceedings cases are quite different from Articles 2 or 3 ECHR cases.

KELLER: That was my question.

FURA: Then, you have to be much more cautious. I would be more reluctant to press on in Articles 2 and 3 ECHR cases and even in Article 8 ECHR cases. However, these technical breaches, such as length of proceedings, are very different. We have a number of settlements and even unilateral declarations in cases against Sweden concerning tax surcharges. These are of a very technical nature. Naturally, there can also be human suffering in these cases, but in the end, they are about money. These cases are easier to settle than mistreatment or torture cases.

KELLER: When negotiations fail, what instructions are given to the parties?

FURA: Well, frankly speaking, I do not deal with that normally. I do not see the case at that stage unless the lawyers come to see me for advice, but normally they do not.

KELLER: They do not?

FURA: No.

KELLER: They make it on their own.

FURA: I do not think that it is my job to get involved at that stage. If everything fails, including the unilateral declaration, then I would have to judge or adjudicate the case and I have to remain impartial. However, the Case Lawyer is not alone in this. Naturally, you will have to ask the other people that you will interview, but they have superiors that they can talk to and they can discuss these cases with them. I think that negotiations are some kind of an oddity and you have to know how to conduct them. You cannot expect a young lawyer to know how to deal with these situations unless he, or she, will get instructions.

KELLER: Let us now turn to the content. Normally, the content of a settlement consists of money. What else can be included in the settlement?

FURA: The settlement can include recognition that there was a violation. It can also include silence or discretion, but that would normally occur in a different context. For instance, in a commercial context, one of the major benefits of a friendly settlement is that you keep it out of the public eye. I think you can agree on that if it is important for the applicant and worthwhile for the Government. Of course, it also depends on the domestic legislation. Although I do not exclude silence, I have not seen it as a condition. A promise made by the country concerned to prepare a legislative amendment is, of course, possible. However, it would be more frequent as part of the pilot judgment procedure. Why not in a friendly settlement? I mean, I do not exclude it. I have never seen the reduction of a criminal sanction in the national criminal procedure because normally that stage has already passed. You have seen, I guess, in some friendly settlements or even in judgments that, when we decide, for instance, that the applicant did not get a fair trial because the judges were not impartial, then we state that the best remedy for this violation is to give the person a new trial. I do not think that the Court has gone this way so far in the context of friendly settlements. In the cases, where we decide that the best remedy is a new trial, it is also specified "if the applicant so wishes". I mean, you cannot force the applicant, especially if you are not sure that he, or she, would be acquitted. Why should he, or she, go through a new trial? Payments in kind and right to visit would occur in Article 8 ECHR cases. Access to a child could be included, but I have never seen it.

KELLER: But you would not exclude it?

FURA: No. Again, a fine line needs to be drawn here, because we cannot substitute ourselves for the domestic courts. This resembles what happened in and after the *Görgülü* case.[1] I think that we should be cautious. We can give some hints to the domestic courts as to what could be done. I think nonetheless that, we should be

---

[1] *Görgülü v. Turkey* (Appl. No. 6802/03), Decision (Third Section–Arrangement), 30 September 2008, not yet reported; Decision of the German Constitutional Court (Second Senate), 14 October 2004, 2 BvR 1481/04, Human Rights Law Journal 25 (2004) 99.

very careful to press it, because this is a very concrete issue. We have to know for sure all the relevant factors and all the relevant information when we render the decision or when the deal is concluded. Very often, we assess a situation that occurred several years ago. It becomes especially absurd in child custody cases when we say: "Yes, the courts should have done more when it comes to the possibility for the father or the mother to visit his, or her, child." I am among those Judges who are very reluctant to be too specific because we have never seen the parties. Also, we assess the other party and we take into account the reality that existed three years ago. The case could concern a child who was then three years old and is now six years old. You should never rule out such a possibility, but I have not seen it thus far.

KELLER: Let us turn to the conclusion of a friendly settlement. You mentioned earlier that lengthy proceedings are a good area for a friendly settlement. Could you tell us more? Are there typical cases which are especially appropriate for friendly settlements?

FURA: Property cases and property rights. I am now in the Section dealing with the Romanian cases. There are many of them. A great portion of them deal with property rights. One typical problem is that property, which was nationalized and then denationalized, is now owned by two owners. Two persons are entitled to the same piece of property. As they cannot both claim this right, the Government has to compensate one of them. I think that these cases are much better suited for friendly settlements than for judgments. One of the reasons for this is that we have become some kind of a real estate agency. We sit here and we say: "Well yes, here we have an apartment in Bucharest located on this street on the third floor. It is worth this much money." We do not have the required expertise and it is not a task for which we should be responsible. I think that, once the situation is assessed, the parties should go back and settle. We can facilitate the settlement, but the negotiations should be done between the parties. This is very typical.

KELLER: Did this occur in the *Hutten-Czapska* case?[2]

FURA: No, it is not quite the same. It is rather like the *Brumarescu* case.[3]

KELLER: Do you know how often you will succeed?

FURA: No. I do not have any exact record of the cases where I was involved and instructed the lawyers to try to settle. My feeling is that 95 per cent of the cases are settled.

[2] *Hutten-Czapska v. Poland* (Appl. No. 35014/97), Judgment (Grand Chamber–Pilot Judgment), 19 June 2006, Reports 2006-VIII, 57; *Hutten-Czapska v. Poland* (Appl. No. 35014/97), Judgment (Grand Chamber–Friendly Settlement), 28 April 2008, not yet reported.
[3] *Brumarescu v. Romania* (Appl. No. 28342/95), Judgment (Grand Chamber), 28 October 1999, Reports 1999-VII, 201.

KELLER: Only five per cent of these failed?

FURA: Yes or 10 per cent maybe. I think that we are rather conservative in our approach. I think that we could be braver. So far, we have only tried to settle those cases in which we are sure that it would work.

KELLER: How often has the Court disapproved of a friendly settlement? Did you ever encounter such a situation?

FURA: I have seen one case, I believe, but I do not exactly remember what the problem was.

KELLER: So not very often?

FURA: No, it does not occur very often. However, there has been a case, or a few cases, where it was not regarded proper to settle.

KELLER: Is it the *Göçmen* case?[4] Is it a Turkish case?

FURA: Yes, I think so.

KELLER: Yes, I know that one. Did you encounter such issues as part of your experience?

FURA: No.

KELLER: What problems emerge at enforcement?

FURA: I suppose one problem could be that the payment is not paid on time. However, normally there is a condition on interest in the settlement agreement. Of course, this interest must be high enough to incite the Government to pay out promptly.

KELLER: Do we know, for instance, whether in Turkey, where friendly settlements occur very often, these amounts are really paid out?

FURA: I guess so. As you know, it is not our primary concern to look after the enforcement. This comes under the competence of the Committee of Ministers. Still, we would hear – I am sure – if the applicants were unhappy. They would come back to us and say: "Well, I know that this is settled, but I did not get my payment." As far as my cases are concerned, the payments are made.

KELLER: Would you consider that there is *res judicata* when the money is not paid out following a friendly settlement judgment? Would you declare a case inadmissible because the award was not paid out?

FURA: No, I do not think so. I have never seen such a case. If an applicant

---

[4] *Göçmen and Others v. Turkey* (Appl. No. 19279/92), Judgment (First Section), 30 January 2001, not reported.

returns and indicates that he, or she, has not received the payment: "Yes, there is a friendly settlement agreement but I have not received the payment and this is confirmed", then the settlement is broken. The case is open again. We can just restore it to the docket because nothing has changed. If it is a strike out, it can of course be restored. This is provided for in the Convention and the Rules of Court.

KELLER: Are the negotiations more or less laborious than the preparation of a judgment?

FURA: I think that they could be more laborious, but not for me or the Court. Nonetheless, I think that friendly settlements may be worthwhile for the reasons that I explained.

KELLER: Do you have any criticism of the friendly settlement procedure? Should friendly settlements be avoided in certain cases?

FURA: Yes. As already mentioned, a recent Swedish report[5] seems to indicate that a broad application of the settlement policy could lead to the disappearance of case law. There would be no guidance for the domestic courts and it is one of our primary tasks as a court to give guidance. I therefore think that the friendly settlement procedure should only be used in areas where the case law is settled. In those cases, the drafting of judgments would only consist of copying and pasting templates. Such areas exist, for instance, in length of proceedings and property cases. I do not think that it would be appropriate to conclude friendly settlements in new areas because the Court could be deprived of the possibility of developing its case law. This is a very important task.

KELLER: Do you think that it is appropriate to conclude friendly settlements in, for instance, Articles 2 or 3 ECHR cases?

FURA: That is a really tough question. I would take a very cautious approach. I would say that there could be Articles 2 and 3 ECHR cases where it would be acceptable and even good to have a friendly settlement. Nonetheless, we have to be very careful. The Court should not become a money machine. Then, we would stop being a court of human rights. It would just be a matter of paying damages, which would be a very unfortunate development. It is part of the pressure to which we are subjected. I have not seen any such tendencies. However, I am also of the opinion that there is no area to be excluded. There might be specific circumstances where the applicants who seek relief would not be better served by a judgment but rather by a friendly settlement. It all depends on the circumstances and on what you put into this settlement. As you have hinted in your questions, there are a lot of other aspects apart from money that you can include in a friendly settlement. The recognition of a violation and future undertakings can

---

[5] Röttorp, P./Rogalska Hedlund, A. (2007).

also be part of a settlement. In certain circumstances, this could be much more important for an applicant.

KELLER: Could you think of any measures that would improve friendly settlements at the Court?

FURA: If we could process applications more quickly, then friendly settlements could also be handled more rapidly. It is almost a fact of life that, when a case is allowed to rot, then it becomes much more difficult to settle because the parties have been fighting for years. It does not bother them to keep on fighting for another couple of years. If the process is started early on, the parties are much more flexible. They can be massaged more easily and they are more open-minded. If you wait too long and the parties develop very strong beliefs, it will not be possible to settle. I am sure that there might be other ways of improving settlements. We have also discussed the possibility of setting up a special unit. It might be something to explore. I think that we definitely should look into it at some point. I am not so sure whether we will go down this road because negotiations require a certain amount of expertise and experience. In addition, it is also necessary to know the country and the case law. If a special unit is established, there will be some overlap in its work. It is unavoidable.

KELLER: Would you have some concrete wishes for the State representatives or the applicants concerning their friendly settlements?

FURA: It would be to come with an open mind. Many people – including those who apply too late or too early and those with unsuccessful complaints concerning rights which are not protected under the Convention – perceive themselves as having been violated. They are hurt in their feelings and they do not want to hear about a friendly settlement. There is no such thing as a "friendly" settlement for them. It is for this reason that they come to the Court. When they are here and they fill in their application, they are already beyond the friendly settlement stage. Ideally, alternative dispute resolution proceedings should be conducted at the domestic level and many countries do conduct them, but not in the human rights field.

KELLER: Should they be conducted in cases concerning human rights?

FURA: Yes, I think so. However, it is important to first acknowledge that there is a problem. The earlier this issue is addressed, the better. At the same time, it may never be too late. It depends on how much effort this Court or the Registrar can put into this process. There is a theory according to which it is always possible to find a compromise suitable for both parties. It takes a long time and the Court has to hear the parties out. It also takes a long time if you never meet, if you speak on the phone or if you just exchange letters.

KELLER: This was a very interesting interview. Thank you very much.

II. Interview with Jakub Wołąsiewicz

Respondent: Jakub Wołąsiewicz, Government Agent for Poland
Interviewer: Helen Keller
Assistant: Daniel Decurtins
Date: 30 January 2009
Time: 09:00–10:23
Interview time: 1:23 hrs
Place: Office of Helen Keller at the ECtHR, Strasbourg

JAKUB WOŁĄSIEWICZ: My name is Jakub Wołąsiewicz. I was born in Zielona Gora in 1960. I was educated at the Faculty of Law at Warsaw University. I graduated in 1984, and then I started my career in diplomacy. I have been working as a Government Agent since 2003.

HELEN KELLER: Do you have any special education in mediation or alternative dispute resolution?

WOŁĄSIEWICZ: No, but I have the personal skills that are required in this field. I was a negotiator or a mediator when I worked for the Ministry of Foreign Affairs. I took part in the negotiations of the main Polish treaties. For four years, I negotiated with Russians and I took part in the withdrawal of the Russian troops. Following the collapse of communism, I participated in the negotiations of all the treaties that replaced the former Polish and Soviet treaties with the new countries, new members of CIS (Commonwealth of Independent States) and also with other States. I have no special training in this field, but I was chosen to negotiate and I think that I was quite successful.

KELLER: From your experience, what are the main reasons leading Poland to conclude friendly settlements? What are the motives of applicants in seeking settlements instead of judgments?

WOŁĄSIEWICZ: In my opinion, it is not a policy of the State to conclude friendly settlements. It is rather a choice of the Government Agent. In my country, politicians are only interested in very important cases. I have an important margin of discretion in the resolution of routine cases: I can either wait for the judgment or conclude a friendly settlement. As you know, we have a lot of cases and we tried from the very beginning to regroup cases dealing with the same violations. We started concluding friendly settlements in areas where there was previous case law.

We decided to start the friendly settlement procedure in order to save time. For the Government, friendly settlements do not only save time but also money. According to the jurisprudence, the amount of money granted to the applicant in a friendly settlement can be lower than in a regular judgment. It is approximately 20–25 per cent lower. It is thus possible to save money in such cases.

This is also beneficial for the applicant. Once again, there is a delay in the proceedings in Polish cases. A few years ago, an applicant had to wait five, six and sometimes even eight, nine years for a judgment since the introduction of the application. If I conclude a friendly settlement after a communication with the Court and both sides agree on the amount of just satisfaction, they could receive this amount much quicker.

I must say that, for Polish applicants, the question of money is one of the most important ones. Poland is also a Party to the ICCPR, but few Poles bring complaints before the United Nations Human Rights Committee. I have approximately 300 new communications per year from the Court and only one complaint from the Human Rights Committee.

There are also applicants who are less interested in money and more in other individual measures. There is a third group which is connected to the pilot procedure. In such cases, the interest on each side is much deeper because it is not only connected to individual measures but also to the general ones.

KELLER: May I come back to the question of money? I am not sure that I understood you correctly. If you compare the amounts obtained in friendly settlements and in judgments, which one is higher?

WOŁĄSIEWICZ: Of course, the one in the judgment.

KELLER: Would you say that it is about 20 per cent higher?

WOŁĄSIEWICZ: Yes, approximately. There is also a benefit for the Court in this procedure. The Court saves time when it does not have to deal with the details of a specific case. In my opinion, this is a very important factor.

The friendly settlement procedure is at times complicated when the applicant, the Government Agent and the Court do not share the same views. However, we held last year quite a comprehensive discussion with the Court. The Registrars visited Poland and met with, not only me, but also the Minister of Justice, his Deputies and other experts. We discussed the possibility of enhancing the friendly settlement procedure to settle groups of cases.

The first group which we identified was composed of cases concerning the length of proceedings. We have a new Act on individual complaints against the excessive delay of judicial proceedings. It was enacted in 2004, but we had some implementation problems in the last three or four years. We have this domestic remedy, but there is a malfunction in some cases. Cases and complaints appeared again before the Court. We decided that it was necessary to amend the 2004 Act. The amended Act is currently considered by the Parliament. At the same time, we decided together with the Registry of the Court that the Government Agent could settle all the new complaints dealing with the former law.

The amount of the compensation granted by the Court in recent judgments in this type of case went up to 30,000 PLN (Polish Złoty). At the moment, the maximum amount is 10,000 PLN under the Polish law. We agreed with the Registry to take into account the fact that the amount of compensation has been raised up to 20,000 PLN under the new Act. This sum of money is lower than the average compensation that can be obtained in a judgment handed down by the Court in similar cases. At the moment, I am involved in a friendly settlement which concerns more than 100 applicants. From time to time, the applicants refuse the proposed amounts. In such situations, I use unilateral declarations. As part of the agreement with the Registry, it is understood that, if I offer the maximum amount (i.e. 20,000 PLN) and the applicant refuses this money, my unilateral declaration for 20,000 PLN will be accepted by the Court. This occurs in one group of cases which I mentioned, namely the cases concerning the length of proceedings.

We also have an agreement with the Registry in cases concerning a malfunction in the cassation procedure before Polish courts. We have no remedy in those cases. This problem was already handled by the Court in the *Staroszczyk*[1] and *Siałkowska*[2] cases. We did not find any problems with law, but rather with the practice. There was therefore no necessity to establish an exclusive remedy. In co-operation with the Supreme Court, we changed the practice. I believe that, there will not be any new cases now, but there are still some cases pending (approximately 50 similar cases). In those cases, we agreed to conclude a friendly settlement instead of creating a special remedy. It was less time-consuming.

The third group of cases relates to the length of detention. Here, we also established a scheme under which I propose an amount of money to the applicant as part of the friendly settlement proceedings. If he, or she, refuses this amount, I then make a unilateral declaration. We determined certain groups of cases where there was already established case law. We agreed on the amounts of money that the Government Agent could propose to the applicant. If the applicant opposes this kind of solution, I send a unilateral declaration to the Court and the Court accepts this proposal.

Given the existence of this scheme, I presume that there will no longer be any problems or any judgments handed down by the Court in these kinds of cases. We are now dealing with old cases which were already communicated to the Government. We have shown to the Court how we will deal with the new cases and what kind of remedies we will establish at the domestic level. The Court decided that this practice was sufficient and that there was an effective remedy. This is not strictly connected to the rules established in the case law of the Court:

---

[1] *Staroszczyk v. Poland* (Appl. No. 59519/00), Judgment (First Section), 22 March 2007, not yet reported.
[2] *Siałkowska v. Poland* (Appl. No. 8932/05), Judgment (First Section), 22 March 2007, not yet reported.

It is rather a sort of pilot project that the Court decided to carry out. Once again, the Court and I believe that approximately 50 per cent of all cases coming from the Polish system can be resolved on the basis of this pilot procedure. Of course, a very important part of this agreement is the confidence between the parties, namely the Government Agent and the Court.

KELLER: You said that a group from the Registry came to Warsaw. There were therefore no Judges involved.

WOŁĄSIEWICZ: Yes. According to the Rules of Court, Judges must be absolutely impartial. The friendly settlement procedure is not a part of the judicial discretion of the Court. It is rather part of proceedings conducted by the Registry. There was therefore no agreement with Judges, but rather with the Registry.

KELLER: Is this agreement written or oral?

WOŁĄSIEWICZ: We did not conclude any written agreement. We have, of course, the minutes of the meeting. Both sides have the memos. That is all. Once again, the ECtHR does not give me the right to conclude any agreements in this matter. It was a question of confidence. Both sides know on what we agreed, and I have no problem with this.

KELLER: Do you have a concrete mandate from the Polish Government? For example, are you allowed to proceed alone with the negotiations in length cases amounting to 20,000 PLN?

WOŁĄSIEWICZ: This is also a question of confidence, but this time it is between me and the Government. In this type of case, I negotiate alone with the Registry. Some high-ranking officials from the Ministry of Justice are also involved in this process as supervisors.

KELLER: Is the Treasurer involved?

WOŁĄSIEWICZ: The Treasurer was also involved in the discussion on the length of proceedings. We discussed the general measures, i.e. the draft Act amending the 2004 Act. There was a discussion on how high the amount of just satisfaction should be. From the very beginning of these negotiations, the Treasurer proposed a maximum amount of 12,000 PLN. The Court and I proposed a maximum amount of 20,000 PLN and following negotiations, the Treasurer agreed. When the draft Act went to the Government, the Treasurer said: "Yes, this is part of the agreement. We do not oppose the quota of 20,000 PLN."

KELLER: Is this method of settlement only used in Poland?

WOŁĄSIEWICZ: Yes, it is only used in Poland. All experiments with pilot proceedings were initiated in Poland.

KELLER: That is very useful information. You have spoken about the procedure followed in areas where there are routine friendly settlements. Do you also have friendly settlements in problematic areas where there is no established case law?

WOŁĄSIEWICZ: No. We use the friendly settlement procedure in cases where there is established case law concerning Poland. It is then much easier for me to justify, for instance, a compensation proposal in this kind of procedure. Of course, I am not controlled by the Government. No one asks me to justify this kind of procedure. In all friendly settlement cases, I prepare a kind of reasoning. In some cases, I also ask the Ministry of Justice for some kind of advice. Ninety-five per cent of all complaints are connected to the Polish system of justice and therefore my main partner in friendly settlements is the Ministry of Justice.

KELLER: Let us go back to the negotiations in – as I call them – class or mass friendly settlements, such as in the *Broniowski* case.[3] Can you tell us how you deal with a group of dozens or hundreds of applicants in cases where you have to conclude a friendly settlement?

WOŁĄSIEWICZ: Well, in pilot proceedings, I have much less discretion, because this is the collective responsibility of the entire Government. Further, an important part of the pilot proceedings concerns the question of general measures. These individual or general measures are also part of the negotiations and of the friendly settlement. As you may be aware, I only negotiate with one applicant during the pilot procedure. This applicant does not have any contact with the others.

On the one hand, the Government must realize that there is a serious issue at stake and that it has to take full responsibility. On the other hand, the applicant should also be aware that the settlement will have an important bearing on cases of many other people who are suffering from the same systemic malfunction.

Applicants usually have very good lawyers, such as Mr Hermeliński who is now a member of the Constitutional Court. Thus, the best advocates are against me. The individual applicant is not alone against the entire State machinery. It is not easy, because the point of view of an applicant can sometimes differ from the point of view of his, or her, counsel. The lawyers' knowledge of the procedure and of all the implications is much better than that of the applicant. Usually, there are no negotiations between the applicant and the Government. There could also be problems between the applicant and his counsel. In a pilot procedure, it is necessary to have someone from the Registry. This person then acts as a mediator.

KELLER: Where do you negotiate?

WOŁĄSIEWICZ: In Warsaw.

---

[3] *Broniowski v. Poland* (Appl. No. 31443/96), Judgment (Grand Chamber–Pilot Judgment), 22 June 2004, Reports 2004-V, 1; *Broniowski v. Poland* (Appl. No. 31443/96), Judgment (Grand Chamber–Friendly Settlement), 28 September 2005, Reports 2005-IX, 1.

KELLER: And how many persons represent the Registry?

WOŁĄSIEWICZ: Usually, there are two persons: the Registrar, it could be Michael O'Boyle or Paul Mahoney, and one lawyer from the Section dealing with Polish cases. In both Polish pilot judgments, it was the same person, Ms Renata Degener. On the applicant's side, there is the applicant and his, or her, lawyer. There are sometimes two or three lawyers. On the Government's side, there were once 15 people. This was an unbalanced situation, but it did not mean that the rights at stake were adjudicated in a disproportionate manner. This is precisely the role of the Registry, namely, to find a balance on both sides.

I never encountered a situation where the Government tried to put pressure on the applicant. I cannot vouch that it will be the same in all future cases. The applicant mainly plays a role at the level of the individual measures, whereas the lawyer can also have a bearing on the general measures. The role of the Registry is very open; it does not only mediate in the negotiations, but it also gives advice and information about previous case law. In friendly settlements, all sides are equal and also very patient. In the *Broniowski* case,[4] we had two rounds of negotiations. In the following pilot procedure, in *Hutten-Czapska*,[5] one round of negotiations was sufficient. Those rounds took place in Warsaw, given that it was much easier for the Government and the applicant to meet there. Those negotiations never took place at the Government's offices; they were held at the Information Office of the Council of Europe.

KELLER: They took place in a neutral place.

WOŁĄSIEWICZ: Yes, it was absolutely neutral.

KELLER: Do you negotiate in Polish?

WOŁĄSIEWICZ: Well, the negotiations are in Polish and that is the only interference on the Government's side. We offered an interpreter, which was needed for Michael O'Boyle and another person. The Registry fully knows and understands what goes on between the parties. In a friendly settlement, we have no official lunches or anything of the sort. The Registry is absolutely independent. We only meet at the place where negotiations are held. The Registry also gives this kind of recommendation. There should be no links.

KELLER: Did you notice any differences between the applicants and the lawyers?

WOŁĄSIEWICZ: Yes. As I told you, for the applicant, the most important aspect is

---

    [4] Ibid.
    [5] *Hutten-Czapska v. Poland* (Appl. No. 35014/97), Judgment (Grand Chamber–Pilot Judgment), 19 June 2006, Reports 2006-VIII, 57; *Hutten-Czapska v. Poland* (Appl. No. 35014/97), Judgment (Grand Chamber–Friendly Settlement), 28 April 2008, not yet reported.

the individual measure, that is, money. For the lawyer, the general measures are much more important.

KELLER: Do you sometimes sense more reluctance from one side than the other?

WOŁĄSIEWICZ: We feel reluctance from both sides.

KELLER: What do you do when you feel that the negotiations come to a dead point and that there is a risk that they will fail? Can you intervene or do you just sit quietly and wait for the Registry to move forward with the negotiations?

WOŁĄSIEWICZ: Well, there was never a dead point. It has never happened in my life. It may look as though there is a dead point, but this is strategy. Also, the applicant uses these kinds of tricks to pretend that we have come to a dead point. In reality, it is not a dead point; it is part of the negotiations. I use this as part of my negotiating skills and nothing more. Both sides do the same. Of course, if it looks as if it is a dead point, the Registry is a little bit nervous and is much more active in these situations than an ordinary mediator. In such situations, the Registry decides to close negotiations and to hold bilateral talks. That means that they try to present the situation to the applicant once again and then to me. Thus, the mediation goes on in such situations as perhaps an arbitration procedure would. The arbitrator is the Registry. This is a combination of different kinds of settlement procedures. It is not only mediation, conciliation or negotiation. From time to time, it also resembles to an arbitration procedure. However, we do not have any specific rules, terms of reference or anything of the sort. The procedure is absolutely open and both sides decide which kinds of negotiation techniques they prefer to use.

KELLER: Did you ever encounter a situation where a group of applicants among hundreds of others would not agree on the general friendly settlement?

WOŁĄSIEWICZ: Yes, always.

KELLER: How do you deal with such a situation?

WOŁĄSIEWICZ: This is a normal situation. The remedy is always connected to some kind of financial benefit. It is not possible to satisfy all people with a remedy agreed to in a pilot procedure settlement. However, this is part of the game. We understand that potential applicants want to receive much more than the pilot applicant received. We cannot satisfy all the needs of those individuals. Once again, the Registry plays a very important role in such situations. Following the friendly settlement, there is a judgment of the Court (i.e. the Judges decide whether the friendly settlement is fair). If there is a final judgment approving the friendly settlement, then this is the end of the story.

KELLER: Let us discuss the content of a friendly settlement. What is the content of a friendly settlement in a pilot judgment? What do you agree on?

WOŁĄSIEWICZ: We agree on individual and general measures.

KELLER: Do you agree to acknowledge that the Convention has been violated?

WOŁĄSIEWICZ: Yes.

KELLER: And this is part of the written procedure?

WOŁĄSIEWICZ: Absolutely, in pilot judgment settlements. We also have regular friendly settlements in which we do not acknowledge violations of the Convention, because according to the Rules of Court, there is no such need in this context. However, part of the settlement in a pilot judgment is that there was a violation and that the Government understands the genesis of the violation. The Government therefore proposes individual measures to the applicant and general measures to the other people involved.

KELLER: Let us discuss these two rules of content. Are there other individual measures which could be included in a friendly settlement apart of money?

WOŁĄSIEWICZ: There could be, but they are very difficult to agree on. For instance, in cases relating to detention, a possible individual measure could be the release of a person or the reduction of a sentence. I have no permission from the Minister of Justice to interfere with the work of the Polish judicial system. I can offer money or apologies. I remember that, from time to time, a component of the agreement was that I visited the person concerned and apologized.

KELLER: Can you explain how the general measures fit into the friendly settlement?

WOŁĄSIEWICZ: The friendly settlement in pilot judgments is concluded after the main judgment where the violation and its source are mentioned. There is no reason to determine the kind of remedy that should be used or the kind of general measure that should be implemented by the Government just to fulfil the requirement of the Convention and of the Court's case law. Before the Government enters into negotiations, we determine the general measures as part of a draft law or as part of a scheme included in this draft law. During the friendly settlement negotiations, this draft is commented on by the applicant and by the Registry. The Registry decides at this preliminary stage whether the proposed draft is compatible with the remedy used in these kinds of cases. Usually, the general measure is the most important for the Government. Individual measures are of lesser interest because they concern only one person.

From time to time, I raise a little the level of compensation in individual measures. This was criticized by ECtHR lawyers. They said that the Government gave more money to individuals because they agreed on general measures that would not be acceptable to other applicants. It needs to be emphasized, however, that every friendly settlement is evaluated by the Court, which then decides whether it is fair or not. From the very beginning, an explanation was also included as to the differences in levels of compensation. For instance, in the *Broniowski* case, only one person, Mr Broniowski, received just satisfaction in the ECtHR proceedings. The explanation for this was that it was a benefit for the first applicant. He could have received more in domestic proceedings.

KELLER: You told us that you discuss draft legislation with the applicant and the Registry. Nonetheless, there is the risk that this draft legislation will go to Parliament and that Parliament will amend it.

WOŁĄSIEWICZ: There is such a risk.

KELLER: And how do you deal with this risk?

WOŁĄSIEWICZ: I always say before the Parliament: "I have an agreement with the Court. If you wish to break this agreement, I will commit suicide in the Parliament's main room. It will be a scandal." It works.

KELLER: This is interesting because the Convention system in the particular case of pilot judgments has a more or less direct effect on the legislative procedure at the national level.

WOŁĄSIEWICZ: It represents a huge interference in the domestic legal system, especially in countries like Germany. It is a very sensitive question. I am aware of the problem that Ms Wittling-Vogel has, for instance, with the law on length of proceedings. It is a nightmare. However, it is specific to Germany. It involves difficult work!

KELLER: It is particularly difficult for you because you are in between. You have the Court on the one side and you have the national political bodies, such as the Government and the Parliament, on the other.

WOŁĄSIEWICZ: I withdrew Soviet soldiers, thousands of them.

KELLER: You can surely handle this. Could you tell us how many friendly settlements you would be able to bring to a successful end in ordinary cases? Do they represent 50 per cent or 60 per cent of these cases?

WOŁĄSIEWICZ: I do not know. In the previous years, I did not frequently conclude friendly settlements. Since then, we are still waiting for the case law. Approximately two years ago, I started thinking precisely about this kind of pilot procedure, about the negotiations with the Registry and about the policy of friendly settlements.

KELLER: Was it your idea?

WOŁĄSIEWICZ: Yes.

KELLER: Really? You personally? (*respondent nods*) That is good to know!

WOŁĄSIEWICZ: I remember the first meeting with President Costa when he said: "No, no, no. This is a problem." Finally, at the beginning of the year, I sent to President Costa an invitation to Poland saying: "This time, I am not looking for your presence as a President. I would like you to work with the Polish authorities in order to find a solution in these three groups of cases." He did not agree, saying that he is a known person and that he could not participate in this kind of negotiation. And then, Michael O'Boyle said: "Well, if you wish, we can visit Poland and start thinking about how to reduce the amount of cases."

I was interested in holding a consultation on general remedies with the Court. It was absolutely clear for me that Poland would have to amend its laws. Fortunately, we do not have the same problems as other countries where the newly enacted law does not comply with the case law and the Convention. In my opinion, it is much better to consult with the Registry before an important law is changed, as this could potentially generate new cases.

During the consultations with the Court, the Ministry of Justice presented some ideas and advanced some very "Polish" justifications for the changes introduced. The Registry found that this explanation was not appropriate, as Poland had to follow European standards in this case. The personnel of the Ministry of Justice then started to realize that there were problems with domestic legislation. As I mentioned, the same happened to the Treasurer who was opposing the payment of a high amount of money. Thus, the first part allows us to hold consultations on future remedies. At the same time, however, if we have a perfect remedy, should we not find some kind of solution for the cases which are connected to the previous law? How should these cases be resolved?

There are two possibilities; they can be settled or resolved on a case-by-case basis by the Court. However, we need some kind of scheme for friendly settlements. Let us say, for instance, that I propose some quotas which are not acceptable to the Court. Then, the applicant refuses the amount of money, I reiterate the same proposal in the unilateral declaration and the Court finally rejects it. It is therefore senseless. From the very beginning, we should have a mutual understanding. We should establish that we finalize all groups of cases according to some sort of scheme which is acceptable to the Court and the Government Agent. The Government Agent would then be able to propose an amount which would not be rejected by the Court.

KELLER: Let us go back to the decision process before the Court. You said that you approached President Costa. He was reluctant at the beginning, but then he came to Poland. Did he finally authorize Mr O'Boyle and Ms Degener to come to Poland, or was this the initiative of the Registry?

WOŁĄSIEWICZ: Well, the decision finally came from the Registry.

KELLER: President Costa and the Judges were not involved?

WOŁĄSIEWICZ: This happened for the very first time. They were a little anxious as to the outcome of this process. They did not know how it would end. They were in an uncomfortable situation. Following the consultations, they were enthusiastic about the implementation of the scheme. There is nonetheless a small problem. Yesterday, I had a meeting with Lawrence Early and he said it was an excellent procedure, but that it may not be possible to replicate it with other countries. As part of such a process, there needs to be confidence and the will to co-operate.

KELLER: Did you have any problems with the enforcement of friendly settlements?

WOŁĄSIEWICZ: No, it has never happened.

KELLER: The Government paid and the general measures were implemented.

WOŁĄSIEWICZ: Well, not in connection to the pilot judgments. Do you remember the *Tysiąc* case?[6]

KELLER: No.

WOŁĄSIEWICZ: It concerned abortion. There was a lack of remedy for pregnant women who have the right to abortion under the law. This remedy is still not implemented. It largely depends on the Minister who is dealing with the measure.

KELLER: Was the *Tysiąc* case combined with a friendly settlement?

WOŁĄSIEWICZ: No, this was a judgment. As I said, I never introduced general measures in friendly settlements. They are only part of regular judgments. They may, exceptionally, be part of friendly settlements concluded in pilot proceedings.

KELLER: What measures would improve friendly settlement proceedings and would make your life or the applicant's easier?

WOŁĄSIEWICZ: I think that the procedure launched last year in regular cases is absolutely satisfactory. It has played an important role in reducing my workload as well as that of the Court. In my country, and perhaps in other countries as well, it is thought to be senseless to wait and to proceed on a judgment-by-judgment basis once a group of cases has been identified. It is much better to agree on individual measures as part of a general scheme. This is a new procedure, and it is not regulated by the Convention or the Rules of Court. I think, however, it is effective. Until now, I did not receive any criticism on behalf of the applicants regarding this proposal. Many applicants would be much happier if they could

---

[6] *Tysiąc v. Poland* (Appl. No. 5410/03), Judgment (Fourth Section), 20 March 2007, not yet reported.

receive the money quicker. Unfortunately, the cases that are communicated to me already have a five-year delay. Applicants then wait eight years on average.

KELLER: What do you think of this proactive approach which consists of sending a proposal for a friendly settlement with the first communication? Are you satisfied with it?

WOŁĄSIEWICZ: Yes! Yes!

KELLER: Do you find yourself to be overwhelmed by the Court?

WOŁĄSIEWICZ: No, I do not accept everything blindly. I must of course check if there is a real violation. It is senseless to launch the regular procedure and wait for the judgment. Thus, in a situation where the complaint is absolutely justified, I proceed with a friendly settlement. As regards these groups of cases, it is considered from the very beginning that the regular procedure will definitely not be followed. The amount of just satisfaction obtained in a judgment is much higher than in a friendly settlement. Thus, all parties are satisfied.

KELLER: Is there anything else that you would like to say?

WOŁĄSIEWICZ: During the Stockholm Colloquy last year, I proposed a so-called simplified procedure for pilot judgments.

KELLER: Do you have any written documents about it?

WOŁĄSIEWICZ: You could find it on the Court's website. It was published under the title "Stockholm Colloquy"[7] in June. It contains my statement about the pilot procedure.[8] My experience with the *Broniowski*[9] and the *Hutten-Czapska*[10] cases allowed me to have a critical point of view on the matter. First of all, it is a time-consuming procedure. It took about ten years from the moment when the application was lodged to the final decision approving the friendly settlement. This was not the end of the matter, because there were still proceedings in the clone cases. My proposal was to simplify the procedure. In the *Broniowski* and *Hutten-Czapska* cases, I did not agree with the violation at the initial stage. There was thus a judgment.

KELLER: Was it necessary?

WOŁĄSIEWICZ: Yes, it is necessary in all sorts of situations. I could do the same with some of the cases that have just been concluded. For instance, the length of proceedings cases concern a malfunction in the 2004 Act. Thus, taking into account that there was a violation, I can conclude it on the same basis. It was a

---

[7] Council of Europe (2008).
[8] Wołąsiewicz, J. (2008), p. 94 et seq.
[9] *Broniowski v. Poland*, note 3 *supra*.
[10] *Hutten-Czapska v. Poland*, note 5 *supra*.

malfunction and the rights of the applicant were violated. In a situation where there is no question of a violation, it is not necessary to wait for the first judgment. After the communication, we can immediately proceed with the friendly settlement. This reduces the amount of time required to resolve a case. I introduced this idea at the Stockholm Colloquy and in the reflection group.

DANIEL DECURTINS: With which Section do you mostly work?

WOŁĄSIEWICZ: I do not even know. My main partner is Lawrence Early, but from time to time, another Section of the Registry is also involved.

DECURTINS: Are there any cases which you would refuse to settle?

WOŁĄSIEWICZ: Yes, cases concerning sensitive issues, such as abortion.

DECURTINS: Do you refuse friendly settlements in cases where a murderer has undergone lengthy proceedings and is currently in prison?

WOŁĄSIEWICZ: Once again, these are the priorities. I did not mention such cases as they did not give rise to a friendly settlement scheme.

A very important part of the consultation with the Registry was the question of prison conditions. The Polish prisons are overcrowded. According to the Polish law, each prisoner should have three square meters. In other countries, there are different standards. However, Poland has been violating this rule for five years. I tried to change the prison situation, but once again, these are financial decisions. I have not received any positive response from the Ministry of Justice for these cases for four years. However, this has changed in the last year. The Ministry of Justice decided to follow my advice. Overcrowding is part of the problem of prison conditions, but it is also connected to other violations. Thus, these are some of the priorities.

I won the first fight against overcrowding. The Minister of Justice prepared an action plan. We had more than 100,000 prisoners for 70,000 places. There were 30,000 too many detainees for the places available. Yesterday, we finally achieved the right balance. An important issue during our consultations was that we present to the Court (to the Registry) this action plan with the promise that the situation is temporary. Otherwise, the Court could expect 200,000 potential applications. We had the feeling that, for the Court, this kind of massive violation is very dangerous. We prepared the action plan and we introduced an effective remedy. We had the feeling that one judgment from the Court would have a domino effect. Thus, we asked the Court – and this was part of very confidential negotiations – not to hand down any judgments regarding overcrowding until we change the prison situation. Currently, the situation has changed, and there could be a judgment on the matter.

I launched the project concerning prison overcrowding after Mr Hammarberg visited Poland. For me, the work of Mr Hammarberg was a warning signal. He indicated the possible violations that could reach the Court and give rise to a judgment. If I did not quickly react to the Hammarberg recommendation, 300,000 applications could have appeared before the Court. I was therefore very satisfied with the work of Mr Hammarberg and his recommendations during the visit. Of course, he held meetings with the Minister of Justice and other important officials. Following this visit, we prepared this action plan as well as introduced the remedy. I believe that there will be no judgments regarding prison overcrowding. Nevertheless, the most important question was that the Court agreed during this consultation not to adjudicate these cases. Once again, this was an important sign of confidence. The Court did not have to do this. It could have announced the judgment five months ago. However, the Court approves of us and trusts us. Once again, I have the impression that the question of confidence is very important in the work of the Court, especially between the Government and the Court.

KELLER: We thank you for this very interesting interview.

III. Entretien avec Frank Schürmann

Interviewé: Frank Schürmann, agent du gouvernement suisse
Intervieweur: Helen Keller
Assistant: Daniel Decurtins
Date: 30 janvier 2009
Heure: 08:30–09:30
Durée: 00:50 hrs
Endroit: bureau de Helen Keller à la Cour, Strasbourg

FRANK SCHÜRMANN: Je m'appelle Frank Schürmann. Je suis né le 21 février 1955. Je suis l'agent du gouvernement suisse devant la Cour. J'occupe cette fonction depuis trois ans; je travaille pour le bureau de l'agent depuis 18 ans avec une interruption de trois ans. Durant ces trois années, je me suis occupé de l'unification des codes de procédure pénale.

HELEN KELLER: Avez-vous une formation dans la médiation ou dans les règlements amiables?

SCHÜRMANN: Je n'ai aucune formation spécifique dans ce domaine.

KELLER: Selon votre expérience, quels sont les motifs – surtout pour le gouvernement suisse, mais aussi pour les requérants – pour conclure un règlement amiable?

SCHÜRMANN: Il faut d'abord dire que très peu d'affaires suisses ont été réglées à Strasbourg par un règlement amiable. C'était le cas pour 11 affaires seulement (parmi plus de 4000 requêtes enregistrées depuis l'entrée en vigueur de la Convention en 1974). Si l'on ajoutait les affaires dans lesquelles on a concrètement discuté la possibilité d'un règlement amiable (mais qui n'a pas été réalisée), on arriverait à une quinzaine d'affaires au total.

Du côté du gouvernement, il est rare de prendre l'initiative. On l'a fait lorsque, par exemple, la législation avait changé depuis l'introduction de la requête. C'était le cas dans l'affaire *D. c. Suisse*[1] qui soulevait la même question juridique que l'affaire *Huber*[2] tranchée par la Cour en 1990 (question de l'impartialité du *Bezirksanwalt* du canton de Zurich sous l'angle de l'article 5 (3) CEDH). Le requérant D. a saisi la Cour après cet arrêt, mais les faits se sont produits avant. On s'est dit que cela ne servirait à rien de poursuivre la procédure à Strasbourg et nous avons pris contact avec l'avocat du requérant avant même d'attendre la décision sur la recevabilité de la Commission.

---

[1] *D. c. Suisse* (req. no. 15736/89), rapport (commission–règlement amiable), 1 avril 1992, D.R. 73, 102.
[2] *Huber c. Suisse* (req. no. 12794/87), arrêt (plénière), 23 octobre 1990, séries A, vol. 188.

KELLER: C'est le principe, mais la pratique est différente avec cette approche pro-active du greffe.

SCHÜRMANN: Je sais qu'il y a des États qui concluent de plus en plus de règlements amiables dans le cadre de cette approche (qu'on appelle parfois un règlement "hors procédure" pour le distinguer du règlement amiable au sens technique qui n'intervient dès lors que la décision sur la recevabilité a été prise, cf. article 38 (1) (b) CEDH).

KELLER: Comment réagissez-vous quand la Cour vous propose un règlement amiable? Est-ce que cela arrive parfois?

SCHÜRMANN: Quand on est invité à déposer nos observations sur la recevabilité et le bien fondé d'une affaire, on est également invité à se prononcer sur la possibilité d'un règlement amiable. La réponse standard est la suivante: "À ce stade de la procédure, nous n'envisageons pas de régler la présente affaire à l'amiable."

KELLER: Est-ce le standard suisse?

SCHÜRMANN: Oui, pour la simple raison qu'en règle générale, il y a une affaire défendable et à défendre, tranchée au préalable par le Tribunal fédéral.

KELLER: L'arrêt et la loi?

SCHÜRMANN: L'arrêt et l'application de la loi dans le cas d'espèce. Il est rare que la loi en tant que telle soit mise en cause.

KELLER: Passons à la procédure. Quels sont les pas à prendre pour conclure un règlement amiable?

SCHÜRMANN: On parle de la procédure du règlement amiable proprement dite où il y a un échange entre les parties par l'intermédiaire de la Cour. La Cour nous invite à prendre position et alors on déclare à quelles conditions on pourrait conclure un règlement amiable.

KELLER: Par le biais de la Cour? Cela veut dire le biais de qui?

SCHÜRMANN: Du greffe de la Cour. L'engagement concret de la Cour en faveur d'un règlement amiable nous indique qu'il pourrait y avoir une violation de la Convention. On a eu des affaires, dans lesquelles le gouvernement était prêt à conclure un règlement amiable qui n'a pourtant pas pu être mis en œuvre.

KELLER: Parce que les requérants l'ont refusé?

SCHÜRMANN: Oui, parce que les requérants ont émis des conditions tellement exagérées qu'on n'a pas pu les accepter.

KELLER: Parlez-vous parfois directement avec le requérant ou avec l'avocat du requérant?

SCHÜRMANN: Oui, cela arrive. Il arrive qu'on contacte directement le requérant ou son avocat, ou que l'avocat du requérant nous appelle. Cela peut arriver même avant que la Cour ou le greffe concrétisent la possibilité de conclure un règlement amiable. C'était le cas dans une affaire suisse dans laquelle on n'avait même pas déposé nos observations sur la recevabilité et le bien fondé (affaire *D*.).[3] Dans une autre affaire, c'était l'avocat qui nous a appelé en soulignant l'intérêt de son client de terminer au plus vite la procédure à Strasbourg. Il sied toutefois de souligner que ces affaires sont restées l'exception. Notre philosophie est basée sur la prudence.

KELLER: Lorsque vous négociez, vous avez à vos côtés deux personnes, notamment l'avocat et le requérant. Est-ce qu'il y a une différence dans l'attitude de ces deux personnes? Négociez-vous avec l'avocat? Est-ce qu'il faut plutôt convaincre l'avocat ou le requérant?

SCHÜRMANN: Notre interlocuteur est toujours l'avocat.

KELLER: Même dans les cas ou il n'y a pas d'avocat?

SCHÜRMANN: Non. Dans ce cas, on serait évidemment obligé de contacter directement le requérant. Mais à ma connaissance cela n'a jamais été le cas et aucun requérant ne nous a jamais contactés.

KELLER: La procédure de négociation est-elle écrite? Est-ce que vous vous rencontrez pour négocier?

SCHÜRMANN: On ne l'a jamais fait. Tout se passe par le biais du greffe de la Cour. Ceci n'exclut pas le contact direct.

KELLER: Les négociations sont-elles confidentielles?

SCHÜRMANN: Oui.

KELLER: Est-ce que vous avez des problèmes quand vous n'avez pas pu conclure un règlement amiable et que la procédure normale continue? Est-ce qu'il arrive que vous possédez des informations confidentielles qui rendent la procédure subséquente plus difficile?

SCHÜRMANN: À mon souvenir, cette situation ne s'est jamais présentée.

KELLER: Pour les parties, je pense que ce n'est pas tellement intéressant. Pour quelles raisons croyez-vous que les négociations échouent?

SCHÜRMANN: Il y avait deux affaires dans lesquelles on a vraiment essayé de conclure un règlement amiable, sans y arriver. Les motifs étaient différents. L'objet de la première affaire, l'affaire *Kessler*,[4] était le droit de répliquer (article 6 (1)

---

[3] *D. c. Suisse*, note 1 *supra*.
[4] *Kessler c. Suisse* (req. no. 10577/04), arrêt (première section), 26 juillet 2007, pas encore publié.

CEDH), problème que la Cour avait déjà tranché à plusieurs reprises. Le requérant insistait d'avoir un arrêt sur le fond.

KELLER: Et puis?

SCHÜRMANN: Le greffe nous a signalé que la chose était mûre et nous a conseillé de faire une déclaration unilatérale. On l'a fait; pourtant, l'affaire s'est terminée par un arrêt de la Cour.

KELLER: Ça, c'est intéressant.

SCHÜRMANN: Dans cet arrêt, la Cour a indiqué que le requérant pourrait tout de même avoir besoin d'un arrêt de la Cour pour pouvoir entamer la procédure de révision en vertu de l'article 122 de la loi sur le Tribunal fédéral (ce qui ne correspond d'ailleurs pas à la jurisprudence du Tribunal fédéral, cf. ATF B 57/06 du 28 juin 2006). L'idée derrière un règlement amiable est de clore l'affaire au niveau international et national. C'est évident. On ne peut pas aller devant le Tribunal fédéral sur la base d'un règlement amiable et demander la révision de son arrêt. On était un peu surpris parce que cette affaire aurait pu être réglée à l'amiable. La deuxième affaire était *Hadri-Vionnet*.[5] Malgré les efforts, le règlement amiable n'a pas pu être réalisé.

KELLER: C'est un point intéressant. Je voudrais bien revenir sur l'affaire *Kessler*. Est-ce qu'il est clair dans l'arrêt *Kessler* que le gouvernement suisse voulait conclure un règlement amiable et qu'il proposait une déclaration unilatérale? Est-ce mentionné dans le texte de l'arrêt?

SCHÜRMANN: Cela ressort effectivement du paragraphe 15 de l'arrêt de la Cour.

KELLER: En termes de temps et d'énergie, est-ce qu'il est plus difficile de préparer un jugement ou un règlement amiable? Est-ce que cela vous prend plus de temps pour préparer des observations pour une procédure normale que de négocier avec le requérant?

SCHÜRMANN: Cela prend beaucoup plus de temps pour préparer des observations. Les observations sur la recevabilité et le bien fondé, les observations complémentaires, les observations sur l'article 41 CEDH prennent beaucoup plus de temps. C'est lié au fait qu'on envisage la possibilité d'un règlement amiable que dans les cas très clairs. À part des cas exceptionnels, il n'y a pas grande chose à examiner et à expliquer.

KELLER: Pour les cas ayant trait à la longueur des procédures, le gouvernement suisse refuse en principe de conclure des règlements amiables et de suivre l'approche pro-active du greffe.

---

[5] *Hadri-Vionnet c. Suisse* (req. no. 55525/00), arrêt (cinquième section), 14 février 2008, pas encore publié.

Schürmann: On ne l'a jamais fait pour une question de longueur de procédure. Il y en a très peu d'ailleurs.

Keller: Mais il y en a?

Schürmann: Il y en a eu dans le cadre de l'article 5 (3) CEDH pour la longueur de la détention préventive. Une affaire est d'ailleurs pendante devant la Cour. C'est une affaire qui a été jugée par le Tribunal pénal de Bellinzona. Elle concernait le trafic de 1,500 kilos d'héroïne par un clan du Kosovo. Le requérant avait été maintenu pendant une durée de temps considérable (plus de cinq ans) en détention provisoire. Même dans ce genre d'affaires qui soulèvent, à première vue, des questions sérieuses quant à la compatibilité de la mesure incriminée avec la Convention, notre approche vis-à-vis la conclusion d'un règlement amiable reste prudente: on défend la position des autorités nationales – tant qu'elle est défendable.[6]

Keller: Est-ce qu'il y a des arrêts où la Cour a constaté une violation mais a décidé de reporter sa décision en ce qui concerne l'article 41 CEDH? Est-ce que le gouvernement suisse et le requérant commencent à négocier à ce stade un règlement amiable? Est-ce que cela arrive?

Schürmann: En tout cas, ce n'est pas la pratique dans les affaires suisses. Certes, il y a eu l'affaire *Schuler-Zgraggen*.[7] Dans ce cas, toutefois, c'était le gouvernement suisse qui a demandé à la Cour de ne pas trancher la question de l'article 41 CEDH parce que la procédure de révision était entrée en vigueur juste avant l'audience devant la Cour. On avait plaidé que, si la Cour constatait une violation, il y aurait la possibilité d'une procédure de révision permettant au Tribunal fédéral de se prononcer sur la question de la satisfaction équitable. Étant donné que la requérante n'était pas satisfaite du montant qu'elle avait obtenu dans le cadre de la procédure de révision, il y a eu l'affaire *Schuler-Zgraggen (Article 50)*.[8] Il s'agit donc d'une affaire assez particulière, la seule dans laquelle la question de la satisfaction équitable a été tranchée séparément du fonds.

Keller: Le contenu d'un règlement amiable inclut toujours l'argent. Vous avez dit que lorsque vous acceptez une proposition pour un règlement amiable, le montant est le même que le requérant recevrait dans une procédure normale? Ou est-ce un montant plus élevé?

Schürmann: C'est difficile à dire. Il est difficile de prévoir les montants que la Cour va octroyer. En ce qui concerne les frais et dépenses pour les juridictions

---

[6] *Shabani c. Suisse* (req. no. 29044/06), arrêt (première section), 5 novembre 2009, pas encore publié.
[7] *Schuler-Zgraggen c. Suisse* (req. no. 14518/89), arrêt (chambre), 24 juin 1993, séries A, vol. 263.
[8] *Schuler-Zgraggen c. Suisse* (req. no. 14518/89), arrêt (chambre), 31 janvier 1995, séries A, vol. 305-A.

nationales et internationales, les choses sont relativement simples. Dans le cadre du dommage matériel, c'est souvent le lien de causalité qui prête à discussion. En ce qui concerne le tort moral, on a l'impression que la Cour, de plus en plus, accorde des montants à ce titre. Par le passé et pour les affaires suisses, la règle était que la publication de l'arrêt est susceptible de réparer le tort moral. En tout cas, il est difficile de prévoir les montants. De façon générale, je dirais qu'on n'a pas tendance à offrir des montants sensiblement plus élevés par rapport à ceux qu'on soumet à la Cour dans le cadre de nos observations sous l'article 41 CEDH, pour arriver à tout prix à un règlement amiable.

KELLER: Est-ce que d'autres choses peuvent se trouver dans un règlement amiable? Est-ce que vous acceptez de reconnaître que la CEDH a été violée dans le cadre d'un règlement amiable?

SCHÜRMANN: Non, mais cela fait parti des règles du jeu. Je crois qu'on ne l'a jamais fait, à une exception près.[9]

KELLER: Est-ce qu'on peut trouver autre chose dans un règlement amiable?

SCHÜRMANN: Oui. Il y avait autre chose que l'argent dans l'affaire *Tatete*.[10] Ce cas concernait une requérante d'asile qui était atteinte du SIDA. Sa demande d'asile a été refusée et puis elle avait fait une demande de reconsidération (*Wiedererwägungsgesuch*). Au lieu de poursuivre la procédure de reconsidération, on a entamé des négociations pour conclure un règlement amiable. Le contenu de ce règlement amiable était l'admission provisoire de la requérante.

KELLER: Dans quel endroit avez-vous commencé les négociations? C'était suite à la communication de l'affaire à la Cour?

SCHÜRMANN: Oui. Je crois même après la décision sur la recevabilité. À l'époque c'était toujours séparé. Tant que l'avis de la Cour n'est pas connu, l'issue de la procédure est formellement ouverte. Je crois qu'il y a différents types de règlements amiables qui sont conclus pour différents motifs.

KELLER: Je suis absolument d'accord.

SCHÜRMANN: Vous êtes mieux placée que moi pour le savoir. Il y a des affaires dans lesquelles on peut sans autre admettre qu'il y a eu violation.

KELLER: Est-ce qu'il y a d'autres éléments qui sont inclus dans les règlements amiables?

SCHÜRMANN: Oui, par exemple dans l'affaire *Waser et Steiger*.[11] Il s'agissait de

---

[9] *Kessler c. Suisse*, note 4 *supra*, para. 15.
[10] *Tatete c. Suisse* (req. no. 41874/98), arrêt (deuxième section–arrangement), 6 juillet 2000, non publié.
[11] *Waser et Steiger c. Suisse* (req. no. 31990/02), décision (cinquième section–arrangement), 23 octobre 2006, non publié.

l'interdiction du mariage entre un père et sa belle-fille (*Stieftochter*). Le législateur fédéral avait saisi l'occasion des travaux en cours dans le cadre de la loi sur le partenariat enregistré, pour introduire une dispositon permettant une telle union. On a tout de suite conclu un règlement hors procédure et l'interdiction du mariage a été levée.

KELLER: Dans le cadre de l'article 8 CEDH, est-il est possible d'accepter un droit de visite?

SCHÜRMANN: Oui, pourquoi pas? A condition que la situation se présente d'une façon claire.

KELLER: Silence des parties? Est-ce accepté dans les règlements amiables?

SCHÜRMANN: Silence?

KELLER: Silence sur le cas, sur l'affaire?

SCHÜRMANN: Oui, la confidentialité est respectée. En tout cas, de notre côté. Et je n'ai pas de raison de croire qu'il en irait autrement du côté des requérants.

KELLER: Par exemple, destruction des documents des autorités nationales, tel le casier judiciaire ou les écoutes téléphoniques? Est-ce que cela pourrait faire part du contenu d'un règlement amiable?

SCHÜRMANN: Oui, si le requérant le propose et dans la mesure où de telles mesures pourrait faire l'objet des mesures individuelles revendiquées par le Comité des Ministres dans le cadre de ces compétences en vertu de l'article 46 CEDH.

KELLER: Est-ce que le gouvernement suisse a déjà proposé dans un règlement amiable de changer la loi?

SCHÜRMANN: Non, pas à ma connaissance. Dans les affaires pertinentes, la loi était soit en cours de modification ou venait d'être adoptée, mais n'était pas encore entrée en vigueur. Un exemple de ce cas de figure est l'affaire *I.O.*[12] qui concernait la procédure pénale bernoise, notamment le droit absolu de réplique dans le cadre de la procédure de *habeas corpus*. Les bernois avaient entre-temps changé la loi. Dans ce cas de figure, il est facile de conclure un règlement amiable.

KELLER: Quels sont les facteurs qui favorisent la conclusion d'un règlement amiable selon vous?

SCHÜRMANN: Du côté du gouvernement, le facteur principal est la prévisibilité de l'arrêt constatant une violation de la Convention pour quelque raison que ce soit. Du côté du requérant, je crois que les motifs sont assez différents. On a eu une affaire dans laquelle le requérant avait fait pression parce qu'il avait purgé sa

---

[12] *I.O. c. Suisse* (req. no. 21529/93), arrêt (deuxième section–règlement amiable), 8 mars 2001, non publié.

peine en Suisse et avait l'intention de retourner, le plus vite possible, dans son pays d'origine sans attendre l'issue définitive de la procédure à Strasbourg.

KELLER: Mais cette affaire s'est terminée par un règlement amiable?

SCHÜRMANN: Oui, devant la Cour. La Commission avait constaté une violation de la Convention. C'était d'ailleurs la seule affaire jusqu'à maintenant où on avait invité un canton à payer une partie des frais.

KELLER: C'est une chose intéressante. Nous savons que les Allemands ont des problèmes parce qu'il arrive que les *Bundesländer* ne permettent pas à l'agent du gouvernement de conclure un règlement amiable parce qu'ils devront en payer une partie. Est-ce que cela cause aussi des problèmes en Suisse à cause du fédéralisme?

SCHÜRMANN: C'est une question difficile. Les Allemands ont une loi depuis quelque temps.[13] Ils sont dans une situation plus solide. Nous avons toujours défendu la position que, comme la requête est dirigée contre la Suisse, c'est le Tribunal fédéral qui, en règle générale, est la dernière instance ayant eu l'occasion de se prononcer. En plus, c'est la Confédération qui défend la Suisse à Strasbourg, et non pas les cantons. Jusqu'à maintenant, ces arguments étaient suffisants pour maintenir la position selon laquelle on ne fait recours au canton qu'à titre tout à fait exceptionnel.

KELLER: Même dans les affaires ou la faute était sur le plan communal ou cantonal?

SCHÜRMANN: Oui. Cela dit, la question est discutable. Personnellement, je pense que l'existence d'une base légale précisant les conditions auxquelles le recours aux autorités cantonales est possible, aurait quelques mérites.

KELLER: Dans l'affaire mentionnée tout à l'heure, le canton a payé finalement?

SCHÜRMANN: Oui, la moitié, sauf erreur.

KELLER: C'était sans base légale?

SCHÜRMANN: Oui, et c'était même sans discussion. Les représentants du canton ont dit que le canton serait prêt à payer.

KELLER: C'est généreux.

KELLER: Est-ce qu'il y a des problèmes avec l'exécution des règlements amiables?

SCHÜRMANN: Non.

---

[13] *Gesetz zur Lastentragung im Bund-Länder-Verhältnis bei Verletzung von supranationalen oder völkerrechtlichen Verpflichtungen (Lastentragungsgesetz, LastG) vom 5. September 2006* (BGBl. I S. 2098, 2105), éntrée en vigeur le 12 séptembre 2006.

KELLER: Non. Vous payez sans problèmes.

SCHÜRMANN: Ce n'est pas pareil pour tout le monde.

KELLER: Oui, exactement. Quelles mesures pourraient améliorer ou faciliter un règlement amiable? Est-ce que vous constatez qu'il y a des obstacles?

SCHÜRMANN: Ces derniers temps, la Cour et le greffe sont devenus plus actif. C'est une très bonne chose parce qu'on est quasiment sous l'autorité de la Cour. C'est différent lorsqu'on contacte le requérant en tant que représentant d'une autorité fédérale et de la partie adverse afin de le convaincre. Nous avons reçu des lettres de la Cour indiquant clairement à l'avocat du requérant d'essayer de convaincre son client parce que c'était la meilleure solution. Ces lettres n'étaient pas écrites en ces termes, mais tel était leur sens. C'était nouveau, mais c'était très utile pour des raisons évidentes et pour tous les intéressés, y compris la Cour.

KELLER: Lorsque vous recevez une proposition pour un règlement amiable, vous ne vous sentez pas brusqué par le fait qu'elle suggère un montant d'argent à payer?

SCHÜRMANN: Je crois que, dans les affaires suisses, la Cour n'a jamais indiqué de montant précis.

KELLER: Vraiment?

SCHÜRMANN: Je n'ai effectivement pas de souvenir d'une telle proposition de la Cour à l'attention du gouvernement.

KELLER: Comment pourrait-on améliorer la procédure de règlements amiables tant pour vous que pour les requérants? Avez-vous d'autres idées?

SCHÜRMANN: Je n'ai pas ressenti le besoin d'améliorer la procédure dans les affaires suisses. Je crois que c'est un instrument important et qu'il est utilisé de manière satisfaisante. Il en va peut-être autrement pour les États ayant des affaires répétitives. Un grand nombre des affaires déclarées recevables sont des cas répétitifs. On pourrait probablement trouver des moyens pour optimiser le processus de conclusion d'un règlement amiable. Étant donné qu'il y a peu de cas suisses, il est difficile pour moi de dire quelles modifications seraient appropriées dans le cadre de cette procédure.

KELLER: Êtes-vous en mesure de clore définitivement un règlement amiable ou devez-vous demander l'avis d'un autre organisme, tel le Ministre des Affaires étrangères ou le gouvernement? Qui décide de cela?

SCHÜRMANN: Bonne question. En tout cas, je discute avec mon supérieur, le directeur de l'Office fédéral de la Justice, qui est l'Office compétent pour la représentation de la Suisse devant la Cour. Lorsqu'une question de règlement amiable (ou de la saisie de la Grande Chambre) survient, j'en discute avec le directeur de l'Office. Il n'est pas exclu qu'on soumette la question, à la suite de cette discussion, à notre Conseillère fédérale, cheffe du Département fédéral de Justice et Police.

KELLER: Et pas au gouvernement?

SCHÜRMANN: Non.

KELLER: Mais elle pourrait soumettre l'affaire au gouvernement?

SCHÜRMANN: Oui, elle le pourrait.

KELLER: Est-ce que le Ministre des Finances est compétent dans ce domaine? Est-ce qu'il pourrait intervenir?

SCHÜRMANN: Il pourrait. Mais cela n'est jamais arrivé.

KELLER: Avez-vous des remarques supplémentaires?

SCHÜRMANN: J'ai noté que nous avons un taux de succès très élevé. Ce n'est pas très pertinent parce qu'on a eu peu d'affaires. À part quelques exceptions, elles ont toutes abouti. De plus, il y a une certaine réticence à conclure des règlements amiables. L'approche pro-active du greffe n'entre pas en ligne de compte tant que l'affaire paraît défendable, ce qui est le cas dans une très large mesure en Suisse. Il ne faut pas oublier que tout règlement amiable met en question, en quelque sorte, le bien-fondé de l'arrêt national qui fait l'objet de la requête. Et cette question n'obtiendra plus de réponse.

KELLER: Il est intéressant de connaître votre point de vue car il est complètement différent de celui des polonais.

SCHÜRMANN: Oui, j'imagine que la situation en Pologne est différente à certains égards.

KELLER: Bien sûr, on ne peut pas généraliser. Il y a différents types de règlements amiables et il y a différents pays. Pour cette raison, la fonction des règlements amiables varie selon les problèmes. En Suisse, c'est typiquement un problème intertemporel. Pour les Polonais, on pourrait dire également que c'est un problème intertemporel, mais sur une plus grande échelle. C'est différent. Je vous remercie pour cet entretien intéressant.

IV. Interview with Serkan Cengiz

Interviewee: Serkan Cengiz, human rights lawyer based in İzmir, Turkey
Interviewer: Magdalena Forowicz
Date: 30 March 2009
Time: 13:00–14:20
Interview time: 1:20 hrs
Telephone interview

SERKAN CENGIZ: My name is Serkan Cengiz. I was born on 4 June 1974. I am a lawyer in private practice in Izmir, Turkey. I have graduated from the University of Selçuk in 1996 and I was admitted to the İstanbul Bar Association in 1998. I did research for an NGO in London. I returned in 2001 to İzmir and I have been practicing human rights law since then. One of my applications so far has been concluded with a friendly settlement (*Albayrak v. Turkey*[1]). Since 2002, I have been running my own office and representing a number of applicants before the ECtHR.

MAGDALENA FOROWICZ: Since when have you been dealing with mediation and friendly settlements?

CENGIZ: I have dealt with friendly settlements when I did research for a NGO in London. I have also dealt with them since 2002 as part of my private practice in Izmir.

FOROWICZ: In your country of origin, in which fields are mediation, alternative dispute resolution as well as judicial and extrajudicial settlements employed?

CENGIZ: They are used in every field pursuant to the provisions of the advocacy law. Furthermore, in 2005, a new criminal procedure law was put into place which allows us to settle cases for certain crimes through mediation. Those are the crimes where investigation and/or prosecution is dependent upon the will of the victim, as well as the crimes set forth in Articles 253 of the Criminal Procedure Law, namely causing injury with intention (Article 86 except sub-paragraph 3 and Article 88 of the Penal Code), causing injury with negligence, trespassing, disclosure of commercial and banking secrets, etc.

FOROWICZ: Let us now turn to the motives of the parties. From your experience, why do the applicants and the Government conclude friendly settlements?

CENGIZ: Friendly settlements before the ECtHR and other courts are generally concluded with the intention of saving time. This applies to both parties. The

---

[1] *Albayrak v. Turkey* (Appl. No. 70151/01), Decision (Fourth Section–Arrangement), 21 March 2006, not reported.

friendly settlement procedure is generally shorter. It takes about a year and a half to conclude a friendly settlement. However, the proceedings before the ECtHR come to this stage three and four years after lodging an application with the Registry. The conclusion of friendly settlements loses its attractiveness because of its length and its current structure.

FOROWICZ: Why do State representatives conclude friendly settlements?

CENGIZ: They do not want to take responsibility and to have a judgment of the Court finding a violation. In the *Tahsin Acar* case,[2] this aspect became quite apparent. The applicant did not want to conclude a friendly settlement, as for him an apology was not sufficient. He wanted the Government to acknowledge the violation in full and to find out what had happened to his brother. He also wanted to know who the abductors were.

FOROWICZ: Let us now turn to the procedure. Which procedure is usually followed in friendly settlements?

CENGIZ: There are generally two procedures. According to the first one, we enter into negotiations following an invitation from the Registry and we make a proposal. When we receive the observations of the Government, the Registry requests us to submit our observations, a just satisfaction claim and a friendly settlement proposal. We therefore submit our friendly settlement proposals together with our observations. Then, the Registry sends our observations, including friendly settlement proposals, to the Government. Sometimes, the Government may send its friendly settlement proposals with its observations and we send back our comments and/or rejection arguments and/or acceptance.

As part of the second procedure, the Registry sends its friendly settlement proposals to the parties. The proposals offered by the Registry only contain the payment of some amount to the applicant by the Government. In both procedures, we usually have no chance to discuss the offer with the Government and the Registry, since the negotiations are conducted through documents. However, the Government and the applicant's representatives may hold face-to-face meetings in some cases, but this is very rare (see *Yağcı and Sargın v. Turkey*[3]).

Most of the negotiations are conducted through the exchange of papers. These procedures do not require so much preparation. The proposal is usually based on our claims under Article 41 ECHR. Just satisfaction claims are prepared at the same time as friendly settlement claims. We do not usually know the level of compensation (pecuniary and non-pecuniary) that we could obtain in a friendly settlement; we usually look at the case law of the Court to claim the approximate

    [2] *Tahsin Acar v. Turkey* (Appl. No. 26307/95), Judgment (Grand Chamber), 6 May 2003, Reports 2003-VI, 1.
    [3] *Yağcı and Sargın v. Turkey* (Appl. Nos. 16419/90; 16426/90), Report (Commission), 30 November 1993, not reported, para. 12.

figures and decide whether the offer of the Government or the Registry is reasonable. This is especially the case if the Registry prepares the proposal. When the case concerns Articles 2 and 3 ECHR, the Government usually offers a reasonable amount. My personal opinion is that the Government does not want a judgment in these cases, as this would damage its reputation. Further, a judgment finding an ECHR violation would give the applicant the right to re-open the case at the domestic level.

Turkey currently has approximately 10,000 applications pending before the Court. The proceedings before the ECtHR are all delayed for this reason. When I draft a proposal, I take into account the moral and financial expectations of the applicants. My clients tend to regard the ECtHR mainly as a Court which can remedy all of their losses, including their pecuniary and non-pecuniary ones. They generally see the Court as a compensation court, but it clearly is not a court of this type.

FOROWICZ: Let us now turn to the position of the parties. Have you noticed a disequilibrium between the applicant and the State representative?

CENGIZ: The State is generally more powerful than the applicant. This can be noticed in the *Hutton* and *Arrondelle* cases.[4] Further, the applicant is in an inherently weaker position, as he/she will be unable to re-open the case at the domestic level when a friendly settlement is concluded.

FOROWICZ: Do you know of any cases where the negotiations were unsuccessful? Did the parties ever interrupt the negotiations because they were unhappy and did not agree with the negotiator?

CENGIZ: When the negotiations fail, the Court proceeds with the case as usual. We do not know if the negotiations have failed. I only know when I receive a document to sign. If I do not receive any document to sign, I understand that the negotiations have not commenced at all. The negotiations could fail when there is an imbalance between the proposal of the Government and of the applicant.

FOROWICZ: What is usually stipulated in a friendly settlement? The usual component is money. Could there be anything else?

CENGIZ: It could be an apology. Sometimes, the Government also indicates that it will introduce a new law or that it will review the old one. It has also been mentioned previously that a review has taken place and that the situation is now better. A major problem in this area is that the Government undertakes in a friendly settlement to pass a new law as part of the general measures. It is often difficult to enforce individual measures, which are based on this general measure. This

---

[4] *Hutton v. United Kingdom* (Appl. No. 28014/02), Decision (Fourth Section–Arrangement), 24 June 2008, not yet reported; *Arrondelle v. United Kingdom* (Appl. No. 7889/77), Decision (Commission), 15 July 1980, D.R. 19, 186.

occurred in the *Ülke* case,[5] which made it impossible to pursue the individual cases further. The Court found a violation under Article 3 ECHR in this application. The Committee of Ministers has been monitoring this case and the Government has not taken any individual steps since then. In such cases, the Government sometimes obviates the individual responsibility by undertaking that it will introduce general measures. However, as it has not taken this general measure, it was impossible to introduce the individual measures, which were based on it.

Another relevant example in this context is the *Hulki Güneş* case.[6] The Committee of Ministers expected Turkey to implement the general measures, but the Government has failed to do this until now. As a result, it was impossible to implement individual measures, as there were no provisions under domestic law. Of course, the proceedings for both cases mentioned above gave rise to findings of a violation.

FOROWICZ: We have seen friendly settlement cases with Turkey where the Government had to acknowledge the violation of the ECHR. What do you think about this practice?

CENGIZ: These are not acknowledgments of violations. They are apologies and perhaps indirect acknowledgments of violations. As such, they do not give the applicant the right to re-open his, or her, case at the domestic level. According to the Turkish domestic law, only the judgments of the Court which find a violation can be used as an instrument to re-open the relevant domestic proceedings. However, the relevant provisions have a very limited scope. For instance, only the applicants who were party to the domestic proceedings as defendants have the right to re-open the domestic proceedings (Article 311/1-f of the Criminal Procedure Law). The victims do not have such a right. This fact becomes very important in cases where the Court finds a violation under Articles 2 and 3 ECHR, since the victims/applicants were not defendants but interveners in the domestic proceedings against State agents. For instance, I tried to re-open the domestic proceedings after the judgment of the Court in the *Fahriye Çalışkan v. Turkey* case.[7] The competent public prosecutor dismissed my application for re-opening the domestic proceedings. The Assize Court which heard my objection against the decision of the prosecutor concluded that there was no domestic remedy to re-open criminal proceedings against a Superintendant. The Assize Court referred to the wording of the same provision (CPC Article 3211/1f).

---

[5] *Ülke v. Turkey* (Appl. No. 39437/98), Judgment (Second Section), 24 January 2006, not reported.
[6] *Hulki Güneş v. Turkey* (Appl. No. 28490/95), Judgment (Third Section), 19 June 2003, Reports 2003-VII (extracts), 187.
[7] *Fahriye Calişkan v. Turkey* (Appl. No. 40516/98), Judgment (Fourth Section), 2 October 2007, not yet reported.

FOROWICZ: The ECtHR has sometimes used the pilot judgment procedure in cases involving systemic violations. Are there proceedings against Turkey which resemble this procedure?

CENGIZ: There were proceedings of this type with regard to the situation in south-east Turkey. People had been evacuated from their houses because it was suspected that the PKK had carried out terror activities in the area. There was no compensation provided. An important case in this area was the *Doğan* case.[8] The Government had passed a new law to remedy the suffering of approximately 1,500 applicants. The applicants would have to present their case to a new institution established at the domestic level in order to obtain compensation. This resembled a pilot procedure.

Another type of pilot procedure was used with regard to a situation in northern Cyprus. This happened in the *Loizidou v. Turkey* case.[9] Following this judgment, some of the applicants were redirected to a compensation commission established at the domestic level. The *Demades v. Turkey*[10] judgment was also part of these cases. Further cases followed in January 2009.

FOROWICZ: Are there enforcement problems in Turkish friendly settlement cases?

CENGIZ: There is no problem with regard to the payment of the compensation, but there are problems with the taking of individual measures and with the prevention of similar violations. There is often no law on the basis of which these individual measures could be taken. I have touched upon these problems earlier.

FOROWICZ: When should friendly settlements be concluded?

CENGIZ: A friendly settlement should be concluded if it is faster than a regular proceeding. Sometimes, it takes four or five years to discuss the possibility of concluding a friendly settlement. This is not very advantageous.

I do not advise friendly settlements when a case could be re-opened at the domestic level. A friendly settlement would prevent such a re-opening. I advise them when the applicant has no financial means, when the case is weak, when there is no need to re-open the case or when there is no moral intention behind the application. Cases concerning Article 3 ECHR have recently become rather weak, as the required evidence is often missing. The burden of proof in those cases is rather heavy on the applicant, as the ECtHR in some judgments seems to expect applicants to prove that they were subjected to torture. In many of these

---

[8] *Doğan and Others v. Turkey* (Appl. Nos. 8803–11/02; 8813/02; 8815–19/02), Judgment (Third Section), 29 June 2004, Reports 2004-VI (extracts), 81.

[9] *Loizidou v. Turkey* (Appl. No. 15318/89), Judgment (Grand Chamber), 18 December 1996, Reports 1996-VI, 2216.

[10] *Demades v. Turkey* (Appl. No. 16219/90), Judgment (Third Section), 31 July 2003, not reported.

cases, there is no longer any evidence as time has passed and no traces of torture are left.

Friendly settlement decisions or judgments should have the same authority as ordinary judgments. They should not be ineffective just because they cannot re-open cases at the domestic level. Friendly settlement cases are not binding under Turkish law. The payment is made *ex gratia*.

Another problem is that the level of compensation that could be obtained has been reduced by the ECtHR in the recent years. Further, the ECtHR seems to have shifted the burden of proof to the applicant. It currently requires more evidence from the applicant than previously.

FOROWICZ: What factors promote the conclusion of a friendly settlement? What should be improved about friendly settlements?

CENGIZ: A special Court Section should be set up for friendly settlement negotiations.

The applicants and the relevant Governments should be invited to friendly settlement negotiations as quickly as possible. This time period should not be extended beyond one year following the introduction of an application. Thus, an application should be settled through friendly settlement within two years after the introduction date.

Judgments or decisions issued by the Court in respect of friendly settlements should carry the same effects and authority as the ordinary judgments finding an ECHR violation. Applicants should be entitled to re-open domestic proceedings following a friendly settlement.

States should undertake serious obligations (not as *ex gratia*) in order to prevent the recurrence of similar violations.

The Committee of Ministers should be more active in monitoring the implementation process. Otherwise, the Court's backlog will continue to rise as a result of similar applications.

FOROWICZ: Do you consider that friendly settlements are a sensible solution to the heavy workload of the Court?

CENGIZ: Yes, if the shortcomings that I mentioned are met.

2

Statistics

I. Explanatory Note

The appendix includes statistics on friendly settlements, arrangements, unilateral declarations and judgments.[1] The tables concern data concerning the overall statistics as well as country-specific statistics for Poland and Turkey. The research for this volume was solely based on information that was publicly available, as the Court did not grant us access to the case files.

1. General Indications

The statistics included in this appendix were collected from the following sources: *HUDOC* (online database of the ECtHR); *European Court of Human Rights Series A: Judgments and Decisions*; *Reports of Judgments and Decisions of the European Court of Human Rights*; *European Commission of Human Rights Decisions and Reports*, *European Court of Human Rights Annual Reports*; *European Court of Human Rights Survey of Activities* (annual); *Yearbook of the European Convention on Human Rights*. We searched for cases which mentioned the terms "friendly settlement", "*règlement amiable*", "struck off the list", "*radiation du rôle*". Judgments, Decisions and Reports of the Commission were included as part of our study.

All the awards mentioned in the statistics are indicated in Euros. When an award was made in a different currency, we converted it into Euros on the basis of the average exchange rate for the respective year.[2] Some of the yearly statistics do not refer to an annual exchange rate as the awards were made in Euros and did not need to be converted. We also applied an inflation rate which only concerned the Euro area.[3] We thus left aside the financial turbulences in Poland and Turkey

---

[1] Abbreviations: a. O. = and Others; Arr. = Arrangement; Art. = Article; Arts. = Articles; BpR = Benefit per Recipient; C/E = Damages for Costs and Expenses; CB = Cash Benefit; Dec = Decision; ECtHR = European Court of Human Rights; FS = Friendly Settlement; Judg. = Judgment; NoC = Number of Cases; NoR = Number of Recipients; nPD = non-Pecuniary Damage; P. 1 = Protocol no 1; P. 2 = Protocol no 2; P. 4 = Protocol no 4; PD = Pecuniary Damage; TA = Total Amount; ToD = Type of Document.

[2] See <http://www.oanda.com/currency/historical-rates> (last visited 25 May 2010). We calculated with the interbank rate.

[3] In percentages 1998–2008: 1.1 per cent (1998); 1.1 per cent (1999); 2.1 per cent (2000);

around the year 2000. This inflation rate was applied once the awards were converted into Euros.

The cases in each category were listed in accordance to the date of the ruling. When two cases had the same ruling date, they were listed in alphabetical order. The date of application was sometimes uncertain and various cases with different application dates were successively merged into one case. In such a situation, a footnote was included with the required explanation. Long case titles were abbreviated due to the lack of space in the layout of the tables.[4] The application numbers were also simplified when this was required.[5] Further, the number of recipients in the context of compensation awarded to the different persons involved in the case (applicants and others) required an important discretion on our part. We sometimes had to regroup several recipients and count them as one.[6] Finally, the category of non-cash benefits (including the statement of regret from the Government) was mentioned in the footnotes, as their random appearance did not require a separate column.

2. Case Analysis

1. Friendly Settlements

Pursuant to Article 38 ECHR, friendly settlements were understood as a procedure where the Court contributes to the settlement and reviews whether it complies with the Convention. Hence, a case was considered to be a friendly settlement when the following conditions were met:

- the settlement process was facilitated by the Court; and
- the Court ensured that the friendly settlement was concluded on the basis of respect for human rights, as defined in the Convention and the protocols thereto.

In addition, we also considered that an application was terminated via a friendly settlement when:

- the Court mentioned that it "placed itself at the disposal of the parties with a view to securing a (…)":

2.3 per cent (2001); 2.2 per cent (2002); 2.1 per cent (2003); 2.1 per cent (2004); 2.2 per cent (2005); 2.2 per cent (2006); 2.1 per cent (2007); 3.3 per cent (2008), see <http://epp.eurostat.ec.europa.eu/tgm/table.do?tab=table&language=en&pcode=tsieb060&tableSelection=1&footnotes=yes&labeling=labels&plugin=1> (last visited 25 May 2010).

[4] If a case involved several applicants, we would use the acronym "a. O." for "and Others". The title of the case would then be: Applicant a. O. v. State.

[5] See for example, 16064–66/90 means 16064/90, 16065/90, and 16066/90.

[6] The specific information concerning this division is available from the authors upon request. The Turkish cases are especially affected in this context. The Polish cases mostly follow the formula of "one applicant–one recipient".

- "(…) friendly settlement" and "contacted the parties to explore the possibilities of reaching a (…)"
- "(…) friendly settlement";
- the Court proposed a friendly settlement procedure;
- the Court proposed the content of a friendly settlement;
- the Court made their good offices available;
- the friendly settlement was negotiated together with the Court;
- the Court attended the meeting between the parties which led to a friendly settlement.

The Court's contribution was a key element in deciding whether a case was a friendly settlement or an arrangement. As the information provided by the Court in its decisions was scarce, we used a low threshold when classifying cases as friendly settlements. Any sign that the Court contributed to the settlement was interpreted as an indication that the case was a friendly settlement. While numerous decisions contained the text of a settlement or referred to a settlement as a "friendly settlement", they lacked any indication as to the contribution of the Court. We therefore assumed that it depended largely on the Registrar who drafted the decision whether such information was included. Given the notorious lack of information, the classification system that we sued was sometimes difficult to follow.

2. Arrangements

For the purposes of our research, arrangements were considered to be settlements reached outside of the Court. In such cases, the Court only approved the settlement and was not involved in the proceedings.

A case constituted an arrangement when the following conditions were met:

- there was no indication of the role or contribution of the Court;
- it was noted that the parties had reached a settlement;
- it was mentioned that the correspondence between the parties was forwarded by the Court.

These indications did not provide sufficient information as to the contribution or involvement of the Court in the settlement process.

The statistics collected for this study differ from the official statistics available to the public. Frequently, a case that we considered to be an arrangement was classified as a friendly settlement in the official statistics.

While arrangements were sometimes included in the form of a judgment, the language used often seemed to indicate that they were in effect decisions. Further, numerous arrangements were struck out of the list because the parties decided to withdraw their application. This often occurred even when the parties did not formally agree on a settlement. There were also arrangements where the Government was ready to settle, but on condition that the case was first struck out of the list of cases. As the applicant was ready to withdraw his complaint, the Court agreed to strike out, finding that the parties had reached a settlement.

II. Overall Statistics

Table II/1. Statistics 1998–2008

Year	Judgments delivered[1]	Total number of decisions adopted[2]	Friendly Settlements/ Arrangements[3]	Friendly Settlements[3]	Arrangements[3]	Unilateral Declarations[3]
2008	1,543	30,240	670	12	658	78
2007	1,503	27,244	389	27	362	47
2006	1,560	29,796	275	24	251	2
2005	1,105	28,648	202	40	162	3
2004	718	21,181	269	36	233	1
2003	703	18,034	266	96	170	2
2002	844	18,450	320	174	146	3
2001	888	9,728	191	124	67	1
2000	695	7,862	248	206	42	No indication
1999	177	4,251	115	105	10	No indication
1998	0	144	7	7	0	No indication
Total	4,025	195,428	2,952	851	2,101	137

[1] This statistical information is based on the chart "Judgments (1959–2008)" in European Court of Human Rights, Annual Report 2008, Registry of the European Court of Human Rights, Strasbourg 2009, p. 151. A judgment may concern more than one application.

[2] The statistical information for the years 2007 and 2008 is based on the table "Events in total (2007–2008)" in European Court of Human Rights, Annual Report 2008, Registry of the European Court of Human Rights, Strasbourg 2009, p. 137. The statistical information for the period between 1999 and 2006 is based on the table "Events (1955–2006)" in European Court of Human Rights, Annual Report 2006, Registry of the European Court of Human Rights, Strasbourg 2007, p. 123. This data includes applications that were declared admissible and inadmissible, as well as applications that were struck out. The statistical information for the year 1998 is based on European Court of Human Rights, Survey of Activities 1998 (November–December 1998), p. 24, available at <http://www.echr.coe.int/NR/rdonlyres/2CF1D16E-F763-46B6-82FC-AAEE9F7ACA4B/0/SurveyofActivities1998.pdf> (last visited 7 May 2010). A decision may concern more than one application.

[3] This information is based on data collected for this study.

Table II/2. Statistics per Country 1998–2008: Friendly Settlements

Friendly Settlements	1998	1999	2000	2001	2002	2003	2004	2005	2006	2007	2008
Andorra		1									
Austria	5	1	6	1	5	1	1				
Belgium	1	1	1	1						1	
Bulgaria	1										1
Croatia					3						
Czech Republic				1		1	1	4			1
Denmark			2								
Estonia											
France	15	65	10	3	3	4	1		3		1
Finland			2			1		1			
Germany	1								2		
Greece			1							1	
Hungary	1	1				2					
Italy	1	27	160	17	7						
Lithuania			1			1	1				
Luxembourg											
Macedonia					1						1
Netherlands	2		1	1							
Poland					1	14	5	1			
Portugal	9	6	9	13	16	1	2	3			1

Friendly Settlements	1998	1999	2000	2001	2002	2003	2004	2005	2006	2007	2008
Romania						2	3	5	11	16	7
Russia										1	
San Marino	1										
Slovakia		1	3		3	1	1	1			
Slovenia					1						
Sweden	1		1				2			1	
Turkey	1		4	81	130	66	18	23	8	4	
United Kingdom	4	2	2		4	1	1	2		2	

Table II/3. Statistics per Country 1998–2008: Arrangements

Arrangements	1998	1999	2000	2001	2002	2003	2004	2005	2006	2007	2008
Andorra									1		
Austria	1					4	6	4	2	4	10
Belgium						2	3	1	6	4	1
Bulgaria	1		1	1	1		1			5	11
Croatia							37	21	14	31	14
Czech Republic							7	23	25	4	3
Cyprus		1	1	1	1			1	16	1	3
Denmark			4	2	1		1	1		3	
Estonia			1					1			1
France	1		1	5	3	10	9	12	11	3	7
Finland			1		1	1			3	6	7
Germany				2		2	1	3	1	8	5
Greece	2	1	3	4	3	14	2	1	2	3	3
Hungary					2	2	5	3		8	18
Ireland	1							1		1	1
Italy			5	26	43	29	5	9	5	9	4
Latvia				1					1	4	7
Lithuania									1	1	
Luxembourg					1						1
Macedonia											19

Arrangements	1998	1999	2000	2001	2002	2003	2004	2005	2006	2007	2008
Moldova								2	3	20	17
Netherlands			1	2	2		2		1	1	2
Norway	1						1				
Poland			3	7	5	23	11	5	31	92	297
Portugal	1	2		1	2					1	
Romania							5	2	2	3	53
Russia			1	1			1	4	17	21	14
San Marino						1	1	1		1	
Slovakia			1		1	7		11	4	22	11
Slovenia						2	24	13	15	1	21
Spain		1	1								
Sweden	1				1	1	5	12	14	2	3
Switzerland			1						1		
Turkey			8	4	68	72	99	26	49	43	33
United Kingdom	3	5	9	7	10	2	3	4	9	32	79
Ukraine				1					15	26	2

III. Poland – Yearly Statistics Concerning Friendly Settlements and Arrangements

Table III/1. 2001 for Poland: Article 6 (1) ECHR (Length of Civil Proceedings) – Friendly Settlements and Arrangements[1,2]

Applicant v. State	Appl. No.	Date of Ruling	ToD	Length of Negotiations	ECHR	Total CB	NoR	BpR
ARRANGEMENTS								
Lewandowska v. Poland	55204/00	27/11/01	Dec.	2y 3m 7d	6 (1)	2,731	1	2,731
Chlewicki v. Poland	54676/00	29/11/01	Dec.	2y 9m 6d	6 (1)	2,731	1	2,731
Borowski v. Poland	52072/99	11/12/01	Dec.	2y 9m 23d	6 (1)	2,594	1	2,594
Grabowska v. Poland	61818/00	11/12/01	Dec.	1y 8m 19d	6 (1)	2,731	1	2,731
Oleś v. Poland	53267/99	11/12/01	Dec.	2y 7m 26d	6 (1)	2,731	1	2,731
Patys v. Poland	51669/99	11/12/01	Judg.	2y 7m 28d	6 (1)	6,827	1	6,827

[1] There were no friendly settlements that year.
[2] Annual Average Exchange Rate: 0.27307 (PLN).

Table III/2. 2002 for Poland: Article 6 (1) ECHR (Length of Civil Proceedings) – Friendly Settlements and Arrangements[1,2]

Applicant v. State	Appl. No.	Date of Ruling	ToD	Length of Negotiations	ECHR	Total CB	NoR	BpR
ARRANGEMENTS								
K.R. v. Poland	39189/98	21/03/02	Dec.	4y 8m 2d	6 (1)	2,604	1	2,604
Górka v. Poland	55106/00	05/11/02	Judg.	3y 9m 4d	6 (1)	2,604	1	2,604
Ferenstein v. Poland	52499/99	12/11/02	Dec.	3y 7m 4d	6 (1)	2,604	1	2,604

[1] There were no friendly settlements that year.
[2] Annual Average Exchange Rate: 0.26042 (PLN).

Table III/3. 2003 for Poland: Article 6 (1) ECHR (Length of Civil Proceedings) – Friendly Settlements and Arrangements[1]

Applicant v. State	Appl. No.	Date of Ruling	ToD	Length of Negotiations	ECHR	Total CB	NoR	BpR
FRIENDLY SETTLEMENTS								
Sędek v. Poland	67165/01	06/05/03	Judg.	3y 0m 1d	6 (1)	3,877	1	3,877
Szymikowska and Szymikowski v. Poland	43786/98	06/05/03	Judg.	4y 10m 27d	6 (1)	3,421	2	1,711
Sagan v. Poland	6901/02	24/06/03	Judg.	1y 9m 18d	6 (1)	3,991	1	3,991
Skóra v. Poland	67162/01	01/07/03	Judg.	3y 1m 16d	6 (1)	3,193	1	3,193
Wysocka-Cysarz v. Poland	61888/00	01/07/03	Judg.	3y 6m 1d	6 (1)	2,851	1	2,851
Godlewski v. Poland	53551/99	08/07/03	Judg.	4y 1m 19d	6 (1)	3,649	1	3,649
Dragan v. Poland	58780/00	15/07/03	Judg.	4y 4m 26d	6 (1)	3,649	1	3,649
Nisiuk v. Poland	64120/00	15/07/03	Judg.	3y 9m 21d	6 (1)	3,421	1	3,421
Janowski v. Poland (No. 2)	49033/99	23/09/03	Judg.	4y 6m 18d	6 (1)	3,877	1	3,877
Piotr Mazurkiewicz v. Poland	72662/01	14/10/03	Judg.	3y 5m 22d	6 (1)	1,482	1	1,482
Szymański v. Poland	75929/01	21/10/03	Judg.	2y 4m 20d	6 (1)	2,965	1	2,965
Krzysztof Piemiążek v. Poland	57465/00	28/10/03	Judg.	4y 4m 11d	6 (1)	3,193	1	3,193
Stańczyk v. Poland	50511/99	02/12/03	Judg.	5y 0m 11d	6 (1)	5,132	1	5,132
Cuyl v. Poland	49920/99	09/12/03	Judg.	4y 10m 14d	6 (1)	5,702	1	5,702
Strzałkowska v. Poland	52586/99	21/01/03	Dec.	3y 8m 14d	6 (1), 13	2,281	1	2,281
Ruchlewicz v. Poland	71205/01	03/07/03	Dec.	2y 11m 8d	3, 6 (1), 13, 14	2,737	1	2,737
Pawlinkowska v. Poland	45957/99	08/07/03	Judg.	4y 9m 3d	6 (1) (also impartiality)	2,281	1	2,281

[1] Annual Average Exchange Rate: 0.22807 (PLN).

Case	Application no.	Date		Length	Article		Amount	No.	Amount
M.M. and E.M.M. v. Poland	76158/01	29/07/03	Judg.	2y 7m 21d	6 (1)		2,737	1	2,737
Mikulska v. Poland	8205/02	29/07/03	Judg.	1y 5m 14d	6 (1)		3,421	1	3,421
Nowakowski v. Poland	71009/01	29/07/03	Judg.	3y 3m 18d	6 (1)		3,421	1	3,421
Chudyba v. Poland	71621/01	23/09/03	Judg.	3y 0m 12d	6 (1)		3,421	1	3,421
Górecka v. Poland	73009/01	23/09/03	Judg.	3y 3m 30d	6 (1)		2,965	1	2,965
Kledzik v. Poland	75098/01	23/09/03	Judg.	2y 9m 2d	6 (1), 13		2,851	1	2,851
Walczuk v. Poland[2]	49911/99	23/09/03	Dec.	1y 7m 28d	6 (1)		0	0	0
Czyżewski v. Poland	7453/02	13/11/03	Dec.	1y 9m 13d	6 (1)		2,737	1	2,737
J.P. v. Poland	18855/02	13/11/03	Dec.	1y 6m 14d	6 (1)		3,421	1	3,421
Jurdziak v. Poland	65873/01	13/11/03	Dec.	3y 7m 15d	6 (1)		2,281	1	2,281
Kornecki v. Poland	75075/01	13/11/03	Dec.	3y 7m 3d	6 (1)		3,421	1	3,421
Krug and Krug-Cupryś v. Poland	53019/99	13/11/03	Dec.	4y 9m 24d	6 (1)		3,421	2	1,711
Andrzejewska v. Poland	15153/02	18/11/03	Dec.	1y 8m 4d	6 (1)		3,079	1	3,079
Kisielewicz v. Poland	9348/02	02/12/03	Dec.	1y 9m 18d	6 (1)		3,649	1	3,649
ARRANGEMENTS									
Krynicki v. Poland	75100/01	02/12/03	Dec.	2y 10m 11d	6 (1)		2,281	1	2,281
Nowak v. Poland	58778/00	02/12/03	Dec.	4y 7m 5d	6 (1)		3,421	1	3,421
Kardzis v. Poland	5696/02	16/12/03	Dec.	1y 10m 22d	6 (1)		3,649	1	3,649
Kowalski v. Poland	52504/99	16/12/03	Dec.	4y 11m 2d	6 (1)		3,421	1	3,421

[2] An arrangement was planned, but the applicant no longer replied to letters.

Table III/4. 2004 for Poland: Article 6 (1) ECHR (Length of Civil Proceedings) – Friendly Settlements and Arrangements[1]

Applicant v. State	Appl. No.	Date of Ruling	ToD	Length of Negotiations	ECHR	Total CB	NoR	BpR
FRIENDLY SETTLEMENTS								
Jagiełło v. Poland[2]	61437/00	17/02/04	Dec.	8y 9m 30d	6 (1), 1 P. 1	0	0	0
Skowroński v. Poland	52595/99	17/02/04	Judg.	4y 11m 25d	6 (1)	3,322	1	3,322
Radek v. Poland	30311/02	20/07/04	Judg.	5y 7m 2d	6 (1)	3,322	1	3,322
Ostrowski v. Poland	63389/00	28/09/04	Judg.	5y 11m 11d	6 (1)	3,322	1	3,322
ARRANGEMENTS								
Napiórkowski v. Poland	62108/00	27/01/04	Dec.	4y 0m 12d	6 (1)	4,429	1	4,429
Rekus v. Poland	72163/01	27/01/04	Dec.	3y 1m 29d	6 (1)	1,550	1	1,550
Wojdalska and Wojdalski v. Poland	34824/02	27/01/04	Dec.	1y 2m 15d	6 (1)	3,322	2	1,661
Konieczka v. Poland	70206/01	23/03/04	Dec.	3y 7m 26d	6 (1)	3,101	1	3,101
Kępka v. Poland	49180/99	04/05/04	Dec.	5y 3m 29d	6 (1) (also unfairness)	4,429	1	4,429
Grodzicki v. Poland	61435/00	04/05/04	Dec.	4y 6m 0d	6 (1)	3,765	1	3,765
Fusiarz v. Poland	65015/01	01/06/04	Dec.	4y 10m 9d	6 (1)	3,322	1	3,322
Ławicka-Poplewska v. Poland	58777/00	07/09/04	Dec.	4y 11m 14d	6 (1)	2,658	1	2,658
Jura v. Poland	20202/02	28/09/04	Dec.	3y 0m 10d	6 (1)	3,322	1	3,322

1 Annual Average Exchange Rate: 0.22147 (PLN).
2 The case was struck out because the applicant no longer replied to communications.

Table III/5. 2005 for Poland: Article 6 (1) ECHR (Length of Civil Proceedings) – Friendly Settlements and Arrangements[1,2]

Applicant v. State	Appl. No.	Date of Ruling	ToD	Length of Negotiations	ECHR	Total CB	NoR	BpR
ARRANGEMENTS								
Misiewicz v. Poland	16742/02	11/01/05	Dec.	3y 6m 21d	6 (1)	4,234	1	4,234
Szczepaniec v. Poland	61278/00	18/01/05	Dec.	5y 0m 26d	6 (1)	4,981	1	4,981
Gola v. Poland	75183/01	22/02/05	Dec.	4y 3m 2d	6 (1)	3,487	1	3,487
Lubera v. Poland	13050/02	15/03/05	Dec.	3y 10m 18d	6 (1), 8, 13, 34	1,494	1	1,494

[1] There were no friendly settlements that year.
[2] Annual Average Exchange Rate: 0.24906 (PLN).

Table III/6. 2006 for Poland: Article 6 (1) ECHR (Length of Civil Proceedings) – Friendly Settlements and Arrangements[1,2]

Applicant v. State	Appl. No.	Date of Ruling	ToD	Length of Negotiations	ECHR	Total CB	NoR	BpR
ARRANGEMENTS								
Gosławski v. Poland	20192/02	07/02/06	Dec.	4y 8m 0d	6 (1) (also errors of fact and law)	2,060	1	2,060
Mączyński v. Poland	1084/02	07/02/06	Dec.	5y 4m 25d	6 (1)	2,575	1	2,575
Nowacka v. Poland	3233/02	14/02/06	Dec.	4y 1m 7d	6 (1)	2,575	1	2,575
Gaurysek v. Poland	21640/02	07/03/06	Dec.	4y 6m 3d	6 (1) (also unfairness), 1 P. 1	1,545	1	1,545
Hamerski v. Poland	6718/02	14/03/06	Dec.	4y 1m 11d	6 (1)	2,060	1	2,060
Temnicka v. Poland	76100/01	28/03/06	Dec.	4y 8m 10d	6 (1)	2,400	1	2,400
Szczęśniak v. Poland	67974/01	04/04/06	Dec.	5y 11m 18d	6 (1)	6,900	1	6,900
Karnas v. Poland	17189/02	04/04/06	Dec.	4y 0m 6d	6 (1) (also unfairness)	2,575	1	2,575
Wójcik v. Poland	10851/02	04/04/06	Dec.	4y 1m 7d	6 (1)	669	1	669
Kiczko v. Poland	77712/01	09/05/06	Dec.	5y 1m 6d	? (probably length)	2,575	1	2,575
Bukowski v. Poland	71150/01	16/05/06	Dec.	5y 3m 6d	6 (1) (also impossibility to enforce judgment)	2,575	1	2,575
Witmoń v. Poland[3]	7541/03	23/05/06	Dec.	3y 3m 20d	6 (1)	2,060	1	2,060
Cieślak v. Poland	12386/03	30/05/06	Dec.	3y 2m 2d	6 (1), 1 P. 1	4,635	1	4,635
Zielonkiewicz v. Poland	25656/05	19/09/06	Dec.	1y 2m 18d	6 (1)	2,575	1	2,575
Wiśniewski v. Poland	64205/01	17/10/06	Dec.	6y 7m 18d	6 (1)	3,862	1	3,862

[1] There were no friendly settlements that year.
[2] Annual Average Exchange Rate: 0.25748 (PLN).
[3] The applicant also complained that there was no effective remedy in case of a breach of the right to a trial within reasonable time.

Bojarski v. Poland	68755/01	07/11/06	Dec.	5y 9m 15d	6 (1)		2,317	1	2,317
Skiba a. O. v. Poland	70474/01	07/11/06	Dec.	5y 10m 23d	6 (1), 13		18,024	7	2,575
Skórzybót v. Poland	3858/05	21/11/06	Dec.	1y 10m 11d	5, 6 (1) (also unfairness), 8, 14, 1 P. 1		2,060	1	2,060
Bogucka v. Poland	27754/05	28/11/06	Dec.	1y 4m 21d	6 (1), 13		8,000	1	8,000
Wasilewski v. Poland[4]	4661/04	05/12/06	Dec.	2y 10m 10d	6 (1)		2,575	1	2,575
Sarnowski v. Poland	3879/05	12/12/06	Dec.	1y 10m 24d	6 (1)		2,500	1	2,500
Strzelecki v. Poland	23051/05	12/12/06	Dec.	1y 5m 27d	6 (1)		2,575	1	2,575

[4] The applicant also complained that the domestic courts had rejected his complaints and ignored the Court's judgment concerning the same proceedings, thus rendering ineffective the length remedy available under domestic law; he further complained about the outcome of the proceedings.

Table III/7. 2007 for Poland: Article 6 (1) ECHR (Length of Civil Proceedings) – Friendly Settlements and Arrangements[1,2]

Applicant v. State	Appl. No.	Date of Ruling	ToD	Length of Negotiations	ECHR	Total CB	NoR	BpR
ARRANGEMENTS								
Wasielewski v. Poland	3494/02	09/01/07	Dec.	5y 0m 30d	6 (also unfairness)	2,653	1	2,653
Broszczakowska v. Poland	18262/05	13/03/07	Dec.	1y 10m 12d	6 (1), 13	2,122	1	2,122
Szymanowicz v. Poland	16658/04	20/03/07	Dec.	2y 10m 20d	6 (1)	4,775	1	4,775
Osmakiewicz v. Poland	34635/02	12/04/07	Dec.	4y 7m 2d	6 (1)	3,979	1	3,979
Wróblewski v. Poland	9359/03	12/04/07	Dec.	4y 1m 10d	6 (1)	2,122	1	2,122
Sypka v. Poland	11062/06	10/05/07	Dec.	1y 2m 0d	6 (1), 13	1,592	1	1,592
Mikołajczyk v. Poland	12351/02	22/05/07	Dec.	5y 10m 18d	?	2,388	1	2,388
Wiland v. Poland	14312/02	05/06/07	Dec.	6y 0m 12d	6 (1) (also ineffectiveness of remedy)	5,306	1	5,306
Blachnio v. Poland	11123/02	12/06/07	Dec.	5y 8m 16d	6 (1)	3,979	1	3,979
Kos v. Poland	36240/03	26/06/07	Dec.	3y 9m 1d	6 (1)	5,571	1	5,571
Witer v. Poland	39814/03	18/09/07	Dec.	3y 9m 14d	6 (1)	2,255	1	2,255
Franosz v. Poland	17992/03	02/10/07	Dec.	4y 4m 19d	6 (1)	3,000	2	1,500
Jakubowski v. Poland	20959/06	02/10/07	Dec.	1y 6m 16d	6 (1)	3,979	1	3,979
Kuberski v. Poland	33099/03	02/10/07	Dec.	4y 0m 1d	6 (1)	2,653	1	2,653
Bąk v. Poland	21092/04	16/10/07	Dec.	3y 4m 18d	6 (1)	3,714	1	3,714
Falkowski v. Poland	32743/06	23/10/07	Dec.	1y 2m 21d	6 (1) (also unfairness)	5,836	1	5,836

[1] There were no friendly settlements that year.
[2] Annual Average Exchange Rate: 0.26528 (PLN).

Stanek v. Poland	16244/03	06/11/07	Dec.	4y 5m 28d	6 (1) (also outcome)	4,244	1	4,244
Marchel v. Poland	31119/02	13/11/07	Dec.	6y 11m 16d	?	3,714	1	3,714
Poniatowski v. Poland	39970/03	13/11/07	Dec.	3y 11m 19d	6 (1)	3,979	1	3,979
Militowska v. Poland	10002/05	11/12/07	Dec.	2y 10m 20d	6 (1)	2,653	1	2,653

Table III/8. 2008 for Poland: Article 6 (1) ECHR (Length of Civil Proceedings) – Friendly Settlements and Arrangements[1,2]

Applicant v. State	Appl. No.	Date of Ruling	ToD	Length of Negotiations	ECHR	Total CB	NoR	BpR
ARRANGEMENTS								
Piekarczyk v. Poland	47727/06	29/01/08	Dec.	1y 2m 19d	6 (also outcome)	2,864	1	2,864
Laskowski v. Poland	17220/03	12/02/08	Dec.	5y 2m 9d	6 (1) (also unfairness, judgment unjust), 13	3,437	1	3,437
Kornacki v. Poland	2967/05	27/03/08	Dec.	3y 2m 25d	6 (1)	7,160	1	7,160
Antkowiak v. Poland	14056/06	22/04/08	Dec.	2y 0m 24d	6 (also outcome)	2,864	1	2,864
Lisiecki v. Poland	18034/05	06/05/08	Dec.	3y 0m 14d	6 (1), 13	2,291	1	2,291
Olewiński v. Poland	8158/06	06/05/08	Dec.	2y 7m 8d	6 (1) (also unfairness), 13	3,437	1	3,437
Pawłowska v. Poland	37991/04	10/06/08	Dec.	3y 8m 20d	6 (1), 8	3,437	1	3,437
Śliwa v. Poland	42001/06	10/06/08	Dec.	1y 7m 30d	6 (1)	2,864	1	2,864
Wiktor v. Poland	42178/05	10/06/08	Dec.	2y 7m 8d	6 (1)	4,010	1	4,010
Bienkowski v. Poland	39010/05	17/06/08	Dec.	2y 8m 3d	6 (1), 1 P. 1	7,876	2	3,938
Strzoda a. O. v. Poland	36055/06	17/06/08	Dec.	1y 9m 26d	6 (1), 1 P. 1	8,592	3	2,864
Śliwa v. Poland	6738/07	01/07/08	Dec.	1y 5m 12d	6 (1)	2,864	1	2,864
Smolińska v. Poland	2410/07	01/07/08	Dec.	1y 5m 27d	6 (1)	2,349	1	2,349
Tokaj v. Poland	23952/05	08/07/08	Dec.	3y 0m 17d	6 (1), 13	2,005	1	2,005
Czemarnik-Noga v. Poland	21905/06	02/09/08	Dec.	2y 3m 15d	6 (1)	4,296	1	4,296
Bzowy v. Poland	32343/04	09/09/08	Dec.	4y 0m 22d	6 (1) (also access to court, unfairness)	2,000	1	2,000

[1] There were no friendly settlements that year.
[2] Annual Average Exchange Rate: 0.28641 (PLN).

Piórkowski v. Poland	20000/07	09/09/08	Dec.	1y 4m 17d	6 (1)	2,578	1	2,578
Ciechanowski v. Poland	2863/06	16/09/08	Dec.	6y 0m 14d	6 (1)	4,296	1	4,296
Makowska v. Poland	34762/06	16/09/08	Dec.	2y 7m 9d	6 (1)	5,442	1	5,442
Woźniak v. Poland	10511/07	14/10/08	Dec.	1y 8m 0d	6 (1)	3,523	1	3,523
Małagocki v. Poland	53122/07	21/10/08	Dec.	0y 10m 24d	6 (1)	2,434	1	2,434
Markieta v. Poland	49718/06	21/10/08	Dec.	1y 10m 24d	6 (1), 1 P. 1	2,578	1	2,578
Remesz a. O. v. Poland	32224/04	09/12/08	Dec.	4y 4m 0d	6 (1), 13	10,884	4	2,721
Adamska v. Poland	13314/07	16/12/08	Dec.	1y 9m 4d	6 (1)	3,437	1	3,437

IV. Poland – Cumulative Statistics Concerning Friendly Settlements and Arrangements

Table IV/1. Number of Recipients

Year	Judgments	Arrangements	Total
1999			
2000			
2001		6	6
2002		3	3
2003	16	21	37
2004	3	10	13
2005		4	4
2006		28	28
2007		21	21
2008		30	30
Total	19	123	142

Table IV/2. Average Length of Negotiations

Year	Judgments Art. 6 (1)	NoC	Arrangements Art. 6 (1)	NoC	∅ Length
1999					
2000					
2001			907 d	6	907 d
2002			1,464 d	3	1,464 d
2003	1,340 d	15	1,090 d	21	1,194 d
2004	2,315 d	4	1,409 d	9	1,688 d
2005			1,532 d	4	1,532 d
2006			1,452 d	22	1,452 d
2007			1,419 d	20	1,419 d
2008			2,578 d	24	2,578 d
∅ Length	1,545 d	19	1,594 d	109	1,587 d

Table IV/3. Damages Paid by Poland in Friendly Settlements and Arrangements: Article 6 (1) ECHR (Length of Civil Proceedings)

YEAR	JUDGMENTS		ARRANGEMENTS		TA	ACTUAL 2008	NoR	BpR	ACTUAL 2008
	BpR	TA	BpR	TA					
1999									
2000									
2001			3,391	20,344	20,344	23,639	6	3,391	3,940
2002			2,604	7,813	7,813	8,906	3	2,604	2,969
2003	3,343	53,482	2,900	60,895	114,377	127,988	37	3,091	3,459
2004	3,322	9,966	2,990	29,898	39,865	43,771	13	3,067	3,367
2005			3,549	14,196	14,196	15,275	4	3,549	3,819
2006			2,846	79,690	79,690	83,993	28	2,846	3,000
2007			3,358	70,514	70,514	72,841	21	3,358	3,469
2008			3,251	97,518	97,518	97,518	30	3,251	3,251
NoR / TA	19	63,449	123	380,868	416,160	441,387	142	2,931	3,108
BpR / TA Actual 2008	3,339	70,790	3,096	403,143					
BpR Actual 2008	3,726		3,278						

V. Poland – Yearly Statistics Concerning Judgments

Table V/1. 2000 for Poland: Article 6 (1) ECHR (Length of Civil Proceedings) – Judgments[1]

Applicant v. State	Appl. No.	Date of Judgment	Length of Negotiations	ECHR	Cash Benefits						Total CB	NoR	BpR
					PD	NoR	nPD	NoR	C/E	NoR			
Dewicka v. Poland	38670/97	04/04/00	3y 1m 8d	6 (1)			3,557	1			3,557	1	3,557
Wojnowicz v. Poland	33082/96	21/09/00	4y 11m 9d	6 (1)			5,928	1	608	1	6,536	1	6,536
Sobczyk v. Poland	25693/94; 27387/95	26/10/00	8y 7m 24d	6 (1)			4,742	1	474	1	5,217	1	5,217
Malinowska v. Poland	35843/97	14/12/00	4y 0m 28d	6 (1)			5,928	1			5,928	1	5,928
Wasilewski v. Poland	32734/96	21/12/00	4y 7m 3d	6 (1)			4,742	1			4,742	1	4,742

[1] Annual Average Exchange Rate: 0.23712 (PLN).

Table V/2. 2001 for Poland: Article 6 (1) ECHR (Length of Civil Proceedings) – Judgments[1]

Applicant v. State	Appl. No.	Date of Judgment	Length of Negotiations	ECHR	PD	NoR	nPD	NoR	C/E	NoR	Total CB	NoR	BpR
Kurzac v. Poland	31382/96	22/02/01	5y 9m 13d	6 (1)			5,461	1	1,693	1	7,155	1	7,155
C. v. Poland	27918/95	03/05/01	6y 7m 8d	6 (1)			5,461	1	492	1	5,953	1	5,953
Kreuz v. Poland	28249/95	19/06/01	6y 1m 9d	6 (1)			8,192	1	2,421	1	10,613	1	10,613
Zwierzyński v. Poland	34049/96	19/06/01	5y 0m 4d	6 (1)			4,096	1	6,827	1	10,923	1	10,923
Pogorzelec v. Poland	29455/95	17/07/01	6y 1m 25d	6 (1)			13,654	1		1	13,654	1	13,654
Jedamski v. Poland	29691/96	26/07/01	6y 1m 25d	6 (1)			5,461	1			5,461	1	5,461
Bejer v. Poland	38328/97	04/10/01	4y 3m 0d	6 (1)			4,096	1	1,229	1	5,325	1	5,325
Parciński v. Poland	36250/97	18/12/01	4y 11m 6d	6 (1)			1,502	1			1,502	1	1,502
Zawadzki v. Poland	34158/96	20/12/01	6y 2m 19d	6 (1)			13,654	1	2,731	1	16,384	1	16,384

[1] Annual Average Exchange Rates: 0.27307 (PLN), 0.15245 (FRF).

Table V/3. 2002 for Poland: Article 6 (1) ECHR (Length of Civil Proceedings) – Judgments

Applicant v. State	Appl. No.	Date of Judgment	Length of Negotiations	ECHR	Cash Benefits						Total CB	NoR	BpR
					PD	NoR	nPD	NoR	C/E	NoR			
Mączyński v. Poland	43779/98	15/01/02	3y 9m 9d	6 (1)			5,500	1			5,500	1	5,500
Goc v. Poland	48001/99	16/04/02	3y 10m 10d	6 (1)			5,569	1			5,569	1	5,569
Szarapo v. Poland	40835/98	23/05/02	4y 5m 21d	6 (1)			6,500	2			6,500	2	3,250
Gromuś v. Poland	29695/96	28/05/02	6y 9m 3d	6 (1)			5,000	1			5,000	1	5,000
Ustke v. Poland	48684/99	18/06/02	3y 6m 11d	6 (1)			5,000	1			5,000	1	5,000
Hałka a. O. v. Poland	71891/01	02/07/02	2y 3m 17d	6 (1)			10,000	4			10,000	4	2,500
Sawicka v. Poland	37645/97	01/10/02	5y 6m 21d	6 (1)			6,000	1			6,000	1	6,000
W.Z. v. Poland	65660/01	24/10/02	2y 2m 10d	6 (1)			10,000	1			10,000	1	10,000
Koral v. Poland	52518/99	05/11/02	3y 5m 25d	6 (1)			5,000	1			5,000	1	5,000
Piechota v. Poland	40330/98	05/11/02	5y 0m 21d	6 (1)			6,500	1			6,500	1	6,500

Table V/4. 2003 for Poland: Article 6 (1) ECHR (Length of Civil Proceedings) – Judgments

Applicant v. State	Appl. No.	Date of Judgment	Length of Negotiations	ECHR	Cash Benefits						Total CB	NoR	BpR
					PD	NoR	nPD	NoR	C/E	NoR			
Rawa v. Poland	38804/97	14/01/03	5y 8m 27d	6 (1)			4,00	1			4,000	1	4,000
W.M. v. Poland	39505/98	14/01/03	5y 4m 18d	6 (1)			5,000	1			5,000	1	5,000
Sobański v. Poland	40694/98	21/01/03	5y 4m 6d	6 (1)			5,000	1	1,000	1	6,000	1	6,000
Kubiszyn v. Poland	37437/97	30/01/03	6y 4m 25d	6 (1)			3,750	1			3,750	1	3,750
Bukowski v. Poland	38665/97	11/02/03	5y 10m 23d	6 (1)			8,000	1			8,000	1	8,000
Fuchs v. Poland	33870/96	11/02/03	7y 9m 10d	6 (1)			8,000	1	870	1	8,870	1	8,870
Kroenitz v. Poland	77746/01	25/02/03	2y 6m 28d	6 (1)			4,000	1			4,000	1	4,000
Orzeł v. Poland	74816/01	25/03/03	2y 8m 24d	6 (1)			10,000	1			10,000	1	10,000
R.O. v. Poland	77597/01	25/03/03	2y 8m 25d	6 (1)			6,000	1			6,000	1	6,000
Andrzej and Barbara Piłka v. Poland	39619/98	06/05/03	5y 8m 21d	6 (1)			8,500	2			8,500	2	4,250
Gryziecka and Gryziecki v. Poland	46034/99	06/05/03	5y 3m 6d	6 (1)			6,250	2	1,500	2	7,750	2	3,875
Majkrzyk v. Poland	52168/99	06/05/03	4y 4m 2d	6 (1)			4,000	1			4,000	1	4,000
Maliszewski v. Poland	40887/98	06/05/03	5y 4m 28d	6 (1)			4,000	1			4,000	1	4,000
Paśnicki v. Poland	51429/99	06/05/03	4y 1m 19d	6 (1)			4,500	1			4,500	1	4,500
Sobierajska-Nierzwicka v. Poland	49349/99	27/05/03	4y 4m 24d	6 (1)			6,700	1	162	1	6,862	1	6,862
Górska v. Poland	53698/00	03/06/03	4y 1m 28d	6 (1)			6,500	1			6,500	1	6,500

Continued from Table V/4. 2003 for Poland: Article 6 (1) ECHR (Length of Civil Proceedings) – Judgments

Applicant v. State	Appl. No.	Date of Judgment	Length of Negotiations	ECHR	Cash Benefits						Total CB	NoR	BpR
					PD	NoR	nPD	NoR	C/E	NoR			
Wyłęgły v. Poland	33334/96	03/06/03	7y 6m 27d	6 (1)			3,000	2			3,000	2	1,500
R.W. v. Poland	41033/98	15/07/03	5y 6m 21d	6 (1)			8,000	1			8,000	1	8,000
Sitarek v. Poland	42078/98	15/07/03	5y 11m 25d	6 (1)			6,500	1	262	1	6,762	1	6,762
Biskupska v. Poland	39597/98	22/07/03	6y 0m 7d	6 (1)			4,500	1	1,140	1	5,640	1	5,640
Sienkiewicz v. Poland	52468/99	30/09/03	4y 6m 0d	6 (1)			2,000	1			2,000	1	2,000
D.M. v. Poland	13557/02	14/10/03	2y 11m 14d	6 (1), 13			5,000	1			5,000	1	5,000
Dybo v. Poland	71894/01	14/10/03	3y 10m 14d	6 (1)			1,000	1			1,000	1	1,000
Gidel v. Poland	75872/01	14/10/03	2y 9m 25d	6 (1)			6,000	1			6,000	1	6,000
Henryka Malinowska v. Poland	76446/01	14/10/03	2y 8m 20d	6 (1)			4,800	1	140	1	4,940	1	4,940
I.P. v. Poland	77831/01	14/10/03	3y 2m 17d	6 (1)			9,000	1	30	1	9,030	1	9,030
Matasiewicz v. Poland	22072/02	14/10/03	1y 7m 19d	6 (1)			5,000	1			5,000	1	5,000
Porembska v. Poland	77759/01	14/10/03	2y 10m 24d	6 (1)			6,000	1			6,000	1	6,000
Cegielski v. Poland	71893/01	21/10/03	3y 5m 12d	6 (1), 13			8,000	1			8,000	1	8,000
Ciborek v. Poland	52037/99	04/11/03	4y 10m 30d	6 (1)			5,500	1	300		5,800	1	5,800
Łobarzewski v. Poland	77757/01	25/11/03	2y 0m 23d	6 (1), 13			11,000	1	1,500		12,500	1	12,500
Wierciszewska v. Poland	41431/98	25/11/03	5y 11m 15d	6 (1)			3,600	1	1,000		4,600	1	4,600
Peryt v. Poland	42042/98	02/12/03	6y 1m 2d	6 (1)									
Mianowski v. Poland	42083/98	16/12/03	6y 2m 18d	6 (1), 8			10,000	1			10,000	1	10,000

Table V/5. 2004 for Poland: Article 6 (1) ECHR (Length of Civil Proceedings) – Judgments

Applicant v. State	Appl. No.	Date of Judgment	Length of Negotiations	ECHR	Cash Benefits						Total CB	NoR	BpR
					PD	NoR	nPD	NoR	C/E	NoR			
Grela v. Poland	73003/01	13/01/04	4y 6m 22d	6 (1)			6,000	1	40	1	6,040	1	6,040
Kranz v. Poland	6214/02	17/02/04	2y 0m 19d	6 (1)			5,000	1			5,000	1	5,000
Kaszubski v. Poland	35577/97	24/02/04	8y 3m 14d	6 (1)			4,300	1			4,300	1	4,300
Jablonski v. Poland	60225/00	09/03/04	3y 10m 18d	6 (1)			6,000	1			6,000	1	6,000
Hulewicz v. Poland	35656/97	30/03/04	7y 9m 20d	6 (1)			3,500	1	1,500	1	5,000	1	5,000
Pachnik v. Poland	53029/99	30/03/04	5y 4m 17d	6 (1)			9,000	1	100	1	9,100	1	9,100
Krzak v. Poland	51515/99	06/04/04	5y 3m 23d	6 (1)			3,500	1			3,500	1	3,500
Góra v. Poland	38811/97	27/04/04	7y 4m 15d	6 (1)			7,000	1			7,000	1	7,000
Janik v. Poland	38564/97	27/04/04	6y 10m 28d	6 (1)			8,000	1			8,000	1	8,000
Krzewicki v. Poland	37770/97	27/04/04	6y 9m 8d	6 (1)			2,400	1			2,400	1	2,400
Politikin v. Poland	68930/01	27/04/04	3y 9m 23d	6 (1)			4,700	1			4,700	1	4,700
Sarman-Januszewska v. Poland	52478/99	27/04/04	4y 11m 10d	6 (1)			3,300	1			3,300	1	3,300
Gęsiarz v. Poland	9446/02	18/05/04	2y 3m 2d	6 (1)			5,000	1			5,000	1	5,000
Rychliccy v. Poland	51599/99	18/05/04	5y 4m 10d	6 (1)			8,000	2			8,000	2	4,000
Domańska v. Poland	74073/01	25/05/04	4y 0m 7d	6 (1)			1,800	1			1,800	1	1,800
Hajnrich v. Poland	44181/98	25/05/04	6y 9m 17d	6 (1)			3,500	1	150	1	3,650	1	3,650
Urbańczyk v. Poland	33777/96	01/06/04	7y 8m 30d	6 (1)			5,000	1			5,000	1	5,000

Continued from Table V/5. 2004 for Poland: Article 6 (1) ECHR (Length of Civil Proceedings) – Judgments

Applicant v. State	Appl. No.	Date of Judgment	Length of Negotiations	ECHR	Cash Benefits						Total CB	NoR	BpR
					PD	NoR	nPD	NoR	C/E	NoR			
Leszczyńska v. Poland	47551/99	22/06/04	6y 3m 30d	6 (1)			3,000	1	50	1	3,050	1	3,050
Gruzicka v. Poland	55383/00	13/07/04	5y 1m 19d	6 (1)			3,500	1			3,500	1	3,500
Lisawska v. Poland	37761/97	13/07/04	7y 7m 18d	6 (1), 13			10,000	1			10,000	1	10,000
Zynger v. Poland	66096/01	13/07/04	2y 8m 12d	6 (1), 13			7,200	1	2,000	1	9,200	1	9,200
Bednarska v. Poland	53413/99	15/07/04	5y 3m 29d	6 (1), 13			2,000	1			2,000	1	2,000
Kreuz v. Poland (No. 2)	46245/99	20/07/04	6y 9m 3d	6 (1)			3,600	1			3,600	1	3,600
Wróbel v. Poland	46002/99	20/07/04	6y 3m 23d	6 (1)			4,000	1			4,000	1	4,000
Adamscy v. Poland	49975/99	27/07/04	5y 3m 7d	6 (1)			5,000	2			5,000	2	2,500
Biały v. Poland	52040/99	27/07/04	5y 3m 12d	6 (1)			2,500	1			2,500	1	2,500
L. v. Poland	44189/98	27/07/04	6y 8m 9d	6 (1)			6,600	2			6,600	2	3,300
Marszał v. Poland	63391/00	14/09/04	5y 2m 7d	6 (1)			5,000	1	300	1	5,300	1	5,300
Fojcik v. Poland	57670/00	21/09/04	5y 0m 25d	6 (1)			10,000	1			10,000	1	10,000
Janas v. Poland	61454/00	21/09/04	4y 8m 8d	6 (1)			4,500	1	500	1	5,000	1	5,000
Korbel v. Poland	57672/00	21/09/04	5y 2m 14d	6 (1)			3,600	2			3,600	2	1,800
Kusiak v. Poland	50424/99	21/09/04	2y 3m 10d	6 (1)			7,000	2			7,000	2	3,500
Kaśmierek v. Poland	10675/02	21/09/04	2y 6m 24d	6 (1)			4,000	1			4,000	1	4,000
Romanow v. Poland	45299/99	21/09/04	6y 7m 4d	6 (1)			2,800	1			2,800	1	2,800
Związek Nauczycielstwa Polskiego v. Poland	42049/98	21/09/04	6y 9m 11d	6 (1)			10,000	1	916	1	10,916	1	10,916

Durasik v. Poland	6735/03	28/09/04	1y 7m 22d	6 (1)	5,000	1			5,000	1	5,000
Izykowska v. Poland	7530/02	28/09/04	3y 1m 23d	6 (1)	8,500	1	300	1	8,800	1	8,800
Jastrzębska v. Poland	72048/01	28/09/04	4y 6m 4d	6 (1)	3,000	1			3,000	1	3,000
Koblański v. Poland	59445/00	28/09/04	4y 9m 30d	6 (1)	5,000	1			5,000	1	5,000
Król v. Poland	65017/01	28/09/04	4y 4m 25d	6 (1)	4,500	1	1,500	1	6,000	1	6,000
Pieniążek v. Poland	62179/00	28/09/04	5y 1m 27d	6 (1)	2,500	1	100	1	2,600	1	2,600
Zys-Kowalski a. O. v. Poland	70213/01	28/09/04	4y 4m 18d	6 (1)	3,600	4			3,600	4	900
Dudek v. Poland	2560/02	05/10/04	2y 9m 7d	6 (1)	5,000	1			5,000	1	5,000
Falęcka v. Poland	52524/99	05/10/04	7y 2m 27d	6 (1)	3,600	1			3,600	1	3,600
Kruk v. Poland	67690/01	05/10/04	4y 0m 3d	6 (1)	3,600	1			3,600	1	3,600
Kuśmierkowski v. Poland	63442/00	05/10/04	4y 5m 24d	6 (1)	3,500	1			3,500	1	3,500
Lizut-Skwarek v. Poland	71625/01	05/10/04	4y 6m 28d	6 (1), 13	2,750	1	500	1	3,250	1	3,250
Malinowska-Biedrzycka v. Poland	63390/00	05/10/04	5y 8m 16d	6 (1)	10,000	1	1,000	1	11,000	1	11,000
Nowak v. Poland	27833/02	05/10/04	2y 2m 18d	6 (1)	3,600	1			3,600	1	3,600
Przygodzki v. Poland	65719/01	05/10/04	5y 9m 14d	6 (1)	2,500	1			2,500	1	2,500
Sikora v. Poland	64764/01	05/10/04	4y 6m 21d	6 (1)	6,000	1			6,000	1	6,000
Lipowicz v. Poland	57467/00	19/10/04	5y 5m 9d	6 (1)	4,000	1			4,000	1	4,000
Mejer and Jałoszyńska v. Poland	62109/00	19/10/04	5y 4m 25d	6 (1)	5,000	2			5,000	2	2,500
R.P.D. v. Poland	77681/01	19/10/04	4y 10m 4d	6 (1)	5,500	1			5,500	1	5,500
Wiatrzyk v. Poland	52074/99	26/10/04	5y 5m 28d	6 (1)	3,000	1	120	1	3,120	1	3,120
Dojs v. Poland	47402/99	02/11/04	5y 11m 21d	6 (1)	2,500	1			2,500	1	2,500
Sikorski v. Poland	46004/99	09/11/04	6y 3m 3d	6 (1)	6,000	1			6,000	1	6,000

Table V/6. 2005 for Poland: Article 6 (1) ECHR (Length of Civil Proceedings) – Judgments

Applicant v. State	Appl. No.	Date of Judgment	Length of Negotiations	ECHR	Cash Benefits						Total CB	NoR	BpR
					PD	NoR	nPD	NoR	C/E	NoR			
Beller v. Poland	51837/99	01/02/05	5y 10m 21d	6 (1), 1 P. 1			7,000	1	2,000	1	9,000	1	9,000
Kolasiński v. Poland	46243/99	01/02/05	6y 11m 23d	6 (1)			4,000	1	530	1	4,530	1	4,530
Brudnicka a. O. v. Poland	54723/00	03/03/05	5y 1m 20d	6 (1)			73,600	16			73,600	16	4,600
Szenk v. Poland	67979/01	22/03/05	4y 7m 24d	6 (1)			5,000	1			5,000	1	5,000
Zmaliński v. Poland	52039/99	22/03/05	6y 0m 24d	6 (1)			4,500	1	200	1	4,700	1	4,700
J.S. and A.S. v. Poland	40732/98	24/05/05	6y 6m 23d	6 (1)			5,500	2			5,500	2	2,750
Turczanik v. Poland	38064/97	05/07/05	8y 4m 22d	6 (1) (also un-fairness), 13			7,500	1	40	1	7,540	1	7,540
Siemianowski v. Poland	45972/99	06/09/05	10y 5m 8d	6 (1)			2,000	1	500	1	2,500	1	2,500
H.N. v. Poland	77710/01	13/09/05	4y 10m 21d	6 (1), 8			10,000	1	12,000	1	22,000	1	22,000
Sibilski v. Poland	64207/01	04/10/05	5y 6m 25d	6 (1)			3,000	1			3,000	1	3,000
Majewski v. Poland	52690/99	11/10/05	7y 3m 23d	6 (1)			6,000	1	500	1	6,500	1	6,500
Palka v. Poland	49176/99	11/10/05	9y 6m 6d	6 (1)			4,000	1	1,000	1	5,000	1	5,000
Szczeciński v. Poland	73864/01	11/10/05	4y 4m 20d	6 (1)			2,000	1			2,000	1	2,000
Badowski v. Poland	47627/99	08/11/05	6y 8m 14d	6 (1)			3,000	1			3,000	1	3,000
Kaniewski v. Poland	38049/02	08/11/05	3y 0m 25d	6 (1)			8,000	1	500	1	8,500	1	8,500
Majewski a. O. v. Poland	64204/01	08/11/05	5y 1m 24d	6 (1)			9,000	3			9,000	3	3,000
Bogucki v. Poland	49961/99	15/11/05	6y 4m 28d	6 (1)			4,000	1	1,500	1	5,500	1	5,500

Czech v. Poland	49034/99	15/11/05	7y 4m 21d	6 (1)	3,500	1	3,500	1
Wyszczelski v. Poland	72161/01	29/11/05	5y 2m 24d	6 (1)	4,000	1	4,000	1

Table V/7. 2006 for Poland: Article 6 (1) ECHR (Length of Civil Proceedings) – Judgments

Applicant v. State	Appl. No.	Date of Judgment	Length of Negotiations	ECHR	Cash Benefits						Total CB	NoR	BpR
					PD	NoR	nPD	NoR	C/E	NoR			
Kreuz v. Poland (No. 3)	75888/01	24/01/06	4y 10m 15d	6 (1)			3,000	1			3,000	1	3,000
Maria Kaczmarczyk v. Poland	13026/02	24/01/06	4y 4m 19d	6 (1)			2,600	1			2,600	1	2,600
Skowroński v. Poland	36431/03	24/01/06	2y 2m 15d	6 (1)			3,500	1			3,500	1	3,500
Kranc v. Poland	12888/02	31/01/06	4y 5m 3d	6 (1)			2,800	1			2,800	1	2,800
Koss v. Poland	52495/99	28/03/06	6y 10m 9d	6 (1)			7,000	1			7,000	1	7,000
Barszcz v. Poland	71152/01	30/05/06	5y 7m 12d	6 (1)			3,000	1			3,000	1	3,000
Dzierżanowski v. Poland	2983/02	27/06/06	4y 6m 8d	6 (1)			3,000	1			3,000	1	3,000
Ratajczyk v. Poland	11215/02	18/07/06	4y 11m 25d	6 (1)			4,200	1			4,200	1	4,200
Sitarski v. Poland	71068/01	08/08/06	5y 2m 30d	6 (1)			2,600	1			2,600	1	2,600
Chyb v. Poland	20838/02	22/08/06	4y 8m 26d	6 (1), 13			8,000	1			8,000	1	8,000
Majchrzak v. Poland	1524/02	22/08/06	5y 1m 30d	6 (1)			3,500	1			3,500	1	3,500
Nierojewska v. Poland	77835/01	22/08/06	5y 9m 17d	6 (1)			4,500	1			4,500	1	4,500
Nowak and Zajączkowski v. Poland	12174/02	22/08/06	4y 11m 25d	6 (1)			6,000	2			6,000	2	3,000
Rybczyńscy v. Poland	3501/02	03/10/06	4y 8m 24d	6 (1)			2,400	2	363	2	2,763	2	1,382
Cichla v. Poland	18036/03	10/10/06	3y 4m 20d	6 (1)			7,000	1			7,000	1	7,000
Jeruzal v. Poland	65888/01	10/10/06	5y 11m 9d	6 (1)			3,300	1			3,300	1	3,300

Jończyk v. Poland	75870/01	10/10/06	6y 3m 13d	6 (1)	2,500	1			2,500	1	2,500
Kędra v. Poland	1564/02	10/10/06	4y 9m 21d	6 (1)	4,000	1	70	1	4,070	1	4,070
Kuźniak v. Poland	13861/02	10/10/06	5y 2m 15d	6 (1)	4,200	1			4,200	1	4,200
Rybczyńska v. Poland	57764/00	10/10/06	6y 10m 22d	6 (1)	3,500	1			3,500	1	3,500
Szymoński v. Poland	6925/02	10/10/06	5y 10m 19d	6 (1)	4,500	1			4,500	1	4,500
Augustyniak v. Poland	5413/02	17/10/06	5y 8m 26d	6 (1)	1,800	1	100	1	1,900	1	1,900
Chodzyńscy v. Poland	17484/02	17/10/06	5y 1m 27d	6 (1)	1,500	2			1,500	2	750
Czerwiński v. Poland	10384/02	17/10/06	5y 2m 15d	6 (1)	4,400	1			4,400	1	4,400
Grabiński v. Poland	43702/02	17/10/06	3y 11m 2d	6 (1)	10,000	1	1,000	1	11,000	1	11,000
Kwiatkowski v. Poland	4560/04	17/10/06	2y 8m 27d	6 (1)	2,500	1	1,500	1	4,000	1	4,000
Nowak v. Poland	8612/02	17/10/06	4y 8m 0d	6 (1)	3,000	1	600	1	3,600	1	3,600
Zielonka v. Poland	7313/02	17/10/06	5y 2m 2d	6 (1)	2,400	1	100	1	2,500	1	2,500
Atut Sp. z o.o. v. Poland	71151/01	24/10/06	5y 6m 28d	6 (1)	3,000	1			3,000	1	3,000
Baranowska v. Poland	72994/01	24/10/06	5y 5m 21d	6 (1)	2,000	1			2,000	1	2,000
Orzechowski v. Poland	77795/01	24/10/06	5y 2m 10d	6 (1)	6,000	1			6,000	1	6,000
Romaniak v. Poland	53284/99	24/10/06	7y 7m 2d	6 (1)	7,000	1			7,000	1	7,000
Sokołowski v. Poland	15337/02	24/10/06	5y 0m 23d	6 (1)	3,600	1			3,600	1	3,600
Stevens v. Poland	13568/02	24/10/06	4y 7m 12d	6 (1)	5,600	1	1,035	1	6,635	1	6,635
Łukjaniuk v. Poland	15072/02	07/11/06	5y 6m 5d	6 (1)	1,000	1			1,000	1	1,000
Romejko v. Poland	74209/01	07/11/06	5y 9m 21d	6 (1)	6,000	1			6,000	1	6,000
Drabicki v. Poland	15464/02	14/11/06	5y 1m 6d	6 (1)	1,200	1			1,200	1	1,200
Wróblewska v. Poland	22346/02	28/11/06	5y 0m 12d	6 (1)	2,500	1	100	1	2,600	1	2,600
Akerblom v. Poland	64974/01	05/12/06	6y 6m 0d	6 (1)	3,000	1	1,700	1	4,700	1	4,700
Boszko v. Poland	4054/03	05/12/06	3y 10m 18d	6 (1)	3,000	1	500	1	3,500	1	3,500

Continued from Table V/7. 2006 for Poland: Article 6 (1) ECHR (Length of Civil Proceedings) – Judgments

Applicant v. State	Appl. No.	Date of Judgment	Length of Negotiations	ECHR	Cash Benefits						Total CB	NoR	BpR
					PD	NoR	nPD	NoR	C/E	NoR			
Zdeb v. Poland	72998/01	05/12/06	6y 6m 6d	6 (1)			3,000	1			3,000	1	3,000
Zygmunt v. Poland	69128/01	05/12/06	6y 1m 9d	6 (1)			1,800	1	100	1	1,900	1	1,900
Wojtunik v. Poland	64212/01	12/12/06	7y 6m 8d	6 (1)			1,200	1			1,200	1	1,200

Table V/8. 2008 for Poland: Article 6 (1) ECHR (Length of Civil Proceedings) – Judgments

Applicant v. State	Appl. No.	Date of Judgment	Length of Negotiations	ECHR	Cash Benefits						Total CB	NoR	BpR
					PD	NoR	nPD	NoR	C/E	NoR			
Stukus a. O. v. Poland	12534/03	01/04/08	5y 0m 2d	6 (1)			20,000	8			20,000	8	2,500
Krawczak v. Poland	40387/06	08/04/08	1y 6m 17d	6 (1), 13			7,000	1	500	1	7,500	1	7,500
Borysiewicz v. Poland	71146/01	01/07/08	7y 5m 0d	6 (1)			10,000	1			10,000	1	10,000
Beata Bogusław v. Poland	34105/03	29/07/08	4y 9m 13d	6 (1)			1,000	1			1,000	1	1,000
Marek Bogusław v. Poland	34103/03	29/07/08	4y 9m 13d	6 (1)			1,000	1			1,000	1	1,000

VI. Poland – Cumulative Statistics Concerning Judgments

Table VI/1.
Number of Recipients

Year	Total
1999	0
2000	5
2001	9
2002	14
2003	37
2004	72
2005	37
2006	48
2007	0
2008	12
Total	505

Table VI/2.
Average Length of Negotiations

Year	ø Length	NoC
1999		
2000	1,859 d	5
2001	2,079 d	9
2002	1,497 d	10
2003	1,681 d	34
2004	1,886 d	63
2005	2,302 d	19
2006	1,921 d	45
2007		
2008	1,719 d	5
ø Length	1,883 d	190

Table VI/3. Damages Paid by Poland in Judgments:
Article 6 (1) ECHR (Length of Civil Proceedings)

Year	BpR	TA	TA	Actual 2008	NoR	BpR	Actual 2008
1999							
2000	5,196	25,979	25,979	30,786	5	5,196	6,157
2001	8,552	76,969	76,969	89,439	9	8,552	9,938
2002	4,648	65,069	65,069	74,179	14	4,648	5,298
2003	5,433	201,004	201,004	224,923	37	5,433	6,079
2004	4,332	311,936	311,936	342,506	72	4,332	4,757
2005	4,983	184,370	184,370	198,382	37	4,983	5,362
2006	3,620	173,768	173,768	183,151	48	3,620	3,816
2007							
2008	3,292	39,500	39,500	39,500	12	3,292	3,292
NoR / TA	234	*1,078,596*	1,078,596	1,182,866	234	4,609	5,055
BpR / TA Actual 2008	4,609	*1,182,866*					
BpR Actual 2008	5,055						

VII. Poland – Yearly Statistics Concerning Unilateral Declarations

Table VII/1. 2007 for Poland: Article 6 (1) ECHR (Length of Civil Proceedings) – Unilateral Declarations[1]

Applicant v. State	Appl. No.	Date of Ruling	ToD	Length of Negotiations	FS Proposed	ECHR	Total CB	NoR	BpR
ACCEPTED UNILATERAL DECLARATIONS									
Waza v. Poland[2]	11602/02	26/06/07	Dec.	5y 3m 19d	Yes	6 (1), 13	5,306	1	5,306
Maj v. Poland[2]	15071/02	02/10/07	Dec.	6y 4m 4d	Yes	6 (1), 13	2,653	1	2,653
Nowak v. Poland[3]	12958/02	02/10/07	Dec.	5y 10m 25d	Yes	6 (1)	2,653	1	2,653
Popiel v. Poland[3]	19560/02	09/10/07	Dec.	6y 1m 19d	Yes	6 (1)	2,653	1	2,653
Andrzejczyk v. Poland[2]	45982/06	06/11/07	Dec.	0y 11m 28d	Yes	6 (1)	3,979	1	3,979
Wydmański v. Poland[2]	17965/06	06/11/07	Dec.	1y 6m 10d	Yes	6 (1), 13	2,653	1	2,653
REJECTED UNILATERAL DECLARATIONS									
Wawrzynowicz v. Poland[4]	73192/01	17/07/07	Judg.	6y 4m 22d	?	6 (1)	2,653	1	2,653
Tur v. Poland[4]	21695/05	23/10/07	Judg.	2y 4m 23d	?	6 (1), 13	2,653	1	2,653

1234

1 Annual Average Exchange Rate: 0.26528 (PLN).
2 The Government acknowleged the unreasonable duration of domestic proceedings and interference with Art. 13 ECHR.
3 The Government acknowledged the unreasonable duration of the domestic proceedings.
4 The Government was willing to accept a violation of Art. 6 (1) ECHR.

Table VII/2. 2008 for Poland: Article 6 (1) ECHR (Length of Civil Proceedings) – Unilateral Declarations[1]

Applicant v. State	Appl. No.	Date of Ruling	ToD	Length of Negotiations	FS Proposed	ECHR	Total CB	NoR	BpR
ACCEPTED UNILATERAL DECLARATIONS									
M.M. v. Poland[2]	37850/03; 37850/03	04/01/08	Dec.	2y 1m 3d	?	6 (1), 8, 13	4,296	1	4,296
Modłkowska v. Poland[3]	6420/02	29/01/08	Dec.	6y 0m 18d	?	6 (1)	2,864	1	2,864
Bończa Rutkowski v. Poland[4]	15530/02	11/03/08	Dec.	6y 5m 16d	Yes	6 (1)	5,728	1	5,728
Aruniti v. Poland[5]	20797/06	18/03/08	Dec.	1y 10m 20d	?	6 (1), 13	5,442	1	5,442
Hryniewicki v. Poland[4]	18779/02	22/04/08	Dec.	5y 11m 30d	?	6 (1)	4,296	1	4,296
Seweryn v. Poland[5]	38620/06	13/05/08	Dec.	1y 7m 23d	?	6 (1), 13	6,301	1	6,301
Kwaśnik v. Poland[5]	6480/04	20/05/08	Dec.	4y 3m 16d	?	6 (1), 13	5,299	1	5,299
Sakowski and Sakowska v. Poland[3]	5201/06	10/06/08	Dec.	2y 4m 14d	?	6 (1), 13	2,148	2	1,074
Lewandowski v. Poland[4]	12526/02	01/07/08	Dec.	7y 6m 27d	?	6 (1)	2,291	1	2,291
E. Figiel and W. Figiel v. Poland[5]	10281/03	08/07/08	Dec.	5y 3m 19d	?	6 (1), 13	6,015	2	3,007
Sierzputowska v. Poland[4]	18053/06	08/07/08	Dec.	2y 3m 6d	?	6 (1)	5,155	1	5,155
Broszczakowska and Rupniccy v. Poland[4]	19797/02	02/09/08	Dec.	7y 5m 4d	?	6 (1)	1,432	3	477
Burbulis v. Poland[5]	3987/04	09/09/08	Dec.	5y 7m 28d	?	6 (1), 13	6,874	1	6,874

1 Annual Average Exchange Rate: 0.28641 (PLN).
2 The Government acknowledged the unreasonable duration of domestic proceedings and violations of Arts. 8 and 13 ECHR.
3 The Government acknowledged the unreasonable duration of the domestic proceedings and admitted that there was no redress available.
4 The Government acknowledged the unreasonable duration of domestic proceedings.
5 The Government acknowledged the unreasonable duration of domestic proceedings and the interference with Art. 13 ECHR.

Accepted Unilateral Declarations

Case	App. no.	Date	Type	Duration		Article	Amount	No.	Amount
Janik v. Poland[5]	3015/06	09/09/08	Dec.	2y 8m 4d	?	6 (1), 13	4,010	1	4,010
Gwardyan v. Poland[5]	14894/03	16/09/08	Dec.	5y 4m 25d	?	6 (1), 13	2,864	1	2,864
Toborek v. Poland[4]	31835/03	30/09/08	Dec.	5y 0m 0d	?	6 (1)	5,155	1	5,155
Zakrzewska v. Poland[5]	22515/06	30/09/08	Dec.	2y 9m 23d	?	6 (1), 13	2,864	1	2,864
Nowiński v. Poland[6]	14883/04	07/10/08	Dec.	4y 5m 18d	?	6 (1), 13	4,010	1	4,010
Mamzer and Dylich v. Poland[4]	12447/04	21/10/08	Dec.	4y 7m 5d	?	6 (1), 13	5,728	2	2,864
Tomula v. Poland[4]	38595/05	21/10/08	Dec.	3y 0m 23d	?	6 (1)	4,296	1	4,296
Galusiewicz v. Poland[5]	8651/04	09/12/08	Dec.	4y 9m 16d	?	6 (1), 13	4,296	1	4,296
Zaremba v. Poland[4]	38019/07	09/12/08	Dec.	1y 7m 23d	?	6 (1)	3,723	1	3,723

Rejected Unilateral Declarations

Case	App. no.	Date	Type	Duration		Article	Amount	No.	Amount
Kyziol v. Poland[7]	24203/05	12/02/08	Judg.	2y 7m 26d	Yes	6 (1)	2,864	1	2,864
Sadura v. Poland[7]	35382/06	01/07/08	Judg.	1y 11m 0d	?	6 (1), 13	4,296	1	4,296
Figiel v. Poland (No. 1)[7]	38190/05	17/07/08	Judg.	3y 5m 18d	?	6 (1), 13	2,864	1	2,864
Zając v. Poland[7]	19817/04	29/07/08	Judg.	4y 2m 18d	?	6 (1)	1,432	1	1,432
Figiel v. Poland (No. 2)[7]	38206/05	16/09/08	Judg.	3y 7m 18d	?	6 (1), 13	2,864	1	2,864
Krzysztof Kaniewski v. Poland[7]	49788/06	30/09/08	Judg.	1y 9m 25d	?	6 (1)	4,583	1	4,583
Lidia Nowak v. Poland[7]	38426/03	21/10/08	Judg.	5y 0m 12d	?	6 (1), 13	4,296	1	4,296

6 The Government acknowledged the unreasonable duration of domestic proceedings, restriction of access to court and interference with Art. 13 ECHR.
7 The Government was willing to accept a violation of Art. 6 (1) ECHR.

Continued from Table VII/2. 2008 for Poland: Article 6 (1) ECHR (Length of Civil Proceedings) – Unilateral Declarations

Applicant v. State	Appl. No.	Date of Ruling	ToD	Length of Negotiations	FS Proposed	ECHR	Total CB	NoR	BpR
REJECTED UNILATERAL DECLARATIONS									
Śliwa v. Poland[8]	10265/06	02/12/08	Judg.	8y 6m 2d	?	6 (1), 13	2,864	1	2,864
Ludwiczak v. Poland[9]	31748/06	16/12/08	Judg.	2y 4m 29d	?	6 (1)	5,728	1	5,728

[8] The Government was willing to accept a violation of Arts. 6 (1) and 13 ECHR.
[9] The Government was willing to accept a violation of Art. 6 (1) ECHR.

VIII. Poland – Cumulative Statistics Concerning Unilateral Declarations

Table VIII/1.
Number of Recipients

Year	Total
2001	
2002	
2003	
2004	
2005	
2006	
2007	6
2008	27
Total	33

Table VIII/2.
Average Length of Negotiations

Year	ø Length	NoC
2001		
2001		
2003		
2004		
2005		
2006		
2007	1,595 d	6
2008	1,590 d	22
ø Length	1,591 d	28

Table VIII/3. Damages Paid by Poland in Unilateral Declarations: Article 6 (1) ECHR (Length of Civil Proceedings)[1]

Year	BpR	Total	TA	Actual 2008	NoR	BpR	Actual 2008
2001							
2002							
2003							
2004							
2005							
2006							
2007	3,316	19,896	19,896	20,553	6	3,316	3,425
2008	3,522	95,088	95,088	95,088	27	3,522	3,522
NoR / TA	33	*114,984*	114,984	115,641	33	3,484	3,504
BpR / TA Actual 2008	3,484	*115,641*					
BpR Actual 2008	3,504						

[1] This table does not include the rejected unilateral declarations. They were, nonetheless, included in the yearly statistics.

IX. Turkey – Yearly Statistics Concerning Friendly Settlements and Arrangements

Table IX/1. 2000 for Turkey: Articles 2 and 3 ECHR – Friendly Settlements and Arrangements[1,2]

Applicant v. State	Appl. No.	Date of Ruling	ToD	Length of Negotiations	ECHR	Total CB	NoR	BpR
FRIENDLY SETTLEMENTS – ARTICLE 3 ECHR								
Denmark v. Turkey[3]	34382/97	05/04/00	Judg.	3y 2m 29d	3	60,354	1	60,354
Karataş and Boğa v. Turkey	24669/94	17/10/00	Judg.	6y 3m 6d	3	25,916	2	12,958
Gündüz a. O. v. Turkey	31249/96	14/11/00	Judg.	5y 1m 19d	3, 5 (3)	28,965	6	4,828

[1] There were no friendly settlements concerning Art. 2 ECHR and Arts. 2 and 3 ECHR combined that year. There were also no arrangements.
[2] Annual Average Exchange Rates: 0.13421 (DKK), 0.152449 (FRF).
[3] The friendly settlement includes a statement of regret, a statement concerning the change in legislation and a statement regarding the continued participation in the Council of Europe's police-training project.

Table IX/2. 2001 for Turkey: Articles 2 and 3 ECHR – Friendly Settlements and Arrangements[1,2]

Applicant v. State	Appl. No.	Date of Ruling	ToD	Length of Negotiations	ECHR	Total CB	NoR	BpR
FRIENDLY SETTLEMENTS – ARTICLE 2 ECHR								
I.I., I.Ş., K.E. and A.Ö. v. Turkey[3]	30953–56/96	06/11/01	Judg.	5y 7m 19d	2, 5	54,708	4	13,677
FRIENDLY SETTLEMENTS – ARTICLE 3 ECHR								
Gelgeç and Özdemir v. Turkey	27700/95	01/03/01	Judg.	5y 8m 24d	3	24,136	2	12,068
Çavuşoğlu v. Turkey	32983/96	06/03/01	Judg.	4y 6m 8d	3	11,434	1	11,434
Akan, Satan a. O. v. Turkey	30839/96; 30841/69, etc.	22/03/01	Dec.	5y 3m 7d	3, 5, 6, 13, 14, 17, 18, 1 P. 1	217,222	12	18,102
Akkala, Kayir a. O. v. Turkey	30828–35/96, etc.	22/03/01	Dec.	5y 3m 7d	3, 5, 6, 13, 14, 17, 18, 1 P. 1	160,905	10	16,091
Can, Güneş a. O. v. Turkey	30662–67/96, etc.	22/03/01	Dec.	5y 3m 7d	3, 5, 6, 13, 14, 17, 18, 1 P. 1	185,041	10	18,504
Dakman, Össucu a. O. v. Turkey	30741–43/96, etc.	22/03/01	Dec.	5y 3m 7d	3, 5, 6, 13, 14, 17, 18, 1 P. 1	164,123	10	16,412
Delidere v. Turkey	32016/96	22/03/01	Dec.	5y 0m 0d	3, 5, 6, 13, 14, 17, 18, 1 P. 1	80,453	5	16,091
Delidere, Işiktaş a. O. v. Turkey	30773–78/96, etc.	22/03/01	Dec.	5y 3m 7d	3, 5, 6, 13, 14, 17, 18, 1 P. 1	160,905	10	16,091
Demirbaş, Suişmez a. O. v. Turkey	30730–33/96, etc.	22/03/01	Dec.	5y 3m 7d	3, 5, 6, 13, 14, 17, 18, 1 P. 1	172,168	10	17,217
Erdoğan, Taruk a. O. v. Turkey	30808–17/96	22/03/01	Dec.	5y 3m 7d	3, 5, 6, 13, 14, 17, 18, 1 P. 1	160,905	10	16,091

[1] There were no arrangements that year.
[2] Annual Average Exchange Rates: 1.60905 (GBP), 0.152449 (FRF).
[3] The Government acknowledged and regretted the ECHR violations. The Government promised to take the necessary measures to prevent future violations.

Case	Application no.	Date		Duration	Articles			
Gözen, Akan a. O. v. Turkey	30710–19/96	22/03/01	Dec.	5y 3m 7d	3, 5, 6, 13, 14, 17, 18, 1 P. 1	168,950	10	16,895
Gündan, Karadağ a. O. v. Turkey	30674–77/96, etc.	22/03/01	Dec.	5y 3m 7d	3, 5, 6, 13, 14, 17, 18, 1 P. 1	185,041	10	18,504
Kaçmaz, Ekmekçi a. O. v. Turkey	30699/96; 30701/96, etc.	22/03/01	Dec.	5y 3m 7d	3, 5, 6, 13, 14, 17, 18, 1 P. 1	160,905	9	17,878
Kutludemir, Nergis a. O. v. Turkey	30795/96; 30797/96, etc.	22/03/01	Dec.	5y 3m 7d	3, 5, 6, 13, 14, 17, 18, 1 P. 1	176,996	10	17,700
Laçin, Dansuk a. O. v. Turkey	30686–95/96, etc.	22/03/01	Dec.	5y 3m 7d	3, 5, 6, 13, 14, 17, 18, 1 P. 1	188,259	10	18,826
Laçin, Gözen a. O. v. Turkey	30785–94/96	22/03/01	Dec.	5y 3m 7d	3, 5, 6, 13, 14, 17, 18, 1 P. 1	176,956	10	17,696
Orakçi, Korkusuz a. O. v. Turkey	30763–72/96	22/03/01	Dec.	5y 3m 7d	3, 5, 6, 13, 14, 17, 18, 1 P. 1	172,168	10	17,217
Özkan, Yalçin a. O. v. Turkey	30818–27/96	22/03/01	Dec.	5y 3m 7d	3, 5, 6, 13, 14, 17, 18, 1 P. 1	168,950	10	16,895
Özsucu, Aksucu a. O. v. Turkey	32002/96	22/03/01	Dec.	5y 0m 0d	3, 5, 6, 13, 14, 17, 18, 1 P. 1	242,967	15	16,198
Özsucu, Hamazay a. O. v. Turkey	30753–62/96	22/03/01	Dec.	5y 3m 7d	3, 5, 6, 13, 14, 17, 18, 1 P. 1	160,905	10	16,091
Şaşmaz, Karadağ a. O. v. Turkey	30652–61/96	22/03/01	Dec.	5y 3m 7d	3, 5, 6, 13, 14, 17, 18, 1 P. 1	185,041	10	18,504
Şengezer, Izgi a. O. v. Turkey	28512–15/96, etc.	22/03/01	Dec.	5y 7m 19d	3, 5, 6, 13, 14, 17, 18, 1 P. 1	201,131	10	20,113
Uruç, Cantürk a. O. v. Turkey	30720–29/96	22/03/01	Dec.	5y 3m 7d	3, 5, 6, 13, 14, 17, 18, 1 P. 1	176,996	10	17,700
Ağgül a. O. v. Turkey	33324/96	22/05/01	Judg.	4y 8m 17d	3, 5, 6, 8, 13, 14, 1 P. 1	144,815	9	16,091
Aygördü a. O. v. Turkey	33323/96	22/05/01	Judg.	4y 8m 17d	3, 5, 6, 8, 13, 14, 1 P. 1	80,453	5	16,091
Cemal and Nurhayat Güven v. Turkey	31848/96	22/05/01	Judg.	5y 1m 10d	3, 5, 6, 8, 13, 14, 1 P. 1	16,091	2	8,045
Ince a. O. v. Turkey	33325/96	22/05/01	Judg.	4y 8m 17d	3, 5, 6, 8, 13, 14, 1 P. 1	53,099	3	17,700
Kemal Güven v. Turkey	31847/96	25/05/01	Judg.	5y 1m 13d	3, 5, 6, 8, 13, 14, 1 P. 1	16,091	1	16,091
Firat Koç v. Turkey	24937/94	05/06/01	Judg.	6y 9m 24d	3, 5 (3), 6 (1), 6 (3) (c), 13, 14	7,775	1	7,775
Lalihan Ekinci v. Turkey	24947/94	05/06/01	Judg.	6y 9m 24d	3, 5 (3), 6 (1), 6 (3) (c), 13, 14	7,318	1	7,318

Continued from Table IX/2. 2001 for Turkey: Articles 2 and 3 ECHR – Friendly Settlements and Arrangements

Applicant v. State	Appl. No.	Date of Ruling	ToD	Length of Negotiations	ECHR	Total CB	NoR	BpR
FRIENDLY SETTLEMENTS – ARTICLE 3 ECHR								
*Avcı v. Turkey*³	24935/94	10/07/01	Judg.	6y 10m 28d	3, 5 (3), 6 (1), 6 (3) (c), 13, 14	31,404	1	31,404
*Boğ v. Turkey*³	24946/94	10/07/01	Judg.	6y 10m 28d	3, 5 (3), 6 (1), 6 (3) (c), 13, 14	29,575	1	29,575
*Boğa v. Turkey*³	24938/94	10/07/01	Judg.	6y 10m 28d	3, 5 (3), 6 (1), 6 (3) (c), 13, 14	30,947	1	30,947
*Değer v. Turkey*³	24934/94	10/07/01	Judg.	6y 10m 28d	3, 5 (3), 6 (1), 6 (3) (c), 13, 14	31,404	1	31,404
*Demir v. Turkey*³	24990/94	10/07/01	Judg.	6y 10m 28d	3, 5 (3), 6 (1), 6 (3) (c), 13, 14	29,118	1	29,118
*Doğan v. Turkey*³	24939/94	10/07/01	Judg.	6y 10m 28d	3, 5 (3), 6 (1), 6 (3) (c), 13, 14	31,404	1	31,404
*Kızılgedik v. Turkey*³	24944/94	10/07/01	Judg.	6y 10m 28d	3, 5 (3), 6 (1), 6 (3) (c), 13, 14	30,490	1	30,490
Kürküt v. Turkey	24933/94	10/07/01	Judg.	6y 10m 28d	3, 5 (3), 6 (1), 6 (3) (c), 13, 14	5,488	1	5,488
*Orak v. Turkey*³	24936/94	10/07/01	Judg.	6y 10m 28d	3, 5 (3), 6 (1), 6 (3) (c), 13, 14	35,063	1	35,063
*Parlak a. O. v. Turkey*³	24942-43/94, etc.	10/07/01	Judg.	6y 10m 28d	3, 5 (3), 6 (1), 6 (3) (c), 13, 14	96,348	3	32,116
*Şenses v. Turkey*³	24991/94	10/07/01	Judg.	6y 10m 28d	3, 5 (3), 6 (1), 6 (3) (c), 13, 14	28,660	1	28,660
Ercan v. Turkey	31246/96	25/09/01	Judg.	5y 7m 30d	3, 5 (1) (a), 5 (1) (b), 5 (3), 5 (4), 6 (1), 6 (3) (c)	48,272	1	48,272
İşçi v. Turkey	31849/96	25/09/01	Judg.	5y 5m 13d	3, 5, 6, 8, 13, 14	24,136	1	24,136
*Akbay v. Turkey*³	32598/96	02/10/01	Judg.	5y 6m 27d	3, 5 (1) (c), 5 (3), 5 (4), 5 (5), 13	38,115	1	38,115
*Saki v. Turkey*³	29359/95	30/10/01	Judg.	6y 1m 29d	3, 13	8,385	1	8,385
*Acar v. Turkey*³	24940/94	18/12/01	Judg.	7y 4m 6d	3, 5 (2), 6 (1), 6 (3) (c), 13, 14	28,660	1	28,660
*Güngü v. Turkey*³	24945/94	18/12/01	Judg.	7y 4m 6d	3, 5 (2), 6 (1), 6 (3) (c), 13, 14	29,118	1	29,118

FRIENDLY SETTLEMENTS – ARTICLES 2 AND 3 ECHR

Canpolat v. Turkey	28506/95 30780/96	22/03/01	Dec.	5y 7m 18d	2, 3, 5, 6, 13, 14, 18, 1 P. 1	40,226	1	40,226
Cantürk v. Turkey	30779/96	22/03/01	Dec.	5y 3m 7d	2, 3, 5, 6, 13, 14, 18, 1 P. 1	80,453	1	80,453
Kıraç v. Turkey	30844/96	22/03/01	Dec.	5y 3m 7d	2, 3, 5, 6, 13, 14, 18, 1 P. 1	28,963	1	28,963
Şanli v. Turkey	30957/96	22/03/01	Dec.	5y 3m 7d	2, 3, 5, 6, 13, 14, 18, 1 P. 1	28,963	1	28,963
Aydin v. Turkey[3]	28293/95; 29494/95; 30219/96	10/07/01	Judg.	6y 4m 7d	2, 3, 5, 6, 8, 13, 14, 18, 1 P. 1	109,415	12	9,118

Table IX/3. 2002 for Turkey: Articles 2 and 3 ECHR – Friendly Settlements and Arrangements[1, 2]

Applicant v. State	Appl. No.	Date of Ruling	ToD	Length of Negotiations	ECHR	Total CB	NoR	BpR
FRIENDLY SETTLEMENTS – ARTICLE 2 ECHR								
Onal a. O. v. Turkey[3]	27735/95	28/03/02	Judg.	6y 9m 9d	2	76,225	4	19,056
Siddik Yaşa v. Turkey[3]	22281/93	27/06/02	Judg.	9y 0m 6d	2, 5, 6, 8, 13, 14, 18, 33	141,657	1	141,657
Yakar v. Turkey[3]	36189/97	26/11/02	Judg.	5y 7m 18d	2	40,000	1	40,000
Adali v. Turkey[3]	31137/96	12/12/02	Judg.	6y 8m 4d	2	87,541	1	87,541
Şen v. Turkey	31154/96	12/12/02	Judg.	6y 8m 4d	2	111,416	1	111,416
Soğukpinar v. Turkey[3]	31153/96	12/12/02	Judg.	6y 8m 4d	2	87,541	1	87,541
Yalçin v. Turkey[3]	31152/96	12/12/02	Judg.	6y 8m 4d	2	87,541	1	87,541
FRIENDLY SETTLEMENTS – ARTICLE 3 ECHR								
Özbey v. Turkey[3]	31883/96	31/01/02	Judg.	5y 8m 7d	3, 6	15,245	1	15,245
Kaplan v. Turkey	24932/94	26/02/02	Judg.	7y 6m 14d	3, 5 (3), 6 (1), 6 (3) (c), 13, 14	3,659	1	3,659
Erat and Sağlam v. Turkey[3]	30492/96	26/03/02	Judg.	6y 3m 7d	3	45,735	2	22,867
Mehmet Özcan v. Turkey[3]	29856/96	09/04/02	Judg.	6y 3m 12d	3, 5 (3), 5 (4), 6 (1), 6 (3), 14	30,490	1	30,490
Z.Y. v. Turkey[3]	27532/95	09/04/02	Judg.	6y 11m 19d	3	30,490	1	30,490

[1] There were no arrangements concerning Art. 2 ECHR and Arts. 2 and 3 ECHR combined that year.

[2] Annual Average Exchange Rates: 1.59165 (GBP), 0.152449 (FRF).

[3] The Government acknowledged and regretted the ECHR violation. The Government promised to take the necessary measures to prevent future violations.

Yıldız v. Turkey[3]	32979/96	16/07/02	Judg.	5y 11m 2d	3, 6	30,490	1	30,490
Önder v. Turkey[3]	31136/96	25/07/02	Judg.	6y 3m 25d	3	16,800	1	16,800
Süleyman Kaplan v. Turkey[3]	38578/97	10/10/02	Judg.	6y 8m 12d	3	28,000	1	28,000
Keçeci v. Turkey[3]	38588/97	26/11/02	Judg.	5y 2m 6d	3, 5 (1), 5 (3), 6	15,000	1	15,000
Kınay and Kınay v. Turkey[3]	31890/96	26/11/02	Judg.	6y 6m 5d	3, 5, 6, 8, 13, 14	59,000	2	29,500

FRIENDLY SETTLEMENTS – ARTICLES 2 AND 3 ECHR

Erdoğan v. Turkey[3]	26337/95	20/06/02	Judg.	7y 8m 13d	2, 3, 5, 6 (1), 6 (3), 13	100,000	1	100,000
N.Ö. v. Turkey[3]	33234/96	17/10/02	Judg.	6y 1m 4d	2, 3	100,000	1	100,000
Mahmut Demir v. Turkey[3]	22280/93	05/12/02	Judg.	9y 5m 14d	2, 3, 5, 6, 8, 13, 14, 18, 1 P. 1	184,631	1	184,631

ARRANGEMENTS – ARTICLE 3 ECHR

Külekçi a. O. v. Turkey[3]	39330/98	12/12/02	Dec.	5y 2m 2d	3	66,000	3	22,000

Table IX/4. 2003 for Turkey: Articles 2 and 3 ECHR – Friendly Settlements and Arrangements[1]

Applicant v. State	Appl. No.	Date of Ruling	ToD	Length of Negotiations	ECHR	Total CB	NoR	BpR
FRIENDLY SETTLEMENTS – ARTICLE 2 ECHR								
Eren a. O. v. Turkey	42428/98	02/10/03	Judg.	5y 3m 29d	2, 5 (1)	30,000	8	3,750
Kara a. O. v. Turkey	37446/97	25/11/03	Judg.	6y 6m 16d	2	93,000	22	4,227
FRIENDLY SETTLEMENTS – ARTICLE 3 ECHR								
Özkur and Göksungur v. Turkey	37088/97	04/03/03	Judg.	5y 9m 25d	3, 5 (3), 5 (4), 13, 14	16,500	2	8,250
Ateş v. Turkey	28292/95	22/04/03	Judg.	8y 1m 19d	3, 5, 6 (?), 8, 13, 14, 18, 1 P. 1	49,000	1	49,000
Yıldız v. Turkey	28308/95	22/04/03	Judg.	7y 8m 26d	3	30,500	1	30,500
Ö.Ö. and S.M. v. Turkey	31865/96	29/04/03	Judg.	7y 5m 30d	3	30,000	2	15,000
Dilek v. Turkey	31845/96	17/06/03	Judg.	7y 2m 5d	3, 5, 6 (?), 8, 13, 14, 18, 1 P. 1	25,000	1	25,000
Merinç v. Turkey	28504/95	17/06/03	Judg.	8y 0m 3d	3, 13	26,000	1	26,000
Toktaş v. Turkey	38382/97	29/07/03	Judg.	7y 7m 10d	3, 6 (1), 6 (3), 14	26,000	1	26,000
Kalin, Gezer and Orebay v. Turkey	24849/94; 24850/94; 24941/94	28/10/03	Judg.	9y 2m 17d	3, 5 (3)	81,000	3	27,000

[1] There were no arrangements concerning Art. 2 ECHR that year.

FRIENDLY SETTLEMENTS – ARTICLES 2 AND 3 ECHR

H.K. a. O. v. Turkey	29864/96	12/01/03	Judg.	7y 2m 3d	2, 3, 5	60,000	3	20,000
Macir v. Turkey	28516/95	22/04/03	Judg.	7y 9m 23d	2, 3	70,000	1	70,000
Başak a. O. v. Turkey	29875/96	16/10/03	Judg.	7y 11m 3d	2, 3, 8, 13, 1 P. 1	130,000	7	18,571

ARRANGEMENTS – ARTICLE 3 ECHR

Özgür Kiliç v. Turkey	42591/98	22/07/03	Judg.	5y 0m 13d	3	27,000	1	27,000
Sünnetçi v. Turkey	28632/95	22/07/03	Judg.	8y 0m 4d	3	25,000	1	25,000
Ramazan Sari v. Turkey	41926/98	31/07/03	Judg.	5y 2m 25d	3, 5, 6, 13	23,000	1	23,000

ARRANGEMENTS – ARTICLES 2 AND 3 ECHR

Yaman v. Turkey	37049/97	22/05/03	Judg.	5y 10m 18d	2, 3, 6 (?), 13	60,000	1	60,000
Oğraş a. O. v. Turkey	39978/98	28/10/03	Judg.	5y 10m 17d	2, 3, 13, 14, 5 (4), 6 (1), 6 (2), 6 (?), 9	76,000	4	19,000
Hanim Tosun v. Turkey	31731/96	06/11/03	Judg.	7y 6m 29d	2, 3, 5, 13, 14	40,000	1	40,000
Yurtseven a. O. v. Turkey	31730/96	18/12/03	Judg.	7y 7m 22d	2, 3, 5, 6, 7	160,000	4	40,000

Table IX/5. 2004 for Turkey: Articles 2 and 3 ECHR – Friendly Settlements and Arrangements[1]

Applicant v. State	Appl. No.	Date of Ruling	ToD	Length of Negotiations	ECHR	Total CB	NoR	BpR
FRIENDLY SETTLEMENTS – ARTICLE 2 ECHR								
Boztaş a. O. v. Turkey	40299/98	09/03/04	Judg.	6y 1m 18d	2, 6 (1), 14, 1 P. 1	68,000	3	22,667
Çelik v. Turkey	41993/98	27/07/04	Judg.	6y 3m 0d	2, 6 (1)	60,000	2	30,000
FRIENDLY SETTLEMENTS – ARTICLE 3 ECHR								
Şahmo v. Turkey	37415/97	22/06/04	Judg.	6y 11m 13d	3, 13	26,000	1	26,000
Temel v. Turkey	37047/97	13/07/04	Judg.	7y 0m 16d	3, 8, 13	6,000	1	6,000
Örnek and Eren v. Turkey	41306/98	15/07/04	Judg.	6y 4m 6d	3, 6, 13, 14	50,000	2	25,000
Karakoç v. Turkey	28294/95	02/11/04	Judg.	9y 6m 22d	3, 5, 6 (?), 8, 13, 14, 18, 1 P. 1	48,000	1	48,000
Kaptan v. Turkey	46749/99	22/12/04	Judg.	6y 0m 21d	3, 5 (3), 6 (1)	18,000	1	18,000
ARRANGEMENTS – ARTICLE 3 ECHR								
Aruç v. Turkey	39675/98	06/04/04	Dec.	6y 3m 14d	3, 5 (3), 6 (1)	16,500	1	16,500
ARRANGEMENTS – ARTICLES 2 AND 3 ECHR								
Binbay v. Turkey	24922/94	21/10/04	Judg.	10y 2m 10d	2, 3, 5, 6 (?), 8, 10, 13, 18, 1 P. 1	45,000	1	45,000

[1] For this year, there were no friendly settlements concerning Arts. 2 and 3 ECHR combined and there were no arrangements concerning Art. 2 ECHR.

Table IX/6. 2005 for Turkey: Articles 2 and 3 ECHR – Friendly Settlements and Arrangements[1]

Applicant v. State	Appl. No.	Date of Ruling	ToD	Length of Negotiations	ECHR	Total CB	NoR	BpR
FRIENDLY SETTLEMENTS – ARTICLE 3 ECHR								
Mahmut Keskin v. Turkey	40156/98	29/03/05	Judg.	8y 0m 25d	3, 5, 6 (1), 9, 10	17,000	1	17,000
ARRANGEMENTS – ARTICLE 3 ECHR								
Bozkurt v. Turkey[2]	35851/97	31/03/05	Dec.	8y 6m 13d	3, 6, 13	20,000	1	20,000
Yücetürk v. Turkey	76089/01	04/10/05	Dec.	4y 2m 16d	3	10,000	1	10,000

[1] For this year, there were no friendly settlements and arrangements concerning Art. 2 ECHR and Arts. 2 and 3 ECHR combined.
[2] The Government acknowledged and regretted the ECHR violation. The Government promised to take the necessary measures to prevent future violations. The case is considered to be a friendly settlement in the official statistics of the Court.

Table IX/7. 2006 for Turkey: Articles 2 and 3 ECHR – Friendly Settlements and Arrangements[1,2]

Applicant v. State	Appl. No.	Date of Ruling	ToD	Length of Negotiations	ECHR	Total CB	NoR	BpR
FRIENDLY SETTLEMENTS – ARTICLE 2 ECHR								
Arslan and Arslan v. Turkey	57908/00	10/01/06	Judg.	6y 0m 0d	2	13,000	2	6,500
FRIENDLY SETTLEMENTS – ARTICLE 3 ECHR								
Berk v. Turkey	41973/98	20/04/06	Judg.	7y 11m 23d	3, 13, 5 (1), 8	5,000	2	2,500
Okatan v. Turkey	40996/98	13/07/06	Judg.	8y 4m 10d	3, 5	6,000	1	6,000
ARRANGEMENTS – ARTICLE 2 ECHR								
Memiş v. Turkey[3]	42593/98	21/02/06	Judg.	7y 7m 12d	2, 13	22,009	1	22,009
ARRANGEMENTS – ARTICLE 3 ECHR								
Yazici v. Turkey	73033/01	11/07/06	Dec.	5y 5m 11d	3, 5, 6 (1)	15,000	1	15,000
Kölge v. Turkey	20227/02	21/11/06	Dec.	4y 6m 23d	3, 5 (3), 5 (4), 5 (5), 13	8,000	1	8,000
Tekmek v. Turkey	50035/99	28/11/06	Dec.	7y 5m 20d	3, 5 (1) (a), 5 (1) (b), 6 (1), 6 (3) (d)	6,000	1	6,000
ARRANGEMENTS – ARTICLES 2 AND 3 ECHR								
Karakoyun v. Turkey	51285/99	30/03/06	Dec.	7y 7m 7d	2, 3, 5, 14	30,000	2	15,000

[1] There were no friendly settlements concerning Arts. 2 and 3 ECHR combined that year.
[2] Annual Average Exchange Rate: 1.46725 (GBP).
[3] The Government acknowledged and regretted the ECHR violations. The Government promised to take all the necessary measures to prevent future violations.

Table IX/8. 2007 for Turkey: Articles 2 and 3 ECHR – Friendly Settlements and Arrangements[1]

Applicant v. State	Appl. No.	Date of Ruling	ToD	Length of Negotiations	ECHR	Total CB	NoR	BpR
FRIENDLY SETTLEMENTS – ARTICLE 2 ECHR								
Hacıoğlu a. O. v. Turkey[2]	7253/04; 7260/04, etc.	04/01/07	Dec.	3y 0m 4d	2, 13	325,000	15	21,667
ARRANGEMENTS – ARTICLE 2 ECHR								
Çardakçı a. O. v. Turkey	39224/98	23/01/07	Judg.	9y 3m 21d	2, 8, 13, 1 P. 1	20,000	4	5,000
Yağcı a. O. v. Turkey	5974/02	22/03/07	Dec.	5y 11m 27d	2, 6 (1), 8, 13, 1 P. 1	61,500	3	20,500
Pektaş a. O. v. Turkey	73722/01	04/12/07	Dec.	6y 4m 17d	2, 6, 8, 13	20,000	7	2,857
ARRANGEMENTS – ARTICLE 3 ECHR								
Salman v. Turkey	63745/00	03/04/07	Dec.	6y 4m 17d	3, 6 (1)	10,000	1	10,000
Acar v. Turkey	74941/01	30/08/07	Dec.	6y 0m 10d	3, 6, 13	9,000	1	9,000
Sumak v. Turkey	29735/03	11/10/07	Dec.	4y 1m 14d	3, 5 (1) (b), (c), 13	5,000	1	5,000
ARRANGEMENTS – ARTICLES 2 AND 3 ECHR								
Kabul a. O. v. Turkey[1]	24873/02	04/09/07	Dec.	5y 3m 0d	2, 3, 6, 8, 13, 14	20,000	7	2,857

[1] There were no friendly settlements concerning Art. 3 ECHR and Arts. 2 and 3 ECHR combined that year.
[2] The Government undertook to issue appropriate instructions and to adopt all necessary measures to ensure that the right to life is respected.

Table IX/9. 2008 for Turkey: Articles 2 and 3 ECHR – Friendly Settlements and Arrangements[1]

Applicant v. State	Appl. No.	Date of Ruling	ToD	Length of Negotiations	ECHR	Total CB	NoR	BpR
ARRANGEMENTS – ARTICLE 3 ECHR								
İçen v. Turkey	10268/02	06/05/08	Dec.	6y 2m 22d	3, 4, 5 (1) (c), 13	5,200	2	2,600
Kaya v. Turkey	20981/03	13/05/08	Dec.	4y 10m 24d	3, 5 (5), 6 (1), 6 (3), 13	5,000	1	5,000

[1] For this year, there were no arrangements concerning Art. 2 ECHR and Arts. 2 and 3 ECHR combined. There were also no friendly settlements.

X. Turkey – Cumulative Statistics Concerning Friendly Settlements and Arrangements

Table X/1. Number of Recipients

Year	Friendly Settlements			Arrangements			Total
	Art. 2	Art. 3	Arts. 2 and 3	Art. 2	Art. 3	Arts. 2 and 3	
1999							
2000		9					9
2001	4	270	16				290
2002	10	13	3		3		29
2003	30	12	11		3	10	66
2004	5	6			1	1	13
2005		1			2		3
2006	2	3		1	3	2	11
2007	15			14	3	7	39
2008					3		3
Total	66	314	30	15	18	20	463

Table X/2. Average Length of Negotiations

Year	FRIENDLY SETTLEMENTS						ARRANGEMENTS						Ø LENGTH
	Art. 2	NoC	Art. 3	NoC	Arts. 2 and 3	NoC	Art. 2	NoC	Art. 3	NoC	Arts. 2 and 3	NoC	
1999													
2000	2,059 d	1	1,783 d	3									1,783 d
2001	2,512 d	7	2,120 d	48	1,957 d	5							2,104 d
2002	2,169 d	2	2,332 d	11	2,831 d	3			1,889 d	1			2,437 d
2003	2,262 d	2	2,794 d	8	2,789 d	3			2,226 d	3	2,464 d	4	2,580 d
2004			2,628 d	5					2,296 d	1	3,724 d	1	2,632 d
2005			2,947 d	1					2,328 d	2			2,534 d
2006	2,192 d	1	2,984 d	2			2,784 d	1	2,128 d	3	2,776 d	1	2,513 d
2007	1,100 d	1					2,640 d	3	2,012 d	3	1,918 d	1	2,122 d
2008									2,032 d	2			2,032 d
Ø Length	2,271 d	14	2,271 d	78	2,422 d	11	2,676 d	4	2,134 d	15	2,611 d	7	2,299 d

Table X/3. Damages Paid by Turkey in Friendly Settlements: Articles 2 and 3 ECHR

FRIENDLY SETTLEMENTS

Year	Art. 2 BpR	Art. 2 TA	Art. 3 BpR	Art. 3 TA	Arts. 2 and 3 BpR	Arts. 2 and 3 TA
1999						
2000			12,804	115,236		
2001	13,677	54,708	17,845	4,818,094	18,001	288,020
2002	63,192	631,919	23,609	306,922	128,210	384,631
2003	4,100	123,000	23,667	284,000	23,636	260,000
2004	25,600	128,000	24,667	148,000		
2005			17,000	17,000		
2006	6,500	13,000	3,667	11,000		
2007	21,667	325,000				
2008						
NoR / TA	66	1,275,627	314	5,700,252	30	932,651
BpR / TA Actual 2008	19,328	1,411,566	18,154	6,595,257	31,088	1,064,099
BpR Actual 2008	21,387		21,004		35,470	

Table X/4. Damages Paid by Turkey in Arrangements: Articles 2 and 3 ECHR

	ARRANGEMENTS										
	Art. 2		Art. 3		Arts. 2 and 3						
Year	BpR	TA	BpR	TA	BpR	TA	TA	Actual 2008	NoR	BpR	Actual 2008
1999											
2000							115,236	136,554	9	12,804	15,173
2001							5,160,822	5,996,875	290	17,796	20,679
2002			22,000	66,000			1,389,473	1,583,999	29	47,913	54,621
2003			25,000	75,000	33,600	336,000	1,078,000	1,206,282	66	16,333	18,277
2004			16,500	16,500	45,000	45,000	337,500	370,575	13	25,962	28,506
2005			15,000	30,000			47,000	50,572	3	15,667	16,857
2006	22,009	22,009	9,667	29,000	15,000	30,000	105,009	110,679	11	9,546	10,062
2007	7,250	101,500	8,000	24,000	2,857	20,000	470,500	486,027	39	12,064	12,462
2008			3,400	10,200			10,200	10,200	3	3,400	3,400
NoR/TA	*15*	*123,509*	*18*	*250,700*	*20*	*431,000*	8,713,739	9,951,762	463	18,820	21,494
BpR/TA Actual 2008	*8,234*	*128,047*	*13,928*	*275,120*	*21,550*	*477,674*					
BpR Actual 2008	*8,536*		*15,284*		*23,884*						

XI. Turkey – Yearly Statistics Concerning Judgments

Table XI/1. 1999 for Turkey: Articles 2 and 3 ECHR – Judgments[1,2]

Applicant v. State	Appl. No.	Date of Judgment	Length of Negotiations	ECHR	PD	NoR	nPD	NoR	C/E	NoR	Total CB	NoR	BpR
ARTICLE 2 ECHR													
Tanrikulu v. Turkey	23763/94	08/07/99	5y 1m 13d	2, 13, former 25 (1)			22,787	4	20,729	1	43,516	4	10,879
ARTICLES 2 AND 3 ECHR													
Çakıcı v. Turkey	23657/94	08/07/99	5y 2m 6d	2, 3, 5, 13	17,522	2	41,776	2	29,315	1	88,613	3	29,538

[1] There were no judgments concerning Art. 3 ECHR on its own that year.
[2] Annual Average Exchange Rates: 1.51912 (GBP), 0.15245 (FRF).

Table XI/2. 2000 for Turkey: Articles 2 and 3 ECHR – Judgments[1]

Applicant v. State	Appl. No.	Date of Judgment	Length of Negotiations	ECHR	Cash Benefits						Total CB	NoR	BpR
					PD	NoR	nPD	NoR	C/E	NoR			
ARTICLE 2 ECHR													
Ertak v. Turkey	20764/92	09/05/00	7y 7m 8d	2	24,638	5	36,957	6	15,012	1	76,607	6	12,768
Demiray v. Turkey	27308/95	21/11/00	5y 7m 3d	2	21,700	1	21,700	1	1,606	1	45,006	1	45,006
Gül v. Turkey	22676/93	14/12/00	7y 3m 19d	2, 13	57,489	5	49,276	6	34,493	1	141,258	6	23,543
ARTICLE 3 ECHR													
Sevtap Veznedaroğlu v. Turkey	32357/96	11/04/00	4y 0m 5d	3			2,170	1	1,085	1	3,255	1	3,255
Ilhan v. Turkey	22277/93	27/06/00	7y 0m 3d	3, 13	128,904	1	41,064	1	26,201	1	196,168	2	98,084
Dikme v. Turkey	20869/92	11/07/00	7y 8m 19d	3, 5 (3)			30,490	1	1,524	1	32,014	1	32,014
Jabari v. Turkey[2]	40035/98	11/07/00	2y 4m 15d	3 (in case of expulsion), 13							0	1	0
Sattık a. O. v. Turkey	31866/96	10/10/00	5y 2m 14d	3			82,127	10	8,213	10	90,340	10	9,034
Bilgin v. Turkey	23819/94	16/11/00	6y 7m 23d	3, 8, 13, 1 P. 1	19,710	1	16,425	1	33,265	1	69,401	1	69,401
Büyükdağ v. Turkey	28340/95	21/12/00	5y 4m 12d	3, 6 (1), 13			15,245	1	2,287	1	17,532	1	17,532

[1] Annual Average Exchange Rates: 1.64254 (GBP), 0.1524490 (FRF), 1.085 (USD).
[2] The Court held that the finding of a potential breach of Art. 3 ECHR and an actual breach of Art. 13 ECHR constitute in themselves sufficient just satisfaction for any non-pecuniary damage sustained by the applicant.

Articles 2 and 3 ECHR

Case	App. no.	Date	Duration	Articles											
Mahmut Kaya v. Turkey	22535/93	28/03/00	6y 7m 8d	2, 3, 13			28,744		1	33,835	1	62,579	1	62,579	
Timurtaş v. Turkey	23531/94	13/06/00	6y 4m 4d	2, 3, 5, 13			49,276	2	31,289	1	80,565	2	40,283		
Salman v. Turkey	21986/93	27/06/00	7y 1m 7d	2, 3, 13, former 25 (1)	64,586	1	57,489	1	33,681	1	155,756	1	155,756		
Akkoç v. Turkey	22947/93; 22948/93	10/10/00	6y 11m 9d	2, 3, 13, former 25 (1)	57,489	1	65,702	1	21,869	1	145,059	1	145,059		
Taş v. Turkey	24396/94	14/11/00	6y 5m 7d	2, 3, 5 (1), 5 (3), 5 (4), 5 (5), 13			49,276	2	22,899	1	72,175	2	36,088		

Table XI/3. 2001 for Turkey: Articles 2 and 3 ECHR – Judgments[1]

Applicant v. State	Appl. No.	Date of Judgment	Length of Negotiations	ECHR	Cash Benefits						Total CB	NoR	BpR
					PD	NoR	nPD	NoR	C/E	NoR			
ARTICLE 2 ECHR													
Tanlı v. Turkey	26129/95	10/04/01	6y 3m 19d	2, 13	62,358	1	48,272	2	19,309	1	129,938	2	64,969
Avşar v. Turkey	25657/94	10/07/01	6y 9m 0d	2, 13	64,362	3	36,203	4	28,030	1	128,595	4	32,149
ARTICLE 3 ECHR													
Dulaş v. Turkey	25801/94	31/01/01	6y 8m 29d	3, 8, 13, 1 P. 1	20,274	1	16,091	1	22,831	1	59,196	1	59,196
Berktay v. Turkey	22493/93	01/03/01	7y 6m 29d	3, 5, 13	36,204	1	40,226	2	15,248	2	91,678	2	45,839
Altay v. Turkey	22279/93	22/05/01	8y 1m 8d	3, 5 (3), 6 (1)		1	15,245	1	1,524	1	16,769	1	16,769
ARTICLES 2 AND 3 ECHR													
Çiçek v. Turkey	25704/94	27/02/01	6y 3m 19d	2, 3, 5, 13	16,091	2	80,453	3	16,091	1	112,634	3	37,545
Cyprus v. Turkey	25781/94	10/05/01	6y 5m 18d	2, 3, 5, 6, 8, 9, 10, 13, 1 P. 1, 2 P. 2								0	0
Akdeniz a. O. v. Turkey	23954/94	31/05/01	7y 1m 26d	2, 3, 5 (1), 13, former Art. 25	615,204	12	325,833	18	39,167	9	980,204	18	54,456

[1] Annual Average Exchange Rates: 1.60905 (GBP), 0.1524490 (FRF).

Table XI/4. 2002 for Turkey: Articles 2 and 3 ECHR – Judgments[1]

Applicant v. State	Appl. No.	Date of Judgment	Length of Negotiations	ECHR	Cash Benefits						Total CB	NoR	BpR
					PD	NoR	nPD	NoR	C/E	NoR			
ARTICLE 2 ECHR													
Öneryıldız v. Turkey[2]	48939/99	18/06/02	3y 5m 0d	2, 1 P. 1	77,000	1	77,000	1	7,714	1	161,714	1	161,714
Ülkü Ekinci v. Turkey	27602/95	16/07/02	7y 2m 12d	2, 13			15,590	1	8,278	1	23,868	1	23,868
ARTICLE 3 ECHR													
Algür v. Turkey	32574/96	22/10/02	6y 10m 3d	3, 5 (1)	12,500	1	12,500	1	2,270	1	27,270	1	27,270
ARTICLES 2 AND 3 ECHR													
Abdurrahman Orak v. Turkey	31889/96	14/02/02	5y 8m 9d	2, 3, 13	45,457	1	26,500	2	2,035	1	73,992	1	73,992
Şemsi Önen v. Turkey	22876/93	14/05/02	8y 7m 29d	2, 3, 8, 13			149,000	11	26,110	2	175,110	11	15,919
Orhan v. Turkey	25656/94	18/06/02	7y 6m 25d	2, 3, 5, 8, 13, 34, 1 P. 1	47,750	4	60,900	4	46,158	1	154,807	4	38,702

[1] Annual Average Exchange Rates: 1.59165 (GBP), 0.152449 (FRF).
[2] This case was referred to the Grand Chamber, which delivered a judgment in the case on 30 November 2004.

Table XI/5. 2003 for Turkey: Articles 2 and 3 ECHR – Judgments

Applicant v. State	Appl. No.	Date of Judgment	Length of Negotiations	ECHR	Cash Benefits						Total CB	NoR	BpR
					PD	NoR	nPD	NoR	C/E	NoR			
ARTICLE 2 ECHR													
Tepe v. Turkey	27244/95	09/05/03	8y 0m 5d	2, 13, 38			14,500	1	11,577	1	26,077	1	26,077
ARTICLE 3 ECHR													
Öcalan v. Turkey[2]	46221/99	12/03/03	4y 0m 24d	3, 5 (1), 5 (3), 6 (1), 6 (3) (b), 6 (3) (c)					100,000	1	100,000	1	100,000
Ayşe Tepe v. Turkey	29422/95	22/07/03	7y 9m 27d	3, 5 (3)			20,000	1	1,780	1	21,780	1	21,780
Esen v. Turkey	29484/95	22/07/03	7y 10m 7d	3			17,718	1	1,884	1	19,602	1	19,602
Yaz v. Turkey	29485/95	22/07/03	7y 10m 7d	3			32,000	1	1,884	1	33,884	1	33,884
Yöyler v. Turkey	26973/95	24/07/03	8y 3m 20d	3, 8, 13, 1 P. 1	25,000	1	14,500	1	14,084	1	53,584	1	53,584
Elci a. O. v. Turkey	23145/93; 25091/94	13/11/03	9y 10m 23d	3, 5 (1), 8	23,665	16	225,400	16	46,240	16	295,305	16	18,457
ARTICLES 2 AND 3 ECHR													
Aktaş v. Turkey	24351/94	24/04/03	8y 10m 16d	2, 3, 13, 38	226,065	1	62,000	2	29,275	1	317,340	2	158,670

[1] The Court held unanimously that findings of Arts. 3, 5 and 6 ECHR violations constituted in themselves sufficient just satisfaction for any damage sustained by the applicant; this case was referred to the Grand Chamber which delivered a judgment in the case on 5 May 2005.

Table XI/6. 2004 for Turkey: Articles 2 and 3 ECHR – Judgments

Applicant v. State	Appl. No.	Date of Judgment	Length of Negotiations	ECHR	Cash Benefits						Total CB	NoR	BpR
					PD	NoR	nPD	NoR	C/E	NoR			
ARTICLE 2 ECHR													
Tekdağ v. Turkey	27699/95	15/01/04	8y 6m 20d	2, 13, 38 (1)(a)			14,000	1	12,487	1	26,487	1	26,487
Nuray Şen v. Turkey (No. 2)	25354/94	30/03/04	9y 11m 26d	2, 13			14,500	1	32,034	1	46,534	1	46,534
Özalp a. O. v. Turkey	32457/96	08/04/04	8y 1m 4d	2, 13	30,000	7	25,000	7	6,000	7	61,000	7	8,714
Tashin Acar v. Turkey	26307/95	08/04/04	9y 5m 10d	2, 38			10,000	1	7,700	1	17,700	1	17,700
Buldan v. Turkey	28298/95	20/04/04	9y 4m 18d	2, 13			16,000	2	10,000	1	26,000	2	13,000
Erkek v. Turkey	28637/95	13/07/04	9y 2m 23d	2			10,000	1			10,000	1	10,000
O. v. Turkey	28497/95	15/07/04	8y 11m 19d	2			25,000	1			25,000	1	25,000
Ağdaş v. Turkey	34592/97	27/07/04	7y 7m 23d	2			15,000	1			15,000	1	15,000
İkincisoy v. Turkey	26144/95	27/07/04	10y 2m 8d	2, 5 (3), 5 (4), 5 (5), 13, former 25 (1)	25,000	1	11,000	2	15,000	2	51,000	3	17,000
Şirin Yılmaz v. Turkey	35875/97	29/07/04	7y 3m 21d	2, 13			35,000	2	10,000	1	45,000	2	22,500
Zengin v. Turkey	46928/99	28/10/04	5y 9m 19d	2, 13			12,000	1	2,270	1	14,270	1	14,270
Seyhan v. Turkey	33384/96	02/11/04	8y 3m 7d	2			10,000	1	4,375	1	14,375	1	14,375
A.K. and V.K. v. Turkey	3841/97	30/11/04	7y 4m 8d	2, 13			15,000	2	3,500	2	18,500	2	9,250
Öneryıldız v. Turkey	48939/99	30/11/04	5y 10m 12d	2, 13, 1 P. 1	23,430	1	124,680	4	12,006	1	160,116	4	40,029

Continued from Table XI/6. 2004 for Turkey: Articles 2 and 3 ECHR – Judgments

Applicant v. State	Appl. No.	Date of Judgment	Length of Negotiations	ECHR	Cash Benefits						Total CB	NoR	BpR
					PD	NoR	nPD	NoR	C/E	NoR			
ARTICLE 3 ECHR													
Ayder a. O. v. Turkey	23656/94	08/01/04	9y 8m 19d	3, 8, 13, 1 P. 1	113,009	5	72,500	5	39,275	5	224,784	5	44,957
Çolak and Filizer v. Turkey	32578/96; 32579/96	08/01/04	8y 0m 11d	3			24,000	2	2,500	2	26,500	2	13,250
Sadık Önder v. Turkey	28520/95	08/01/04	8y 4m 11d	3			5,000	1	2,500	1	7,500	1	7,500
Altun v. Turkey	24561/94	01/06/04	9y 11m 2d	3, 8, 13, 1 P. 1	22,000	1	14,500	1	15,000	1	51,500	1	51,500
Batı a. O. v. Turkey	33097/96; 57834/00	03/06/04	7y 10m 16d	3, 5 (3), 13	93,500	8	95,500	10	18,580	14	207,580	8	25,948
Aydın and Yunus v. Turkey	32572/96; 33366/96	22/06/04	8y 5m 25d	3			40,000	2	5,000	2	45,000	2	22,500
Bakbak v. Turkey	39812/98	01/07/04	6y 5m 22d	3			10,000	1	1,530	1	11,530	1	11,530
Mehmet Emin Yüksel v. Turkey	40154/98	20/07/04	6y 6m 1d	3			10,000	1	3,000	1	13,000	1	13,000
Çelik and İmret v. Turkey	44093/98	26/10/04	6y 1m 19d	3, 13			15,000	2	2,375	2	17,375	2	8,688
Abdülsamet Yaman v. Turkey	32446/96	02/11/04	8y 9m 30d	3, 5 (3), 5 (4), 5 (5), 13			17,700	1	7,934	1	25,634	1	25,634
Tuncer and Durmuş v. Turkey	30494/96	02/11/04	8y 8m 7d	3, 5			26,000	2	2,000	2	28,000	2	14,000
Hasan İlhan v. Turkey	22494/93	09/11/04	11y 4m 17d	3, 8, 13, 1 P. 1	33,500	1	14,500	1	12,348	1	60,348	2	30,174

ARTICLES 2 AND 3 ECHR

Ipek v. Turkey	25760/94	17/02/04	9y 2m 30d	2, 3, 5, 13, 38 (1) (a), 1 P. 1	43,500	3	15,000	1	12,080	1	70,580	4	17,645
Ahmet Özkan a. O. v. Turkey	21689/93	06/04/04	10y 11m 29d	2, 3, 5 (1), 5 (3), 8	206,650	26	655,300	34	58,574	34	920,524	34	27,074
A.A. a. O. v. Turkey	30015/96	27/07/04	8y 6m 28d	2, 3			25,000	4	1,875	4	26,875	4	6,719

Table XI/7. 2005 for Turkey: Articles 2 and 3 ECHR – Judgments

Applicant v. State	Appl. No.	Date of Judgment	Length of Negotiations	ECHR	Cash Benefits						Total CB	NoR	BpR
					PD	NoR	nPD	NoR	C/E	NoR			
ARTICLE 2 ECHR													
Menteşe a. O. v. Turkey	36217/97	18/01/05	10y 2m 6d	2, 13			60,000	4	10,000	4	70,000	4	17,500
Gezici v. Turkey	34594/97	17/03/05	8y 3m 25d	2, 13			15,000	1	2,375	1	17,375	1	17,375
Tırkoğlu v. Turkey	34506/97	17/03/05	8y 5m 16d	2			10,000	1			10,000	1	10,000
Güngör v. Turkey[1]	28290/95	22/03/05	9y 8m 8d	2, 14					2,000	1	2,000	1	2,000
Adalı v. Turkey	38187/97	31/03/05	7y 6m 19d	2, 11, 13			20,000	1	67,763		87,763	1	87,763
Acar a. O. v. Turkey	36088/97; 38417/97	24/05/05	6y 6m 23d	2, 13	130,700	7	215,000	10	6,638	10	352,338	10	35,234
Çelikbilek v. Turkey	27693/95	31/05/05	9y 11m 18d	2, 13, 38	60,000	1	23,500	2	8,000	1	91,500	2	45,750
Koku v. Turkey	27305/95	31/05/05	10y 1m 12d	2, 13, 38	60,000	1	23,500	2	15,000	1	98,500	2	49,250
Toğcu v. Turkey	27601/95	31/05/05	10y 0m 6d	2, 13, 38			13,500	1	9,242	1	22,742	2	11,371
Yasin Ateş v. Turkey	30949/96	31/05/05	9y 5m 18d	2, 5 (1), 13, 38	60,000	1	23,500	2	11,723	1	95,223	3	31,741
Fatma Kaçar v. Turkey	35838/97	15/07/05	8y 4m 27d	2, 13			10,000	1	2,375	1	12,375	2	6,187
Hamiyet Kaplan a. O. v. Turkey	36749/97	13/09/05	8y 3m 24d	2, 13	35,500	3	42,700	10	3,674	8	81,874	10	8,187
Dündar v. Turkey	26972/95	20/09/05	10y 6m 17d	2, 14			13,500	2	10,000	2	23,500	2	11,750

[1] The Court indicated that the finding of violation constituted in itself just satisfaction.

Özgen a. O. v. Turkey	38607/97	20/09/05	8y 1m 0d	2, 13	20,000	3	1,875	3	21,875	3	7,292
H.Y. and Hü.Y. v. Turkey	40262/98	06/10/05	7y 8m 24d	2	20,000	2	2,485		22,485	2	11,243
Nesibe Haran v. Turkey	28299/95	06/10/05	10y 3m 14d	2	10,000	1	4,000	1	14,000	1	14,000
Belkıza Kaya a. O. v. Turkey	33420/96; 36206/97	22/11/05	9y 5m 10d	2, 5, 13	135,000	9	8,160	9	143,160	9	15,907
Kakoulli v. Turkey	38595/97	22/11/05	8y 8m 3d	2	30,500	4	20,000	4	50,500	4	12,625

ARTICLE 3 ECHR

Sunal v. Turkey	43918/98	25/01/05	6y 5m 15d	3, 13	10,000	1	2,370	1	12,370	1	12,370
Biyan v. Turkey	56363/00	03/02/05	5y 7m 9d	3, 6 (1)	9,000	1	2,315	1	11,315	1	11,315
Şahin a. O. v. Turkey	53147/99	03/02/05	7y 3m 20d	3, 13	115,000	9	10,000	9	125,000	9	13,889
Öcalan v. Turkey[1]	46221/99	12/05/05	6y 2m 26d	3, 5 (3), 5 (4), 6 (1), 6 (3)			120,000	4	120,000	4	30,000
Gültekin a. O. v. Turkey[1]	52941/99	31/05/05	5y 8m 7d	3, 6 (1), 13	50,000	4	3,000	4	53,000	4	13,250
Dalan v. Turkey	38585/97	07/06/05	9y 4m 10d	3, 13	8,000	1	1,370	1	9,370	1	9,370
Hasan Kılıç v. Turkey	35044/97	28/06/05	9y 7m 4d	3, 13	15,000	1	1,500	1	16,500	1	16,500
Karakaş and Yeşilırmak v. Turkey	43925/98	28/06/05	6y 10m 14d	3, 6 (1)	10,000	2	2,815	2	12,815	2	6,408
S.B. and H.T. v. Turkey	54430/00	05/07/05	9y 8m 5d	3	30,000	2	3,000	2	33,000	2	16,500
Soner Önder v. Turkey[1]	39813/98	12/07/05	7y 6m 6d	3, 6 (1)	8,000	1	2,000	1	10,000	1	10,000

Continued from Table XI/7. 2005 for Turkey: Articles 2 and 3 ECHR – Judgments

Applicant v. State	Appl. No.	Date of Judgment	Length of Negotiations	ECHR	Cash Benefits						Total CB	NoR	BpR
					PD	NoR	nPD	NoR	C/E	NoR			
ARTICLE 3 ECHR													
Karayiğit v. Turkey	63181/00	20/09/05	4y 10m 11d	3, 14			15,000	1	2,815	1	17,815	1	17,815
Cangöz v. Turkey[2]	28039/95	04/10/05	10y 3m 15d	3, 5 (3)									
Günaydın v. Turkey	27526/95	13/10/05	10y 6m 10d	3, 6 (1)			10,000	1	2,000	2	12,000	2	6,000
Akdoğdu v. Turkey	46747/99	18/10/05	6y 11m 18d	3			9,000	1	720	1	9,720	2	4860
Orhan Aslan v. Turkey	48063/99	20/10/05	6y 7m 24d	3, 6 (1)			10,000	1	2,370	1	12,370	1	12,370
Gürbüz v. Turkey	26050/04	10/11/05	1y 4m 29d	3			3,000	1	1,285	1	4,285	1	4,285
Kuruçay v. Turkey	24040/04	10/11/05	1y 4m 16d	3			3,000	1	1,285	1	4,285	1	4,285
Tekin Yıldız v. Turkey	22913/04	10/11/05	1y 5m 3d	3			10,000	1	1,285	1	11,285	1	11,285
Uyan v. Turkey	7454/04	10/11/05	1y 8m 9d	3			3,000	1	1,285	1	4,285	1	4,285
ARTICLES 2 AND 3 ECHR													
Ceyhan Demir a. O. v. Turkey	34491/97	13/01/05	8y 1m 7d	2, 3	50,000	19	38,000	19	4,162	19	92,162	19	4,851
Akkum a. O. v. Turkey	21894/93	24/03/05	11y 10m 20d	2, 3, 13, 38, 1 P. 1	57,300	1	81,000	6	17,000	3	155,300	6	25,883

2 The applicant did not request any compensation for costs and expenses.

Süheyla Aydın v. Turkey	25660/94	24/05/05	10y 7m 20d	2, 3, 13, 38	30,000	1	24,500	2	20,000	1	74,500	2	37,250
Akdeniz v. Turkey	25165/94	31/05/05	10y 9m 13d	2, 3, 5, 13	16,500	1	33,500	2	15,000	1	65,000	2	32,500
Kişmir v. Turkey	27306/95	31/05/05	10y 2m 0d	2, 3, 13, 38	16,500	1	33,500	2	14,120	1	64,120	2	32,060
Tanış a. O. v. Turkey	65899/01	02/08/05	4y 5m 24d	2, 3, 5, 13, 38	90,000	3	80,000	4	17,995	4	187,995	6	31,333
Kanlıbaş v. Turkey	32444/96	08/12/05	9y 4m 29d	2, 3			20,000	2	10,000	1	30,000	2	15,000

Table XI/8. 2006 for Turkey: Articles 2 and 3 ECHR – Judgments

Applicant v. State	Appl. No.	Date of Judgment	Length of Negotiations	ECHR	PD	NoR	nPD	NoR	C/E	NoR	Total CB	NoR	BpR
Article 2 ECHR													
Bişkin v. Turkey	45403/99	10/01/06	7y 1m 17d	2							0	0	0
Mordeniz v. Turkey	49160/99	10/01/06	6y 8m 18d	2, 13							0	0	0
Şeker v. Turkey	52390/99	21/02/06	6y 3m 17d	2, 13			10,000	1	7,000	1	17,000	1	17,000
Perk a. O. v. Turkey	50739/99	28/03/06	7y 7m 10d	2							0	0	0
Ataman v. Turkey	46252/99	27/04/06	7y 5m 14d	2, 13			20,000	1	7,000	1	27,000	1	27,000
Cennet Ayhan and Mehmet Salih Ayhan v. Turkey	41964/98	27/06/06	8y 2m 1d	2, 13			21,800	2	9,375	2	31,175	2	15,587
Kavak v. Turkey	53489/99	06/07/06	6y 11m 2d	2, 13			10,000	2	2,370	2	12,370	2	6,185
Diril v. Turkey	68188/01	19/10/06	5y 7m 22d	2, 5, 13			50,000	6	5,000	6	55,000	6	9,167
Kamer Demir a. O. v. Turkey	41335/98	19/10/06	8y 9m 3d	2, 13			50,000	9	4,261	9	54,261	9	6,029
Selim Yildirim a. O. v. Turkey	56154/00	19/10/06	6y 8m 17d	2, 13			20,000	7	6,000	7	26,000	7	3,714
Kaya a. O. v. Turkey	4451/02	24/10/06	5y 2m 27d	2, 13							0	0	0
Yazici v. Turkey	48884/99	05/12/06	7y 6m 7d	2, 13			10,000	1	4,000	1	14,000	1	14,000
Anter a. O. v. Turkey	55983/00	19/12/06	4y 9m 27d	2, 13			25,000	3	3,500	3	28,500	3	9,500
Article 3 ECHR													
Güler v. Turkey	49391/99	10/01/06	6y 7m 18d	3, 13	10,000	1			2,500	1	12,500	1	12,500

Yavuz v. Turkey	67137/01	10/01/06	4y 11m 2d	3, 13			10,000	1	2,500	1	12,500	1	12,500
Nazif Yavuz v. Turkey	69912/01	12/01/06	4y 9m 8d	3, 13			50,000	1	1,000	1	51,000	1	51,000
Ülke v. Turkey	39437/98	24/01/06	9y 0m 2d	3			10,000	1	1,000	1	11,000	1	11,000
Bilen v. Turkey	34482/97	21/02/06	9y 5m 8d	3, 5 (3), 5 (4)			15,000	1	870	1	15,870	1	15,870
Çalışır v. Turkey	52165/99	21/02/06	6y 4m 15d	3	700	1	10,000	1	1,500	1	12,200	1	12,200
Doğanay v. Turkey	50125/99	21/02/06	10y 7m 16d	3, 13			4,000	1	870	1	4,870	1	4,870
Murat Demir v. Turkey	42579/98	02/03/06	8y 8m 10d	3, 6 (1), 13			17,500	1			17,500	1	17,500
Kekil Demirel v. Turkey	48581/99	11/04/06	6y 10m 28d	3			12,000	1	870	1	12,870	1	12,870
Soner a. O. v. Turkey	40986/98	27/04/06	8y 7m 11d	3, 6 (1), 13			3,000	1	170	1	3,170	3	1,057
Akkurt v. Turkey	47938/99	04/05/06	7y 5m 2d	3, 13			15,000	1	3,000	1	18,000	1	18,000
Saygılı v. Turkey	57916/00	04/05/06	5y 11m 17d	3, 13			5,000	1	285	1	5,285	1	5,285
D a. O. v. Turkey	24245/03	22/06/06	2y 10m 18d	3					4,143	3	4,143	3	1,381
Hüseyin Karakaş v. Turkey	69988/01	22/06/06	5y 1m 29d	3, 13			10,000	1	1,785	1	11,785	1	11,785
Köylüoğlu v. Turkey	45742/99	22/06/06	7y 9m 16d	3, 13			5,000	1			5,000	1	5,000
Uçkan v. Turkey	42594/98	22/06/06	7y 11m 15d	3, 6 (1)			10,000	1	1,500	1	11,500	1	11,500
Avci a. O. v. Turkey	70417/01	27/06/06	5y 1m 3d	3, 13			4,000	4	370	4	4,370	7	624
Hüseyin Esen v. Turkey	49048/99	08/08/06	7y 2m 13d	3, 5 (3), 5 (4), 6 (1), 13			10,000	1	1,000	1	11,000	1	11,000
Söylemez v. Turkey	46661/99	21/09/06	7y 9m 19d	3, 6 (1), 6 (3), 13			8,000	1	3,000	1	11,000	1	11,000
Göçmen v. Turkey	72000/01	17/10/06	5y 4m 23d	3, 13, 6 (1), 6 (3)	20,000	1			1,285	1	21,285	1	21,285
Okkali v. Turkey	52067/99	17/10/06	7y 0m 25d	3			10,000	1			10,000	1	10,000
Sultan Öner a. O. v. Turkey	73792/01	17/10/06	5y 6m 5d	3, 5 (1), 13			25,000	3	2,315	3	27,315	3	9,105
Öktem v. Turkey	74306/01	19/10/06	5y 4m 25d	3, 13			15,000	1	1,500	1	16,500	1	16,500

Continued from Table XI/8. 2006 for Turkey: Articles 2 and 3 ECHR – Judgments

Applicant v. State	Appl. No.	Date of Judgment	Length of Negotiations	ECHR	Cash Benefits						Total CB	NoR	BpR
					PD	NoR	nPD	NoR	C/E	NoR			
ARTICLE 3 ECHR													
Dilek Yilmaz v. Turkey	58030/00	31/10/06	6y 6m 6d	3, 13			4,000	1	799	1	4,799	1	4,799
Emirhan Yildiz a. O. v. Turkey	61898/00	05/12/06	6y 9m 9d	3			27,000	3	1,285	3	28,285	3	9,428
Türkmen v. Turkey	43124/98	19/12/06	8y 4m 19d	3, 6 (1)	25,000	2	25,000	2	2,340	2	52,340	2	26,170
Güzel Şahin a. O. v. Turkey	68263/01	21/12/06	5y 9m 0d	3, 13			39,000	5	3,000	5	42,000	5	8,400
ARTICLES 2 AND 3 ECHR													
Gömi a. O. v. Turkey	35962/97	21/12/06	9y 11m 26d	2, 3							0	0	0

Table XI/9. 2007 for Turkey: Articles 2 and 3 ECHR – Judgments

Applicant v. State	Appl. No.	Date of Judgment	Length of Negotiations	ECHR	Cash Benefits						Total CB	NoR	BpR
					PD	NoR	nPD	NoR	C/E	NoR			
ARTICLE 2 ECHR													
Kamil Uzun v. Turkey	37410/97	10/05/07	2y 1m 25d	2	10,000	2	10,000	2	5,000	2	25,000	2	12,500
ARTICLE 3 ECHR													
Erdoğan Yağız v. Turkey	27473/02	06/03/07	4y 8m 12d	3	1,000	1	1,000	1			2,000	1	2,000
Haci Özen v. Turkey	46286/99	12/04/07	8y 3m 21d	3, 5 (3), 6 (1), 6 (3)(c), 13			15,000	1	1,115	1	16,115	1	16,115
Uslu v. Turkey	33168/03	12/04/07	3y 6m 17d	3, 12			10,000	1	150	1	10,150	1	10,150
Hüseyin Yıldırım v. Turkey	2778/02	03/05/07	5y 3m 11d	3			10,000	1	5,000	1	15,000	1	15,000
Fahriye Çalışkan v. Turkey	40516/98	02/10/07	9y 10m 4d	3, 12	3,500	1	3,500	1			7,000	1	7,000
Necdet Bulut v. Turkey	77092/01	20/11/07	6y 3m 11d	3			5,000	1			5,000	1	5,000
Balçık a. O. v. Turkey	25/02	29/11/07	6y 2m 9d	3, 11			6,000	2			6,000	2	3,000

[1] The case was referred to the Grand Chamber.

Continued from Table XI/9. 2007 for Turkey: Articles 2 and 3 ECHR – Judgments

Applicant v. State	Appl. No.	Date of Judgment	Length of Negotiations	ECHR	Cash Benefits						Total CB	NoR	BpR
					PD	NoR	nPD	NoR	C/E	NoR			
ARTICLES 2 AND 3 ECHR													
Akpinar and Altun v. Turkey	56760/00	27/02/07	6y 10m 30d	2, 3			40,000	2	3,215	2	43,215	2	21,608
Teren Aksakal v. Turkey[1]	51967/99	11/09/07	8y 1m 13d	2, 3			45,000	4	5,000	1	50,000	4	12,500

Special case: *Yüksel Erdoğan a. O. v. Turkey* (Appl. No. 57049/00), Judgment (Third Section), 15 February 2007, not yet reported, para. 118: The Court found a violation of Art. 2 ECHR but struck the case out of the list because "[t]he applicants did not submit any claim for just satisfaction under Article 41 of the Convention taken together with Rule 60 of the Rules of Court". Thus, the Court considered that there was "(...) no reason to award any sum under Article 41 of the Convention (see Ciucci v. Italy, no. 68345/01, § 33, 1 June 2006)".

Table XI/10. 2008 for Turkey: Articles 2 and 3 ECHR – Judgments[1]

Applicant v. State	Appl. No.	Date of Judgment	Length of Negotiations	ECHR	Cash Benefits							Total CB	NoR	BpR
					PD	NoR	nPD	NoR	C/E	NoR	C/E	NoR		
ARTICLE 2 ECHR														
Abdullah Yilmaz v. Turkey	21899/02	17/06/08	6y 4m 6d	2	3,000	1	12,000	1	408	1			15,408	1	15,408
Isaak v. Turkey	44587/98	24/06/08	11y 4m 24d	2	80,000	1	135,000	5	12,000	5			227,000	5	45,400
Solomou a. O. v. Turkey	36832/97	24/06/08	11y 4m 11d	2			125,000	7	12,000	7			137,000	7	19,571
Yürkeli v. Turkey	48913/99	17/07/08	9y 3m 3d	2			3,000	1					3,000	1	3,000
Kılavuz v. Turkey	8327/03	21/10/08	5y 8m 11d	2	3,000	1	10,000	2	1,150	1			14,150	2	7,075
Ömer Aydın v. Turkey	34813/02	25/11/08	6y 4m 23d	2			2,500	1					2,500	1	2,500
ARTICLE 3 ECHR														
Taştan v. Turkey	63748/00	04/03/08	7y 6m 23d	3, 13			5,000	1	1,000	1			6,000	1	6,000
Hüseyin Şimşek v. Turkey	68881/01	20/05/08	7y 1m 28d	3, 6 (1)			5,000	1	2,000	1			7,000	1	7,000
Karaduman a. O. v. Turkey	8810/03	17/06/08	5y 4m 11d	3, 5 (1)(c), 5 (4), 5 (5)			23,000	3	1,150	3			24,150	3	8,050
Nurgül Doğan v. Turkey	72194/01	08/07/08	7y 1m 28d	3, 13			5,000	1	1,650	1			6,650	1	6,650
Çamdereli v. Turkey	28433/02	17/07/08	6y 2m 13d	3			5,000	1	1,000	1			6,000	1	6,000

[1] Annual Average Exchange Rate: 0.68341 (USD).

Continued from Table XI/10. 2008 for Turkey: Articles 2 and 3 ECHR – Judgments

Applicant v. State	Appl. No.	Date of Judgment	Length of Negotiations	ECHR	Cash Benefits						Total CB	NoR	BpR
					PD	NoR	nPD	NoR	C/E	NoR			
ARTICLE 3 ECHR													
Saya a. O. v. Turkey	4327/02	07/10/08	6y 10m 17d	3, 11			21,000	11			21,000	11	1,909
Mehmet Eren v. Turkey	32347/02	14/10/08	6y 2m 17d	3			7,500	1			7,500	1	7,500
Uyan v. Turkey (No. 2)	15750/02	21/10/08	6y 7m 25d	3			5,000	1			5,000	1	5,000
ARTICLES 2 AND 3 ECHR													
Varnava a. O. v. Turkey[2]	16064–66/90; 16068–73/90	10/01/08	17y 11m 16d	2, 3, 5					36,000	9	36,000	9	4,000
Osmanoğlu v. Turkey	48804/99	24/01/08	11y 3m 30d	2, 3	60,000	1	30,000	1	15,000	1	105,000	1	105,000
Mansuroğlu v. Turkey	43443/98	26/02/08	9y 7m 4d	2, 3	50,103	2	22,000	2			72,103	2	36,051
Ali and Ayşe Duran v. Turkey	42942/02	08/04/08	5y 7m 2d	2, 3	22,000	1	20,000	2	4,000	2	46,000	3	15,333
Nebyet Günay a. O. v. Turkey	51210/99	21/10/08	9y 1m 7d	2, 3	15,000	1	45,000	6	2,000	6	62,000	6	10,333

[2] The case was referred to the Grand Chamber.

XII. Turkey – Cumulative Statistics Concerning Judgments

Table XII/1. Number of Recipients

Year	JUDGMENTS			TOTAL
	Art. 2	Art. 3	Arts. 2 and 3	
1999	4		3	7
2000	13	17	7	37
2001	6	4	21	31
2002	2	1	16	19
2003	1	21	2	24
2004	28	28	42	98
2005	60	37	39	136
2006	32	46	0	78
2007	2	8	6	16
2008	17	21	21	59
Total	165	183	157	505

Table XII/2. Average Length of Negotiations

Year	JUDGMENTS						Ø LENGTH
	Art. 2	NoC	Art. 3	NoC	Arts. 2 and 3	NoC	
1999	1,870 d	1			1,893 d	1	1,882 d
2000	2,496 d	3	2,001 d	7	2,442 d	5	2,247 d
2001	2,383 d	2	2,732 d	3	2,426 d	3	2,530 d
2002	1,939 d	2	2,499 d	1	2,669 d	3	2,397 d
2003	2,927 d	1	2,787 d	6	3,242 d	1	2,861 d
2004	3,029 d	14	3,056 d	12	3,509 d	3	3,090 d
2005	3,284 d	18	2,374 d	20	3,416 d	7	2,900 d
2006	2,500 d	13	2,490 d	27	3,648 d	1	2,521 d
2007	787 d	1	2,303 d	7	2,747 d	2	2,240 d
2008	3,072 d	6	2,382 d	9	3,914 d	5	2,972 d
Ø Length	2,855 d	61	2,504 d	92	3,090 d	31	2,719 d

Table XII/3. Damages Paid by Turkey in Judgments: Articles 2 and 3 ECHR

Year	Art. 2		Art. 3		Arts. 2 and 3		TA	Actual 2008	NoR	BpR	Actual 2008
	BpR	TA	BpR	TA	BpR	TA					
1999	10,879	43,516			29,538	88,613	132,129	159,348	7	18,876	22,764
2000	20,221	262,871	24,042	408,709	73,733	516,134	1,187,715	1,407,442	37	32,100	38,039
2001	43,089	258,533	41,911	167,643	52,040	1,092,838	1,519,014	1,765,095	31	49,000	56,939
2002	92,791	185,581	27,270	27,270	25,244	403,909	616,761	703,107	19	32,461	37,006
2003	26,077	26,077	24,960	524,155	158,670	317,340	867,572	970,813	24	36,149	40,451
2004	18,964	530,983	25,670	718,751	24,238	1,017,979	2,267,713	2,489,948	98	23,140	25,408
2005	20,287	1,217,210	12,135	449,010	17,156	669,077	2,335,296	2,512,779	136	17,171	18,476
2006	8,291	265,306	9,524	438,087			703,393	741,376	78	9,018	9,505
2007	12,500	25,000	7,658	61,265	15,536	93,215	179,480	185,403	16	11,218	11,588
2008	23,474	399,058	4,514	94,800	15,291	321,103	814,961	814,961	59	13,813	13,813
NoR / TA	165	3,214,136	183	2,889,690	157	4,520,208	10,624,033	11,750,271	505	21,038	23,268
BpR / TA Actual 2008	19,480	3,474,913	15,791	3,188,893	28,791	5,058,985					
BpR Actual 2008	21,060		17,426		32,223						

XIII. Turkey – Yearly Statistics Concerning Unilateral Declarations

Table XIII/1. 2001 for Turkey: Articles 2 and 3 ECHR – Unilateral Declarations[1,2]

Applicant v. State	Appl. No.	Date of Ruling	ToD	Length of Negotiations	FS Proposed	ECHR	Total CB	NoR	BpR
ACCEPTED UNILATERAL DECLARATIONS – ARTICLE 2 ECHR									
Akman v. Turkey[3]	37453/97	26/06/01	Judg.	2y 1m 3d	Yes	2	136,769	1	136,769

[1] For this year, there were no unilateral declarations concerning Art. 3 ECHR and Arts. 2 and 3 ECHR combined.
[2] Average Annual Exchange Rate: 1.60905 (GBP).
[3] The Government regrets the occurrence of death, acknowledges that the use of excessive or disproportionate force resulting in death constitutes a violation of Art. 2 ECHR and adopts all necessary measures to prevent future violations.

Table XIII/2. 2002 for Turkey: Articles 2 and 3 ECHR – Unilateral Declarations[1,2]

Applicant v. State	Appl. No.	Date of Ruling	ToD	Length of Negotiations	FS Proposed	ECHR	Total CB	NoR	BpR
ACCEPTED UNILATERAL DECLARATIONS – ARTICLE 2 ECHR									
T.A. v. Turkey[3,4]	26307/95	09/04/02	Judg.	7y 5m 11d	Yes	2, 5, 13	111,416	1	111,416
Toğçu v. Turkey[4,5]	27601/95	09/04/02	Judg.	6y 10m 15d	Yes	2, 5, 13	111,416	1	111,416
Haran v. Turkey[6]	25754/94	26/03/02	Judg.	7y 4m 15d	Yes	2	127,332	1	127,332

[1] For this year, there were no unilateral declarations concerning Art. 3 ECHR and Arts. 2 and 3 ECHR combined.

[2] Average Annual Exchange Rate: 1.59165 (GBP).

[3] The unilateral declaration was rejected by the Grand Chamber on 6 May 2003. The case was not struck out.

[4] The Government regrets the occurrence of actions giving rise to the application, acknowledges that unrecorded deprivations of liberty and insufficient investigations into allegations of disappearance constitute violations of Arts. 2, 5 and 13 ECHR and undertakes to adopt all necessary measures.

[5] This case was subsequently restored to the list, and the Court delivered a judgment, see *Toğçu v. Turkey* (Appl. No. 27601/95), Judgment (Second Section), 31 May 2005, not reported.

[6] The Government regrets the occurrence of individual cases of death, acknowledges that the use of unjustified force resulting in death constitutes a violation of Art. 2 ECHR and undertakes to take all the necessary measures.

Table XIII/3. 2003 for Turkey: Articles 2 and 3 ECHR – Unilateral Declarations[1,2]

Applicant v. State	Appl. No.	Date of Ruling	ToD	Length of Negotiations	FS Proposed	ECHR	Total CB	NoR	BpR
ACCEPTED UNILATERAL DECLARATIONS – ARTICLES 2 AND 3 ECHR									
Tahsin Acar v. Turkey	26307/95	06/05/03	Judg.	8y 6m 7d	Yes (Government)	2, 3, 5, 6, 8, 13, 14, 18, 34, 38	101,231	1	101,231

Table XIII/4. 2005 for Turkey: Articles 2 and 3 ECHR – Unilateral Declarations[1]

Applicant v. State	Appl. No.	Date of Ruling	ToD	Length of Negotiations	FS Proposed	CHR	Total CB	NoR	BpR
REJECTED UNILATERAL DECLARATIONS – ARTICLES 2 AND 3 ECHR									
Akdeniz v. Turkey[3,4]	25165/94	31/05/05	?	10y 9m 13d	?	2, 3, 5, 6, 13, 14	?	1	?

[1] For this year, there were no unilateral declarations concerning Art. 2 ECHR and Arts. 2 and 3 ECHR combined.

[2] Average Annual Exchange Rate: 1.44615 (GBP).

[3] The decision mentions that the Chamber rejected a unilateral declaration submitted by the Government. Unfortunately, the Chamber's decision could not be located.

[4] The same judgment was also included in the table "Table XI/7. 2005 for Turkey: Articles 2 and 3 ECHR – Judgments".

XIV. Turkey – Cumulative Statistics Concerning Unilateral Declarations

Table XIV/1. Number of Recipients

Year	Unilateral Declarations			Total
	Art. 2	Art. 3	Arts. 2 and 3	
1999				
2000				
2001	1			1
2002	3			3
2003			1	1
2004				
2005				
2006				
2007				
2008				
Total	4		1	5

Table XIV/2. Average Length of Negotiations

Year	Judgments						ø Length
	Art. 2	NoC	Art. 3	NoC	Arts. 2 and 3	NoC	
1999							
2000							
2001	764 d	1					764 d
2002	2,641 d	3					2,641 d
2003					3,111 d	1	
2004							
2005							
2006							
2007							
2008							
ø Length	2,172 d	4			3,111 d	1	2,360 d

Table XIV/3. Damages Paid by Turkey in Unilateral Declarations: Articles 2 and 3 ECHR[1]

Year	Art. 2 BpR	Art. 2 TA	Art. 3 BpR	Art. 3 TA	Arts. 2 and 3 BpR	Arts. 2 and 3 TA	TA	Actual 2008	NoR	BpR	Actual 2008
1999											
2000											
2001	136,769	136,769					136,769	158,926	1	136,769	158,926
2002	116,721	350,163					350,163	399,186	3	116,721	133,062
2003					101,231	101,231	101,231	113,277	1	101,231	113,277
2004											
2005											
2006											
2007											
2008											
NoR/ TA	4	486,932			1	*101,231*	588,163	671,389	5	117,633	134,278
BpR/ *TA Actual 2008*	121,733	*558,112*			101,231	*113,277*					
BpR Actual 2008	139,528				113,277						

[1] The rejected unilateral declarations were not included in this table. They appear, however, in the yearly statistics.

3

Legal Basis for Friendly Settlements

I. European Convention on Human Rights

CONVENTION FOR THE PROTECTION
OF HUMAN RIGHTS AND FUNDAMENTAL FREEDOMS

Text amended according to the provisions of Protocol no 8 which entered into force on January 1990

Article 28

1. In the event of the Commission accepting a petition referred to it:

   (a) it shall, with a view to ascertaining the facts, undertake together with the representatives of the parties an examination of the petition and, if need be, an investigation, for the effective conduct of which the States concerned shall furnish all necessary facilities, after an exchange of views with the Commission;
   (b) it shall at the same time place itself at the disposal of the parties concerned with a view to securing a friendly settlement of the matter on the basis of respect for human rights as defined in this Convention.

2. If the Commission succeeds in effecting a friendly settlement, it shall draw up a report which shall be sent to the States concerned, to the Committee of Ministers and to the Secretary General of the Council of Europe for publication. This report shall be confined to a brief statement of the facts and of the solution reached.

CONVENTION FOR THE PROTECTION OF HUMAN RIGHTS
AND FUNDAMENTAL FREEDOMS, AS AMENDED BY PROTOCOL NO 11

Article 37 Striking out applications

1. The Court may at any stage of the proceedings decide to strike an application out of its list of cases where the circumstances lead to the conclusion that

   (a) the applicant does not intend to pursue his application; or
   (b) the matter has been resolved; or
   (c) for any other reason established by the Court, it is no longer justified to continue the examination of the application.

However, the Court shall continue the examination of the application if respect for human rights as defined in the Convention and the protocols thereto so requires.

2. The Court may decide to restore an application to its list of cases if it considers that the circumstances justify such a course.

Article 38 Examination of the case and friendly settlement proceedings

1. If the Court declares the application admissible, it shall

   (a) pursue the examination of the case, together with the representatives of the parties, and if need be, undertake an investigation, for the effective conduct of which the States concerned shall furnish all necessary facilities;

   (b) place itself at the disposal of the parties concerned with a view to securing a friendly settlement of the matter on the basis of respect for human rights as defined in the Convention and the protocols thereto.

2. Proceedings conducted under paragraph 1.b shall be confidential.

Article 39 Finding of a friendly settlement

If a friendly settlement is effected, the Court shall strike the case out of its list by means of a decision which shall be confined to a brief statement of the facts and of the solution reached.

PROTOCOL No 14 TO THE CONVENTION FOR THE PROTECTION OF HUMAN RIGHTS AND FUNDAMENTAL FREEDOMS, AMENDING THE CONTROL SYSTEM OF THE CONVENTION

13 May 2004 (entered into force on 1 June 2010)

Article 15

Article 39 of the Convention shall be amended to read as follows:

"Article 39 Friendly settlements

1. At any stage of the proceedings, the Court may place itself at the disposal of the parties concerned with a view to securing a friendly settlement of the matter on the basis of respect for human rights as defined in the Convention and the Protocols thereto.

2. Proceedings conducted under paragraph 1 shall be confidential.

3. If a friendly settlement is effected, the Court shall strike the case out of its list by means of a decision which shall be confined to a brief statement of the facts and of the solution reached.

4. This decision shall be transmitted to the Committee of Ministers, which shall supervise the execution of the terms of the friendly settlement as set out in the decision."

II. Rules of the European Court of Human Rights

RULES OF COURT OF THE EUROPEAN COURT OF HUMAN RIGHTS

18 September 1959

Rule 52[1] (Publication of judgments, decisions and other documents)

1. The Registrar shall be responsible for the publication of:

  – judgments and other decisions of the Court;
  – documents relating to the proceedings including the report of the Commission but excluding any particulars relating to the attempt to reach a friendly settlement;
  – reports of public hearings;
  – any document the publication of which is considered as useful by the President of the Court. (...)

(...)

(...)

RULES OF COURT OF THE EUROPEAN COURT OF HUMAN RIGHTS

as amended on 27 August 1974

Rule 47 (Striking out of the list)

1. When the Party which has brought the case before the Court notifies the Registrar of its intention not to proceed with the case and when the other Parties agree to such discontinuance, the Chamber shall, after having obtained the opinion of the Commission, decide whether or not it is appropriate to approve the discontinuance and accordingly to strike the case out of its list. In the affirmative, the Chamber shall give a reasoned decision which shall be communicated to the Committee of Ministers in order to allow them to supervise, in accordance with Article 54 of the Convention, the execution of any undertakings which may have been attached to the discontinuance by the order or with the approval of the Chamber.

2. When, in a case brought before the Court by the Commission, the Chamber is informed of a friendly settlement, arrangement or other fact of a kind to provide a solution of the matter, it may, after having obtained the opinion, if necessary, of the delegates of the Commission, strike the case out of its list.

(...)

---

[1] As amended by the Court on 24 October 1961.

RULES OF COURT A[2]

as in force at 23 May 1996

Rule 49 (Striking out of the list)

1. When the Party which has brought the case before the Court notifies the Registrar of its intention not to proceed with the case and when the other Parties agree to such discontinuance, the Chamber shall, after consulting the Commission and the applicant, decide whether or not it is appropriate to approve the discontinuance and accordingly to strike the case out of its list.

2.[3] When the Chamber is informed of a friendly settlement, arrangement or other fact of kind to provide a solution of the matter, it may, after consulting, if necessary, the Parties, the Delegates of the Commission and the applicant, strike the case out of the list.

The same shall apply where the circumstances warrant the conclusion that the applicant does not intend to pursue his complaints or if, for any other reason, further examination of the case is not justified.

3. The striking out of a case shall be effected by means of a judgment which the President shall forward to the Committee of Ministers in order to allow them to supervise, in accordance with Article 54 of the Convention, the execution of any untertakings which may have been attached to the discontinuance or solution of the matter.

4. The Chamber may, having regard to the responsibilities of the Court under Article 19 of the Convention, decide that, notwithstanding the notice of discontinuance, friendly settlement, arrangement or other fact referred to in paragraphs 1 and 2 of this Rule, it should proceed with the consideration of the case.

RULES OF COURT B

as in force at 23 May 1996

Rule 51 (Striking out of the list)

1. When a party which has brought the case before the Court notifies the Registrar of its intention not to proceed with the case and when the other party or parties agree to such discontinuance, The Chamber shall, after consulting the Commission, decide whether or not it is appropriate to approve the discontinuance and accordingly to strike the case out of its list.

2. When the Chamber is informed of a friendly settlement, arrangement or other fact of a kind to provide a solution of the matter, it may, after consulting, if necessary, the parties and the Delegates of the Commission, strike the case out of the list.

---

[2] Rules A apply to all cases referred to the Court before the entry into force of Protocol no 9 (1 October 1994) and thereafter only to cases concerning States not bound by that Protocol. They correspond to the Rules that came into force on 1 January 1983, as amended several times subsequently.

[3] As amended on 27 May 1993.

The same shall apply where the circumstances warrant the conclusion that a party who filed an application by virtue of Article 48 § 1 (e) of the Convention does not intend to pursue the application or if, for any other reason, further examination of the case is not justified.

3. The striking out of a case shall be effected by means of a judgment which the President shall forward to the Committee of Ministers in order to allow them to supervise, in accordance with Article 54 of the Convention, the execution of any undertakings which may have been attached to the discontinuance or solution of the matter.

4. The Chamber may, having regard to the responsibilities of the Court under Article 19 of the Convention, decide that, notwithstanding the notice of discontinuance, friendly settlement, arrangement or other fact referred to in paragraphs 1 and 2 of this Rule, it should proceed with the consideration of the case.

RULES OF COURT

4 November 1998

Rule 33 (Public character of proceedings)

(…)

(…)

3. Following registration of an application, all documents deposited with the Registry, with the exception of those deposited within the framework of friendly-settlement negotiations as provided for in Rule 62, shall be accessible to the public unless the President of the Chamber, for the reasons set out in paragraph 2 of this Rule, decides otherwise, either of his or her own motion or at the request of a party or any other person concerned.

(…)

Rule 44 (Striking out and restoration to the list)

1. When an applicant Contracting Party notifies the Registrar of its intention not to proceed with the case, the Chamber may strike the application out of the Court's list under Article 37 of the Convention if the other Contracting Party or Parties concerned in the case agree to such discontinuance.

2. The decision to strike out an application which has been declared admissible shall be given in the form of a judgment. The President of the Chamber shall forward that judgment, once it has become final, to the Committee of Ministers in order to allow the latter to supervise, in accordance with Article 46 § 2 of the Convention, the execution of any undertakings which may have been attached to the discontinuance, friendly settlement or solution of the matter.

3. When an application has been struck out, the costs shall be at the discretion of the Court. If an award of costs is made in a decision striking out an application which has not been declared admissible, the President of the Chamber shall forward the decision to the Committee of Ministers.

4. The Court may restore an application to its list if it considers that exceptional circumstances justify such a course.

Rule 62 (Friendly settlement)

1. Once an application has been declared admissible, the Registrar, acting on the instructions of the Chamber or its President, shall enter into contact with the parties with a view to securing a friendly settlement of the matter in accordance with Article 38 § 1 (b) of the Convention. The Chamber shall take any steps that appear appropriate to facilitate such a settlement.

2. In accordance with Article 38 § 2 of the Convention, the friendly-settlement negotiations shall be confidential and without prejudice to the parties' arguments in the contentious proceedings. No written or oral communication and no offer or concession made in the framework of the attempt to secure a friendly settlement may be referred to or relied on in the contentious proceedings.

3. If the Chamber is informed by the Registrar that the parties have agreed to a friendly settlement, it shall, after verifying that the settlement has been reached on the basis of respect for human rights as defined in the Convention and the Protocols thereto, strike the case out of the Court's list in accordance with Rule 44 § 2.

RULES OF COURT

of December 2008 as in force of 1 January 2009

Rule 33[4] (Public character of documents)

1. All documents deposited with the Registry by the parties or by any third party in connection with an application, except those deposited within the framework of friendly-settlement negotiations as provided for in Rule 62, shall be accessible to the public in accordance with arrangements determined by the Registrar, unless the President of the Chamber, for the reasons set out in paragraph 2 of this Rule, decides otherwise, either of his or her own motion or at the request of a party or any other person concerned.

(…)

(…)

(…)

Rule 43[5] (former Rule 44) (Striking out and restoration to the list)

(…)

(…)

3. The decision to strike out an application which has been declared admissible shall be given in the form of a judgment. The President of the Chamber shall forward that judg-

---

[4] As amended by the Court on 17 June and 8 July 2002, 7 July 2003, 4 July 2005 and 14 May 2007.
[5] As amended by the Court on 17 June and 8 July 2002 and on 7 July 2003.

ment, once it has become final, to the Committee of Ministers in order to allow the latter to supervise, in accordance with Article 46 § 2 of the Convention, the execution of any undertakings which may have been attached to the discontinuance, friendly settlement or solution of the matter.

(...)

Rule 54A[6] (Joint examination of admissibility and merits)

1. When deciding to give notice of the application to the responding Contracting Party pursuant to Rule 54 § 2 (b), the Chamber may also decide to examine the admissibility and merits at the same time in accordance with Article 29 § 3 of the Convention. In such cases the parties shall be invited to include in their observations any submissions concerning just satisfaction and any proposals for a friendly settlement. The conditions laid down in Rules 60 and 62 shall apply *mutatis mutandis*.

2. If no friendly settlement or other solution is reached and the Chamber is satisfied, in the light of the parties' arguments, that the case is admissible and ready for a determination on the merits, it shall immediately adopt a judgment including the Chamber's decision on admissibility.

3. Where the Chamber considers it appropriate, it may, after informing the parties, proceed to the immediate adoption of a judgment incorporating the decision on admissibility without having previously applied the procedure referred to in § 1 above.

Rule 62[7] (Friendly settlement)

1. Once an application has been declared admissible, the Registrar, acting on the instructions of the Chamber or its President, shall enter into contact with the parties with a view to securing a friendly settlement of the matter in accordance with Article 38 § 1 (b) of the Convention. The Chamber shall take any steps that appear appropriate to facilitate such a settlement.

2. In accordance with Article 38 § 2 of the Convention, the friendly-settlement negotiations shall be confidential and without prejudice to the parties' arguments in the contentious proceedings. No written or oral communication and no offer or concession made in the framework of the attempt to secure a friendly settlement may be referred to or relied on in the contentious proceedings.

3. If the Chamber is informed by the Registrar that the parties have agreed to a friendly settlement, it shall, after verifying that the settlement has been reached on the basis of respect for human rights as defined in the Convention and the Protocols thereto, strike the case out of the Court's list in accordance with Rule 43 § 3.

4. Paragraphs 2 and 3 apply *mutatis mutandis* to the procedure under Rule 54A.

---

[6] Inserted by the Court on 17 June and 8 July 2002 and amended on 13 December 2004.
[7] As amended by the Court on 17 June and 8 July 2002.

RULES OF COURT

1 June 2010

Rule 33[8] (Public character of documents)

1. All documents deposited with the Registry by the parties or by any third party in connection with an application, except those deposited within the framework of friendly-settlement negotiations as provided for in Rule 62, shall be accessible to the public in accordance with arrangements determined by the Registrar, unless the President of the Chamber, for the reasons set out in paragraph 2 of this Rule, decides otherwise, either of his or her own motion or at the request of a party or any other person concerned.

(…)

(…)

(…)

Rule 43[9] (former Rule 44) (Striking out and restoration to the list)

(…)

(…)

3. If a friendly settlement is effected, the application shall be struck out of the Court's list of cases by means of a decision. In accordance with Article 39 § 4 of the Convention, this decision shall be transmitted to the Committee of Ministers, which shall supervise the execution of the terms of the friendly settlement as set out in the decision. In other cases provided for in Article 37 of the Convention, the decision to strike out an application which has been declared admissible shall be given in the form of a judgment. The President of the Chamber shall forward that judgment, once it has become final, to the Committee of Ministers in order to allow the latter to supervise, in accordance with Article 46 § 2 of the Convention, the execution of any undertakings which may have been attached to the discontinuance or solution of the matter.

(…)

Rule 54A[10] (Joint examination of admissibility and merits)

1. When giving notice of the application to the responding Contracting Party pursuant to Rule 54 § 2 (b), the Chamber may also decide to examine the admissibility and merits at the same time in accordance with Article 29 § 1 of the Convention. The parties shall be invited to include in their observations any submissions concerning just satisfaction and any proposals for a friendly settlement. The conditions laid down in Rules 60 and 62

---

[8] As amended by the Court on 17 June and 8 July 2002, 7 July 2003, 4 July 2005, 13 November 2006 and 14 May 2007.

[9] As amended by the Court on 17 June and 8 July 2002, 7 July 2003 and 13 November 2006.

[10] Inserted by the Court on 17 June and 8 July 2002 and amended on 13 December 2004 and 13 November 2006.

shall apply, mutatis mutandis. The Court may, however, decide at any stage, if necessary, to take a separate decision on admissibility.

2. If no friendly settlement or other solution is reached and the Chamber is satisfied, in the light of the parties' arguments, that the case is admissible and ready for a determination on the merits, it shall immediately adopt a judgment including the Chamber's decision on admissibility, save in cases where it decides to take such a decision separately.

Rule 56[11] (Decision of a Chamber)

(...)

2. The decision of the Chamber shall be communicated by the Registrar to the applicant. It shall also be communicated to the Contracting Party or Parties concerned and to any third party, including the Commissioner for Human Rights, where these have previously been informed of the application in accordance with the present Rules. If a friendly settlement is effected, the decision to strike an application out of the list of cases shall be forwarded to the Committee of Ministers in accordance with Rule 43 § 3.

Rule 62[12] (Friendly settlement)

1. Once an application has been declared admissible, the Registrar, acting on the instructions of the Chamber or its President, shall enter into contact with the parties with a view to securing a friendly settlement of the matter in accordance with Article 39 § 1 of the Convention. The Chamber shall take any steps that appear appropriate to facilitate such a settlement.

2. In accordance with Article 39 § 2 of the Convention, the friendly-settlement negotiations shall be confidential and without prejudice to the parties' arguments in the contentious proceedings. No written or oral communication and no offer or concession made in the framework of the attempt to secure a friendly settlement may be referred to or relied on in the contentious proceedings.

3. If the Chamber is informed by the Registrar that the parties have agreed to a friendly settlement, it shall, after verifying that the settlement has been reached on the basis of respect for human rights as defined in the Convention and the Protocols thereto, strike the case out of the Court's list in accordance with Rule 43 § 3.

4. Paragraphs 2 and 3 apply, *mutatis mutandis*, to the procedure under Rule 54A.

Practice Direction[13] – Written Pleadings

(16) In view of the confidentiality of friendly-settlement proceedings (see Article 38 § 2 of the Convention and Rule 62 § 2), all submissions and documents filed within the framework of the attempt to secure a friendly settlement should be submitted separately from the written pleadings.

---

[11] As amended by the Court on 17 June and 8 July 2002 and 13 November 2006.
[12] As amended by the Court on 17 June and 8 July 2002 and 13 November 2006.
[13] Issued by the President of the Court in accordance with Rule 32 of the Rules of Court on 1 November 2003, amended on 10 December 2007.

(17) No reference to offers, concessions or other statements submitted in connection with the friendly settlement may be made in the pleadings filed in the contentious proceedings.

III. Rules of Procedure of the European Commission of Human Rights

RULES OF PROCEDURE OF THE EUROPEAN COMMISSION OF HUMAN RIGHTS

2 April 1955

Rule 63

If a Sub-Commission fails to effect a friendly settlement, it shall submit the case to the Commission.

RULES OF PROCEDURE OF THE EUROPEAN COMMISSION OF HUMAN RIGHTS

as in force on 28 June 1993

Rule 53

1. After deciding to admit an application, the Commission shall decide on the procedure to be followed:
   - (a) for the examination of the application under Article 28, paragraph 1.a, of the Convention;
   - (b) with a view to securing a friendly settlement under Article 28, paragraph 1.b, of the Convention.

2. In order to accomplish its tasks under Article 28, paragraph 1.a, of the Convention, the Commission may invite the parties to submit further evidence and observations

3. The Commission shall decide in each case whether observations should be submitted in writing or orally at a hearing.

4. The President shall lay down the time-limits within which the parties shall submit evidence and written observations.

Rule 58

1. When the Commission has found that no friendly settlement in accordance with Article 28, paragraph 1.b, of the Convention can be reached, it shall consider a draft Report drawn up by the Rapporteur on the basis of any provisional opinion reached by the Commission in its deliberations under Rule 55.

2. Where the Commission has been divided in its provisional opinion, the draft Report shall include alternative opinions, if the Commission so decides.

4

Charts for the Use of Friendly Settlements

Any individual claiming to be a victim of a violation of the Convention can lodge an application directly with the Court. Friendly settlements occur at different stages in the proceedings before the Court. Legally, there are no time or other constraints to conclude a friendly settlement. As long as the Court has not decided the case, the parties can conclude a friendly settlement if the rights in the Convention and the Additional Protocols are respected. However, friendly settlements are typically concluded at a specific point in the proceedings. The following charts show the progression of an application through the different judicial stages and the most common scenarios. In order to facilitate understanding, the charts omit certain stages of the procedure (such as, the so-called communication of an application to the respondent State Party) and focus on the most frequently encountered types of friendly settlements.

The first two charts demonstrate the various patterns concerning routine friendly settlements, real friendly settlements and follow-up friendly settlements. The latter occur after a judgment on the merits and settle only the financial aspects of an application. The third chart illustrates the intrinsic link between friendly settlements and unilateral declarations. Although the two forms of decisions are legally different, they are closely related. Unilateral decisions typically follow failed negotiations for a friendly settlement. Finally, the fourth chart exhibits the most spectacular type of friendly settlements: a pilot friendly settlement can serve as a basis for follow-up procedures at the national level.

Chart I In General under Protocol No 11

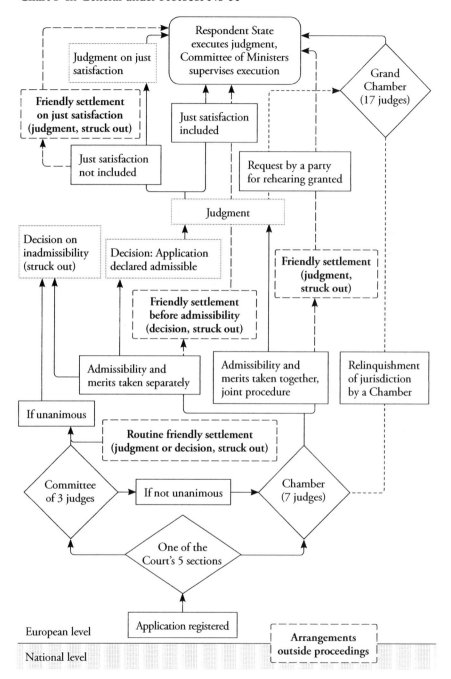

Chart II In General after Protocol No 14

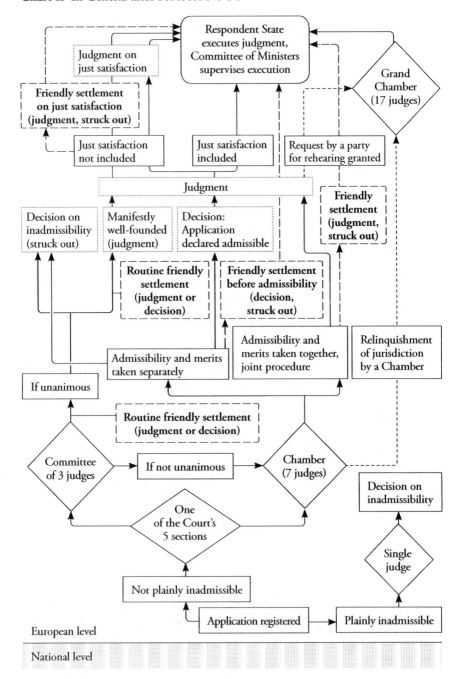

Chart III Unilateral Declaration

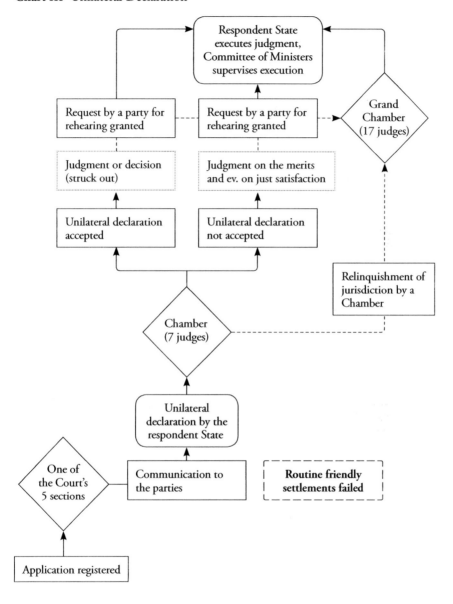

European level

National level

Chart IV After a Pilot Judgment by the Grand Chamber[1]

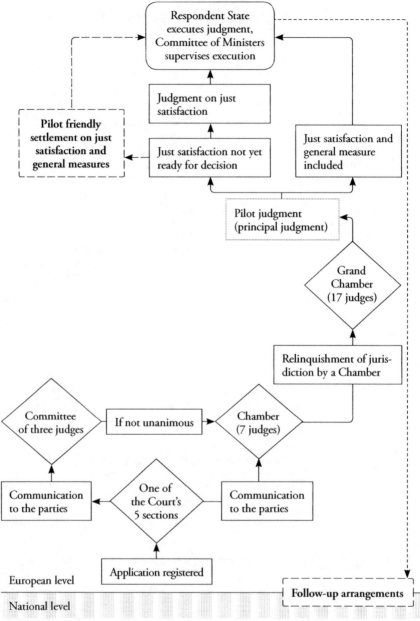

[1] Pilot Judgments are not always handed down by the Grand Chamber. See *Burdov v. Russia* (No. 2) (Appl. No. 33509/04), Judgment (First Section–Pilot Judgment), 15 January 2009, not yet reported.

Bibliography

Alexander, Larry and Moore, Michael, "Deontological Ethics" in Edward N Zalta (ed) *The Stanford Encyclopedia of Philosophy* (Winter 2009 Edition), available at <http://plato.stanford.edu/archives/win2009/entries/ethics-deontological/> (last visited 27 May 2010).

Allen, Tom, "Restitution and Transitional Justice in the European Court of Human Rights" Columbia Journal of European Law 13 (2007) 1.

Ang, Fiona and Berghmans, Eva, "Friendly Settlements and Striking Out of Applications" in Paul Lemmens and Wouter Vandenhole (eds) *Protocol No. 14 and the Reform of the European Court of Human Rights* (Antwerp: Intersentia, 2005) 89.

Becker, Lawrence C and Becker, Charlotte B (eds) *Encyclopedia of Ethics* (2nd edn, New York: Routledge, 2001).

Bentham, Jeremy, *An Introduction to the Principles of Morals and Legislation* [1789] edited by James Henderson Burns and Herbert Lionel Adolphus Hart (London: Athlone, 1970).

Berger, Vincent, "Le règlement amiable devant la Cour" in Louis-Edmond Pettiti, Emmanuel Decaux and Pierre-Henri Imbert, *La Convention européenne des droits de l'homme. Commentaire article par article* (Paris: Economica, 1995) 783.

Brown, Henry J and Marriott, Arthur L, *ADR Principles and Practice* (2nd edn, London: Sweet and Maxwell, 1999).

Brownlie, Ian, *Principles of Public International Law* (7th edn, Oxford: Oxford University Press, 2008).

Bryman, Alan, *Social Research Methods* (3rd edn, Oxford: Oxford University Press, 2008).

Cabral Barreto, Ireneu, "Friendly Settlement before the European Court of Human Rights" in Council of Europe (ed) *Alternatives to Litigation between Administrative Authorities and Private Parties: Conciliation, Mediation and Arbitration – Proceedings, Multilateral Conference Lisbon (Portugal), 31 May–2 June 1999* (Strasbourg: Council of Europe Publishing, 2000).

Caflisch, Lucius, "The Reform of the European Court of Human Rights: Protocol No. 14 and Beyond" Human Rights Law Review 6 (2006) 403.

Camilleri, Joseph A and Falk, Jim, *The End of Sovereignty? The Politics of a Shrinking and Fragmenting World* (Aldershot: Elgar, 1992).

Candela Soriano, Mercedes, "The Reception Process in Spain and Italy" in Helen Keller and Alec Stone Sweet (eds) *A Europe of Rights: The Impact of the ECHR on National Legal Systems* (Oxford: Oxford University Press, 2008) 393.

Chayes, Abram and Handler Chayes, Antonia, *The New Sovereignty. Compliance with International Regulatory Agreements* (Cambridge, Mass: Harvard University Press, 1995).

Chesebro, James W and Borisoff, Deborah J, "Appendix A: Qualitative Research" in Jason S Wrench, *et al*, *Quantitative Research Methods for Communication. A Hands-On Approach* (New York: Oxford University Press, 2008) 449.

Coleman, Jules and Silver, Charles, "Justice in Settlements" in Jules Coleman and Ellen Frankel Paul (eds) *Philosophy and Law – Social Philosophy and Policy,* Vol. 4 (Oxford: Blackwell, 1987) 102.

Cooter, Robert and Ulen, Thomas, *Law & Economics* (5th edn, Boston: Pearson Addison-Wesley, 2008).

Council of Europe (ed) *Towards Stronger Implementation of the European Convention on Human Rights at National Level. Colloquy organised under the Swedish chairmanship of the Committee of Ministers of the Council of Europe. Stockholm, 9–10 June 2008* (Strasbourg: Council of Europe, 2008), available at <http://www.coe.int/t/E/Human_Rights/h-inf_2008_11.pdf> (last visited 27 May 2010).

Courell, Ann Marie, *The Friendly Settlement Procedure under the European Convention on Human Rights,* Unpublished PhD Thesis, European University Institute (Florence, 2006).

Davis, Nancy, "Contemporary Deontology" in Peter Singer (ed) *A Companion to Ethics* (Oxford: Blackwell, 1991) 205.

De Schutter, Olivier, "Le règlement amiable dans la Convention européenne des droits de l'homme: entre théorie de la fonction de juger et théorie de la négociation" in Patrick de Fontbressin, *et al, Les droits de l'homme au seuil du troisième millénaire. Mélanges en homage à Pierre Lambert* (Brussels: Bruylant, 2000) 225.

Dembour, Marie-Bénédicte and Krzyżanowska-Mierzewska, Magda, "Ten Years On: The Voluminous and Interesting Polish Case Law" European Human Rights Law Review 5 (2004) 517.

Denzin, Norman K and Lincoln, Yvonna S, "Introduction. The Discipline and Practice of Qualitative Research" in Norman K Denzin and Yvonna Lincoln (eds) *The Landscape of Qualitative Research* (3rd edn, London: Sage, 2008) 1.

Dollé, Sally, "Friendly Settlement 14 Years on in the European Commission of Human Rights" in Michele de Salvia and Mark E Villiger (eds) *The Birth of European Human Rights Law – Liber Amicorum Carl Aage Nørgaard* (Baden-Baden: Nomos, 1998) 243.

Doucet, Andrea and Mauthner, Natasha, "Qualitative Interviewing and Feminist Research" in Pertti Alasuutari, Leonard Bickman and Julia Brannen, *The SAGE Handbook of Social Research Methods* (Los Angeles: Sage, 2008) 328.

Duff, Antony and Garland, David (eds) *A Reader on Punishment* (Oxford: Oxford University Press, 1994).

Dworkin, Ronald, *Taking Rights Seriously* (5th edn, London: Duckworth, 1987).

Dyzenhaus, David, "Judicial Independence, Transitional Justice and the Rule of Law" Otago Law Review 4 (2003) 345.

Egli, Patricia, "Protocol No. 14 to the European Convention for the Protection of Human Rights and Fundamental Freedoms: Towards A More Effective Control Mechanism?" Journal of Transnational Law and Policy 17 (2007) 1.

Fassbender, Bardo and Bleckmann, Albert, "Article 2 (1)" in Bruno Simma (ed) *The Charter of the United Nations – A Commentary,* Vol. 1 (2nd edn, Oxford: Oxford University Press, 2002) 68.

Fiss, Owen, "Against Settlement" The Yale Law Journal 93 (1984) 1073.

Frey, Raymond Gillespie, "Act-Utilitarianism" in Hugh LaFollette (ed) *The Blackwell Guide to Ethical Theory* (Malden, Mass: Blackwell, 2000) 165.

Fribergh, Erik and Villiger, Mark E, "The European Commission of Human Rights" in Ronald St John MacDonald, Franz Matscher and Herbert Petzold (eds) *The European System for the Protection of Human Rights* (Dordrecht: Martinus Nijhoff, 1993) 605.

Garlicki, Lech, "Broniowski and After: On the Dual Nature of 'Pilot Judgments'" in Lucius Caflisch, *et al* (eds) *Human Rights – Strasbourg Views / Droits de l'homme – Regards de Strasbourg. Liber Amicorum Luzius Wildhaber* (Kehl: Engel, 2007) 177.

Gattini, Andrea, "Mass Claims at the European Court of Human Rights" in Stephan Breitenmoser, *et al* (eds) *Human Rights, Democracy and the Rule of Law – Liber Amicorum Luzius Wildhaber* (Zurich: Dike and Nomos, 2007) 271.

Gauthier, David, *Morals by Agreement* (Oxford: Oxford University Press, 1986).

Gensler, Harry J and Spurgin, Earl W (eds) *Historical Dictionary of Ethics* (Lanham: Scarecrow Press, 2008).

Goodin, Robert E, "Utility and the Good" in Peter Singer (ed) *A Companion to Ethics* (Oxford: Blackwell, 1991) 241.

Gottlieb, Gidon, *Nation Against State: A New Approach to Ethnic Conflicts and the Decline of Sovereignty* (New York: Council on Foreign Relations Press, 1993).

Greer, Steven, *The European Convention on Human Rights. Achievements, Problems and Prospects* (Cambridge: Cambridge University Press, 2006).

Hart, Herbert Lionel Adolphus, "Between Utility and Rights" in Herbert Lionel Adolphus Hart, *Essays in Jurisprudence and Philosophy* (Oxford: Oxford University Press, 1983) 198.

Henkin, Louis, *The Age of Rights* (New York: Columbia University Press, 1990).

Hill, Jr, Thomas E, "Kantianism" in Hugh LaFollette (ed) *The Blackwell Guide to Ethical Theory* (Malden, Mass: Blackwell, 2000) 227.

Hooker, Brad, "Rule-Consequentialism" in Hugh LaFollette (ed) *The Blackwell Guide to Ethical Theory* (Malden, Mass: Blackwell, 2000) 183.

Hurd, Ian, "Legitimacy and Authority in International Politics" International Organization 53 (1999) 379.

Jackson, Joshua L, "Broniowski v. Poland: A Recipe for Increased Legitimacy of the European Court of Human Rights as a Supranational Constitutional Court" Connecticut Law Review 39 (2006) 759.

Janis, Mark W, Kay, Richard S and Bradley, Anthony W, *European Human Rights Law – Text and Materials* (3rd edn, Oxford: Oxford University Press, 2008).

Kaboğlu, Ibrahim Özden and Koutnatzis, Stylianos-Ioannis, "The Reception Process in Greece and Turkey" in Helen Keller and Alec Stone Sweet (eds) *A Europe of Rights: The Impact of the ECHR on National Legal Systems* (Oxford: Oxford University Press, 2008) 451.

Kamm, Frances M, "Nonconsequentialism" in Hugh LaFollette (ed) *The Blackwell Guide to Ethical Theory* (Malden, Mass: Blackwell, 2000) 205.

Kant, Immanuel, *Groundwork for the Metaphysics of Morals* [1785] edited and translated by Allen W Wood (New Haven: Yale University Press, 2002).

—, *Die Metaphysik der Sitten* [1797], Kants Werke – Akademie-Ausgabe, Band VI (Berlin: de Gruyter, 1968).

Keller, Helen, "Reception of the European Convention for the Protection of Human Rights and Fundamental Freedoms (ECHR) in Poland and Switzerland" Zeitschrift für ausländisches öffentliches Recht und Völkerrecht 65 (2005) 283.

— and Stone Sweet, Alec, "Assessing the Impact of the ECHR on National Legal Systems" in Helen Keller and Alec Stone Sweet (eds) *A Europe of Rights: The Impact of the ECHR on National Legal Systems* (Oxford: Oxford University Press, 2008) 677.

Koopmans, Sven MG, *Diplomatic Dispute Settlement. The Use of Inter-State Conciliation* (The Hague: T.M.C. Asser Press, 2008).

Krüger, Hans Christian and Nørgaard, Carl Aage, "Reflections Concerning Friendly Settlement under the European Convention on Human Rights" in Franz Matscher and Herbert Petzold (eds) *Protecting Human Rights: The European Dimension – Studies in honour of Gérard J. Wiarda* (Köln: Heymann, 1988) 329.

Krzyżanowska-Mierzewska, Magda, "The Reception Process in Poland and Slovakia" in Helen Keller and Alec Stone Sweet (eds) *A Europe of Rights: The Impact of the ECHR on National Legal Systems* (Oxford: Oxford University Press, 2008) 531.

Leach, Philip, *Taking a Case to the European Court of Human Rights* (2nd edn, Oxford: Oxford University Press, 2005).

Locke, John, *Two Treatises of Government* (1690) A Critical Edition with an Introduction and Apparatus Criticus by Peter Laslett (Cambridge: Cambridge University Press, 1960).

Lyons, David, "Human Rights and the General Welfare" Philosophy and Public Affairs 6 (1977) 113.

MacCormick, Neil, *Questioning Sovereignty. Law, State, and Nation in the European Commonwealth* (Oxford: Oxford University Press, 1999).

Mahoney, Paul, "Short Commentary on the Rules of Court: Some of the Main Points" The European Legal Forum 7 (2001) 445.

Marciano, Alain (ed) *Law and Economics: A Reader* (London: Routledge, 2009).

Mathis, Klaus, *Efficiency Instead of Justice? Searching for the Philosophical Foundations of the Economic Analysis of Law* (Berlin: Springer, 2009).

Miceli, Thomas J, *The Economic Approach to Law* (2nd edn, Stanford: Stanford University Press, 2009).

Mill, John Stuart, *Utilitarianism and On Liberty* edited by Mary Warnock (2nd edn, Malden, Mass: Blackwell, 2003).

Mirate, Silvia, *Giustizia amministrativa e convenzione europea dei diritti dell'uomo: L' "altro" diritto europeo in Italia, Francia e Inghilterra* (Naples: Jovene, 2007).

Moore, Michael, *Placing Blame. A General Theory of the Criminal Law* (Oxford: Clarendon Press, 1997).

Myjer, Egbert, "It is Never Too Late for the State – Friendly Settlements and Unilateral Declarations" in Lucius Caflisch, *et al* (eds) *Human Rights – Strasbourg Views / Droits de l'homme – Regards de Strasbourg. Liber Amicorum Luzius Wildhaber* (Kehl: Engel, 2007) 309.

Nozick, Robert, *Anarchy, State, and Utopia* (New York: Blackwell, 1974).

O'Boyle, Michael, "Friendly Settlement and Third Party Intervention" Talk given at the Multilateral Meeting of Government Agents, 8–9 December 2003, The Hague (unpublished paper on file with the authors).

O'Neill, Onora, "Kantian Ethics" in Peter Singer (ed) *A Companion to Ethics* (Oxford: Blackwell, 1991) 175.

Ovey, Clare and White, Robin CA, *Jacobs and White – The European Convention on Human Rights* (4th edn, Oxford: Oxford University Press, 2006).

Paraskeva, Costas, "Human Rights Protection Begins and Ends at Home: The 'Pilot Judgment Procedure' Developed by the European Court of Human Rights", Human Rights Law Commentary 3/2007, available at <http://www.nottingham.ac.uk/shared/shared_hrlcpub/Paraskeva.pdf> (last visited 27 May 2010).

Partsch, Karl Josef, "Individuals in International Law" in Rudolf Bernhardt (ed) *Encyclopedia of Public International Law*, Vol. 2 (Amsterdam: North-Holland Publishers, 1995) 957.

Pettit, Philip, "The Consequentialist Can Recognise Rights" The Philosophical Quarterly 38 (1988) 42.

—, "Consequentialism" in Peter Singer (ed) *A Companion to Ethics* (Oxford: Blackwell, 1991) 230.

Polinsky, A Mitchell and Rubinfeld, Daniel L, "The Deterrent Effects of Settlements and Trials" International Review of Law and Economics 8 (1988) 109.

Posner, Eric A and Vermeule, Adrian, "Transitional Justice as Ordinary Justice" Harvard Law Review 117 (2004) 761.

Posner, Richard A, *Economic Analysis of Law* (7th edn, New York: Aspen Publishers, 2007).

Post, Stephen G (ed) *Encyclopedia of Bioethics* (3rd edn, New York: Macmillan, 2004).

Rawls, John, *A Theory of Justice* (Revised edn, Cambridge, Mass: Belknap Press, 1999).

Reid, Karen, *A Practitioner's Guide to the European Convention on Human Rights* (3rd edn, London: Sweet & Maxwell, 2008).

Reisman, W Michael and Benesch, Susan, "The Use of Friendly Settlements in the Inter-American Human Rights System" in Lal Chand Vohrah, *et al* (eds) *Man's Inhumanity to Man – Essays on International Law in Honour of Antonio Cassese* (The Hague: Kluwer Law International, 2003) 741.

Ress, Georg, "The Effect of Decisions and Judgments of the European Court of Human Rights in the Domestic Legal Order" Texas International Law Journal 40 (2005) 359.

"Review of the Working Methods of the European Court of Human Rights – Lord Woolf Report" Human Rights Law Journal 26 (2005) 447.

Röttorp, Paula and Rogalska Hedlund, Anna, *Tyst rättvisa. Svenska staten köper sig ut ur statistiken* (Stockholm: Timbro, 2007).

Rozakis, Christos L, "Unilateral Declarations as A Means of Settling Human Rights Disputes: A New Tool for the Resolution of Disputes in the ECHR's Procedure" in Marcelo G Kohen (ed) *Promoting Justice, Human Rights and Conflict Resolution through International Law. Liber Amicorum Lucius Caflisch* (Leiden: Nijhoff, 2007) 1003.

Sadurski, Wojciech, "Partnering with Strasbourg: Constitutionalisation of the European Court of Human Rights, the Accession of Central and East European States to the Council of Europe, and the Idea of Pilot Judgments" Human Rights Law Review 9 (2009) 397.

Sardaro, Pietro, "Jus Non Dicere for Allegations of Serious Violations of Human Rights: Questionable Trends in the Recent Case Law of the Strasbourg Court" European Human Rights Law Review 6 (2003) 601.

Sassen, Saskia, *Losing Control? Sovereignty in the Age of Globalization* (New York: Columbia University Press, 1996).

Schreuer, Christoph, "The Waning of the Sovereign State: Towards a New Paradigm for International Law?" European Journal of International Law 4 (1993) 447.

Shelton, Dinah, *Remedies in International Human Rights Law* (2nd edn, Oxford: Oxford University Press, 2005).

Sinnott-Armstrong, Walter, "Consequentialism" in Edward N Zalta (ed) *The Stanford Encyclopedia of Philosophy* (Winter 2009 Edition), available at <http://plato.stanford.edu/archives/win2009/entries/consequentialism/> (last visited 27 May 2010).

Slaughter, Anne-Marie, "International Law in a World of Liberal States" European Journal of International Law 6 (1995) 503.

Standaert, Patricia E, "The Friendly Settlement of Human Rights Abuses in the Americas" Duke Journal of Comparative and International Law 9 (1999) 519.

Stone Sweet, Alec and Keller, Helen, "The Reception of the ECHR in National Legal Orders" in Helen Keller and Alec Stone Sweet (eds) *A Europe of Rights: The Impact of the ECHR on National Legal Systems* (Oxford: Oxford University Press, 2008) 3.

Sweeney, James A, "Divergence and Diversity in Post-Communist European Human Rights Cases" Connecticut Journal of International Law 21 (2005) 1.

Teitel, Ruti G, *Transitional Justice* (New York: Oxford University Press, 2000).

—, "Transitional Justice in a New Era" Fordham International Law Journal 26 (2003) 893.

Villiger, Mark E, "Fair Trail and Excessive Length of Proceedings as Focal Points of the ECtHR's Increasing Caseload" in Rüdiger Wolfrum and Ulrike Deutsch (eds) *The European Court of Human Rights Overwhelmed by Applications: Problems and Possible Solutions* (Berlin: Springer, 2009) 93.

Warbrick, Colin, "The Principle of Sovereign Equality" in Vaughan Lowe and Colin Warbrick (eds) *The United Nations and the Principles of International Law: Essays in Memory of Michael Akehurst* (London: Routledge, 1994) 204.

Weber, Gregory S, "Who Killed the Friendly Settlement? The Decline of Negotiated Resolutions at the European Court of Human Rights" Pepperdine Dispute Resolution Law Journal 7 (2007) 215.

Wildhaber, Luzius, "A Constitutional Future for the European Court of Human Rights?" Human Rights Law Journal 23 (2002) 161.

—, "Pilot Judgments in Cases of Structural or Systemic Problems on the National Level" in Rüdiger Wolfrum and Ulrike Deutsch (eds) *The European Court of Human Rights Overwhelmed by Applications: Problems and Possible Solutions* (Berlin: Springer, 2009) 69.

Wittman, Donald A, *Economic Analysis of the Law: Selected Readings* (Malden, Mass: Blackwell, 2003).

Wołąsiewicz, Jakub, "Pilot Judgments: The Experience of a Government Agent" in Council of Europe (ed) *Towards Stronger Implementation of the European Convention on Human Rights at National Level. Colloquy organised under the Swedish chairmanship of the Committee of Ministers of the Council of Europe. Stockholm, 9–10 June 2008* (Strasbourg: Council of Europe, 2008) 94.

Zagrebelsky, Vladimiro, "Questions autour de Broniowski" in Lucius Caflisch, *et al* (eds) *Human Rights – Strasbourg Views / Droits de l'homme – Regards de Strasbourg. Liber Amicorum Luzius Wildhaber* (Kehl: Engel, 2007) 521.

Zwaak, Leo, "The Procedure Before the European Court of Human Rights" in Pieter van Dijk, *et al* (eds) *Theory and Practice of the European Convention on Human Rights* (4th edn, Antwerp: Intersentia, 2006) 95.

Index

access to court 35, 128
acknowledgment of a Convention breach 4,
    25, 43, 44, 45, 64, 68, 78, 103–105,
    114, 119, 120, 121, 122, 123, 125,
    146, 147, 159, 163, 176, 196
admissibility 15, 34, 37, 53–55, 143,
    184, 188
alternative dispute resolution 5, 38, 77, 138,
    141, 144, 147, 149, 157–158, 168,
    169, 183, 193
apology *see* expression of regret
applicant 92, 98, 141–142
applicant's representation *see* lawyer
arrangement *see* arrangement outside pro-
    ceedings; follow-up arrangement; mass
    arrangement; pilot arrangement; routine
    arrangement; simple arrangement
arrangement outside proceedings 63, 184
asylum 21, 41, 188
attorney *see* lawyer

balance of power 7, 95, 96, 162, 174, 195
binding force and execution of judgments
    (Article 46 ECHR) 39, 45, 47, 48,
    58, 152
Bundesländer 24, 77, 190

Cantons *see Bundesländer*
Case Lawyer 33, 34, 144, 172
caseload of the ECtHR 3, 4, 8, 14–17, 32,
    35, 70, 71, 91, 93, 100, 110–111, 122,
    127–132, 137, 138, 141, 145, 151,
    152, 195, 198
case management function 10, 49–51, 50,
    92, 121
Chamber of the Court 33
clone cases 109, 112, 188
    see also pilot friendly settlement; pilot
    judgment; repetitive cases; systemic
    problems
Committee of Ministers 3, 31, 37, 58,
    71–72, 123, 149, 152, 189, 196, 198
Committee (of three Judges) 33
compensation 11, 12, 19, 20, 26, 47–50,
    56, 64–66, 70, 73, 78, 79, 80, 85,
    89, 92, 95, 98, 99, 103, 104, 110,
    114, 117, 118, 119–118, 129–131,
    136, 137, 142, 147, 152,
    166–167, 187
    see also costs and expenses; non-pecuniary
    compensation; pecuniary compensation

confidentiality 8, 9, 39–40, 57, 58, 68,
    78, 79, 95, 141, 147, 150–151, 161,
    185, 189
conflict of interests 83, 84, 91–95, 100, 106,
    134, 135, 137
consequentialism 87–90, 97
content of friendly settlements 19–24,
    40–47, 136, 139, 152, 188
costs and expenses 49, 66, 109
Council of Europe 15, 63, 74, 149, 150
country situation
    Germany 113–114
    Italy 28, 37, 49, 50, 68, 75, 76, 112–113
    Poland 75, 76, 108–112, 127–137, 145,
        152, 170–178, 181–182, 192
    Russia 54, 56, 75, 81, 82, 114–115
    Sweden 74, 115, 158–159, 163
    Turkey 37, 45, 50–52, 69, 74–76, 80,
        100–102, 108–111, 116–127, 134–137,
        146, 193, 196–197
    United Kingdom 28, 64, 112,
        115–116, 145
criminal record 42

deontology 88–91, 97
disappearance of persons *see* right to life

efficiency 79, 86, 91, 93–94, 96–97, 100,
    118, 132, 137, 159
established case law 47, 63, 65, 68, 69, 99,
    146, 148, 149, 151, 163, 171
ethics *see* legitimacy of friendly settlements
European Commission of Human
    Rights 11–21, 23–25, 26, 29,
    29–31, 109
execution of friendly settlements 79,
    166–167, 179, 184, 190, 197
execution of judgments 45, 46, 152
ex gratia payment 19, 38, 39, 43, 47, 55,
    147, 198
exhaustion of domestic remedies 32, 44,
    71, 132
expression of regret 43, 44, 103, 105,
    119–125, 176, 194, 195, 196
expropriation *see* property rights

fact finding 15, 19, 120
fairness 66, 90, 95, 98
fast-track 67, 82, 138, 139
    see also efficiency; routine friendly settlement
federalism *see Bundesländer*

financial awards *see* compensation
follow-up arrangement 61, 73, 144
follow-up friendly settlement 23, 54, 58, 61, 70, 72, 149
form of settlements 29–31, 58, 59, 139, 143–144, 148, 152
friendly settlement *see* follow-up friendly settlement; interstate friendly settlement; paper friendly settlement; pilot friendly settlement; real friendly settlement; routine friendly settlement

general interests 83, 93, 93–95, 106, 133, 134, 137, 151
general measures *see* measures in friendly settlements
Germany *see* country situation
Government *see* State Parties; State Agent
Government Agent *see* State Agent
Grand Chamber of the Court 33, 35–36, 40, 61–63, 68, 120

Immanuel Kant 88
impartiality 66, 128, 148, 164
inadmissibility 18, 33–34, 57, 166
individual interests 83, 91–93, 94, 134–137
individual measures *see* measures in friendly settlements
inhuman and degrading treatment *see* prohibition of torture and inhuman and degrading treatment (Article 3 ECHR)
Inter-American Court 5
interim measures 53
interstate friendly settlement 6, 7, 74–75
investigation 95, 103, 104, 118–120
Italy *see* country situation

John Locke 88
John Rawls 89
joint procedure on admissibility and merits 34–35, 143
Judge Rapporteur 33, 34, 78
Judges of the ECtHR 9, 27, 31, 33, 36, 59, 82, 83, 138, 148, 149, 157, 168, 172, 178–179

Kantianism *see* deontology
Kurdistan Workers' Party (PKK) 50, 123, 197

lawyer 9, 10, 36–37, 59, 82, 83, 141–142, 149, 157–158, 160, 161, 163, 164, 165, 173, 184, 185, 191, 193–198
legal aid 36, 42
legal character
  of friendly settlements 6, 29, 30, 31, 38–39, 60, 139, 143–144, 147, 176–177, 198
  of international law 86–87

legitimacy of friendly settlements 11, 40, 85, 91, 97–107, 143, 148, 151
  see also consequentialism; deontology
length of proceedings (Article 6 (1) ECHR) 8, 12, 25, 35, 36, 40, 48, 49, 64–66, 69, 78, 100, 108, 109, 112–114, 127–135, 140, 146, 147, 163, 165, 167, 171–172, 181, 186, 187

management function 12
  see also efficiency
manifestly ill-founded 33
manifestly well-founded 57
mass arrangement 60, 70–73
mass friendly settlement 25, 171, 173
measures in friendly settlements
  general measures 11, 23–24, 37, 38, 47, 51, 61–62, 70–75, 77, 83, 117, 120, 145, 152, 164, 170, 173–175, 176–177, 179, 195–196
  individual measures 11, 20–23, 37, 41–46, 55–56, 61, 63, 83, 170, 173–175, 176, 179–180, 189, 195–197
mediator 30, 142, 145, 150, 169, 173–174, 184
  see also Registry
merits 34, 37, 55, 143, 144, 184, 186
monetarization of human rights 6, 11, 47–49, 71, 78, 85, 95, 139, 142, 167, 170, 195

negotiations 26, 29, 34, 39, 40, 51–61, 65, 68, 69, 79–83, 85, 96, 98, 117, 124, 141, 144, 145, 150–152, 160–164, 168, 173–175, 176, 184–187, 188, 194, 195, 198
non-execution of judgments 35, 37, 38, 48, 65, 69, 71
non-pecuniary compensation 49, 66, 71, 109, 194

ordinary proceedings 11, 12, 37, 38, 40, 66, 76–82, 91, 109, 117–127, 131, 136, 137, 139–148, 185, 187

paper friendly settlement *see* routine friendly settlement
pecuniary compensation 49, 55, 109, 170–171, 172–173, 175, 194, 198
pilot arrangement 70–73, 111, 136, 172
pilot friendly settlement 4, 7, 20, 25, 58, 61, 70–74, 77, 83, 111, 136, 139, 141, 144, 145, 149, 152, 172, 175, 179
  see also clone cases; repetitive cases; systemic problems

pilot judgment 4, 11, 20, 34, 47, 50, 51, 70–73, 83, 111, 136, 144, 152, 164, 172, 174, 175–177, 181, 196
see also clone cases; repetitive cases; systemic problems
Pinto Law 113, 128
Poland *see* country situation
policy
  ECtHR 17, 24, 49
  State 62, 75–78, 114
proactive approach 35, 50, 57, 59, 77–78, 140, 186, 191, 192
procedure of friendly settlements 32–38, 52–58, 63–64, 65, 69–70, 77–84, 159–160, 180, 184, 194–195
see also fairness
professional training 144–145
prohibition of torture and inhuman and degrading treatment (Article 3 ECHR) 6, 7, 12, 19, 28, 45, 48, 75–76, 76, 85, 95–107, 109, 111, 116–127, 134–136, 140, 143, 147–148, 163, 167, 181–182, 195–198
property rights 35, 42, 71, 73, 76, 80, 100, 165, 167
see also Protocols, Protocol no 1
Protocols
  in general 14, 38, 68, 80, 82
  Protocol no 1 28, 51, 56, 76, 114, 123
    see also property rights
  Protocol no 11 15, 16, 18–19, 29, 31, 41, 53, 86
  Protocol no 14 16, 17, 57–58, 143, 152
  Protocol no 14bis 16, 17, 57
publicity 58, 76, 159, 164

real friendly settlement 11, 58, 61, 69–70, 76, 139, 144, 145, 149, 151
reasoning 147–148
reform 14–18, 17, 31, 137
Registrar 8, 34, 39, 130, 168, 170, 174
registration 32, 194
Registry 6, 8, 9, 15, 17, 18, 32–37, 48, 50, 59–70, 75, 77–79, 114, 126, 129, 139–152, 161–162, 170–172, 174–175, 178, 181, 184–186, 192, 194–195
regret clause 45, 46, 103, 105, 119–125, 164, 167
re-opening of a case 21, 23, 68, 120, 121, 124, 147, 195–198
reparation *see* non-pecuniary compensation
repetitive cases 11, 35, 68, 73, 79, 94, 105, 109, 112, 120, 121, 123, 124, 127, 135, 145, 191
see also clone cases and pilot judgment
residence permit 21–22, 41

respect for human rights 25, 29, 38, 53, 55, 69, 82, 159
see also legal character of friendly settlements
restoration of a case 55–56
retributivism 90
right to liberty and security (Article 5 ECHR) 44, 48, 65, 68, 69, 71, 123, 171, 176, 183, 187
right to life (Article 2 ECHR) 6, 7, 12, 19, 27, 44–48, 76, 85, 99, 103, 106, 108, 109, 111, 116, 117, 118–122, 124–128, 134–136, 140, 143, 147–148, 163, 167, 195–196
Ronald Dworkin 89
routine arrangement 61, 68–69
routine friendly settlement 7, 34–35, 58, 61, 65–69, 72, 76, 82, 139, 142, 144, 145, 151, 173, 176
Russia *see* country situation

Section (of the ECtHR) 10, 33, 65, 78, 117, 145, 161, 181, 198
separation of powers 11, 21
simple arrangement 61
State Agent 9, 59, 67, 76, 79, 89, 90, 98, 129, 141–142, 146, 149, 151, 152, 169–182, 183–192
State interest 75–78, 86, 92, 194
State Parties 9–19, 23–29, 34, 36, 50, 51, 55, 56, 60, 63, 66, 68–80, 86, 92–93, 95, 98, 105, 108, 112, 117, 120–130, 136, 142, 145, 146, 151, 152, 160–161, 162–163, 186, 191, 192, 195
see also State Agent
strike out 30, 33, 34, 53–56, 61, 69, 167
structural deficiencies *see* clone cases; pilot friendly settlement; pilot judgment; repetitive cases; systemic problems
Sweden *see* country situation
systemic problems 15, 49, 56, 70, 71, 72, 75, 83, 108, 112, 117, 122–121, 123, 124, 127, 131, 133, 152, 173, 180–181
see also clone cases; pilot friendly settlement; pilot judgment; repetitive cases

tableaux 78
tax exemption 47
time 32, 37, 118, 121, 124, 137–136, 137, 138, 140, 142–143, 158, 162, 169–170, 180, 186, 193–194
torture *see* prohibition of torture and inhuman and degrading treatment (Article 3 ECHR)
transitional justice 6, 64
transitional problem 24, 64, 115–116, 161, 171

trust 75–79, 120, 128
Turkey *see* country situation

unilateral declaration 4, 5, 9, 11, 18, 51,
     56, 67, 75, 82, 103–106, 108–119,
     123, 132, 133, 136, 145–147, 150,
     160, 162–163, 171, 186

utilitarianism *see* consequentialism
United Kingdom *see* country situation

waiver of further legal action 39, 61–63, 115
widower's benefits 64, 116
withdrawal of application 59–63, 144
written procedure 25, 79–84, 160, 176, 194